**W9-DIF-510**

# CONTENTS

# SOURCES FOR *OF THE PEOPLE*

## A HISTORY OF THE UNITED STATES
## VOLUME I TO 1877

EDITED BY

*Maxwell Johnson*

NEW YORK   OXFORD
OXFORD UNIVERSITY PRESS

Oxford University Press is a department of the University of Oxford.
It furthers the University's objective of excellence in research, scholarship,
and education by publishing worldwide. Oxford is a registered trade mark of
Oxford University Press in the UK and certain other countries.

Published in the United States of America by Oxford University Press
198 Madison Avenue, New York, NY 10016, United States of America.

For titles covered by Section 112 of the US Higher Education
Opportunity Act, please visit www.oup.com/us/he for the latest
information about pricing and alternate formats.

Library of Congress Cataloging-in-Publication Data

Names: Johnson, Maxwell E., 1952- editor.
Title: Sources for Of the people : a history of the United States / edited by
  Maxwell Johnson.
Description: [Fourth edition] | New York, NY : Oxford University Press, 2019. |
  "Sources for Of the People: A History of the United States, Fourth Edition,
  is a two-volume primary source collection, expertly edited by
  Maxwell Johnson, and specifically designed to accompany
  Of the People." —Publisher. | Includes bibliographical references.
Identifiers: LCCN 2018033866 | ISBN 9780190910143 (volume 1 : pbk.) |
  ISBN 9780190910150 (volume 2 : pbk.)
Subjects: LCSH: United States—History—Sources.
Classification: LCC E178 .O25 2019 Suppl. | DDC 973—dc23 LC record
  available at https://lccn.loc.gov/2018033866

9 8 7 6 5 4

Printed by LSC Communications, Inc., United States of America

# HOW TO READ A PRIMARY SOURCE

This sourcebook is composed of eighty-one primary sources. A primary source is any text, image, or other information that gives us a first-hand account of the past by someone who witnessed or participated in the historical events in question. While such sources can provide significant and fascinating insight into the past, they must also be read carefully to limit modern assumptions about historical modes of thought. Here are a few elements to keep in mind when approaching a primary source.

## AUTHORSHIP

Who produced this source of information? A male or a female? A member of the elite or of the lower class? An outsider looking in at an event or an insider looking out? What profession or lifestyle does the author pursue that might influence how he or she is recording this information?

## GENRE

What type of source are you examining? Different genres—categories of material—have different goals and stylistic elements. For example, a personal letter meant exclusively for the eyes of a distant cousin might include unveiled opinions and relatively trivial pieces of information, like the writer's vacation plans. On the other hand, a political speech intended to convince a nation of a leader's point of view might subdue personal opinions beneath artful rhetoric and focus on large issues like national welfare or war. Identifying genre can be useful for deducing how the source may have been received by an audience.

## AUDIENCE

Who is reading, listening to, or observing the source? Is it a public or a private audience? National or international? Religious or non-religious? The source may be geared toward the expectations of a particular group; it may be recorded in a language that is specific to a particular group. Identifying audience can help us understand why the author chose a certain tone or included certain types of information.

## HISTORICAL CONTEXT

When and why was this source produced? On what date? For what purposes? What historical moment does the source address? It is paramount that we approach primary sources in context to avoid anachronism (attributing an idea or a habit to a past era where it does not belong) and faulty judgment. For example, when considering a medieval history, we must account for the fact that in the Middle Ages, the widespread understanding was that God created the world and could still interfere in the activity of mankind—such as sending a terrible storm when a community had sinned. Knowing the context (Christian, medieval, views of the world) helps us to avoid importing modern assumptions—like the fact that storms are caused by atmospheric pressure—into historical texts. In this way we can read the source more faithfully, carefully, and generously.

## BIAS AND FRAMING

Is there an overt argument being made by the source? Did the author have a particular agenda? Did any political or social motives underlie the reasons for writing the document? Does the document exhibit any qualities that offer clues about the author's intentions?

## STYLISTIC ELEMENTS

Stylistic features such as tone, vocabulary, word choice, and the manner in which the material is organized and presented should also be considered when examining a source. They can provide insight into the writer's perspective and offer additional context for considering a source in its entirety.

# CHAPTER 1

# WORLDS IN MOTION, 1450–1550

## 1.1 LETTER OF CHRISTOPHER COLUMBUS ON HIS FIRST VOYAGE TO AMERICA (1492)

In 1492, the Italian explorer Christopher Columbus (1451–1506) led his first expedition to the Americas on behalf of King Ferdinand III of Spain. In 1493, Columbus wrote the following letter to Luis de Santángel, the Spanish finance minister who had supported Columbus' voyage. Convinced that he had discovered a route to Asia, Columbus termed the Caribbean area he found the "Indies" and its inhabitants "Indians." In the letter, Columbus described the geography of the land, speculated about the nature of its Arawak inhabitants, and sought to convince de Santángel of the future financial benefits the Spanish crown might gain by developing the area's resources.

*Written in 1493, to the Treasurer of Aragon, Luis de Santángel, who had provided Castile Taino Indians his settlement La Navidad on the north coast of present-day Haiti*

SIR:

As I know you will be rejoiced at the glorious success that our Lord has given me in my voyage, I write this to tell you how in thirty-three days I sailed to the Indies with the fleet that the illustrious King and Queen, our Sovereigns, gave me, where I discovered a great many islands inhabited by numberless people; and of all I have taken possession for their Highnesses by proclamation and display of the Royal Standard [Spanish flag] without opposition. To the first island I discovered I gave the name of San Salvador in commemoration of His Divine Majesty, who has wonderfully granted all this. The Indians call it Guanaham.[1] The second I named the Island of Santa Maria de Conception; the third, Fernandina; the fourth, Isabella; the fifth, Juana; and thus to each one I gave a new name.[2]

Source: "Letter of Christopher Columbus on His First Voyage to America, 1492," *National Humanities Center*, https://national-humanitiescenter.org/pds/amerbegin/contact/text1/columbusletter.pdf (Accessed June 4, 2018).

1. Also Guanahani. Columbus made landfall in the Bahamas or the Turks & Caicos, north of the island of Hispaniola (present-day Haiti and the Dominican Republic). While there is insufficient evidence to specify the island, contenders include San Salvador (formerly Watling Island) and Samana Cay in the Bahamas.
2. *Island of Santa Maria de Conception:* Rum Cay, Bahamas. *Fernandina:* Long Island, Bahamas. *Juana:* Cuba.

When I came to Juana, I followed the coast of that isle toward the west and found it so extensive that I thought it might be mainland, the province of Cathay [China]; and as I found no towns nor villages on the seacoast, except a few small settlements, where it was impossible to speak to the people because they fled at once, I continued the said route, thinking I could not fail to see some great cities or towns; and finding at the end of many leagues that nothing new appeared and that the coast led northward, contrary to my wish, because the winter had already set in, I decided to make for the south, and as the wind also was against my proceeding, I determined not to wait there longer and turned back to a certain harbor whence I sent two men to find out whether there was any king or large city. They explored for three days and found countless small communities and people, without number, but with no kind of government, so they returned.

I heard from other Indians I had already taken that this land was an island, and thus followed the eastern coast for one hundred and seven leagues[3] until I came to the end of it. From that point I saw another isle to the eastward, at eighteen leagues' distance, to which I gave the name of Hispaniola.[4] I went thither and followed its northern coast to the east, as I had done in Juana, one hundred and seventy-eight leagues eastward, as in Juana. This island, like all the other, is most extensive. It has many ports along the seacoast excelling any in Christendom—and many fine, large, following rivers. The land there is elevated, with many mountains and peaks incomparably higher than in the centre isle. They are most beautiful, of a thousand varied forms, accessible, and full of trees of endless varieties, so high that they seem to touch the sky, and I have been told that they never lose their foliage. I saw them as green and lovely as trees are in Spain in the month of May. Some of them were covered with blossoms, some with fruit, and some in other conditions, according to their kind. The nightingale and other small birds of a thousand kinds were singing in the month of November when I was there. There were palm trees of six or eight varieties, the graceful peculiarities of each one of them

being worthy of admiration as are the other trees fruits and grasses. There are wonderful pine woods, and very extensive ranges of meadow land. There is honey, and there are many kinds of birds, and a great variety of fruits. Inland there are numerous mines of metals and innumerable people.

Hispaniola is a marvel. Its hills and mountains, fine plains and open country, are rich and fertile for planting and for pasturage, and for building towns and villages. The seaports there are incredibly fine, as also the magnificent rivers, most of which bear gold. The trees, fruits and grasses differ widely from those in Juana. There are many spices and vast mines of gold and other metals in this island. They have no iron, nor steel, nor weapons, nor are they fit for them, because although they are well-made men of commanding stature, they appear extraordinarily timid. The only arms [weapons] they have are sticks of cane, cut when in seed with a sharpened stick at the end, and they are afraid to use these. Often I have sent two or three men ashore to some town to converse with them, and the natives came out in great numbers, and as soon as they saw our men arrive, fled without a moment's delay although I protected them from all injury.

At every point where I landed and succeeded in talking to them, I gave them some of everything I had—cloth and many other things—without receiving anything in return, but they are a hopelessly timid people. It is true that since they have gained more confidence and are losing this fear, they are so unsuspicious and so generous with what they possess, that no one who had not seen it would believe it. They never refuse anything that is asked for. They even offer it themselves, and show so much love that they would give their very hearts. Whether it be anything of great or small value, with any trifle of whatever kind, they are satisfied. I forbade worthless things being given to them, such as bits of broken bowls, pieces of glass, and old straps, although they were as much pleased to get them as if they were the finest jewels in the world. One sailor was found to have got for a leathern strap, gold of the weight of two and a half castellanos, and others

---

3. The Spanish league was about 2.6 miles.
4. . . . [P]resent-day Haiti and the Dominican Republic.

for even more worthless things much more; while for a new *blancas* they would give all they had, were it two or three castellanos of pure gold or an arroba or two of spun cotton.[5] Even bits of the broken hoops of wine casks they accepted, and gave in return what they had, like fools, and it seemed wrong to me. I had to win their love and to induce them to become Christians, and to love and serve their Highnesses and the whole Castilian nation, and help to get for us things they have in abundance, which are necessary to us.

They have no religion nor idolatry, except that they all believe power and goodness to be in heaven. They firmly believed that I, with my ships and men, came from heaven, and with this idea I have been received everywhere, since they lost fear of me. They are, however, far from being ignorant. They are most ingenious men, and navigate these seas in a wonderful way and describe everything well, but they never before saw people wearing clothes, nor vessels like ours. Directly I reached the Indies in the first isle I discovered, I took by force some of the natives, that from them we might gain some information of what there was in these parts; and so it was that we immediately understood each other, either by words or signs. They are still with me and still believe that I come from heaven. They were the first to declare this wherever I went, and the others ran from house to house, and to the towns around, crying out, "Come! Come! and see the men from heaven!" Then all, both men and women, as soon as they were reassured about us, came, both small and great, all bringing something to eat and to drink, which they presented with marvelous kindness.

In these isles there are a great many canoes, something like rowing boats, or all sizes, and most of them are larger than an eighteen-oared galley. They are not so broad, as they are made of a single plank, but a galley could not keep up with them in rowing, because they go with incredible speed, and with these they row about among all these islands, which are innumerable, and carry on their commerce. I have seen some of these canoes with seventy and eighty men in them, and each had an oar. In all the islands I observed little difference in the appearance of the people, or in them, and each had an oar. In all the islands I observed little difference in the appearance of the people, or in their habits and language, except that they understand each other, which is remarkable. Therefore I hope that their Highnesses will decide upon the conversion of these people to our holy faith, to which they seem much inclined.

I have already stated how I sailed one hundred and seven leagues along the seacoast of Juana [Cuba] in a straight line form west to east. I can therefore assert that this island is larger than England and Scotland together, since beyond these one hundred and seven leagues there remained and the west point two provinces where I did not go, one of which they call Avan, the home of men with tails. These provinces are computed to be fifty or sixty leagues in length, as far as can be gathered from the Indians with me, who are acquainted with all these islands. This other, Hispaniola, is larger in circumference than all Spain from Catalonia to Fuentarabia in Biscay, since upon one of its four sides I sailed one hundred and eighty eight leagues from west to east. This is worth having, and must on no account be given up. I have taken possession of all these islands for their Highnesses, and all may be more extensive than I know or can say, and I hold them for their Highnesses, who can command them as absolutely as the kingdoms of Castile.

In Hispaniola, in the most convenient place, most accessible for the gold mines and all commerce with the mainland on this side or with that of the great Khan on the other,[6] with which there would be great trade and profit, I have taken possession of a large town, which I have named the City of Navidad.[7] I began fortifications there which should be completed by this time, and I have left in it men enough to hold it, with arms, artillery, and provisions for more than a year; and a boat with a master seaman skilled in the arts necessary to make others. I am so friendly with the king of that country that he was proud to call me his brother and hold me as such. Even should he change his mind and wish to quarrel with my men, neither he nor his subjects know what arms are nor wear clothes,

---

5. *Blanca:* Spanish copper coin. *Castellano:* Spanish gold coin. *Arroba:* Spanish unit of weight, app. 25 pounds.
6. *Kahn:* Mongol ruler of China.
7. On the north coast of present-day Haiti.

as I have said. They are the most timid people in the world, so that only the men remaining there could destroy the whole region, and run no risk if they know how to behave themselves properly.

In all these islands the men seem to be satisfied with one wife, except they follow as many as twenty to their chief or king. The women appear to me to work harder than the men, and so far as I can hear they have nothing of their own, for I think I perceived that what one had others shared, especially food. In the islands so far I have found no monsters, as come expected, but, on the contrary, they are people of very handsome appearance. They are not black as in Guinea, though their hair is straight and coarse, as it does not grow where the sun's rays are too ardent. And in truth the sun has extreme power here, since it is within twenty-six degrees of the equinoctial line [equator]. In these islands there are mountains where the cold this winter was very severe, but the people endure it from habit, and with the aid of the meat they eat with very hot spices.

As for monsters,[8] I have found no trace of them except at the point in the second isle as one enters the Indies, which is inhabited by a people considered in all the isles as most ferocious, who eat human flesh. They possess many canoes, with which they overrun all the isles of India [West Indies], stealing and seizing all they can. They are not worse looking than the other, except that they wear their hair long like women, and use bows and arrows of the same cane, with a sharp stick at the end for want lack of iron,[9] of which they have none. They are ferocious compared to these other races, who are extremely cowardly, but I only hear this from the others. They are said to make treaties of marriage with the women in the first isle to be met with coming from Spain to the Indies, where there are no men. These women have no feminine occupation, but use bows and arrows of cane like those before mentioned, and cover and arm themselves with plates of copper, of which they have a great quantity. Another island, I am told, is larger than Hispaniola, where the

natives have no hair, and where there is countless gold; and from them all I bring Indians to testify to this.[10]

To speak, in conclusion, only of what has been done during this hurried voyage, their Highnesses will see that I can give them as much gold as they desire, if they will give me a little assistance, spices, cotton, as much as their Highnesses may command to be shipped, and mastic[11] as much as their Highnesses choose to send for, which until now has only been found in Greece, in the isle of Chios, and the Signoria can get its own price for it; as much lign-aloe[12] as they command to be shipped, and as many slaves as they choose to send for, all heathens. I think I have found rhubarb and cinnamon. Many other things of value will be discovered by the men I left behind me, as I stayed nowhere when the wind allowed me to pursue my voyage, except in the City of Navidad, which I left fortified and safe. Indeed, I might have accomplished much more, had the crews served me as they ought to have done.

The eternal and almighty God, our Lord, it is Who gives to all who walk in His way, victory over things apparently impossible, and in this case signally so, because although these lands had been imagined and talked of before they were seen, most men listened incredulously to what was thought to be but an idle tale. But our Redeemer has given victory to our most illustrious King and Queen, and to their kingdoms rendered famous by this glorious event, at which all Christendom should rejoice, celebrating it with great festivities and solemn Thanksgiving to the Holy Trinity, with fervent prayers for the high distinction that will accrue to them turning so many peoples to our holy faith; and also from the temporal benefits that not only Spain but all Christian nations will obtain. Thus I record what has happened in a brief note written on board the *Caravel*, off the Canary Isles, on the 15th of February, 1493.

*Yours to command,*
THE ADMIRAL.

---

8. Many Europeans, including Columbus, predicted that "monstrous races" existed in the unexplored world, including dog-headed men.
9. I.e., due to the lack of iron.
10. Columbus took
11. *Mastic:* valuable resin from a species of gum tree, used in food and medicine at the time.
12. *Lign-aloe:* another tree resin.

*Postscript within the letter*

Since writing the above, being in the Sea of Castile, so much wind arose south southeast, that I was forced to lighten the vessels, to run into this port of Lisbon to-day which was the most extraordinary thing in the world from whence I resolved to write to their Highnesses. In all the Indies I always found the temperature like that of May. Where I went in thirty-three days I returned in twenty-eight, except that these gales have detained me fourteen days, knocking about in this sea. Here all seamen say that there has never been so rough a winter, nor so many vessels lost. Done the 14th day of March.

**QUESTIONS TO CONSIDER**

1. How did Columbus describe the landscape around him? How did Columbus try to sell the area to the Spanish Crown?
2. What did Columbus think of the area's inhabitants?

# 1.2 PONCE DE LEÓN'S ROYAL PATENT (1511)

---

Ponce de León (1471–1521) was a Spanish explorer and political official who spent the last two decades of his life working for Spanish colonial efforts in the Caribbean and North America. In 1512, de León, by then the Governor of Puerto Rico, received a royal patent from King Ferdinand III to explore the island of Bimini, in the Bahamas, and mainland Florida. In 1515, he set out with a small fleet and traveled across the Caribbean and up both coasts of Florida before returning to Spain after Ferdinand's death in 1516. The explorer returned to Florida in 1521, but he died shortly thereafter in a skirmish with Florida's Native American Calusa inhabitants. In the translation of the patent that follows, the Spanish government outlined de León's land rights before the ensuing journey.

---

Whereas you, Juan Ponce de Leon, send to entreat and beg as a favor from me that I grant your permission and authority to go to discover and settle the Islands of Beniny, under certain conditions which will hereafter be declared, therefore, in order to show you favor, I grant you permission and authority so that you may go to discover and settle the island aforesaid, provided that it be not one of those already discovered, and under the conditions and as shall hereafter be set forth, as follows:

Firstly, that, with the ships you wish to take at your own cost and expense you may go to discover, and you shall discover, the island aforesaid; and for it, you may have three years' time counted from the day on which this my patent shall be presented to you, or when the contract shall be made with you in regard to the settlement aforesaid, provided that you shall be obliged to go to discover within the first year of the three years aforesaid, and that on going you may touch at any islands and mainland of the Ocean Sea, both discovered and to be discovered, provided they be not among the islands and mainland of the Ocean Sea belonging to the very serene king of Portugal, our very dear and very beloved son; and it is understood that you may not take or possess any profit or any other thing from them or any of them lying within the limits stipulated between us and him beyond only the things which should

*Source:* T. Frederick Davis, "Ponce de Leon's First Voyage and Discovery of Florida," *The Florida Historical Society Quarterly* 14 no. 1 (July 1935): 7–49.

be necessary for your maintenance and provision of ships and men, by paying for them what they should be worth.

*Item*, That you may take, and there shall be taken on your part in these kingdoms of Castile, or in the said Isla Española, for the abovesaid, the ships, supplies, officers, sailors, and men that you should find necessary, by paying for them in full according to custom, in the presence of our officials in Isla Española at present residing and who should reside in our House of Trade thereof, and in Castile, in the presence of our officials residing and who should reside in our House of Trade of Seville.

*Item*, In order to show you favor, I order that during the period of the three years, no person may go, nor shall he go, to discover the island of Beniny aforesaid; and if any one should go to discover it, or should discover it by accident, the stipulations of this my patent shall be carried out with you and not with the person who should thus discover it; and if another discover it, you shall lose nothing of the right which you have therefor, provided that, as aforesaid, you should set sail to go to discover it within the first year aforesaid, and that it will be of no value in any other way; and provided that it be not one of those of which report and certain knowledge is had.

*Item*, That when you find and discover the island aforesaid in the manner abovesaid, I make you the gift of the government and justice of it for all the days of your life, and for it I give you full power and civil and criminal jurisdiction, with all their incidences and dependencies, and annexes and rights.

*Item*, That when you find the island aforesaid, as abovesaid, you shall be obliged to settle at your cost in the sites and places that you can best do it; and that you may have possession of the houses and farms and settlements and heriditaments that you should make there and of the gain you should have in the island aforesaid, in accordance with the provisions of this contract.

*Item*, That, if fortresses should have to be built in the island aforesaid, they must be and shall be at our cost, and we shall place therein our wardens, as we should see best fulfils our service; and if, while the forts aforesaid are being built, you should build any house or houses for habitation and for defense from the Indians, these shall be your own; and if there should be need thereof for our service, you shall have to give them on being paid their value.

*Item*, That I shall give you, and by the present I do give you, for the space of twelve years, counted from the day on which you should discover the island of Beniny aforesaid, the tenth of all the revenues and profits belonging to us in the island aforesaid, if this is not from the tithes of our profits or in any other manner whatsoever.

*Item*, That I shall order you, and by the present I do order you, that the Indians who should be in the island aforesaid, shall be allotted in accordance with the persons there should be [in your expedition]; and that this be observed and that the first discoverers be provided for before any other persons; and that all the preference that should conveniently be shown in this be given to them.

*Item*, That I grant for the space of the ten years aforesaid that those persons who should go to discover the island aforesaid and who should settle on that voyage, enjoy the gold and other metals and profitable things which should be in the island aforesaid, without paying us from them other fees or tithes the first year; in the second, the ninth part; in the third, the eighth part; in the fourth, the seventh part; in the fifth, the sixth part; and the other five years after that paying the fifth, in accordance with and in the form and manner in which it is now paid in the Isla Española; and that the other settlers who should go later, who are not included among the discoverers should pay the fifth from the first year; for I order another exemption to be given to the latter instead of that from gold.

*Item*, To show greater benefit and favor to you, the said Juan Ponce de Leon, it is my will and pleasure that you are to have the government and settlement of all the islands lying near the island of Beniny aforesaid which you should discover in your person and at your cost and expense in the manner aforesaid, and which are not among those islands of which information is had, as abovesaid, under the conditions and in the form that is set forth in this my agreement; and as, by virtue thereof, you are to have of the island aforesaid.

*Item,* That I grant you the title of our adelantado of the island aforesaid, and of the other islands you shall discover in the manner aforesaid.

*Item,* That you collect the gold, if there should be any, in the same way in which it is now collected in the Isla Española, or in the form and manner that I shall order.

*Item,* That you can not take in your company, for the aforesaid, any person or persons who are foreigners from outside our domains and seigniories.

*Item,* That for assurance that you, the said Juan Ponce and the persons who should go with you will execute, carry out, and perform and that the contents of this patent which it pertains to you to observe and carry out shall be carried out, performed, and observed, before making the said voyage shall give trustworthy and creditable bonds to the satisfaction of our officials residing in the Isla Española.

*Item,* That you, the said Juan Ponce, and the other persons who should go and remain there, shall execute and observe and perform all that is contained in this my said agreement, and every part and parcel of it, any you shall not cause any fraud or deceit, nor shall you give favor, or aid or consent thereto; and if you should learn of any, you will inform us and our officials in our name, under penalty that any person of you who should do the contrary, by that very fact he who does not so act, shall have lost any grace or benefit which we should consider it fitting to order executed on the persons and goods of those who should do it, or consent to it, or conceal it.

*Item,* That after having reached the island and learned what is in it, you shall send me a report of it, and another to our officials who reside in the Isla Española, so that we may know what should have been done and take the measures fitting to our service.

Therefore, if you, the said Juan Ponce carry out all the abovesaid and every part and parcel of it, and shall have given the said bonds or give and pay the things abovesaid, I promise and assure you by the present to order everything contained in this patent and every part and parcel of it to be observed and carried out, and order our officials who reside in the Isla Española that in our name, in accordance with the abovesaid, they should make the said contract and agreement with you and receive the said bonds. For your dispatch, I am ordering Don Diego Colon, our admiral and governor of the said Isla Española, and our appellate judges and the officials of our treasury who reside there, and all the justices of the said Isla Española that they give you all the favor and aid that you should find necessary, and that no impediments be offered you therein or in any part or parcel of it.

Done in Burgos, February twenty-three, one thousand five hundred and twelve.

*I the King*

By command of his Highness
  Lope Conchillos.
Sealed by the Bishop of Palencia.

## QUESTIONS TO CONSIDER

1. What rights did Ponce de León receive in Bimini?
2. How did the Spanish government seek to use the patent to assert its own power on the North American mainland?

# 1.3 BARTOLEMÉ DE LAS CASAS, EXCERPT FROM *A BRIEF ACCOUNT OF THE DESTRUCTION OF THE INDIES* (1552)

Bartolemé de las Casas (1484–1566), a Spanish friar and historian, was the one of the first people to broadcast how Spanish colonial officials abused indigenous populations in the Americas. Appointed "Protector of the Indians," de las Casas set about trying to change Spanish policy toward indigenous populations in the early 1540s. In 1542, de las Casas wrote *A Brief Account of the Destruction of the Indies* and sent the work to Prince Phillip II of Spain. In *A Brief Account*, which he published a decade later, de las Casas outlined Spanish cruelty toward indigenous peoples. *A Brief Account* helped to convince Spanish authorities to create the New Laws of 1542, which, among other things, limited the power of colonial governors and barred Spanish officials from enslaving indigenous people.

America was discovered and found out *Ann. Dom.* 1492, and the Year insuing inhabited by the *Spaniards*, and afterward a multitude of them travelled thither from *Spain* for the space of Nine and Forty Years. Their first attempt was on the *Spanish* Island, which indeed is a most fertile soil, and at present in great reputation for its Spaciousness and Length, containing in Circumference Six Hundred Miles: Nay it is on all sides surrounded with an almost innumerable number of Islands, which we found so well peopled with Natives and Forreigners, that there is scarce any Region in the Universe fortified with so many Inhabitants: But the main Land or Continent, distant from this Island Two Hundred and Fifty Miles and upwards, extends it self above Ten Thousand Miles in Length near the sea-shore, which Lands are some of them already discover'd, and more may be found out in process of time: And such a multitude of People inhabits these Countries, that it seems as if the Omnipotent God has Assembled and Convocated the major part of Mankind in this part of the World.

Now this infinite multitude of Men are by the Creation of God innocently simple, altogether void of and averse to all manner of Craft, Subtlety and Malice, and most Obedient and Loyal Subjects to their Native Sovereigns; and behave themselves very patiently, sumissively and quietly towards the *Spaniards*, to whom they are subservient and subject; so that finally they live without the least thirst after revenge, laying aside all litigiousness, Commotion and hatred.

This is a most tender and effeminate people, and so imbecile and unequal-balanced temper, that they are altogether incapable of hard labour, and in few years, by one Distemper or other soon expire, so that the very issue of Lords and Princes, who among us live with great affluence, and fard deliciously, are not more effiminate and tender than the Children of their Husbandmen or Labourers: This Nation is very Necessitous and Indigent, Masters of very slender Possessions, and consequently, neither Haughty, nor Ambitious. They are parsimonious in their Diet, as the Holy Fathers were in their frugal life in the Desert, known by the name of *Eremites*. They go naked, having no other Covering but what conceals their Pudends from publick sight. An hairy Plad, or loose Coat, about an Ell, or a coarse woven Cloth at most Two Ells long serves

*Source:* Bartolemé de las Casas, *A Brief Account of the Destruction of the Indies* (Urbana-Champaign, IL: Project Gutenberg, 2007), http://www.gutenberg.org/cache/epub/20321/pg20321-images.html (Accessed June 4, 2018).

them for the warmest Winter Garment. They lye on a coarse Rug or Matt, and those that have the most plentiful Estate or Fortunes, the better sort, use Network, knotted at the four corners in lieu of Beds, which the Inhabitants of the Island of *Hispaniola*, in their own proper Idiom, term *Hammacks*. The Men are pregnant and docible. The natives tractable, and capable of Morality or Goodness, very apt to receive the instill'd principles of Catholick Religion; nor are they averse to Civility and good Manners, being not so much discompos'd by variety of Obstructions, as the rest of Mankind; insomuch, that having suckt in (if I may so express my self) the very first Rudiments of the Christian Faith, they are so transported with Zeal and Furvor in the exercise of Ecclesiastical Sacraments, and Divine Service, that the very Religioso's themselves, stand in need of the greatest and most signal patience to undergo such extream Transports. And to conclude, I my self have heard the *Spaniards* themselves (who dare not assume the Confidence to deny the good Nature praedominant in them) declare, that there was nothing wanting in them for the acquisition of Eternal Beatitude, but the sole Knowledge and Understanding of the Deity. . . .

As to the firm land, we are certainly satisfied, and assur'd, that the *Spaniards* by their barbarous and execrable Actions have absolutely depopulated Ten Kingdoms, of greater extent than all *Spain*, together with the Kingdoms of *Arragon* and *Portugal*, that is to say, above One Thousand Miles, which now lye wast and desolate, and are absolutely ruined, when as formerly no other Country whatsoever was more populous. Nay we dare boldly affirm, that during the Forty Years space, wherein they exercised their sanguinary and detestable Tyranny in these Regions, above Twelve Millions (computing Men, Women, and Children) have undeservedly perished; nor do I conceive that I should deviate from the Truth by saying that above Fifty Millions in all paid their last Debt to Nature.

Those that arriv'd at these Islands from the remotest parts of *Spain*, and who pride themselves in the Name of Christians, steer'd Two courses principally, in order to the Extirpation, and Exterminating of this People from the face of the Earth. The first whereof was raising an unjust, sanguinolent, cruel War. The other, by putting them to death, who hitherto, thirsted

after their Liberty, or design'd (which the most Potent, Strenuous and Magnanimous Spirits intended) to recover their pristin Freedom, and shake off the Shackles of so injurious a Captivity: For they being taken off in War, none but Women and Children were permitted to enjoy the benefit of that Country-Air, in whom they did in succeeding times lay such a heavy Yoak, that the very Brutes were more happy than they: To which Two Species of Tyranny as subalternate things to the Genus, the other innumerable Courses they took to extirpate and make this a desolate People, may be reduced and referr'd.

Now the ultimate end and scope that incited the *Spaniards* to endeavor the Extirptaion and Desolation of this People, was Gold only; that thereby growing opulent in a short time, they might arrive at once at such Degrees and Dignities, as were no wayes consistent with their Persons.

Finally, in one word, their Ambition and Avarice, than which the heart of Man never entertained greater, and the vast Wealth of those Regions; the Humility and Patience of the Inhabitants (which made their approach to these Lands more facil and easie) did much promote the business: Whom they so despicably contemned, that they treated them (I speak of things which I was an Eye Witness of, without the least fallacy) not as Beasts, which I cordially wished they would, but as the most abject dung and filth of the Earth; and so sollicitous they were of their Life and Soul, that the above-mentioned number of People died without understanding the true Faith or Sacraments. And this also is as really true as the praecedent Narration (which the very Tyrants and cruel Murderers cannot deny without the stigma of a lye) that the *Spaniards* never received any injury from the *Indians*, but that they rather reverenced them as Persons descended from Heaven, until that they were compelled to take up Arms, provoked thereunto by repeated Injuries, violent Torments, and injust Butcheries.

## OF THE ISLAND HISPANIOLA

In this Isle, which, as we have said, the *Spaniards* first attempted, the bloody slaughter and destruction of Men first began: for they violently forced away Women and

Children to make them Slaves, and ill-treated them, consuming and wasting their Food, which they had purchased with great sweat, toil, and yet remained dissatisfied too, which every one according to his strength and ability, and that was very inconsiderable (for they provided no other Food than what was absolutely necessary to support Nature without superfluity, freely bestow'd on them, and one individual *Spaniard* consumed more Victuals in one day, than would serve to maintain Three Families a Month, every one consisting of Ten Persons. Now being oppressed by such evil usage, and afflicted with such greate Torments and violent Entertainment they began to understand that such Men as those had not their Mission from Heaven; and therefore some of them conceal'd their Provisions and others to their Wives and Children in lurking holes, but some, to avoid the obdurate and dreadful temper of such a Nation, sought their Refuge on the craggy tops of Mountains; for the *Spaniards* did not only entertain them with Cuffs, Blows, and wicked Cudgelling, but laid violent hands also on the Governors of Cities; and this arriv'd at length to that height of Temerity and Impudence, that a certain Captain was so audacious as abuse the Consort of the most puissant King of the whole Isle. From which time they began to consider by what wayes and means they might expel the *Spaniards* out of their Countrey, and immediately took up Arms. But, good God, what Arms, do you imagin? Namely such, both Offensive and Defensive, as resemble Reeds wherewith Boys sport with one another, more than Manly Arms and Weapons.

Which the *Spaniards* no sooner perceived, but they, mounted on generous Steeds, well weapon'd with Lances and Swords, begin to exercise their bloody Butcheries and Strategems, and overrunning their Cities and Towns, spar'd no Age, or Sex, nay not so much as Women with Child, but ripping up their Bellies, tore them alive in pieces. They laid Wagers among themselves, who should with a Sword at one blow cut, or divide a Man in two; or which of them should decollate or behead a Man, with the greatest dexterity; nay farther, which should sheath his Sword in the Bowels of a Man with the quickest dispatch and expedition.

They snatcht young Babes from the Mothers Breasts, and then dasht out the brains of those innocents against the Rocks; others they cast into Rivers scoffing and jeering them, and call'd upon their Bodies when falling with derision, the true testimony of their Cruelty, to come to them, and inhumanely exposing others to their Merciless Swords, together with the Mothers that gave them Life.

They erected certain Gibbets, large, but low made, so that their feet almost reacht the ground, every one of which was so order'd as to bear Thirteen Persons in Honour and Reverence (as they said blasphemously) of our Redeemer and his Twelve Apostles, under which they made a Fire to burn them to Ashes whilst hanging on them: But those they intended to preserve alive, they dismiss'd, their Hands half cut, and still hanging by the Skin, to carry their Letters missive to those that fly from us and lye sculking on the Mountains, as an exprobation of their flight.

The Lords and Persons of Noble Extract were usually expos'd to this kind of Death; they order'd Gridirons to be placed and supported with wooden Forks, and putting a small Fire under them, these miserable Wretches by degrees and with loud Shreiks and exquisite Torments, at last Expir'd.

I once saw Four or Five of their most Powerful Lords laid on these Gridirons, and thereon roasted, and not far off, Two or Three more over-spread with the same Commodity, Man's Flesh; but the shril Clamours which were heard there being offensive to the Captain, by hindring his Repose, he commanded them to be strangled with a Halter. The Executioner (whose Name and Parents at *Sevil* are not unknown to me) prohibited the doing of it; but stopt Gags into their Mouths to prevent the hearing of the noise (he himself making the Fire) till that they dyed, when they had been roasted as long as he thought convenient. I was an Eye-Witness of these and innumerable Number of other Cruelties: And because all Men, who could lay hold of the opportunity, sought out lurking holes in the Mountains, to avoid as dangerous Rocks so Brutish and Barbarous a People, Strangers to all Goodness, and the Extirpaters and Adversaries of Men, they bred up such fierce hunting Dogs as would devour an *Indian* like a Hog, at first sight in less than a moment: Now such kind of Slaughters and Cruelties as these were committed by the Curs, and if at any time it hapned, (which was rarely) that the *Indians* irritated upon a just account destroyd or took away the Life of any *Spaniard,* they promulgated and proclaim›d this Law among them, that One Hundred *Indians* should dye for every individual *Spaniard* that should be slain.

**QUESTIONS TO CONSIDER**

1. How did de las Casas depict indigenous populations? How did he describe Spanish colonizers?
2. What strategy did de las Casas use to try to convince Phillip II of the "Destruction of the Indies"?

# 1.4 LETTER WRITTEN BY JUAN DE OÑATE FROM NEW MEXICO (1599)

Juan de Oñate (1550–1626) was a Spanish conquistador who served as governor of the new Spanish colony in New Mexico from 1598 to 1608. In 1599, early in his tenure, de Oñate wrote the following letter to the former Viceroy of New Spain, Luis de Velasco, who had selected de Oñate as Governor in 1595. In the letter, de Oñate outlined his efforts to instill order in his men, described the indigenous inhabitants, and tried to convince de Velasco of the colony's potential as an economic asset to Spain. In 1601, de Oñate led an expedition to the Great Plains region and fought several skirmishes against the Native Americans he found there. In 1606, he resigned his position and was exiled from New Mexico after an investigation into his leadership revealed mistreatment of colonial and indigenous populations.

*Copy of a letter written by Don Juan de Oñate from New Mexico to the Viceroy, the Count of Monterey, on the second day of March, 1599.*

From Rio de Nombre de Dios I last wrote to you Illustrius Sir, giving you an account of my departure, and of the discovery of a wagon road to the Rio del Norte, and of my certain hopes God has been pleased to grant, may He be forever praised; for greatly to His advantage and that of his royal Majesty, they have acquired a possession so good that none other of his Majesty in these Indies excels it, judging it solely by what I have seen, by things told of in reliable reports, and by things almost a matter of experience, from having been seen by people in my camp and known by me at present.

This does not include the vastness of the settlements or the riches of the West which the natives praise, or the certainty of pearls promised by the South Sea from the many shells containing them possessed by these Indians, or the many settlements called the seven caves, which the Indians report at the head of this river, which is the Rio del Norte; but includes only the provinces which I have seen and traversed, the people of this eastern country, the Apaches, the nation of the Cocoyes, and many others which are daily being discovered in this district and neighborhood, as I shall specify in this letter. I wish to begin by giving your Lordship an account of it, because it is the first since I left New Spain.

I departed, Illustrius Sir, from Rio de Nombre de Dios on the sixteenth of March, with the great

*Source:* "Letter Written by Don Juan de Oñate from New Mexico, 1599," *American Journeys,* http://www.americanjourneys.org/pdf/AJ-010.pdf (Accessed June 4, 2018).

multitude of wagons, women, and children, which your Lordship very well knows, freed from all my opponents, but with a multitude of evil predictions conforming to their desires and not to the goodness of God. His Majesty was pleased to accede to my desires, and to take pity on my great hardships, afflictions, and expenses, bringing me to these provinces of New Mexico with all his Majesty's army enjoying perfect health.

Although I reached these provinces on the twenty-eighth day of May (going ahead with as many as sixty soldiers to pacify the land and free it from traitors, if in it there should be any, seizing Humaña and his followers, to obtain full information, by seeing with my own eyes, regarding the location and nature of the land, and regarding the nature and customs of the people, so as to order what might be best for the army, which I left about twenty-two leagues from the first pueblos, after having crossed the Rio del Norte, at which river I took possession, in the name of his Majesty, of all these kingdoms and pueblos which I discovered before departing from it with scouts), the army did not overtake me at the place where I established it and where I now have it established, in this province of the Teguas, until the nineteenth day of August of the past year. During that time I travelled through settlements sixty-one leagues in extent toward the north, and thirty-five in width from east to west. All this district is filled with pueblos, large and small, very continuous and close together.

At the end of August I began to prepare the people of my camp for the severe winter with which both the Indians and the nature of the land threatened me; and the devil, who has ever tried to make good his great loss occasioned by our coming, plotted, as is his wont, exciting a rebellion among more than forty-five soldiers and captains, who under pretext of not finding immediately whole plates of silver lying on the ground, and offended because I would not permit them to maltreat these natives, either in their persons or in their goods, became disgusted with the country, or to be more exact, with me, and endeavored to form a gang in order to flee to that New Spain, as they proclaimed, although judging from what has since come to light their intention was directed more to stealing slaves and clothing and to other acts of effrontery not

permitted. I arrested two captains and a soldier, who they said were guilty, in order to garrote them on this charge, but ascertaining that their guilt was not so great, and on account of my situation and of the importunate pleadings of the religious and of the entire army, I was forced to forego the punishment and let bygones be bygones.

Although by the middle of September I succeeded in completely calming and pacifying my camp, from this great conflagration a spark was bound to remain hidden underneath the ashes of the dissembling countenances of four of the soldiers of the said coterie. These fled from me at that time, stealing from me part of the horses, thereby violating not only one but many proclamations which, regarding this matter and others, I had posted for the good of the land in the name of his Majesty.

Since they had violated his royal orders, it appeared to me that they should not go unpunished; therefore I immediately sent post-haste the captain and procurator-general Gaspar Perez de Villagran and the captain of artillery Geronimo Marques, with an express order to follow and overtake them and give them due punishment. They left in the middle of September, as I have said, thinking that they would overtake them at once, but their journey was prolonged more than they or I had anticipated, with the result to two of the offenders which your Lordship already knows from the letter which they tell me they wrote from Sancta Barbara. The other two who fled from them will have received the same at your Lordship's hands, as is just. . . .

The people are in general very comely; their color is like those of that land, and they are much like them in manner and dress, in their grinding, in their food, dancing, singing, and many other things, except in their languages, which are many, and different from those there. Their religion consists in worshipping idols, of which they have many; and in their temples, after their temples, after their own manner, they worship them with fire, painted reeds, feathers, and universal offering of almost everything they get, such as small animals, birds, vegetables, etc. In their government they are free, for although they have some petty captains, they obey them badly and in very few things.

We have seen other nations such as the Querechos, or herdsmen, who live in tents of tanned hides, among the buffalo. The Apaches, of whom we have also seen some, are innumerable, and although I heard that they lived in rancherías, a few days ago I ascertained that they live like these in pueblos, one of which, eighteen leagues from here, contains fifteen plazas. They are a people whom I have compelled to render obedience to His Majesty, although not by means of legal instruments like the rest of the provinces. This has caused me much labor, diligence, and care, long journeys, with arms on the shoulders, and not a little watching and circumspection; indeed, because my *maese de campo* was not as cautious as he should have been, they killed him with twelve companions in a great pueblo and fortress called Acóma, which must contain about three thousand Indians. As punishment for its crime and its treason against his Majesty, to whom it had already rendered submission by a public instrument, and as a warning to the rest, I razed and burned it completely, in the way in which your Lordship will see by the process of this cause. All these provinces, pueblos, and peoples, I have seen with my own eyes.

There is another nation, that of the Cocóyes, an innumerable people with huts and agriculture. Of this nation and of the large settlements at the source of the Rio del Norte and of those to the northwest and west and towards the South Sea, I have numberless reports, and pearls of remarkable size from the said sea, and assurance that there is an infinite number of them on the coast of this country. And as to the east, a person in my camp, an Indian who speaks Spanish and is one of those who came with Humaña, has been in the pueblo of the said herdsmen. It is nine continuous leagues in length and two in width, with streets and houses consisting of huts. It is situated in the midst of the multitude of buffalo, which are so numerous that my *sargento mayor*, who hunted them and brought back their hides, meat, tallow, and suet, asserts that in one herd alone he saw more than there are of our cattle in the combined three ranches of Rodrigo del Rio, Salvago, and Jeronimo Lopez, which are famed in those regions.

I should never cease were I to recount individually all of the many things which occur to me. I can only say that with God's help I shall see them all, and give new worlds, new, peaceful, and grand, to his Majesty, greater than the good Marquis gave to him, although he did so much, if you, Illustrious Sir, will give to me the aid, the protection, and the help which I expect from such a hand. And although I confess that I am crushed at having been so out of favor when I left that country, and although a soul frightened by disfavor usually loses hope and despairs of success, it is nevertheless true that I never have and never shall lose hope of receiving many and very great favors at the hand of your Lordship, especially in matters of such importance to his Majesty. And in order that you, Illustrious Sir, may be inclined to render them to me, I beg that you take note of the great increase which the royal crown and the rents of his Majesty have and will have in this land, with so many and such a variety of things, each one of which promises very-great treasures. . . .

## QUESTIONS TO CONSIDER

1. How did de Oñate describe his work? What did he think of the Native American populations he encountered?
2. Does de Oñate's leadership style seem effective?

# 1.5 CONTRASTING VIEWS OF THE SPANISH CONQUEST OF TENOCHTITLÁN (1585, n.d.)

The following two images depict the capture of the Aztec capital at Tenochtitlán by Spanish conquistador Hérnan Cortés in 1521. To take the city, one of the largest in the world at the time, Cortés courted alliances with other indigenous populations and led a coalition force against the Aztecs. The first image, from the *History of Tlaxcala*, created under the direction of the Mexican businessman Diego Muñoz Camargo in 1585, shows a Native American view of the capture of the city. In the top panel, La Malinche, Cortés' enslaved indigenous interpreter and advisor, leads a Spanish ship forward. In the middle panel, indigenous warriors allied with Cortés lead the attack against Aztec warriors. The second image, "The Capture of Tenochtitlan," painted by a Spanish artist in the seventeenth century, shows how the Spanish viewed the city and the conquest. After Cortés' victory, Spanish forces looted the city and slaughtered thousands of inhabitants.

*Sources:* "Anfibian attack of spanish-tlaxcallan forces. Malinche and Cortés," https://commons.wikimedia.org/wiki/Category:Lienzo_de_Tlaxcala#/media/File:Lienzo_de_Tlaxcala_Teciquauhtitla.jpg (Accessed June 4, 2018); "Entrance of Cortés La Conquista de Mexico," https://www.loc.gov/exhibits/exploring-the-early-americas/conquest-of-mexico-paintings.html (Accessed June 4, 2018).

**QUESTIONS TO CONSIDER**

1. How did Camargo view the attack? How did the Spanish view the attack?

2. What differences stand out between the two works? How might you explain these differences?

# CHAPTER 2

# COLONIAL OUTPOSTS, 1550–1650

## 2.1 ROYAL PATENT FROM QUEEN ELIZABETH I TO WALTER RALEIGH (1585)

In 1584, Queen Elizabeth I of England gave the English explorer Walter Raleigh (1554–1618) a royal patent to possession of "such remote, heathen and barbarous lands, countreis, and territories, not actually possessed of any Christian prince, nor inhabited by Christian people" in North America in exchange for one-fifth of any gold and silver found there. Raleigh's patent was part of a broader effort by Elizabeth I to increase England's colonial holdings and global prominence. Patent in hand, Raleigh organized multiple expeditions to Roanoke Island, North Carolina. The Roanoke Colony did not succeed due to consistent scarcity of supplies, but the English interest in the North American southeast would remain. In 1607, the Virginia Company founded a royal colony in Virginia at Jamestown.

Elizabeth by the grace of God of England, France and Ireland Queene, defender of the faith, &c. To all people to whom these presents shal come, greeting. Know ye that of our especial grace, certaine science, & meere motion, we have given and granted, and by these presents for us, our heires and successors doe give and grant to our trusty and welbeloved servant Walter Ralegh Esquire, and to his heires and assignes forever, free liberty & licence from time to time, and at all times for ever hereafter, to discover, search, finde out, and view such remote, heathen and barbarous lands, countreis, and territories, not actually possessed of any Christian prince, nor inhabited by Christian people, as to him, his heires and assignes, and to every or any of them shall seeme good, and the same to have, holde, occupy & enjoy to him, his heires and assignes for ever, with all prerogatives, commodities, jurisdictions, royalties, priviledges, franchises and preeminences, thereto or thereabouts both by sea and land, whatsoever we by our letters patents may grant, and as we or any of our noble progenitors have heretofore granted to any person or persons, bodies politique or corporate: and the saide Walter Ralegh, his heires and assignes, and all such as from time to time, by licence of us, our heires and successors, shal goe or travaile thither to inhabite or remaine, there to build

*Source:* "The letters patents, granted by the Queenes Majestie to M. Walter Ralegh," *Virtual Jamestown,* http://www.virtualjamestown.org/exist/cocoon/jamestown/fha/J1013m (Accessed May 9, 2018).

and fortifie, at the discretion of the said Walter Ralegh, his heires & assignes, the statutes or act of Parliament made against fugitives, or against such as shall depart, remaine or continue out of our Realme of England without licence, or any other statute, act, law, or any ordinance whatsoever to the contrary in any wise notwithstanding.

And we do likewise by these presents, of our especial grace, meere motion, and certaine knowledge for us, our heires and successors, give and graunt full authoritie, libertie and power to the said Walter Ralegh, his heires and assignes, and every of them, that he and they, and every or any of them, shall and may at all and every time and times hereafter, have, take, and leade in the sayde voyage, and travaile thitherward, or inhabite there with him or them, and every or any of them, such, and so many of our subjects as shall willingly accompany him or them, and every or any of them: and to whom also we doe by these presents, give full libertie and authoritie in that behalfe, and also to have, take and employ, and use sufficient shipping and furniture for the transportations, and Navigations in that behalfe, so that none of the same persons or any of them be such as hereafter shall be restrained by us, our heires or successors.

And further that the said Walter Ralegh his heires and assignes, and every of them, shall have, holde, occupie and enjoy to him, his heires and assignes, and every of them for ever, all the soyle of all such landes, territories, and Countreis, so to be discovered and possessed as aforesayd, and of all such Cities, Castles, Townes, Villages, and places in the same, with the right royalties, franchises, and jurisdictions, as well marine as other within the sayd landes, or Countreis, or the seas thereunto adjoyning, to be had, or used, with full power to dispose thereof, and of every part in fee simple or otherwise, according to the order of the lawes of England, as neere as the same conveniently may be, at his, and their wil and pleasure, to any persons then being, or that shall remaine within the allegiance of us, our heires and successors: reserving alwayes to us, our heires and successors, for all services, dueties, and demaunds, the fift part of all the oare of golde and silver, that from time to time, and at all times after such discoverie, subduing and possessing, shall be there gotten and obteined: All which lands, Countries,

and territories shall for ever be holden of the sayd Walter Ralegh, his heires and assignes, of us, our heires and successors, by homage, and by the sayd payment of the sayd fift part, reserved onely for all services.

And moreover, we do by these presents, for us, our heires and succsessors, give and grant licence to the said Walter Ralegh, his heires, and assignes, and every of them, that he, and they, and every or any of them, shall and may from time to time, and at all times for ever hereafter, for his and their defence, encounter and expulse, repell and resist aswell by sea as by lande, and by all other wayes whatsoever, all and every such person and persons whatsoever, as without the especiall liking and license of the sayd Walter Ralegh, and of his heires and assignes, shall attempt to inhabite within the sayde Countryes, or any of them, or within the space of two hundreth leagues neere to the place or places within such Countryes as aforesayde (if they shall not bee before planted or inhabited within the limits as aforesayd with the subjects of any Christian Prince being in amitie with us) where the sayd Walter Ralegh, his heires, or assignes, or any of them, or his, or their, or any of their associats or company, shall within six yeeres (next ensuing) make their dwellings or abidings, or that shall enterprise or attempt at any time hereafter unlawfully to annoy, eyther by Sea or Lande the sayde Walter Ralegh, his heires or assignes, or any of them, or his or their, or any of his or their companies: giving, and graunting by these presents further power and authoritie to the sayd Walter Ralegh, his heires and assignes, and every of them from time to time, and at all times for ever hereafter, to take and surprise by all maner of meanes whatsoever, all and every those person or persons, with their Shippes, Vessels, and other goods and furniture, which without the licence of the sayde Walter Ralegh, or his heires, or assignes, as aforesayd, shalbe found traffiquing into any Harbour, or Harbours, Creeke, or Creekes, within the limits aforesayd, (the subjects of our Realmes and Dominions, and all other persons in amitie with us, trading to the Newfound lands for fishing as heretofore they have commonly used, or being driven by force of a tempest, or shipwracke only excepted and those persons, and every of them, with their shippes, vessels, goods, and furniture to deteine and possesse as of good and lawfull prize, according to the discretion of him the sayd Walter Ralegh, his heires, and assignes, and every, or any of them. And for uniting in more perfect league and amitie, of such Countryes, landes, and territories so to be possessed and inhabited as aforesayd with our Realmes of England and Ireland, and the better incouragement of men to these enterprises: we doe by these presents, graunt and declare that all such Countries, so hereafter to be possessed and inhabited as is aforesayd, from thencefoorth shall be of the allegiance to us, our heires and successours. And wee doe graunt to the sayd Walter Ralegh, his heires, and assignes, and to all, and every of them, and to all, and every other person and persons, being of our allegiance, whose names shall be noted or entred in some of our Courts of recorde within our Realme of England, that with the assent of the sayd Walter Ralegh, his heires or assignes, shall in his journeis for discoverie, or in the journeis for conquest hereafter travail to such lands, countreis and territories, as aforesayd, and to their, and to every of their heires, and they, and every or any of them being eyther borne within our sayde Realmes of England or Irelande, or in any other place within our allegiance, and which hereafter shall be inhabiting within any the Lands, Countryes, and Territories, with such licence, (as aforesayd) shall and may have all the priviledges of free Denizens, and persons native of England, and within our allegiance in such like ample maner and forme, as if they were borne and personally resident within our said Realme of England, any law, custome, or usage to the contrary notwithstanding.

And forasmuch as upon the finding out, discovering, or inhabiting of such remote lands, countries, and territories as aforesaid, it shalbe necessary for the safety of all men, that shall adventure themselves in those journeyes or voyages, to determine to live together in Christian peace, and civill quietnesse eche with other, whereby every one may with more pleasure and profit enjoy that whereunto they shall atteine with great paine and perill, wee for us, our heires and successors, are likewise pleased and contented, and by these presents doe give & grant to the said Walter Ralegh, his heires and assignes for ever, that he and they, and every or any of them, shall and may from time to time for ever hereafter, within the said mentioned remote lands and countries, in the way by the seas thither, and

from thence, have full and meere power and authoritie to correct, punish, pardon, governe, and rule by their and every or any of their good discretions and policies, aswell in causes capitall, or criminall, as civil, both marine and other, all such our subjects, as shal from time to time adventure themselves in the said journeis or voyages, or that shall at any time hereafter inhabite any such lands, countreis, or territories as aforesayd, or that shall abide within 200 leagues of any of the sayd place or places where the sayde Walter Ralegh, his heires or assignes, or any of them, or any of his or their associats or companies, shall inhabite within 6 yeeres next ensuing the date hereof, according to such statutes, lawes and ordinances as shall be by him the sayd Walter Ralegh, his heires and assignes, and every or any of them devised, or established, for the better government of the said people as aforesaid. So always as the said statutes, lawes, and ordinances may be, as nere as conveniently may bee, agreeable to the forme of the lawes, statutes, governement, or pollicie of England, and also so as they be not against the true Christian faith, nowe professed in the Church of England, nor in any wise to withdrawe any of the subjects or people of those lands or places from the alleagance of us, our heires and successours, as their immediate Soveraigne under God.

And further, we doe by these presents for us, our heires and successors, give and grant ful power and authoritie to our trustie and welbeloved Counsailour Sir William Cecill knight, Lorde Burghley, or high Treasourer of England, and to the Lorde Treasourer of England for us, our heires and successors for the time being, and to the privie Counsaile of us, our heires and successors, or any foure or more of them for the time being, that he, they, or any foure or more of them, shall and may from time to time, and at all times hereafter, under his or their handes or Seales by vertue of these presents, authorise and licence the saide Walter Ralegh, his heires and assignes, and every or any of them by him, & by themselves, or by their, or any of their sufficient Atturneis, Deputies, Officers, Ministers, Factors, and servants, to imbarke & transport out of our Realme of England and Ireland, and the Dominions thereof, all or any part of his or their goods, and all or any the goods of his and their associats and companies, and every or any of them, with such other necessaries and commodities of any our Realmes, as to the sayde Lorde Treasurer, or foure or more of the privie Counsaile, of us our heires and successors for the time being (as aforesaid) shalbe from time to time by his or their wisedomes, or discretions thought meete and convenient, for the better reliefe and supportation of him the sayde Walter Ralegh, his heires, and assignes, and every or any of them, and of his or their or any of their associats and companies, any act, statue, law, or any thing to the contrary in any wise notwithstanding.

Provided alwayes, and our wil and pleasure is, and we do hereby declare to all Christian kings, princes, and states, that if the sayde Walter Ralegh, his heires or assignes, or any of them, or any other by their licence or appointment, shall at any time or times hereafter robbe or spoile by sea or by land, or doe any acte of unjust or unlawfull hostilitie, to any of the subjects of us, our heires or successors, or to any of the subjucts of any the kings, princes, rulers, Governours, or estates, being then in perfect league and amitie with us, our heires and successours, and that upon such injurie, or upon just complaint of any such Prince, Ruler, Governour or estate, or their subjects, wee, our heires and successors, shall make open Proclamation within any the portes of our Realme of England, that the saide Walter Ralegh, his heires and assignes, and adherents, or any to whom these our Letters patents may extende, shall within the termes to bee limited, by such Proclamation, make full restitution, and satisfaction of all such injuries done: so as both we and the said Princes, or other so complaining, may hold us and themselves fully contented: And that if the said Walter Ralegh, his heires and assignes, shall not make our cause to be made satisfaction accordingly within such time so

to be limitted, that then it shal be lawful to us, our heires and successors, to put the sayde Walter Ralegh, his heires and assignes, and adherents, and all the inhabitants of the saide places to be discovered (as in aforesaid) or any of them out of our allegeance and protection, and that from and after such time of putting out of protection of the saide Walter Ralegh, his heires, assignes and adherents, and others so to be put out, and the said places within their habitation, possession and rule, shall be out of our allegeance and protection, and free for all Princes and others to pursue with hostilitie, as being not our subjects, nor by us any way to be avouched, maintained, or defended, nor to be holden as any of ours, nor to our protection, or dominion, or allegeance any way belonging: for that expresse mention of the cleere yeerely value of the certaintie of the premisses, or any part thereof, or of any other gift, or grant by us, or any our progenitors, or predecessors to the said Walter Ralegh, before this time made in these presents, bee not expressed, or any other grant, ordinance, provision, proclamation, or restraint to the contrary thereof, before this time, given, ordained, or provided, or any other thing, cause or matter whatsoever, in any wise notwithstanding. In witnesse whereof, wee have caused these our letters to be made Patents. Witnesse our selves, at Westminster the five and twentie day of March, in the sixe and twentith yeere of our Raigne.

## QUESTIONS TO CONSIDER

1. What rights did Raleigh receive?
2. Why was the English crown interested in North America? How did it view North America?

# 2.2 EXCERPT FROM JOHN WHITE'S RECOUNTING OF HIS JOURNEY TO ROANOKE (1590)

The English explorer and painter John White (1540–1593) was one of the men Walter Raleigh enlisted in his attempt to establish a colony at Roanoke, Virginia, after his 1584 Royal Patent (see Reading 2.1). White sailed on an initial voyage to Roanoke in 1585, and in 1586, Raleigh appointed White as Governor of the second attempt at a colony at Roanoke. White's group sailed from England in 1586, but White was forced to return to ask for more supplies just one year later. After multiple delays in making a voyage back to Roanoke due to European warfare, White returned in 1590 to find the colony deserted—it became the "Lost Colony" in the popular imagination. Poor weather forced White to give up searching for the colonists, including his daughter and granddaughter, on nearby islands, and he sailed for England just three months later. In the following document, White recounts his journey to the colony and attempts to locate the "lost" colonists. The population of Roanoke Island likely relocated to the mainland and there merged with various Native American tribes.

The 15 of August towards evening we came to an anker at Hatorask, in 36 degr. and one third, in five fadom water, three leagues from the shore. At our first comming to anker on this shore we saw a great smoke rise in the Ile Roanoak neere the place where I left our Colony in the yeere 1587, which smoake put us in good hope that some of the colony were there expecting my returne out of England.

The 16 and next morning our two boates went a shore & Captaine Cooke, & Cap. Spicer, & their company with me, with intent to passe to the place at Raonoak, where our countreymen were left. At our putting from the ship we commanded our Master gunner to make readie two Minions and a Falkon well loden, and to shoot them off with reasonable space betweene every shot, to the ende that their reportes might bee heard to the place where wee hoped to finde some of our people. This was accordingly performed, & our twoe boats put off unto the shore, in the Admirals boat we sounded all the way and found from our shippe until we came within a mile of the shore nine, eight, and seven fadome: but before we were halfe way betweene our ships and the shore we saw another great smoke to the Southwest of Kindrikers mountes: we therefore thought good to goe to the second smoke first: but it was much further from the harbour where we landed, then we supposed it to be, so that we were very sore tired before wee came to the smoke. But that which grieved us more was that when we came to the smoke, we found no man nor signe that any had bene there lately, nor yet any fresh water in all this way to drinke. Being thus wearied with this journey we returned to the harbour where we left our boates, who in our absence had brought their caske a shore for fresh water, so we deferred our going to Roanoak until the next morning, and caused some of those saylers to digge in those sandie hills for fresh water whereof we found very sufficient. That night wee returned aboord with our boates and our whole company in safety.

The next morning being the 17 of August, or boates and company were prepared againe to goe up to Roanoak, but Captaine Spicer had then sent his boat ashore for fresh water, by meanes whereof it was ten of the clocke aforenoone before we put from our ships which were then come to an anker within two miles of the shore. The Admirals boat was halfe way toward the

*Source:* "The fift voyage of M. John White into the West Indies and parts of America," *Virtual Jamestown,* http://www.virtual-jamestown.org/exist/cocoon/jamestown/fha/J1019 (Accessed May 9, 2018).

shore, when Captaine Spicer put off from his ship. The Admirals boat first passed the breach, but not without some danger of sinking, for we had a sea brake into our boat which filled us halfe full of water, but by the will of God and carefull styrage of Captaine Cooke we came safe ashore, saving onely that our furniture, victuals, match and powder were much wet and spoyled. For at this time the winde blue at Northeast and direct into the harbour so great a gale, that the Sea brake extremely on the barre, and the tide went very forcibly at the entrance. By that time our Admirals boate was halled ashore, and most of our things taken out to dry, Captaine Spicer came to the entrance of the breach with his mast standing up, and was halfe passed over, but by the rash and undiscreet styrage of Ralph Skinner his Masters mate, a very dangerous Sea brake into their boate and overset them quite, the men kept the boat some in it, and some hanging on it, but the next sea set the boat on ground, where it beat so, that some of them were forced to let goe their hold, hoping to wade ashore; but the Sea still beat them downe, so that they could neither stand nor swimme, and the boat twise or thrise was turned the keele upward, whereon Captaine Spicer and Skinner hung untill they sunke, & were seene no more. But foure that could swimme a litle kept themselves in deeper water and were saved by Captain Cookes meanes, who so soone as he saw their oversetting, stripped himselfe, and four other that could swimme very well, & with all haste possible rowed unto them, & saved foure. They were a 11 in all, & 7 of the chiefest were drowned, whose names were Edward Spicer, Ralph Skinner, Edward Kelley, Thomas Bevis, Hance the Surgion, Edward Kelborne, Robert Coleman. This mischance did so much discomfort the saylers, that they were all of one mind not to goe any further to seeke the planters. But in the end by the commandement & perswasion of me and Captaine Cooke, they prepared the boates: and seeing the Captaine and me so resolute, they seemed much more willing. Our boates and all things fitted againe, we put off from Hatorask, being the number of 19 persons in both boates: but before we could get to the place, where our planters were left, it was so exceeding darke, that we overshot the place a quarter of a mile: there we espied towards the North end of the Iland ye light of a great fire thorow the woods, to the which we presently rowed: when wee came right over against it, we

let fall our Grapnel neere the shore, & sounded with a trumpet a Call, & afterwardes many familiar English tunes of Songs, and called to them friendly; but we had no answere, we therefore landed at day-breake, and coming to the fire, we found the grasse & sundry rotten trees burning about the place. From hence we went thorow the woods to that part of the Iland directly over against Dasamongwepeuk, & from thence we returned by the water side, round about the North point of the Iland, untill we came to the place where I left our Colony in the yeere 1586. In all this way we saw in the sand the print of the Salvages feet of 2 or 3 sorts troaden ye night, and as we entred up the sandy banke upon a tree, in the very browe thereof were curiously carved these fair Romane letters C R O: which letters presently we knew to signifie the place, where I should find the planters seated, according to a secret token agreed upon betweene them & me at my last departure from them, which was, that in any wayes they should not faile to write or carve on the trees or posts of the dores the name of the place where they should be seated; for at my comming away they were prepared to remove from Roanoak 50 miles into the maine. Therefore at my departure from them in An. 1587 I willed them, that if they should happen to be distressed in any of those places, that then they should carve over the letters or name, a Crosse in this forme, but we found no such signe of distresse. And having well considered of this, we passed toward the place where they were left in sundry houses, but we found the houses taken downe, and the place very strongly enclosed with a high palisado of great trees, with cortynes and flankers very Fort-like, and one of the chiefe trees or postes at the right side of the entrance had the barke taken off, and 5 foote from the ground in fayre Capitall letters was graven CROATOAN without any crosse or signe of distresse; this done, we entred into the palisado, where we found many barres of Iron, two pigges of Lead, foure yron fowlers, Iron sacker-shotte, and such like heavie things, throwen here and there, almost overgrowen with grasse and weedes. From thence wee went along by the water side, towards the point of the Creeke to see if we could find any of their botes or Pinnisse, but we could perceive no signe of them, nor any of the last Falkons and small Ordinance which were left with them, at my departure from them. At our returne from the Creeke, some of our Saylers meeting us, tolde that they had found where divers chests had bene hidden, and long sithence digged up againe and broken up, and much of the goods in them spoyled and scattered about, but nothing left, of such things as the Savages knew any use of, undefaced. Presently Captaine Cooke and I went to the place, which was in the ende of an olde trench, made two yeeres past by Captaine Amadas: where wee found five Chests, that had bene carefully hidden of the Planters, and of the same chests three were my owne, and about the place many of my things spoyled and broken, and my bookes torne from the covers, the frames of some of my pictures and Mappes rotten and spoyled with rayne, and my armour almost eaten through with rust; this could bee no other but the deede of the Savages our enemies at Dasamongwepeuk, who had watched the departure of our men to Croatoan; and assoone as they were departed, digged up every place where they suspected any thing to be buried: but although it much grieved me to see such spoyle of my goods, yet on the other side I greatly joyed that I had safely found a certaine token of their safe being at Croatoan, which is the place where Manteo was borne, and the Savages of the Iland our friends.

When we had seene in this place so much as we could, we returned to our Boates, and departed from the shoare towards our Shippes, with as much speede as wee could: For the weather beganne to overcast, and very likely that a foule and stormie night would ensue. Therefore the same Evening with much danger and labour, we got our selves aboard, by which time the winde and seas were so greatly risen, that wee doubted our Cables and Anchors would scarcely holde untill Morning: wherefore the Captaine caused the Boate to be manned with five lusty men, who could swimme all well, and sent them to the little Iland on the right hand of the Harbour, to bring aboard six of our men, who had filled our caske with fresh water: the Boate the same night returned aboard with our men, but all our Caske ready filled they left behinde, unpossible to bee had aboard without danger of casting away both men and Boates: for this night prooved very stormie and foule.

**QUESTIONS TO CONSIDER**

1. What does White seem concerned with recording?
2. How does he react to finding Roanoke deserted? What would you have done in his situation?

# 2.3 SELECTION FROM SAMUEL DE CHAMPLAIN'S ACCOUNT OF NATIVE AMERICAN WARFARE (1609)

The French explorer Samuel de Champlain (1574–1635) became renowned for his efforts to establish French colonies in North America. After founding a trading post at Quebec City in 1608, Champlain quickly realized that his "New France" would need to depend on trading with Native American populations and that he would need carefully to construct alliances with friendly Native American tribes. In 1609, as narrated in the following excerpt from his writings, Champlain fought with a Native American coalition against the Iroquois tribe near Lake Champlain. He would remain as the de facto Governor of New France until his return to France in 1620.

*Source: The Works of Samuel De Champlain, Volume II* (Toronto: The Champlain Society, 1925), 94–100. Retrieved from the Internet Archive website, https://archive.org/details/worksofsamueldec02chamuoft (Accessed June 4, 2018).

Now as we began to get within two or three days' journey of the home of their enemy, we proceeded only by night, and during the day we rested. Nevertheless, they kept up their usual superstitious ceremonies in order to know what was to happen to them in their undertakings, and often would come and ask me whether I had had dreams and had seen their enemies. I would tell them that I had not, but nevertheless continued to inspire them with courage and good hope. When night came on, we set off on our way until the next morning. Then we retired into the thick woods where we spent the rest of the day. Towards ten or eleven o'clock, after walking around our camp, I went to take a rest, and while asleep I dreamed that I saw in the lake near a mountain our enemies, the Iroquois, drowning before our eyes. I wanted to succor them, but our Indian allies said to me that we should let them all perish ; for they were bad men. When I awoke they did not fail to ask me as usual whether I had dreamed anything. I told them what I had seen in my dream. This gave them such confidence that they no longer had any doubt as to the good fortune awaiting them.

Evening having come, we embarked in our canoes in order to proceed on our way, and as we were paddling along very quietly, and without making any noise, about ten o'clock at night on the twenty-ninth of the month, at the extremity of a cape which projects into the lake on the west side, we met the Iroquois on the war-path. Both they and we began to utter loud shouts and each got his arms ready. We drew out into the lake and the Iroquois landed and arranged all their canoes near one another. Then they began to fell trees with the poor axes which they sometimes win in war, or with stone axes ; and they barricaded themselves well.

Our Indians all night long also kept their canoes close to one another and tied to poles in order not to get separated, but to fight all together in case of need. We were on the water within bowshot of their barricades. And when they were armed, and everything in order, they sent two canoes which they had separated from the rest, to learn from their enemies whether they wished to fight, and these replied that they had no other desire, but that for the moment nothing could be seen and that it was necessary to wait for daylight

in order to distinguish one another. They said that as soon as the sun should rise, they would attack us, and to this our Indians agreed. Meanwhile the whole night was spent in dances and songs on both sides, with many insults and other remarks, such as the lack of courage of our side, how little we could resist or do against them, and that when daylight came our people would learn all this to their ruin. Our side too was not lacking in retort, telling the enemy that they would see such deeds of arms as they had never seen, and a great deal of other talk, such as is usual at the siege of a city. Having sung, danced, and flung words at one another for some time, when daylight came, my companions and I were still hidden, lest the enemy should see us, getting our fire-arms ready as best we could, being however still separated, each in a canoe of the Montagnais Indians. After we were armed with light weapons, we took, each of us, an arquebus and went ashore. I saw the enemy come out of their barricade to the number of two hundred, in appearance strong, robust men. They came slowly to meet us with a gravity and calm which I admired ; and at their head were three chiefs. Our Indians likewise advanced in similar order, and told me that those who had the three big plumes were the chiefs, and that there were only these three, whom you could recognize by these plumes, which were larger than those of their companions ; and I was to do what I could to kill them. I promised them to do all in my power, and told them that I was very sorry they could not understand me, so that I might direct their method of attacking the enemy, all of whom undoubtedly we should thus defeat ; but that there was no help for it, and that I was very glad to show them, as soon as the engagement began, the courage and readiness which were in me.

As soon as we landed, our Indians began to run some two hundred yards towards their enemies, who stood firm and had not yet noticed my white companions who went off into the woods with some Indians. Our Indians began to call to me with loud cries ; and to make way for me they divided into two groups, and put me ahead some twenty yards, and I marched on until I was within some thirty yards of the enemy, who as soon as they caught sight of me halted and gazed at me and I at them. When I saw them make a move to draw their bows upon us, I took aim with my arquebus and shot straight at one of the three chiefs, and with this shot two fell to the ground and one of their companions was wounded who died thereof as little later. I had put four bullets into my arquebus. As soon as our people saw this shot so favourable for them, they began to shout so loudly that one could not have heard it thunder, and meanwhile the arrows flew thick on both sides. The Iroquois were much astonished that two men should have been killed so quickly, although they were provided with shields made of cotton thread woven together and wood, which were proof against their arrows. This frightened them greatly. As I was reloading my arquebus, one of my companions fired a shot from within the woods, which astonished them again so much that, seeing their chiefs dead, they lost courage and took to flight, abandoning the field and their fort, and fleeing into the depth of the forest, whither I pursued them and laid low still more of them. Our Indians also killed several and took ten or twelve prisoners. The remainder fled with the wounded. Of our Indians fifteen or sixteen were wounded with arrows, but these were quickly healed.

After we had gained the victory, our Indians wasted time in taking a large quantity of Indian corn and meal belonging to the enemy, as well as their shields, which they had left behind, the better to run. Having feasted, danced, and sung, we three hours later set off for home with the prisoners.

**QUESTIONS TO CONSIDER**

1. How does Champlain view the Native Americans he fought with and against?
2. What stands out about Native American warfare at the time?

# 2.4 SELECTION FROM ROBERT JUET'S JOURNAL OF HENRY HUDSON'S VOYAGE (1609)

Henry Hudson (1565–1611) was an English explorer who made several trips to North America as an agent of the Dutch East India Company, a multinational trading company associated with the Dutch government. Hudson sought a Northwest Passage, which would connect the Atlantic Ocean to the Pacific Ocean. The following document is taken from sailor Robert Juet's journal during Hudson's 1609 transatlantic voyage to Nova Scotia, Cape Cod, and up the Hudson River to near present-day Albany, New York. In 1610, Juet again sailed with Hudson on another transatlantic voyage to northern Canada, where Hudson's ship entered the Hudson Bay. After a winter spent on land after their ship became encased in ice, the crew, including Juet, mutinied when Hudson asked them to continue to explore the Bay. Hudson, left in a small boat with a few allies, was never seen again.

Then our Boate went on Land with our Net to Fish, and caught ten great Mullets, of a foot and a halfe long a peece, and a Ray as great as foure men could hale into the ship. So wee trimmed our Boate and rode still all day. At night the wind blew hard at the Northwest, and our Anchor came home, and we droue on

*Source:* "Juet's Journal of Hudson's 1609 Voyage," *The New Netherland Museum/Half Moon,* https://www.halfmoon.mus.ny.us/ Juets-journal.pdf (Accessed June 4, 2018).

shoare, but tooke no hurt, thanked bee God, for the ground is soft sand and Oze. This day the people of the Countrey came aboord of vs, seeming very glad of our coming, and brought greene Tabacco, and gaue vs of it for Kniues and Beads. They goe in Deere skins loose, well dressed. Thay haue yellow Copper. They desire Cloathes, and are very ciuill. They haue great store of Maiz or Indian Wheate, whereof they make good Bread. The Countrey is full of great and tall Oakes.

The fifth, in the morning as soone as the day was light, the wind ceased and the Flood came. So we heaued off our ship againe into fiue fathoms water, and sent our Boate to sound the Bay, and we found that there was three fathoms hard by the Souther shoare. Our men went on Land there, and saw great store of Men, Women, and Children, who gaue them Tabacco at their comming on Land. So they went vp into the Woods, and saw great store of very goodly Oakes, and some Currants. For one of them came aboord and brought some dryed, and gaue me some, which were sweet and good. This day many of the people came aboord, some in Mantles of Feathers, and some in Skins of diuers sorts of good Furres. Some women also came to vs with Hempe. They had red Copper Tabacco pipes, and other things of Copper they did weare about their neckes. At night they went on Land againe, so wee rode very quiet, but durst not trust them.

The sixth, in the morning was faire weather, and our Master sent *Iohn Colman*, with foure other men in our Boate ouer to the North-side, to sound the other Riuer, being foure leagues from vs. They found by the way shoald water two fathomes ; but at the North of the Riuer eighteen, and twentie fathoms, and very good riding for Ships ; and a narrow Riuer to the Westward betweene two Ilands. The Lands trhey told vs were as pleasant with Grasse and Flowers, and goodly Trees, as euer they had seene, and very sweet smells came from them. So they went in two leagues and saw an open Sea, and returned ; and as they came backe, they were set vpon by two Canoes, the one hauing twelue, the other fourteen men. The night came on, and it began to rayne, so that their Match went out; and they had one man slaine in the fight, which was an *English*-man, named *Iohn Colman*, with an Arrow shot into his throat, and two more hurt. It grew so darke that they could not find the ship that night, but labored too and

fro on their Oares. They had so great a streame, that their grapnel would not hold them.

The seuenth, was very faire weather, wee rode still very quietly. The people came aboord vs, and brought Tabacco and *Indian* Wheat, to exchange for Kniues and Beades, and offered vs no violence. So we sitting vp our Boate did marke them, to see if they would make any shew of the Death of our man ; which they did not.

The ninth, faire weather. In the morning, two great Canoes came aboord full of men; the one with their Bowes and Arrowes, and the other in shew of buying of kniues to betray vs; but we perceiued their intent. Wee tooke two of them to haue kept them, and put red Coates on them, and would not suffer the other to come neere vs. So they went on Land, and two other came aboord in a Canoe : we tooke the one and let the other goe ; but hee which wee had taken, got vp and leapt ouer-boord. . . .

The first of October, faire weather, the wind variable between the West and the North. In the morning we weighed at seuen of the clocke with the ebbe, and got downe below the Mountaynes, which was seuen leagues. Then it fell calme and the floud was come, and wee anchored at twelue of the clocke. The people of the Mountaynes came aboord vs, wondering at our ship and weapons. We bought some small skinnes of them for Trifles. This after-noone, one Canoe kept hanging vnder our sterne with one man in it, which we could not keepe from thence, who got vp by our Rudder to the Cabin window, and stole out my Pillow, and two Shirts, and two Bandeleeres. Our Masters Mate shot at him, and stroke him on the brest, and killed him. Whereupon all the rest fled away, some in their Canoes, and so leapt out of them into the water. We manned our Boat, and got our things againe. Then one of them that swamme got hold of our Boat, thinking to ouerthrow it. But our Cooke tooke a Sword, and cut off one of his hands, and he was drowned. By this time the ebbe was come, and we weighed and got downe two leagues, by that time it was darke. So we anchored in foure fathomes water, and rode well.

The second, faire weather. At breake of day wee weighed, the wind being at North-west, and got downe seuen leagues; then the floud was come strong, so we anchored. Then came one of the Sauages that swamme away from vs at our going vp the Riuer with many other, thinking to betray vs. But wee perceiued their intent, and suffered none of them to enter our ship, Whereupon two Canoes full of men, with their Bowes and Arrowes shot at vs after our sterne: in recompence whereof we discharged six Muskets, and killed two or three of them. Then aboue an hundred of them came to a point of Land to shoot at vs. There I shot a Falcon at them, and killed two of them : whereupon the rest fled into the Woods. Yet they manned off another Canoe with nine or ten men, which came to meet vs. So I shot at it also a Falcon and shot it through, and killed one of them Then our men with their Muskets, killed three or foure more of them. So they went their way, within a while after, wee got downe two leagues beyond that place, and anchored in a Bay, cleere from all danger of them on the other side of the Riuer, where we saw a very good piece of ground : and hard by it there was a Cliffe, that looked of the colour of a white greene, as though it were either Copper, or Siluer Myne : and I thinke it to be one of them, by the Trees that grow vpon it. For they be all burned, and the other places are greene as grasse, it is on that side of the Riuer that is called *Manna-hata.* There we saw no people to trouble vs: and rode quietly all night; but had much wind and raine.

The third, was very stormie; the wind at East North-east. In the morning, in a gust of wind and raine our Anchor came home, and we droue on ground, but it was Ozie. Then as we were about to haue out an Anchor, the wind came to the North North-west, and droue vs off againe. Then we shot an Anchor, and let it fall in foure fathomes water, and weighed the other. Wee had much wind and raine, with thicke weather: so we roade still all night.

The fourth, was faire weather, and the wind at North North-west, wee weighed and came out of the Riuer, into which we had runne so farre. Within a while after, we came out also of *The great mouth of the great Riuer,* that runneth vp to the North-west, borrowing vpon the Norther side of the same, thinking to haue deepe water : for wee had sounded a great way with our Boat at our first going in, and found seuen, six, and fiue fathomes. So we came out that way, but we were deceiued, for we had but eight foot & an halfe water: and so to three, fiue, three, and two fathomes and an halfe. And then three, foure, fiue, sixe, seuen, eight, nine and ten fathomes. And by twelue of the clocke we were cleere of all the Inlet. Then we tooke in our Boat, and set our mayne-sayle and sprit-sayle, and our top-sayles, and steered away East South-east, and South-east by East off into the mayne sea : and the Land on the Souther-side of the Bay or Inlet, did beare at noone West and by South foure leagues from vs.

The fift, was faire weather, and the wind variable betweene the North and the East. Wee held on our course South-east by East. At no one I obserued and found our height to bee 39.degrees 30.minutes. Our Compasse varied six degrees to the West.

We continued our course toward *England,* without seeing any Land by the way, all the rest of this moneth of October : And on the seuenth day of Nouember, *stilo nouo,* being Saturday : by the Grace of God we safely arriued in the Range of *Dartmouth* in *Deuonshire,* in the yeere 1609.

## QUESTIONS TO CONSIDER

1. What does Juet seem concerned with recording?
2. How does he describe the surrounding land and Native American populations?

# 2.5 THOMAS MORTON, EXCERPT FROM *THE NEW ENGLISH CANAAN* (1637)

Thomas Morton (1579–1647) was an English colonist who gained notoriety for his denunciation of the Puritan Plymouth Colony. In 1624, Morton arrived in Massachusetts as a member of a trading company sponsored by the English crown. Morton and his compatriots traded with the local Algonquin tribes and infuriated the pious Puritans at Plymouth by supplying Native Americans with guns and liquor and hosting a yearly May Day celebration with the tribes. Plymouth forces captured Morton in 1628 and banished him from Massachusetts in 1629. In 1637, Morton published the *New English Canaan,* from which the following document is taken. The three-volume series attacked Puritan behavior toward Native Americans and lauded Native American culture. In the early 1640s, Morton again returned to Massachusetts and was again captured and imprisoned. He died in Maine in 1647.

The Natives of New England are accuftomed to build them houfes much like the wild Irifh; they gather Poles in the woodes and put the great end of them in the ground, placinge them in forme of a circle or circumference, and, bendinge the topps of them in forme of an Arch, they bind them together with the Barke of Walnut trees, which is wondrous tuffe, fo that they make the fame round on the Topp for the fmooke of their fire to affend and paffe through ; thefe they cover with matts, fome made of reeds and fome of longe flagges, or fedge, finely fowed together with needles made of the fplinter bones of a Cranes legge, with threeds made of their Indian hempe, which their groueth naturally, leaving feverall places for dores, which are covered with mats, which may be rowled up and let downe againe at their pleafures, making ufe of the feverall dores, according as the winde fitts. The fire is alwayes made in the middeft of the houfe, with winde fals commonly : yet fome times they fell a tree that groweth neere the houfe, and, by drawing in the end thereof, maintaine the fire on both fids, burning the tree by Degrees fhorter and fhorter, until it be all confumed ; for it burneth night and day. Their lodging is made in three place of the houfe about the fire ; they lye upon plankes, commonly about a foote or 18. inches aboue the ground, raifed upon railes that are borne up upon forks ; they lay mats under them, and Coats of Deares fkinnes, otters, beavers, Racownes, and of Beares hides, all which they have dreffed and converted into good lether, with the haire on, for their coverings : and in this manner they lye as warme as they defire. In the night they take their reft ; in the day time, either the kettle is on with fifh or flefh, by no allowance, or elfe the fire is imployed in roafting of fifhes, which they delight in. The aire doeth beget good ftomacks, and they feede continually, and are no niggards of their vittels ; for they are willing that any one fhall eate with them. Nay, if any one that fhall come into their houfes and there fall a fleepe, when they fee him difpofed to lye downe, they will fpreade a matt for him of their owne accord, and lay a roule of fkinnes for a boulfter, and let him lye. If hee fleepe until their

*Source:* Thomas Morton, *The New English Canaan* (Boston: The Publications of the Prince Society, 1858), 134–138. Retrieved from the Internet Archive website, https://archive.org/stream/newenglishcanaan00mort/newenglishcanaan00mort_djvu.txt (Accessed June 4, 2018).

meate be difhed up, they will fet a wooden boule of meate by him that fleepeth, and wake him faying, Cattup keene Meckin : That is, if you be hungry, there is meat for you, where if you will eate you may. Such is their Humanity.

Likewife, when they are minded to remoove, they carry away the mats with them ; other materiales the place adjoining will yeald. They ufe not to winter and fummer in one place, for that would be a reafon to make fuell fcarfe ; but, after the manner of the gentry of Civilized natives, remoove for their pleafures ; fome times to their hunting places, where they remaine keeping good hofpitality for that feafon ; and fome-times to their fifhing places, where they abide for that feafon likewife : and at the fpring, when fifh comes in plentifully, they have meetinges from feverall places, where they exercife themfelves in gaminge and playing of juglinge trickes and all manner of Revelles, which they are delighted in ; [fo] that it is admirable to be-hould what paftime they ufe of feverall kindes, every one ftriving to furpaffe each other. After this manner they fpend their time.

## QUESTIONS TO CONSIDER

1. How does Morton describe Native Americans?
2. Do his descriptions make Native American tribes seem, to quote Morton, "civilized"?

CHAPTER 3

# THE ENGLISH COME TO STAY, 1600–1660

## 3.1 JOHN SMITH, "A TRUE RELATION OF SUCH OCCURENCES AND ACCIDENTS OF NOTE, AS HATH HAPNED IN VIRGINIA" (1608) AND "THE GENERAL HISTORIE OF VIRGINIA" (1624)

John Smith (1580–1631) was an explorer who played a crucial role in early English efforts to colonize the east coast of North America. Following its establishment at Jamestown, Virginia, in 1607, the Virginia Colony floundered. Over sixty percent of the colony's first 100 colonists died. In response, Smith instituted martial law and demanded that colonists work if they wanted to eat. The colony subsequently recovered. Smith also brought the colony into tension with the local Powhatan Confederacy, a large Native American group. In 1607, the Powhatans captured and held Smith hostage for several months. In 1608, Smith wrote a report to the colony's financial backers about the incident; this is the first document. Sixteen years later, after Powhatan and his daughter, Pocahontas, had died, Smith again wrote about the incident in a much more embellished tone; this is the second document. In October 1609, Smith left the Virginia Colony after he was injured in a gunpowder explosion. He would later help to map North America's northeast coast before its colonization in the 1620s.

**A TRUE RELATION OF SUCH OCCURRENCES AND ACCIDENTS OF NOTE, AS HATH HAPNED IN VIRGINIA (1608)**

Arriving at Werawocomoco, their Emperour proudly lying upon a Bedstead a foote high upon tenne or twelve Mattes, richly hung with many Chaynes of great Pearles about his necke, and covered with a great Covering of rahaughcums [that is, raccoon pelts]: At his head sat a woman, at his feete another, on each side sitting upon a Matte upon the ground were raunged his chiefe men on each side the fire, tenne in a ranke, and behind them as many young women, each a great Chaine of white Beades over

*Source:* Philip Barbour, ed., *The Complete Works of John Smith* (Williamsburg, VA: Institute of Early American History and Culture, 1986), I: 53 and II: 150–151.

their shoulders, their heads painted in redde, and [he] with such a grave and Majesticall countenance, as drove me into admiration to see such state in a naked Salvage, . . . hee kindly welcomed me with good wordes, and great Platters of sundrie Victuals, assuring mee his friendship, and my libertie within foure dayes; hee much delighted in [his kinsman] Opechancanoughs relation of what I had described to him, and oft examined me upon the same [subjects]. Hee asked me the cause of our coming; I tolde him, being in fight with the Spaniards our enemie, being over powred, near put to retreat, and by extreame weather put to his shore . . .

## THE GENERAL HISTORIE OF VIRGINIA (1624)

At last they brought him to Meronocomoco [sic], where was Powhatan their Emperor. Here more then two hundred of those grim Courtiers stood wondering at him, as [if] he had been a monster; till Powhatan and his trayne had put themselves in their greatest braveries [ie finest attire]. Before a fire upon a seat like a bedsted, he sat covered with a great robe, made of Rarowcun skinnes, and all the tayles hanging by. On either hand did sit a young wench of 16 or 18 yeares, and along on each side the house, two rowes of men, and behind them as many women, with all their heads and shoulders painted red; many of their heads beadecked with the white downe of Birds, but every one with something; and a great chayne of white beads about their necks. At his entrance before the King, all the people gave a great shout. The Queene of Appamatuck was appointed to bring him water to wash his hands, and another brought him a bunch of feathers, in stead of a Towell to dry them; having feasted him after their best barbarous manner they could, a long consultation was held, but the conclusion was, two great stones were brought before Powhatan; then as many as could layd hands on him, dragged him to them, and thereon laid his head, and being ready with their clubs, to beate out his braines, Pocahontas the Kings dearest daughter, when no intreaty could prevaile, got his head in her armes, and laide her owne upon his to save him from death; whereat the Emperour was contented he should live to make him hatchets, and her bells, beads, and copper . . .

### QUESTIONS TO CONSIDER

1.   How does Smith represent the Native Americans in both readings?
2.   In what ways does the 1624 reading differ from the 1608 reading?

# 3.2 JOHN WINTHROP, "A MODEL OF CHRISTIAN CHARITY" (1630)

In 1629, a group of Puritans, who wanted to leave England to form a more pure, religious society in North America, took control over the Massachusetts Bay Company, a nascent trading enterprise. Subsequently, the Puritans, led by lawyer John Winthrop (1587–1649), gained a royal charter to form a colony on a large tract of land in North America. In 1630, the new colonists left England on four ships. Winthrop likely gave the following sermon to the colonists before they crossed. In it, he outlined a vision of a new society centered on "love" that would be a "model" to the world. Winthrop's vision of a "City on a Hill" continues to influence American politicians today.

*Source: Collections of the Massachusetts Historical Society, Volume VII of the Third Series* (Boston: Charles C. Little and James Brown, 1838), 33–48. Retrieved from the Hathi Trust website, https://hdl.handle.net/2027/njp.32101076467495 (Accessed June 4, 2018).

ON BOARD THE ARBELLA,
ON THE ATLANTIC OCEAN.
By the Hon. John Winthrop Esqr. In his passage (with a great company of Religious people, of which Christian tribes he was the Brave Leader and famous Governor ;) from the Island of Great Brittaine to New-England in the North America. Anno 1630.

## CHRISTIAN CHARITIE

## A MODELL HEREOF

GOD ALMIGHTY in his most holy and wise providence, hath soe disposed of the condition of mankind, as in all times some must be rich, some poore, some high and eminent in power and dignitie ; others mean and in submission.

## THE REASON HEREOF

1 *Reas*. First to hold conformity with the rest of his world, being delighted to show forth the glory of his wisdom in the variety and difference of the creatures, and the glory of his power in ordering all these differences for the preservation and good of the whole ; and the glory of his greatness, that as it is the glory of princes to have many officers, soe this great king will haue many stewards, counting himself more honoured in dispensing his gifts to man by man, than if he did it by his owne immediate hands.

2 *Reas*. Secondly that he might haue the more occasion to manifest the work of his Spirit : first upon the wicked in moderating and restraining them : soe that the riche and mighty should not eate upp the poore nor the poore and dispised rise upp against and shake off theire yoake. 21y In the regenerate, in exerciseing his graces in them, as in the grate ones, theire love, mercy, gentleness, temperance &c., in the poore and inferior sorte, theire faithe, patience, obedience &c.

3 *Reas*. Thirdly, that every man might have need of others, and from hence they might be all knitt more nearly together in the Bonds of brotherly affection. From hence it appears plainly that noe man is made more honourable than another or more wealthy &c., out of any particular and singular respect to himselfe, but for the glory of his creator and the common good of the creature, man. Therefore God still reserves the propperty of these gifts to himself as Ezek. 16. 17. he there calls wealthe, *his gold and his silver*, and Prov. 3. 9.

he claims theire service as his due, *honor the Lord with thy riches* &c.—All men being thus (by divine providence) ranked into two sorts, riche and poore ; under the first are comprehended all such as are able to live comfortably by their own meanes duely improved ; and all others are poore according to the former distribution. There are two rules whereby we are to walk one towards another : Justice and Mercy. These are always distinguished in their act and in their object, yet may they both concurre in the same subject in eache respect ; as sometimes there may be an occasion of showing mercy to a rich man in some sudden danger or distresse, and alsoe doeing of meere justice to a poor man in regard of some perticular contract &c. There is likewise a double Lawe by which wee are regulated in our conversation towards another ; in both the former respects, the lawe of nature and the lawe of grace, or the morrall lawe or the lawe of the gospell, to omitt the rule of justice as not properly belonging to this purpose otherwise than it may fall into consideration in some perticular cases. By the first of these lawes man as he was enabled soe withall is commanded to love his neighbor as himself. Upon this ground stands all the precepts of the morrall lawe, which concernes our dealings with men. To apply this to the works of mercy ; this lawe requires two things. First that every man afford his help to another in every want or distresse. Secondly, that hee performe this out of the same affection which makes him carefull of his owne goods, according to that of our Savior, (Math.) *Whatsoever ye would that men should do to you*. . . .

. . . Herein are 4 things to be propounded ; *first* the persons, 21y the worke, 31y the end, 4thly the meanes. 1. For *the persons*. Wee are a company professing ourselves fellow members of Christ, in which respect onely though wee were absent from each other many miles, and had our imployments as farre distant, yet wee ought to account ourselves knitt together by this bond of loue, and, live in the exercise of it, if wee would have comforte of our being in Christ. This was notorious in the practice of the Christians in former times ; as is testified of the Waldenses, from the mouth of one of the adversaries *Æneas sylvius* "mutuo ament pere antequam norunt," they use to loue any of theire owne religion even before they were acquainted with them. 2nly for the *worke* wee have in hand. It is by a mutuall consent, through a speciall overvaluing providence and a more than an ordinary approbation of the Churches of Christ, to seeke out a place of cohabitation and Consorteshipp under a due forme of Government both ciuill and ecclesiasticall. In such cases as this, the care of the publique must oversway all private respects, by which, not only conscience, but meare civill policy, dothe binde us. For it is a true rule that particular Estates cannot subsist in the ruin of the publique. 31y The *end* is to improve our lives to doe more service to the Lord ; the comforte and encrease of the body of Christe, whereof we are members ; that ourselves and posterity may be the better preserved from the common corruptions of this evill world, to serve the Lord and worke out our Salvation under the power and purity of his holy ordinances. 4thly for the *meanes* whereby this must be effected. They are twofold, a conformity with the worke and end wee aime at. These wee see are extraordinary, therefore wee must not content ourselves with usuall ordinary meanes. Whatsoever wee did, or ought to have done, when wee liued in England, the same must wee doe, and more allsoe, where wee goe. That which the most in theire churches mainetaine as truthe in profession onely, wee must bring into familiar and constant practice ; as in this duty of loue, wee must loue brotherly without dissimulation, wee must loue one another with a pure hearte fervently. Wee must beare one anothers burthens. We must not looke onely on our owne things, but allsoe on the things of our brethren. Neither must wee thinke that the Lord will beare with such faileings at our hands as he dothe from those among whome wee have lived ; and that for these 3 Reasons ; 1. In regard of the more neare bond of marriage between him and us, wherein hee hath taken us to be his, after a most strickt and peculiar manner, which will make them the more jealous of our loue and obedience. Soe he tells the people of Israell, *you onely have I knowne of all the families of the Earthe, therefore will I punishe you for your Transgressions.* 21y, because *the Lord will be sanctified in them that come neare him.* We know that there were many that corrupted the service of the Lord ; some setting upp altars before his owne ; others offering both strange fire and strange sacrifices allsoe ; yet there came noe fire from heaven, or other sudden judgement upon them, as did upon Nadab and Abihu, whoe yet wee may think did not sinne presumptuously. 31y When God gives a speciall commission he lookes to have it strictly observed in every article, When he gave Saule a commission to destroy Amaleck, Hee indented

with him upon certain articles, and because hee failed in one of the least, and that upon a faire pretense, it lost him the kingdom, which should have beene his reward, if hee had observed his commission. Thus stands the cause between God and us. We are entered into Covenant with Him for this worke. Wee haue taken out a commission. The Lord hath given us leave to drawe our own articles. Wee haue professed to enterprise these and those accounts, upon these and those ends. Wee have hereupon besought Him of favour and blessing. Now if the Lord shall please to heare us, and bring us in peace to the place we desire, then hath hee ratified this covenant and sealed our Commission, and will expect a strict performance of the articles contained in it ; but if wee shall neglect the observation of these articles which are the ends we have propounded, and, dissembling with our God, shall fall to embrace this present world and prosecute our carnall intentions, seeking great things for ourselves and our posterity, the Lord will surely breake out in wrathe against us ; be revenged of such a [sinful] people and make us knowe the price of the breache of such a covenant.

Now the onely way to avoyde this shipwracke, and to provide for our posterity, is to followe the counsel of Micah, *to doe justly, to love mercy, to walk humbly with our God.* For this end, wee must be knitt together, in this worke, as one man. Wee must entertaine each other in brotherly affection. Wee must be willing to abridge ourselves of our superfluities, for the supply of other's necessities. Wee must uphold a familiar commerce together in all meekeness, gentleness, patience and liberality. Wee must delight in eache other ; make other's conditions our oune ; rejoice together, mourne together, labour and suffer together, allwayes haueving before our eyes our commission and community in the worke, as members of the same body. Soe shall wee *keepe the unitie of the spirit in the bond of peace.* The Lord will be our God, and delight to dwell among us, as his oune people, and will command a blessing upon us in all our ways. Soe that wee shall see much more of his wisdome, power, goodness and truthe, than formerly wee haue been acquainted with. Wee shall finde that the God of Israell is among us, when ten of us shall be able to resist a thousand of our enemies ; when hee shall make us a prayse and glory that men shall say of succeeding plantations, "the Lord make it likely that of *New England.*" For wee must consider that wee shall be as a citty upon a hill. The eies of all people are uppon us. Soe that if wee shall deale falsely with our God in this worke wee haue undertaken, and soe cause him to withdrawe his present help from us, wee shall be made a story and a by-word through the world. Wee shall open the mouthes of enemies to speake evill of the wayes of God, and all professors for God's sake. Wee shall shame the faces of many of God's worthy servants, and cause theire prayers to be turned into curses upon us till wee be consumed out of the good land whither wee are a goeing.

I shall shutt upp this discourse with the exhortation of Moses, that faithfull servant of the Lord, in his last farewell to Israell, Deut. 30. *Beloved there is now sett before us life and good, Death and evill, in that wee are commanded this day to love the Lord our God, and to love one another, to walke in his wayes and to keepe his Commandements and his Ordinance and his lawes*, and the articles of our Covenant with him, that *wee may live and be multiplied, and that the Lord our God may blesse us in the land whither wee goe to possesse it. But if our heartes shall turne away, soe that wee will not obey, but shall be seduced, and worshipp and serve other Gods*, our pleasure and profitts, *and serve them* ; it is propounded unto us this day, *wee shall surely perishe out of the good land whither wee passé over this vast sea to posesse it* ;

Therefore let us choose life
that wee, and our seede
may lieu, by obeyeing His
voyce and cleaveing to Him,
for Hee is our life and
our prosperity.

**QUESTIONS TO CONSIDER**

1. Which qualities, in Winthrop's mind, would allow the colony to survive?
2. What was, in Winthrop's mind, the colony's broader purpose? Why was he so concerned with its survival?

# 3.3 ROGER WILLIAMS, EXCERPT FROM *A KEY INTO THE LANGUAGE OF AMERICA* (1643)

Puritan minister Roger Williams (1603–1683) challenged the pious Puritans to be even more pure. In 1631, Williams moved to the Plymouth Colony to teach and preach. As he gained familiarity with the colony, however, he began to feel that the Plymouth church was not pure enough—that is, it was too closely tied to the purported corruption of the Church of England. Moreover, Williams began to sympathize with the plight of local Native Americans, whose land the Plymouth colonists took possession of without recompense. Local leaders summoned Williams to be questioned multiple times and eventually convicted him of sedition and heresy in 1635. Williams escaped west, where he founded a new colony at Providence, Rhode Island, in 1637. Providence quickly attracted others who were fleeing the Puritan colonies, including Anne Hutchinson, a tremendously devout woman who accused Puritan leaders of promoting a "covenant of works" over a "covenant of grace." In 1643, Williams published *A Key into the Language of America*, a phrase book of Native American languages that included a strong defense of Native American culture and from which the following document is excerpted. Rhode Island would continue to be a haven for independent thought in the years ahead.

*Source:* Roger Williams, *A Key into the Language of America* (London: Gregory Dexter, 1643). Retrieved from the Internet Archive website, https://archive.org/details/keyintolanguage002will (Accessed June 4, 2018).

It is expected, that having had fo much converfe with thefe *Natives*, I fhould write fome litle of them.

Concerning them (a little to gratifie expectation) I fhall touch upon *foure* Heads :

Firft, by what *Names* they are diftinuifhed.

Secondly, Their *Originall* and *Defcent*.

Thirdly, their *Religion, Manners, Cuftumes,* &c.

Fourthly, That great *Point of their Converfion*.

To the firft, their *Names* are of two parts : Firft, thofe the *English* giving : as *Natives, Salvages, Indians, Wild-men*, (to the *Dutch call them Wilden*) *Abergeny men, Pagans, Barbarians, Heathen*.

Secondly, their *Names*, which they give themselves.

I cannot observe, that they ever had (before the comming of the *English, French or Dutch amongst them*) any *Names* to difference *themselves* from *strangers*, for they knew none ; but two forts of *names* they had, and have amongst *themselves*.

Firft, *generall*, belonging to all *Natives*, as *Ninnuock, Ninnimi Binnûwock, Eniskeetompauwog*, which signifies *Men, Folke*, or *People*.

Secondly, particular *names*, peculiar to severall *Nations*, of them amongst *themfelves, as Nanbigganeuck, Maffachusêuck Cawasumsêuck, Cowweseuck, Quintikóock Qunnipieuck, Pequttóog,* &c.

They have often asked mee, why we call them *Indians Natives*, &c. And understanding the reason, they will call themselves *Indians*, in opposition to Eglifh, &c.

For the fecond Head propofed, their Originall and Defcent.

From *Adam* and *Noah* that they fpring, it is granted on all hands.

But for their later *Defcent*, and whence they came into thofe pars, it feemes as hard to finde, as to finde the *wellhead* of fome frefh *Streame*, which running many miles out of the *Countrey* to the falt *Ocean*, hath met with many mixing *Streames* by the way. They fay themfelves, that they have *fprung* and *growne* up in that very place, like the very trees of the *wilderneffe*.

They fay that their *Great God Cawtantowwit* created thofe parts, as I obferved in the Chapter of their *Religion*. They have no *Clothes, Bookes*, nor *Letters*, and conceive their *Fathers* never had ; and therefore they are eafily perfwaded that the *God* that made *Englifh* men is a greater *God*, becaufe Hee hath fo richly endowed the *Englifh* above *themfelves* : But when they hear that about fixteen hundred yeeres agoe, *England* and the *Inbabitants* thereof were like unto *themfelves*, and fince have received from *God, Clothes, Bookes*, &c. they are greatly affected with a secret hope concerning *themfelves*.

*Wife* and *Judicious* men, with whom I have difcourfed, maintain their originall to be *Northward* from *Tartaria* :and at my now taking fhip, at the *Dutch Plantation*, it pleafed the *Dutch Governour*, (in fome difcourse with mee about the *Natives*), to draw their *Line* from *Iceland*, becaufe the name *Sackmakan* (she name for an *Indian* Prince, about the *Dutch*) is the name for a *Prince* in *Iceland*.

Other opinions I could number up : under favour I shall prefent (nor mine opinion, but) my *Obfervations* to the judgement of the Wife.

Firft, others (and my felfe) have conceived fome of their words to hold affinitie with the *Hebrew*.

Secondly, they conftantly *annoint* their *heads* as the *Jewes* did.

Thirdy, they give Dowries for their wives, as the *Jewes* did.

Fourthly (and which I have not fo obferved amongft orher *Nations* as amongft the *Jewes*, and *thefe* :) they conftantly feperate their Women (during the time of their montly fickneffe) in a little house alone by themfelves foure or five dayes, and hold it an *Irreligious thing* for either *Father* or *Husband* or any *Male* to come neere them.

They have often asked me if it bee fo with *women* of other *Nations*, and whether they are fo *feparated* : and for their practice they plead *Nature* and *Tradition*. Yet againe I have found a greater. *Affinity* of their Language with the Greek Tongue.

2. As the *Greekes* and other *Nations*, and ourfelves call the feven *starres* (or Charles Waine the *Beare*), fo doe they *Mosk* or *Paukunnawaw* the Beare.

3. They have many strange Relations of one *Wetucks*, a man that wrought great *Miracles* amongft them, and *walking upon the waters*, &c. with fome kind of broken Refemblance to the *Sonne of God*.

## QUESTIONS TO CONSIDER

1. What types of things does Williams think his Anglo readers ought to know about Native American civilization?

2. How does Williams represent Native American life?

# 3.4 JOHN WINTHROP, "REMARKS ON LIBERTY" (1645)

The Massachusetts colonists did not always achieve the high standards set out in John Winthrop's "A Model of Christian Charity" (see Reading 3.2). In particular, his fellow colonists did not obey their leaders nearly as well as he thought they should. In 1645, Winthrop, by then the Deputy Governor of Massachusetts, was impeached after interfering in a local election. Three months later, the court acquitted Winthrop, and he rose to deliver the following speech. In it, he castigated those who had put him on trial and bemoaned "natural liberty." Just one year later, Winthrop was elected Governor of the Massachusetts Bay Colony, his fourth time in that position and a role he would hold until his death in 1649.

I suppose something may be expected from me, upon this charge that is befallen me, which moves me to speak now to you ; yet I intend not to intermeddle in the proceedings of the court, or with any of the persons concerned therein. Only I bless God, that I see an issue of this troublesome business. I also acknowledge the justice of the court, and, for mine own part, I am well satisfied, I was publicly charged, and I am publicly and legally acquitted, which is all I did expect or desire. And though this be sufficient for my justification before men, yet not so before the God, who hath seen so much amiss in my dispensations (and even in this affair) as calls me to be humble. For to be publicly and criminally charged in this court, is matter of humiliation, (and I desire to make a right use of it,) notwithstanding I be thus acquitted. If her father had spit in her face, (saith the Lord concerning Miriam,) should she not have been ashamed seven days? Shame had lien upon her, whatever the occasion had been. I am unwilling to stay you from your urgent affairs, yet give me leave (upon this special occasion) to speak a little more to this assembly. It may be of some good use, to inform and rectify the judgments of some of the people, and may prevent such distempers as have arisen amongst us. The great question that have troubled the country, are about the authority of the magistrates and the liberty of the people. It is yourselves who have called us to this office, and being called by you, we have our authority from God, in way of an ordinance, such as hath the image of God eminently stamped upon it, the contempt and violation whereof hath been vindicated with examples of divine vengeance. I entreat you to consider, that when you choose magistrates, you take them from among yourselves, men subject to like passions as you are. Therefore when you see infirmities in us, you should reflect upon your own, and that would make you bear the more with us, and not be severe censurers of the failings of your magistrates, when you have continual experience of the like infirmities in yourselves and others. We account him a good servant, who breaks not his covenant. The covenant between you and us is the oath you have taken of us, which is to this purpose, that we shall govern you and judge your causes by the rules of God's laws and our own, according to our best skill. When you agree with a workman to build you a

*Source:* James Savage, ed., *The History of New England from 1630 to 1649 By John Winthrop, Esq.* (Boston: Little Brown and Company, 1858), 279–282. Retrieved from the Hathi Trust website, https://hdl.handle.net/2027/hvd.32044015517436 (Accessed June 4, 2018).

ship or house, etc., he undertakes as well for his skill as for his faithfulness, for it is his profession, and you pay him for both. But when you call one to be a magistrate, he doth not profess nor undertake to have sufficient skill for that office, nor can you furnish him with gifts, etc., therefore you must run the hazard of his skill and ability. But if he fail in faithfulness, which by his oath he is bound unto, that he must answer for. If it fall out that the case be clear to common apprehension, and the rule clear also, if he transgress here, the error is not in the skill, but in the evil of the will : it must be required of him. But if the case be doubtful, or the rule doubtful, to men of such understanding and parts as your magistrates are, if your magistrates should err here, yourselves must bear it.

For the other point concerning liberty, I observe a great mistake in the country about that. There is a twofold liberty, natural (I mean as our nature is now corrupt) and civil or federal. The first is common to man with beasts and other creatures. By this, man, as he stands in relation to man simply, hath liberty to do what he lists; it is a liberty to evil as well as to good. This liberty is incompatible and inconsistent with authority, and cannot endure the least restraint of the most just authority. The exercise and maintaining of this liberty makes men grow more evil, and in time to be worse than brute beasts : omnes sumus licentia deteriores. This is that great enemy of truth and peace, that wild beast, which all the ordinances of God are bent against, to restrain and subdue it. The other kind of liberty I call civil or federal, it may also be termed moral, in reference to the covenant between God and man, in the moral law, and the politic covenants and constitutions, amongst men themselves. This liberty is the proper end and object of authority, and cannot subsist without it ; and it is a liberty to that only which is good, just, and honest. This liberty you are to stand for, with the hazard (not only of your goods, but) of your lives, if need be. Whatsoever crosseth this, is not authority, but a distemper thereof. This liberty is maintained and exercised in a way of subjection to authority ; it is of the same kind of liberty wherewith

Christ hath made us free. The woman's own choice makes such a man her husband ; yet being so chosen, he is her lord, and she is to be subject to him, yet in a way of liberty, not of bondage ; and a true wife accounts her subjection her honor and freedom, and would not think her condition safe and free, but in her subjection to her husband's authority. Such is the liberty of the church under the authority of Christ, her king and husband ; his yoke is so easy and sweet to her as a bride's ornaments ; and if through forwardness or wantonness, etc., she shake it off, at any time, she is at no rest in her spirit, until she take it up again ; and whether her lord smiles upon her, and embraceth her in his arms, or whether he frowns, or rebukes, or smites her, she apprehends the sweetness of his love in all, and is refreshed, supported, and instructed by every such dispensation of his authority over her. On the other side, ye know who they are that complain of this yoke and say, let us break their bands, etc., we will not have this man to rule over us. Even so, brethren, it will be between you and your magistrates. If you stand for your natural corrupt liberties, and will do what is good in your own eyes, you will not endure the least weight of authority, but will murmur, and oppose, and be always striving to shake off that yoke; but if you will be satisfied to enjoy such civil and lawful liberties, such as Christ allows you, then will you quietly and cheerfully submit unto that authority which is set over you, in all the administrations of it, for your good. Wherein, if we fail at any time, we hope we shall be willing (by God's assistance) to hearken to good advice from any of you, or in any other way of God ; so shall your liberties be preserved, in upholding the honor and power of authority amongst you.

**QUESTIONS TO CONSIDER:**

1. What does Winthrop mean by liberty? What kind of liberty is the proper kind, in his mind?
2. Does the Massachusetts Bay Colony seem democratic here?

# 3.5 WILLIAM BRADFORD, EXCERPT FROM *OF PLYMOUTH PLANTATION* (1651)

William Bradford (1590–1647) became a major voice of the Plymouth Colony. In 1608, Bradford and a small group of Puritan separatists left England for the Netherlands, seeking a degree of religious freedom. Ten years later, they began planning for a new colony in North America. In 1620, Bradford signed the Mayflower Compact and helped to found the colony near Cape Cod Bay, Massachusetts. Over the next three decades, Bradford served as Governor of the Plymouth Colony on five different occasions. Perhaps most importantly, his *Of Plymouth Plantation*, from which the following document is excerpted, provides a crucial record of the colonial venture at Plymouth. In this excerpt, Bradford recounts the Pilgrim's arrival and their early efforts to secure a foothold on the North American mainland.

## THE 9. CHAP

*Of their vioage, & how they passed y^e sea, and of their safe arrivall at Cape Codd.*

. . . But to omite other things, (that I may be breefe,) after longe beating at sea they fell with that land which is called Cape Cod; the which being made & certainly knowne to be it, they were not a litle joyfull. After some deliberation had amongst them selves & with y^e m^r. of y^e ship, they tacked aboute and resolved to stande for y^e southward (y^e wind & weather being faire) to finde some place aboute Hudsons river for their habitation. But after they had sailed y^t course aboute halfe y^e day, they fell amongst deangerous shoulds and roring breakers, and they were so farr intangled ther with as they conceived them selves in great danger; & y^e wind shrinking upon them withall, they resolved to bear up againe for the Cape, and thought them selves hapy to gett out of those dangers before night overtooke them, as by Gods providence they did. And y^e next day they gott into y^e Cape-harbor wher they ridd in saftie. A word or too by y^e way of this cape; it was thus first named by Capten Gosnole & his company, Anno: 1602, and after by Capten Smith was caled Cape James; but it retains y^e former name amongst seamen. Also y^t pointe which first shewed those dangerous shoulds unto them, they called Pointe Care, & Tuckers Terrour; but y^e French & Dutch to this day call it Malabarr, by reason of those perilous shoulds, and y^e losses they have suffered their.

Being thus arived in a good harbor and brought safe to land, they fell upon their knees & blessed y^e God of heaven, who had brought them over y^e vast & furious ocean, and delivered them from all y^e periles & miseries therof, againe to set their feete on y^e firme and stable earth, their proper elemente. And no marvell if they were thus joyfull, seeing wise Seneca was so affected with sailing a few miles on y^e coast of his owne Italy; as he affirmed, that he had rather remaine twentie years on his way by land, then pass by sea to any place in a short time; so tedious & dreadfull was y^e same unto him.

But hear I cannot but stay and make a pause, and stand half amased at this poore peoples presente condition; and so I thinke will the reader too, when he well considers y^e same. Being thus passed y^e vast ocean, and a sea of troubles before in their preparation (as may be remembred by y^t which wente before), they had now no freinds to wellcome them, nor inns

*Source:* William Bradford, *Of Plimoth Plantation* (Boston: Wright & Potter, 1898). Retrieved from the Project Gutenberg website, http://www.gutenberg.org/files/24950/24950-h/24950-h.htm (Accessed June 4, 2018).

to entertaine or refresh their weatherbeaten bodys, no houses or much less townes to repaire too, to seeke for succoure. It is recorded in scripture as a mercie to yᵉ apostle & his shipwraked company, yᵗ the barbarians shewed them no smale kindnes in refreshing them, but these savage barbarians, when they mette with them (as after will appeare) were readier to fill their sids full of arrows then otherwise. And for yᵉ season it was winter, and they that know yᵉ winters of yᵗ cuntrie know them to be sharp & violent, & subjecte to cruell & feirce stormes, deangerous to travill to known places, much more to serch an unknown coast. Besids, what could they see but a hidious & desolate wildernes, full of wild beasts & willd men? and what multituds ther might be of them they knew not. Nether could they, as it were, goe up to yᵉ tope of Pisgah, to vew from this willdernes a more goodly cuntrie to feed their hops; for which way soever they turnd their eys (save upward to yᵉ heavens) they could have litle solace or content in respecte of any outward objects. For suer being done, all things stand upon them with a wetherbeaten face; and yᵉ whole countrie, full of woods & thickets, represented a wild & savage heiw. If they looked behind them, ther was yᵉ mighty ocean which they had passed, and was now as a maine barr & goulfe to seperate them from all yᵉ civill parts of yᵉ world. If it be said they had a ship to sucour them, it is trew; but what heard they daly from yᵉ mʳ. & company? but yᵗ with speede they should looke out a place with their shallop, wher they would be at some near distance; for yᵉ season was shuch as he would not stirr from thence till a safe harbor was discovered by them wher they would be, and he might goe without danger; and that victells consumed apace, but he must & would keepe sufficient for them selves & their returne. Yea, it was muttered by some, that if they gott not a place in time, they would turne them & their goods ashore & leave them. Let it also be considred what weake hopes of supply & succoure they left behinde them, yᵗ might bear up their minds in this sade condition and trialls they were under; and they could not but be very smale. It is true, indeed, yᵉ affections & love of their brethren at Leyden was cordiall & entire towards them, but they had litle power to help them, or them selves; and how yᵉ case stode betweene them & yᵉ marchants at their coming away, hath allready

been declared. What could now sustaine them but the spirite of God & his grace? May not & ought not the children of these fathers rightly say: *Our faithers were Englishmen which came over this great ocean, and were ready to perish in this willdernes; but they cried unto yᵉ Lord, and he heard their voyce, and looked on their adversitie, &c. Let them therfore praise yᵉ Lord, because he is good, & his mercies endure for ever. Yea, let them which have been redeemed of yᵉ Lord, shew how he hath delivered them from yᵉ hand of yᵉ oppressour. When they wandered in yᵉ deserte willdernes out of yᵉ way, and found no citie to dwell in, both hungrie, & thirstie, their sowle was overwhelmed in them. Let them confess before yᵉ Lord his loving kindnes, and his wonderfull works before yᵉ sons of men.*

### THE 10. CHAP

*Showing how they sought out a place of habitation, and what befell them theraboute.*

Being thus arrived at Cap-Cod yᵉ 11. of November, and necessitie calling them to looke out a place for habitation, (as well as the maisters & mariners importunitie,) they having brought a large shalop with them out of England, stowed in quarters in yᵉ ship, they now gott her out & sett their carpenters to worke to trime her up; but being much brused & shatered in yᵉ shipe wᵗʰ foule weather, they saw she would be longe in mending. Wheruppon a few of them tendered them selves to goe by land and discovere those nearest places, whilst yᵉ shallop was in mending; and yᵉ rather because as they wente into yᵗ harbor ther seemed to be an opening some 2. or 3 leagues of, which yᵉ maister judged to be a river. It was conceived ther might be some danger in yᵉ attempte, yet seeing them resolute, they were permited to goe, being 16. of them well armed, under yᵉ conduct of Captain Standish, having shuch instructions given them as was thought meete. They sett forth yᵉ 15. of Noveᵇʳ: and when they had marched aboute the space of a mile by yᵉ sea side, they espied 5. or 6. persons with a dogg coming towards them, who were salvages; but they fled from them, & rane up into yᵉ woods, and yᵉ English followed them, partly to see if they could speake with them, and partly to discover if ther might not be more of them lying in ambush. But yᵉ Indeans seeing them selves thus followed, they againe forsooke the woods, & rane away on yᵉ sands as hard as they could, so as they could not come near them, but followed them by yᵉ tracte of their feet sundrie miles, and saw that they had come the same way. So, night coming on, they made their randevous & set out their sentinels, and rested in quiete yᵗ *night*, and the next morning followed their tracte till they had headed a great creake, & so left the sands, & turned an other way into yᵉ woods. But they still followed them by geuss, hoping to find their dwellings; but they soone lost both them & them selves, falling into shuch thickets as were ready to tear their cloaths & armore in peeces, but were most distresed for wante of drinke. But at length they found water & refreshed them selves, being yᵉ first New-England water they drunke of, and was now in thir great thirste as pleasante unto them as wine or bear had been in for-times. Afterwards they directed their course to come to yᵉother shore, for they knew it was a necke of land they were to crosse over, and so at length gott to yᵉ sea-side, and marched to this supposed river, & by yᵉ way found a pond of clear fresh water, and shortly after a good quantitie of clear ground wher yᵉ Indeans had formerly set corne, and some of their graves. And proceeding furder they saw new-stuble wher corne had been set yᵉ same year, also they found wher latly a house had been, wher some planks and a great ketle was remaining, and heaps of sand newly padled with their hands, which they, digging up, found in them diverce faire Indean baskets filled with corne, and some in eares, faire and good, of diverce collours, which seemed to them a very goodly sight, (haveing never seen any shuch before). This was near yᵉ place of that supposed river they came to seeck; unto which they wente and found it to open it selfe into 2. armes with a high cliffe of sand in yᵉ enterance, but more like to be crikes of salte water then any fresh, for ought they saw; and that ther was good harborige for their shalope; leaving it further to be discovered by their shalop when she was ready. So their time limeted them being expired, they returned to yᵉ ship, least they should be in fear of their saftie; and tooke with them parte of yᵉ corne, and buried up yᵉ rest, and so like yᵉ men from Eshcoll carried with them of yᵉ fruits of yᵉ land, & showed their breethren; of which, & their returne, they were marvelusly glad, and their harts incouraged.

After this, yᵉ shalop being got ready, they set out againe for yᵉ better discovery of this place, & yᵉ mʳ. of yᵉ ship desired to goe him selfe, so ther went some 30. men, but found it to be no harbor for ships but only for boats; ther was allso found 2. of their houses covered with matts, & sundrie of their implements in them, but yᵉ people were rune away & could not be seen; also ther was found more of their corne, & of their beans of various collours. The corne & beans they brought away, purposing to give them full satisfaction when they should meete with any of them (as about some 6. months afterward they did, to their good contente). And here is to be noted a spetiall providence of God, and a great mercie to this poore people, that hear they gott seed to plant them corne yᵉ next year, or els they might have starved, for they had none, nor any liklyhood to get any till yᵉ season had beene past (as yᵉ sequell did manyfest). Neither is it lickly they had had this, if yᵉ first viage had not been made, for the ground was now all covered with snow, & hard frozen. But the Lord is never wanting unto his in their greatest needs; let his holy name have all yᵉ praise.

The month of November being spente in these affairs, & much foule weather falling in, the 6. *of Desemr*: they sente out their shallop againe with 10. of their principall men, & some sea men, upon further discovery, intending to circulate that deepe bay of Capcodd. The weather was very could, & it frose so hard as yᵉ sprea of yᵉ sea lighting on their coats, they were as if they had been glased; yet *that night* betimes they gott downe into yᵉ botome of yᵉ bay, and as they drue nere yᵉ shore they saw some 10. or 12. Indeans very busie aboute some thing. They landed aboute a league or 2. from them, and had much a doe to put a shore any wher, it lay so full of flats. Being landed, it grew late, and they made them selves a barricade with loggs & bowes as well as they could in yᵉ time, & set out their sentenill & betooke them to rest, and saw yᵉ smoake of yᵉ fire yᵉ savages made yᵗ night. When *morning* was come they devided their company, some to coaste along yᵉ shore in yᵉ boate, and the rest marched throw yᵉ woods to see yᵉ land, if any fit place might be for their dwelling. They came also to yᵉ place wher they saw the Indans yᵉ night before, & found they had been cuting up a great fish like a grampus, being some 2. inches thike of fate like a hogg, some peeces wher of they had left by yᵉ way; and yᵉ shallop found 2. more of these fishes dead on yᵉ sands, a thing usuall after storms in yᵗ place, by reason of yᵉ great flats of sand that lye of. So they ranged up and doune all yᵗ day, but found no people, nor any place they liked. When yᵉ sune grue low, they hasted out of yᵉ woods to meete with their shallop, to whom they made signes to come to them into a *creeke* hardby, the which they did at highwater; of which they were very glad, for they had not seen each other all yᵗ day, since yᵉ morning. So they made them a barricado (as usually they did every night) with loggs, staks, & thike pine bowes, yᵉ height of a man, leaving it open to leeward, partly to shelter them from yᵉ could & wind (making their fire in yᵉ midle, & lying round aboute it), and partly to defend them from any sudden assaults of yᵉ savags, if they should surround them. So being very weary, they betooke them to rest. But aboute *midnight,* they heard a hideous & great crie, and their sentinell caled, "Arme, arme"; so they bestired them & stood to their armes, & shote of a cupple of moskets, and then the noys seased. They concluded it was a companie of wolves, or such like willd beasts; for one of yᵉ sea men tould them he had often heard shuch a noyse in New-found land. So they rested till about 5. of yᵉ clock in the *morning;* for yᵉ tide, & ther purpose to goe from thence, made them be stiring betimes. So after praier they prepared for breakfast, and it being day dawning, it was thought best to be carring things downe to yᵉ boate. But some said it was not best to carrie yᵉ armes downe, others said they would be the readier, for they had laped them up in their coats from yᵉ dew. But some 3. or 4. would not cary theirs till they wente them selves, yet as it fell out, yᵉ water being not high enough, they layed them downe on yᵉ banke side, & came up to breakfast. But presently, all on yᵉ sudain, they heard a great & strange crie, which they knew to be the same voyces they heard in yᵉ night, though they varied their notes, & one of their company being abroad came runing in, & cried, "Men, Indeans, Indeans"; and wᵗʰall, their arowes came flying amongst them. Their men rane with all speed to recover their armes, as by yᵉ good providence

of God they did. In yᵉ mean time, of those that were ther ready, tow muskets were discharged at them, & 2. more stood ready in yᵉ enterance of ther randevoue, but were comanded not to shoote till they could take full aime at them; & yᵉ other 2. charged againe with all speed, for ther were only 4. had armes ther, & defended yᵉ baricado which was first assalted. The crie of yᵉ Indeans was dreadfull, espetially when they saw ther men rune out of yᵉ randevoue towourds yᵉ shallop, to recover their armes, the Indeans wheeling aboute upon them. But some runing out with coats of malle on, & cutlasses in their hands, they soone got their armes, & let flye amongs them, and quickly stopped their violence. Yet ther was a lustie man, and no less valiante, stood behind a tree within halfe a musket shot, and let his arrows flie at them. He was seen shoot 3. arrowes, which were all avoyded. He stood 3. shot of a musket, till one taking full aime at him, and made yᵉ barke or splinters of yᵉ tree fly about his ears, after which he gave an extraordinary shrike, and away they wente all of them. They left some to keep yᵉ shalop, and followed them aboute a quarter of a mille, and shouted once or twise, and shot of 2. or 3. peces, & so returned. This they did, that they might conceive that they were not affrade of them or any way discouraged. Thus it pleased God to vanquish their enimies, and give them deliverance; and by his spetiall providence so to dispose that not any one of them were either hurte, or hitt, though their arrows came close by them, & on every side them, and sundry of their coats, which hunge up in yᵉ barricado, were shot throw & throw. Aterwards they gave God sollamne thanks & praise for their deliverance, & gathered up a bundle of their arrows, & sente them into England afterward by yᵉ mʳ. of yᵉ ship, and called that place yᵉ first encounter.

## QUESTIONS TO CONSIDER

1. How does Bradford present the Pilgrim's journey and the land they found?
2. What did the colonists do to start to establish a colony? What was most important to do first?

# CHAPTER 4

# CONTINENTAL EMPIRES, 1660–1720

## 4.1 JOHN ELIOT, *A BRIEF NARRATIVE OF THE PROGRESS OF THE* GOSPEL AMONGST *THE INDIANS IN NEW ENGLAND* (1670)

John Eliot (1604–1690) was a Puritan missionary devoted to spreading Christianity to Native American tribes. In 1631, Eliot arrived in Boston, where he became the minister at a nearby church. He also began to learn the Algonquin language as a part of his attempts to teach Native Americans Christianity and established a series of Native American "praying towns," where he sought to establish a Christian society. In 1675, the murder of one "praying Indian," John Sassamon, would spark King Philip's War, between Native Americans and English Colonists and which devastated both populations. The following document is taken from Eliot's 1670 narrative of his missionary work. In it, he reported on the ways in which he tried to convert Native Americans and speculated on best practices going forward.

*To the Right Worſhipful the Commiſſioners under his Ma-jeſties Great-Seal, for Propagation of the Goſpel amongſt the poor blind Indians in New-England.*
*Right Worſhipful and Chriſtian Gentlemen,*

That brief Tract of the preſent ſtate of the *Indian-Work* in my hand, which I did the laſt year on the ſudden preſent you with when you call'd for ſuch a thing ; That falling ſhort of its end, and you calling for a renewal thereof, with opportunity of more time, I ſhall begin with our laſt great motion in that Work done this Summer, becauſe that will lead me to begin with the ſtate of the *Indians* under the hands of my Brethren Mr. *Mahew* and Mr. *Bourn.*

Upon the 17th day of the 6th month 1670, there was a Meeting at *Maktapog* near *Sandwich* in *Plimouth-Pattent,* to gather a Church among the *Indians* : There were preſent ſix of the Magiſtrates, and many Elders, (all of them Meſſengers of the Churches within that Juriſdiction) in whoſe preſence, in a day of Faſting and Prayer, they making confeſſion of the Truth and Grace of Jeſus Chriſt, did in that ſolemn Aſſembly enter into Covenant, to walk together in the Faith and Order of

*Source:* John Eliot, *A Brief Narrative of the Progress of the Gospel Amongst the Indians in New England* (Boston: John K. Wiggins and Wm. Parsons Lunt, 1670), 19–24. Retrieved from the Internet Archive website, https://archive.org/details/39002055099510.med.yale.edu (Accessed June 5, 2018).

the Gofpel ; and were accepted and declared to be a Church of Jefus Chrift. Thefe *Indians* being of kin to our *Maffachufet-Indians* who firft prayed unto God, converfed with them, and received amongft them the light and love of the Truth ; they defired me to write to Mr. *Leveredge* to teach them : He accepted the Motion : and performed the Work with good fuccefs ; but afterwards he left that place, and went to *Long-Ifland*, and there a godly Brother, named *Richard Bourne* (who purpofed to remove with Mr. *Leveredge*, but hindered by Divine Providence) undertook the teaching of thofe *Indians*, and hath continued in the work with good fuccefs to this day ; him we ordained Paftor : and one of the *Indians*, named *Jude*, fhould have been ordained Ruling-Elder, but being fick at that time, advice was given that he fhould be ordained with the firft opportunity, as alfo a Deacon to manage the prefent Sabbath-day Collections, and other parts of that Office in their feafon. The fame day alfo were they, and fuch of their Children as were prefent, baptized.

From them we paffed over to the *Vinyard*, where many were added to the Church both men and women, and were baptized all of them, and their Children alfo with them ; we had the Sacrament of the Lords Supper celebrated in the *Indian-Church*, and many of the *Englifh-Church* gladly joined with them ; for which caufe it was celebrated in both languages. On a day of Fafting and Prayer, Elders were ordained, two Teaching-Elders, the one to be a Preacher of the Gofpel, to do the Office of a Paftor and Teacher ; the other to be a Preacher of the Gofpel, to do the Office of a Teacher and Paftor, as the Lord should give them ability and opportunity ; Alfo two Ruling-Elders, with advice to ordain Deacons alfo, for the Service of Chrift in the Church. Things were fo ordered by the Lord's guidance, that a Foundation is laid for two Churches more ; for firft, thefe of the *Vinyard* dwelling at too great a diftance to enjoy with comfort their Sabbath-communion in one place, Advice was given them, that after fome experience of walking together in the Order and Ordinances of the Gofpel, they fhould iffue fourth into another Church ; and the Officers are fo chofen, that when they fhall do fo, both Places are furnifhed with a Teaching and Ruling-Elder. . . .

In as much as now we have ordained *Indian Officers* unto the Miniftry of the Gofpel, it is needful to add a word or two of Apology : I find it hopelefs to expect *Englifh* officers in our *Indian* Churches ; the work is full of hardfhip, hard labour, and chargeable alfo, and the *Indians* not yet capable to give confiderable fupport and maintenance ; and Men have bodies, and muft live of the Gofpel : And what comes from England is liable to hazard and uncertainties. On fuch grounds as thefe partly, but efpecially from the fecret wife governance of Jefus Chrift, the Lord of the Harveft, there is no appearance of hope for their fouls feeding in that way : they muft be trained up to be able to live of themfelves in the ways of the Gofpel of Chrift ; and through the riches of God's Grace and Love, fundry of themfelves who are expert in the Scriptures, are able to teach each other : An *Englifh* young man raw in that language, coming to teach among our Chriftian-*Indians*, would be much to their lofs ; there be of themfelves fuch as be more able, efpecially being advantaged that he fpeaketh his own language, and knoweth their manners. Such *Englifh* as fhall hereafter teach them, muft begin with a People that begin to pray unto God, (and fuch opportunities we have many) and then as they grow in knowledge, he will grow (if he be diligent) in ability of fpeech to communicate the knowledge of Chrift unto them. And feeing they muft have Teachers amongft themfelves, they muft alfo be taught to be Teachersf: for which caufe I have begun to teach them the Art of Teaching, and I find fome of them very capable. And while I live, my purpofe is, (by the Grace of Chrift affifting) to make it one of my chief cares and labours to teach them fome of the Liberal Arts and Sciences, and the way how to analize, and lay out into particulars both the Works and Word of God ; and how to communicate knowledge to others methodically and fkillfully, and efpecially the method of Divinity. There be fundry Minifters who live in an opportunity of beginning with a People, and for time to come I shall ceafe my importuning of others, and onely fall to perfwade fuch unto this fervice of Jefus Chrift, it being one part of our Minifterial Charge to preach to the World in the Name of Jefus, and from amongft them to gather Subjects to his holy Kingdom. The Bible, and the Catechifm drawn out of the Bible, are general helps to all parts and places about us, and are the groundwork of Community amongft all our *Indian*-Churches and Chriftians.

I find a Bleffing, when our Church of *Natick* doth fend forth fit Perfons unto fome remoter places, to teach them the fear of the Lord. But we want maintenance for that Service ; it is chargeable matter to fend a Man from his Family : The Labourer is worthy of his Hire : And when they go only to the High-wayes and Hedges, it is not to be expected that they fhould reward them : If they believe and obey their Meffage, it is enough. We are determined to fend forth fome (if the Lord will, and that we live) this Autumn, fundry ways. I fee the beft

way is, *up and be doing* : In all labour there is profit; *Seek and ye fhall find*. We have Chrift's Example, his Promife, his Prefence, his Spirit to affift; and I truft that the Lord will find a way for your encouragement. . . .

### QUESTIONS TO CONSIDER

1. How does Eliot view Native Americans? Is he empathetic or condescending?
2. Do his missionary strategies seem effective to you?

# 4.2 NATHANIEL BACON, "THE DECLARATION" (1676)

King Philip's War exposed deep fractures in Massachusetts society, and Bacon's Rebellion did the same for Virginia society. Nathaniel Bacon (1647–1676) was perhaps a surprising revolutionary. Born to a wealthy family, he emigrated to Virginia in 1674, purchased two plantations, and built a home in Jamestown, the capital. Virginia Governor William Berkeley appointed Bacon to his governor's council, and Bacon very easily might have settled in as part of the colonial power structure. Bacon, however, quickly grew angry with Berkeley's inaction toward Native American hostility. He joined up with other similarly minded colonists and formed a militia, made up of both whites and African American indentured servants, to attack local Doeg and Pamunkey populations—actions that led Berkeley to seek Bacon's arrest. Bacon eluded capture, and Bacon's Rebellion continued to disrupt Virginia. In 1676, Bacon wrote the following document, which outlined his issues with the colonial government. Bacon's Rebellion raged for the next few months, until Bacon's untimely death of dysentery in October 1676.

### THE DECLARACON OF Y$^E$ PEOPLE

1$^{st}$. For having vpon specious pretences of publiqe works raised great vniust taxes vpon the Comonality for y$^e$ aduancement of private favorites & other sinister ends, but noe visible effects in any measure adequate, For not having dureing this long time of time of his Gou'nem$^t$ in any measure aduanced this hopefull Colony either by fortificacons Townes of Trade.

2$^d$. For haveing abused & rendred contemptable the Magistrates of Justice, by aduanceing to places of Judicature, scandalous and Ignorant favorites.

3. For haveing wronged his Ma$^{ties}$ prerogative & interest by assumeing Monopolony of y$^e$ Beaver trade, & for having in y$^t$ vniust gaine betrayed & sold his Ma$^{ties}$ Country & y$^e$ lives of his loyall subiects, to the barbarous heathen.

*Source: Collections of the Massachusetts Historical Society, Volume IX—Fourth Series* (Boston: The Massachusetts Historical Society, 1871), 184–187. Retrieved from the Internet Archive website, https://catalog.hathitrust.org/Record/008881846 (Accessed June 5, 2018).

4. For having protected, favoured, & Imboldned the Indians ag$^t$ his Ma$^{ties}$ loyall subiects, never contriveing, requiring, or appointing any due or prop' meanes of sattis faccon for theire many Inuasions, robberies, & murthers comitted vpon vs.

5. For having when the Army of English, was just vpon y$^e$ track of those Indians, who now in all places burne, spoyle, murther when we might with ease have destroyed y$^m$ who then were in open hostility, for then having expressly countermanded, & sent back our Army, by passing his word for y$^e$ peaceable demeanour of y$^e$ said Indians, who immediately p'secuted theire evill intencons, committing horred murthers & robberies in all places, being p'tected by y$^e$ said ingagem.$^t$ & word past of him y$^e$ said S$^r$ W$^m$ Berkeley, having ruined & laid desolate a greate part of his Ma$^{ties}$ Country, & have now drawne y$^m$ selues into such obscure & remote places, & are by theire success soe imboldned & confirmed, by theire confederacy soe strengthen y$^t$ y$^e$ cryes of blood are in all places, & the terror, & constirnacon of y$^e$ people soe great, are now become, not onely a difficult, but a very formidable enemy, who might att first with ease haue beene destroyed.

6$^{th}$ And lately when vpon y$^e$ loud outcryes of blood y$^e$ Assembly had with all care raised & framed an Army for the preventing of further mischeife & safeguard of this his Ma$^{ties}$ Colony.

7$^{th}$ For haveing with onely y$^e$ privacy of some few favorites, w$^{th}$out acquainting the people, onely by the alteracon of a figure, forged a Comission, by we know not what hand, not onely without, but even ag$^t$ the consent of y$^e$ people, for the raiseing & effecting civill war & distruccon, which being happily & without blood shed prevented, for haveing the second time attempted y$^e$ same, thereby calling downe our forces from the defence of y$^e$ fronteeres & most weekely expoased places.

8. For the prevencon of civill mischeife & ruin amongst ourselues, whilst y$^e$ barbarous enimy in all places did invade, murther & spoyle vs, his ma$^{ties}$ most faithfull subiects.

Of this & the aforesaid Articles we accuse S$^r$ William Berkeley as guilty of each & eu$^r$y one of the same, and as one who hath traitorously attempted, violated & Iniured his Ma$^{ties}$ interest here, by a loss of a greate part of this his Colony & many of his faithfull. loyall subiects, by him be trayed & in a barbarous &

shamefull manner exposed to the Incursions & murther of y$^e$ heathen, And we doe further declare these y$^e$ ensueing p'sons in this list, to have beene his wicked & pernicious councell.$^{rs}$ Confederate, aiders, and assisters ag$^t$ Comonality in these our Civill commotions.

| | |
|---|---|
| S$^r$ Henry Chichley | Nich. Spencer |
| L$^t$ Coll, Christop$^r$ Wormeley | Joseph Bridger |
| Phillip Ludwell | W$^m$ Claiburne Jun5 |
| Rob$^t$ Beverley | Tho. Hawkins |
| Ri : Lee | W$^m$ Sherwood |
| Tho: Ballard | Jo$^n$ Page Clerke |
| W$^m$ Cole | Jo$^n$ Cluffe Clerke |
| Rich$^d$ Cole | Jo$^n$ Cluffe Clerke |

John West: —Hubert Farrell: — Tho. Reade — Math. Kempe.

And we doe further demand y$^t$ y$^e$ said S$^r$ W$^m$ Berkeley with all y$^e$ p'sons in this list be forthwith delivered vp or surrender y$^m$ selues within fower days after the notice here of, Or otherwise we declare as followeth

That in whatsoever place, howse, or ship, any of y$^e$ said p'sons shall reside, be hidd, or p'tected, we declaire y$^e$ owners, Masters or Inhabitants of y$^e$ said places, to be confederates & trayters to y$^e$ people & the estates of y$^m$ is alsoe of all y$^e$ aforesaid p'sons to be confiscated, & this we the Comons of Virg$^a$ doe declare, desiring a firme vnion amongst our selues that we may jointly & with one accord defend our selues ag$^t$ the common Enimy, & let not y$^e$ faults of y$^e$ guilty be y$^e$ reproach of y$^e$ innocent, or y$^e$ faults or crimes of y$^e$ oppress$^{rs}$ deuide & sep'ate vs who have suffered by theire oppressions

These are therefore in his ma$^{ties}$ name of command you forthwith to seize y$^e$ p'sons above mencoed as Trayters to y$^e$ King & Country & them to bring to Midle plantacon, & there to secure y$^m$ vntill further order, and in case of opposicon, if you want any further assistance you are forth with to demand itt in y$^e$ name of y$^e$ people in all y$^e$ Counties of Virg$^a$

*NATH. BACON*
*Gen$^{ll}$ by Consent of y$^e$ people.*

## QUESTIONS TO CONSIDER

1. What were Bacon's main grievances?
2. Do his grievances seem reasonable to you?

# 4.3 ANN COTTON, EXCERPT FROM "AN ACCOUNT OF OUR LATE TROUBLES IN VIRGINIA" (1676)

In the following document, colonist Ann Cotton provides a lively, illuminating account of Bacon's Rebellion. Originally written for a friend, Cotton's narrative was eventually published in the *Richmond Enquirer* in 1804. While little is known about Cotton's life, she was married to John Cotton, an attorney and plantation owner. In her narrative, Cotton stresses the complex political negotiations between Bacon's militia and Berkeley's forces and intricately traces the various military engagements between the two sides. As is obvious from the end of her account, Bacon's Rebellion came to a decided head in 1676. In September of that year, Bacon's forces attacked Jamestown and burned it to the ground, forcing Berkeley to retreat. Just one month later, Bacon's death promptly ended the conflict. Bacon's Rebellion, however, terrified the white elite in Virginia and contributed to hardening racial barriers between whites and African Americans and to a more pugnacious attitude by the colonial government toward Native Americans.

*To Mr. C. H., at Yardly, in Northamptonshire :*

SIR : I having seen yours directed to ————, and considering that you cannot have your desires satisfied that way, for the forementioned reasons, I have by his permission adventured to send you this brief account of those affairs, so far as I have been informed.

The Susquehanians and Marylanders of friends being engaged enemies, as hath by former letter been hinted to you, and that the Indians being resolutely bent not to forsake their fort, it came to this point, that the Marylanders were obliged, finding themselves too weak to do the work themselves, to supplicate—too soon granted—aid of the Virginians, put under the conduct of one Colonel Washington, him whom you have sometimes seen at your house, Who, being joined with the Marylanders, invests the Indians in their fort with a negligent siege, upon which the enemy made several sallies, with as many losses to the besiegers, and at last gave them the opportunity to desert the fort, after that the English had, contrary to the law of arms, beat out of brains of six great men sent out to treat a peace ; an action of ill-consequence, as it proved afterwards, for the Indians having in the dark slipped through the Legure, and in their passage knocked ten of the besiegers on the head, whom they found fast asleep, leaving the rest to prosecute the siege (as Scoging's wife brooding the eggs that the fox had sucked), they resolved to employed their liberty in a avenging their commissioners' blood, which they speedily effected in the death of sixty innocent souls, and then sent in their remonstrance to the governor in justification of the fact, with this expostulation annexed : demanding what it was moved him to take up arms against them, his professed friends, in behalf of the Marylanders, their avowed enemies ; declaring their sorrow to see the Virginians of friends to become such violent enemies as to pursue the chase into another's dominions ; complains that their messengers, sent out for peace, were not only knocked on the head, but the fact countenanced by the governor for which, finding no other way to be satisfied, they had revenged themselves by killing then for one of the English, such being the disproportion between their men murdered and those by them slain, theirs being persons of quality, the other of inferior rank ; professing that if they may have a valuable satisfaction for the damage they had sustained by the English, and that the Virginians would withdraw their aid from the Marylanders' quarrel ; that then they would renew the league with Sir W. B.,* otherwise they would prosecute the war to the last man, and the hardest fend of.

This was fair play from foul gamesters. But the proposals not to be allowed of as being contrary to the honor of the English, the Indians proceed, and, having drawn the neighboring Indians into their aid in a short time, they committed abundance of unguarded and unrevenged murders, by which means a great many of the outward plantations were deserted, the doing whereof did not only terrify the whole colony, but supplanted what esteem the people formerly had for Sir W. B., whom they judged too remiss in applying means to stop the fury of the heathen, and to settle their affections and expectations upon one Esquire Bacon, newly come to the country, one of the council, and nearly related to your late wife's father-in-law, whom they desired might be commissioned general for the Indian war, which Sir William, for some reasons best known to himself, denying, the gentleman, without any scruple, accepts of a commission from the people's affections, signed by the emergencies of affairs and the country's danger, and so forthwith advanced with a small party, composed of such that own his authority, against the Indians, on whom, it is said, he did signal execution. In his absence he, and those with him, were declared rebels to the state, May 29th, and forces raised to reduce him to his obedience, at the head of which the governor advanced some thirty or forty miles to find Bacon out, but not knowing which way he was gone, he dismissed his army, retiring himself and council to Jamestown, there to be ready for the assembly, which was now upon the point of meeting, whither Bacon, some few days after his return home from his Indian march, repaired to render an

account of his services, for which he, and most of those with him in the expedition, were imprisoned ; from whence they were freed by a judgment in court upon Bacon's trial, himself readmitted into the council, and promised a commission the Monday following (this was on Saturday) against the Indians ; with which deluded, he smothers his resentments, and begs leave to visit his lady, now sick, as he pretended, which being granted, he returns to town at the head of four or five hundred men, well armed, and resumed his demands for a commission, which, after some hours' struggle with the governor, being obtained, according to his desire, he takes order for the country's security against the attempts of sculking Indians, fills up his numbers and provisions according to the gage of his commission, and so once more advanced against the Indians, who, hearing of his approach, called in their runners and scouts, betaking themselves to their subterfuges and lurking-holes. The general, for so he was now denominated, had not reached the head of York river, but that a post overtakes him and informs him that Sir W. B. was raising the train-bands in Gloucester, with an intent either to fall into his rear, or otherwise to cut him off when of should return, weary and spent from his Indian service. . . . It vexed him to the heart, as he said, to think that while he was as hunting wolves, tigers, and bears, which daily destroyed our harmless and innocent lambs, that he and those with him should be pursued in the rear with a full cry, as more savage beasts ; he perceived, like the corn, he was light between those stones, which might grind him to powder if he did not look the better about him, for the preventing of which, after a short consultation with his officers, he countermarched his army, about five hundred in all, down to the middle plantation, of which the governor being informed, ships himself and adherers for Accomack (for the Gloster men refused to own his quarrel against the general), after he had caused Bacon, in these parts, to be proclaimed a rebel once more, July 29th.

Bacon, being sate down with his army at the middle plantation, sends out an invitation to all the prime gentlemen in these parts, to give him a meeting

---

* Sir William Berkeley, the Governor of Virginia.

in his quarters, there to consult how the Indians were to be proceeded against, and himself and army protected against the designs of Sir W. B., against whose papers of the twenty-ninth of May, and his proclamation since, he puts forth his replication and those papers upon these dilemmas. . . .

This work being over, and orders given for an assembly to sit on the fourth of September, the writs being issued in his majesty's name, and signed by four of the council, before named, the general once more sets out of find the Indians : of which Sir William having gained intelligence, to prevent Bacon's designs by the assembly, returns from Accomack with about one thousand soldiers, and others, in five ships and ten sloops, to Jamestown, in which were some nine hundred Baconians, for so now they began to be called for a mark of distinction, under the command of Colonel Hansford, who was commissioned by Bacon to raise forces, if need were, in his absence, for the safety of the country. Unto these Sir William sends in a summons for a rendition of the place, with a pardon to all that would decline Bacon's and entertain his cause. What was returned to his summons I know not, but in the night the Baconians forsake the town, by the advice of Drommond and Lawrance (who were both excepted in the governor's summons, out of mercy), every one returning to their own abode, excepting Drommond, Hansford, Lawrence, and some few others, who went to find the general, now returned to the head of York river, having spent his provisions in following the Indians, on whom he did some execution, and sent them packing a great way from the borders.

Before that Drommond, and those with him, had reached the general, he had dismissed his army to their respective habitations, to gather strength against the next intended expedition, excepting some few reserved for his guard, and persons living in these parts, unto whom, those that came with Hansford being joined, made about one hundred and fifty in all. With these, Bacon, by a swift march, before any news was heard of his return from the Indians, in these parts, comes to town, to the consternation of all in it, and there blocks the governor up, which he easily effected by this unheard of project : he was no sooner arrived at town, but by several small parties of horse, two or three in a party, for more he could not spare, he fetcheth into

his little Leagure all the prime men's wives, whose husbands were with the governor, as Colonel Bacon's lady, Madame Bray, Madame Page, Madame Ballard, and others, who, the next morning, he presents to the view of their husbands and friends in town, upon the top of the small work he had cast up in the night, where he caused them to tarry until he had finished his defense against his enemies' shot, it being the only place, as you do know well enough, for these in town to make a sally at, which when completed, and the governor understanding that the gentlewomen were withdrawn to a place of safety, he sent out some six or seven hundred of his soldiers, to beat Bacon out of his trench. But it seem that those works, that were protected by such charms while raising, that plugged up the enemy's shot in their guns, could not now be stormed by a virtue less powerful, when finished, than the sight of a few white aprons, otherwise the service had been more honorable and the damage less, several of those who made the sally being slain and wounded, without one drop of blood drawn from the enemy. Within two or three days after this disaster, the governor reships himself, soldiers, and all the inhabitants of the town, and their goods, and so to Accomack again, leaving Bacon to enter the place at his pleasure, which he did the next morning before day, and the night following burned it down to the ground, to prevent a future siege, as he said, which flagrant and flagitious act performed, he draws his men out of town, and marched them over York river, at Tindell's point, to find Colonel Brent, who was advancing fast upon him from Potomack, at the head of twelve hundred men, as he was informed, with a design to raise Bacon's siege from before the town, or otherwise to fight him, as he saw cause ; but Brent's soldiers no sooner heard that Bacon had got on the north side of York river, with an intent to fight them, and that he had beat the governor out of the town, and fearing if he met with them that he might beat them out of their lives, they basely forsook their colors, the greater part adhering to Bacon's cause, resolving with the Persians to go and worship the rising sun, now approaching near their horizon of which Bacon being informed, he stops his proceedings that way, and begins to provide for another expedition against the Indians, of whom he had heard no news since his last march against them ; which while he was a contriving, death summoned him to more urgent affairs, into whose hands, after a short siege, he surrenders his life, leaving his commission in the custody of his lieutenant-general, one Ingram, newly come into the country.

Sir William no sooner had news that Bacon was dead but he sent over a party, in a sloop, to York, who snapped Colonel Hansford and others with him, that kept a negligent guard at Colonel Reade's house, under his command. When Handsford came to Accomack, he had the honor to be the first Virginian born that was ever hanged ; the soldiers, about twenty in all, that were taken with him, were committed to prison, Captain Carver, Captain Wilford, Captain Farloe, with five or six others of less note, taken at other places, ending their days as Hansford did ; Major Cheesman being appointed, but it seems not destined to the like end, which he prevented by dying in prison, through ill-usage, as it is said.

This execution being over, which the Baconians termed cruelty in the abstract, Sir William ships himself and soldiers for York river, casting anchor at Tindell's point, from where he sent up one hundred and twenty men, to surprise, a guard of about thirty men and boys, kept at Colonel Bacon's house, under the command of Major Whaley, who, being forewarned by Hansford's fate, prevented the designed conflict, with the death of the commander-in-chief, and the taking some prisoners ; Major Lawrence Smith, with six hundred men, meeting with the like fate at Colonel Pate's house in Gloster, against Ingram, the Baconian general, only Smith saved himself by leaving his men in the lurch, being all made prisoners, whom Ingram dismissed to their own homes ; Ingram himself, and all under his command, within a few days after, being reduced to his duty, by the well contrivance of Captain Grantham, who was now lately arrived at York river, which put a period to the war . . .

### QUESTIONS TO CONSIDER

1. What events does Cotton especially highlight?
2. How did she view each side in the rebellion?

# 4.4 DON ANTONIO DE OTERMÍN, LETTER ON THE PUEBLO REVOLT (1680)

The Pueblo Revolt, though perhaps less well known than King Philip's War or Bacon's Rebellion, provides another crucial episode that revealed fractures in the North American colonial experiment. The Spanish colony in New Mexico (described by Juan de Oñate in Reading 1.4) thrived by subjugating Native American Pueblo populations. The Spanish forced Pueblo people to pay tribute, virtually enslaved them on encomienda plantations, and demanded that Pueblo populations convert to Catholicism. In the late 1670s, sparked by increasing Spanish oppression and a deadly drought, Pueblo leader Popé began to raise support for a rebellion. Popé promised prosperity if his followers could oust the Spanish from the region. In August 1680, his large force placed Santa Fe under siege and forced colonial governor Antonio de Otermín to retreat from New Mexico entirely. In this document, from a letter written about the attack, Otermín recounts the revolt and bewails his fortune. The Spanish would not fully retake New Mexico until 1692.

*Source:* "Letter of the governor and captain-general, Don Antonio de Otermin, from New Mexico, in which he gives him a full account of what has happened to him since the day the Indians surrounded him," http://www.pbs.org/weta/thewest/resources/archives/one/pueblo.htm (Accessed June 5, 2018).

MY VERY REVEREND FATHER, Sir, and friend, most beloved Fray Francisco de Ayeta: The time has come when, with tears in my eyes and deep sorrow in my heart, I commence to give an account of the lamentable tragedy, such as has never before happened in the world, which has occurred in this miserable kingdom and holy custodia, His divine Majesty having thus permitted it because of my grievous sins. Before beginning my narration, I desire, as one obligated and grateful, to give your reverence the thanks due for the demonstrations of affection and kindness which you have given in your solicitude in ascertaining and inquiring for definite notices about both my life and those of the rest in this miserable kingdom, in the midst of persistent reports which had been circulated of the deaths of myself and the others, and for sparing neither any kind of effort nor large expenditures. For this, only Heaven can reward your reverence, though I do not doubt that his Majesty (may God keep him) will do so. . . .

On Tuesday, the 13th of the said month, at about nine o'clock in the morning, they came in sight of us in the suburb of Analco, in the cultivated field of the hermitage of San Miguel, and on the other side of the river from the villa, all the Indians of the Tanos and Pecos nations and the Queres of San Marcos, armed and giving war whoops. As I learned that one of the Indians who was leading them was from the villa and had gone to join them shortly before, I sent some soldiers to summon him and tell him on my behalf that he could come to see me in entire safety, so that I might ascertain from him the purpose for which they were coming. Upon receiving this message he came to where I was, and, since he was known, as I say, I asked him how it was that he had gone crazy too—being an Indian who spoke our language, was so intelligent, and had lived all his life in the villa among the Spaniards, where I had placed such confidence in him—and was now coming as a leader of the Indian rebels. He replied to me that they had elected him as their captain, and that they were carrying two banners, one white and the other red, and that the white one signified peace and the red one war. Thus if we wished to choose the white it must be upon our agreeing to leave the country, and if we chose the red, we must perish, because the rebels were numerous and we were very

few; there was no alternative, inasmuch as they had killed so many religious and Spaniards.

On hearing this reply, I spoke to him very persuasively, to the effect that he and the rest of his followers were Catholic Christians, asking how they expected to live without the religious; and said that even though they had committed so many atrocities, still there was a remedy, for if they would return to obedience to his Majesty they would be pardoned; and that thus he should go back to this people and tell them in my name all that had been said to him, and persuade them to agree to it and to withdraw from where they were; and that he was to advise me of what they might reply. He came back from thee after a short time, saying that his people asked that all classes of Indians who were in our power be given up to them, both those in the service of the Spaniards and those of the Mexican nation of that suburb of Analco. He demanded also that his wife and children be given up to him, and likewise that all the Apache men and women whom the Spaniards had captured in war be turned over to them, inasmuch as some Apaches who were among them were asking for them. If these things were not done they would declare war immediately, and they were unwilling to leave the place where they were because they were awaiting the Taos, Percuries, and Teguas nations, with whose aid they would destroy us.

Seeing his determination, and what they demanded of us, and especially the fact that it was untrue that there were any Apaches among them, because they were at war with all of them, and that these parleys were intended solely to obtain his wife and children and to gain time for the arrival of the other rebellious nations to join them and besiege us, and that during this time they were robbing and sacking what was in the said hermitage and the houses of the Mexicans, I told him (having given him all the preceding admonitions as a Christian and a Catholic) to return to his people and say to them that unless they immediately desisted from sacking the houses and dispersed, I would send to drive them away from there. Whereupon he went back, and his people received him with peals of bells and trumpets, giving loud shouts in sign of war.

With this, seeing after a short time that they not only did not cease the pillage but were advancing toward the villa with shamelessness and mockery, I ordered all the soldiers to go out and attack them until they succeeded in dislodging them from that place. Advancing for this purpose, they joined battle, killing some at the first encounter. Finding themselves repulsed, they took shelter and fortified themselves in the said hermitage and houses of the Mexicans, from which they defended themselves a part of the day with the firearms that they had and with arrows. We having set fire to some of the houses in which they were, thus having them surrounded and at the point of perishing, there appeared on the road from Tesuque a band of the people whom they were awaiting, who were all the Teguas. Thus it was necessary to go to prevent these latter from passing on to the villa, because the casas reales were poorly defended; whereupon the said Tanos and Pecos fled to the mountains and the two parties joined together, sleeping that night in the sierra of the villa. Many of the rebels remained dead and wounded, and our men retired to the casas reales with one soldier killed and the maese de campo, Francisco Gomez, and some fourteen or fifteen soldiers wounded, to attend them and intrench and fortify ourselves as best we could.

On the morning of the following day, Wednesday, I saw the enemy come down all together from the sierra where they had slept, toward the villa. Mounting my horse, I went out with the few forces that I had to meet them, above the convent. The enemy saw me and halted, making ready to resist the attack. They took up a better position, gaining the eminence of some ravines and thick timber, and began to give war whoops, as if daring me to attack them.

I paused thus for a short time, in battle formation, and the enemy turned aside from the eminence and went nearer the sierras, to gain the one which comes down behind the house of the maese de campo, Francisco Gomez. There they took up their position, and this day passed without our having any further engagements or skirmishes than had already occurred, we taking care that they should not throw themselves upon us and burn the church and the houses of the villa.

The next day, Thursday, the enemy obliged us to take the same step as on the day before of mounting on horseback in fighting formation. There were only some light skirmishes to prevent their burning and sacking some of the houses which were at a distance from the main part of the villa. I knew well enough that these dilatory tactics were to give time for the people of the other nations who were missing to join them in order to besiege and attempt to destroy us, but the height of the places in which they were, so favorable to them and on the contrary so unfavorable to us, made it impossible for us to go and drive them out before they should all be joined together. . . .

On the next day, Saturday, they began at dawn to press us harder and more closely with gunshots, arrows, and stones, saying to us that now we should not escape them, and that, besides their own numbers, they were expecting help from the Apaches whom they had already summoned. They fatigued us greatly on this day, because all was fighting, and above all we suffered from thirst, as we were already oppressed by it. At nightfall, because of the evident peril in which we found ourselves by their gaining the two stations where the cannon were mounted, which we had at the doors of the casas reales, aimed at the entrances of the streets, in order to bring them inside it was necessary to assemble all the forces that I had with me, because we realized that this was their [the Indians'] intention. Instantly all the said Indian rebels began a chant of victory and raised war whoops, burning all the houses of the villa, and they kept us in this position the entire night, which I assure your reverence was the most horrible that could be thought of or imagined, because the whole villa was a torch and everywhere were war chants and shouts. What grieved us most were the dreadful flames from the church and the scoffing and ridicule which the wretched and miserable Indian rebels made of the sacred things, intoning the alabado and the other prayers of the church with jeers.

Finding myself in this state, with the church and the villa burned, and with the few horses, sheep, goats, and cattle which we had without feed or water for so long that many had already died, and the rest were about to do so, and with such a multitude of people, most of them children and women, so that our numbers in all came to about a thousand persons, perishing with thirst—for we had nothing to drink during these two days except what had been kept in some jars and pitchers that were in the casas reales—surrounded by such a wailing of women and children, with confusion everywhere, I determined to take the resolution of going out in the morning to fight with the enemy until dying or conquering. Considering that the best strength and armor were prayers to appease the divine wrath, though on the preceding days the poor women had made them with such fervor, that night I charged them to do so increasingly, and told the father guardian and the other two religious to say mass for us at dawn, and exhort all alike to repentance for their sins and to conformance with the divine will, and to absolve us from guilt and punishment. These things being done, all of us who could mounted our horses, and the rest went on foot with their harquebuses, and some Indians who were in our service with their bows and arrows, and in the best order possible we directed our course toward the house of the maese de campo, Francisco Xavier, which was the place where (apparently) there were the most people and where they had been most active and boldest. On coming out of the entrance to the street it was seen that there was a great number of Indians. They were attacked in force, and though they resisted the first charge bravely, finally they were put to flight, many of them being overtaken and killed. Then turning at once upon those who were in the streets leading to the convent, they also were put to flight with little resistance. The houses in the direction of the house of the said maese de campo, Francisco Xavier, being still full of Indians who had taken refuge in them, and seeing that the enemy with the punishment and deaths that we had inflicted upon them in the first and second assaults were withdrawing toward the hills, giving us a little room, we laid siege to those who remained fortified in the said houses. Though they endeavored to defend themselves, and did so, seeing that they were being set afire and that they would be burned to death, those who remained alive surrendered and much was made of them. The deaths of both parties in this and the other encounters exceeded three hundred Indians.

Finding myself a little relieved by this miraculous event, although I had lost much blood from two arrow wounds which I had received in the face and from a remarkable gunshot wound in the chest on the day before, I immediately had water given to the cattle, the horses, and the people. Because we now found ourselves with very few provisions for so many people, and without hope of human aid, considering that our not having heard in so many days from the people on the lower river would be because of their all having been killed, like the others in the kingdom, or at least of their being or having been in dire straits, with the view of aiding them and joining with them into one body, so as to make the decisions most conducive to his Majesty's service, on the morning of the next day, Monday, I set out for La Isleta, where I judged the said comrades on the lower river would be. I trusted in divine providence, for I left without a crust of bread or a grain of wheat or maize, and with no other provision for the convoy of so many people except four hundred animals and two carts belonging to private persons, and, for food, a few sheep, goats, and cows.

In this manner, and with this fine provision, besides a few small ears of maize that we found in the fields, we went as far as the pueblo of La Alameda, where we learned from an old Indian whom we found in a maizefield that the lieutenant general with all the residents of his jurisdictions had left some fourteen or fifteen days before to return to El Paso to meet the wagons. This news made me very uneasy, alike because I could not be persuaded that he would have left without having news of me as well as of all the others in the kingdom, and because I feared that from his absence there would necessarily follow the abandonment of this kingdom. On hearing this news I acted at once, sending four soldiers to overtake the said lieutenant general and the others who were following him, with orders that they were to halt wherever they should come up with them. Going in pursuit of them, they overtook them at the place of Fray Cristobal. The lieutenant general, Alonso Garcia, overtook me at the place of Las Nutrias, and a few days' march thereafter I encountered the maese de campo, Pedro de Leiva, with all the people under his command, who were escorting these wagons and who came to ascertain whether or not we were dead, as your reverence had charged him to do, and to find me, ahead of the supply train. I was so short of provisions and of everything else that at best I should have had a little maize for six days or so.

Thus, after God, the only succor and relief that we have rests with your reverence and in your diligence.

Wherefore, and in order that your reverence may come immediately, because of the great importance to God and the king of your reverence's presence here, I am sending the said maese de campo, Pedro de Leiva, with the rest of the men whom he brought so that he may come as escort for your reverence and the wagons or mule-train in which we hope you will bring us some assistance of provisions. Because of the haste which the case demands I do not write at more length, and for the same reason I can not make a report at present concerning the above to the senor viceroy, because the autos are not verified and there has been no opportunity to conclude them. I shall leave it until your reverence's arrival here. For the rest I refer to the account which will be given to your reverence by the father secretary, Fray Buenaventura de Verganza. I am slowly overtaking the other party, which is sixteen leagues from here, with the view of joining them and discussing whether or not this miserable kingdom can be recovered. For this purpose I shall not spare any means in the service of God and of his Majesty, losing a thousand lives if I had them, as I have lost my estate and part of my health, and shedding my blood for God. May he protect me and permit me to see your reverence in this place at the head of the relief. September 8, 1680. Your servant, countryman, and friend kisses your reverence's hand.

*DON ANTONIO DE OTERMIN*

**QUESTIONS TO CONSIDER**

1. How does de Otermín portray the Pueblo?
2. What word choices does he use to gain sympathy for his cause?

# 4.5 EXCERPT FROM *THE SALEM WITCHCRAFT PAPERS* (1692)

In 1692, a mass mania about witchcraft broke out in colonial Massachusetts. While explanations for the causes vary—class strife, the long-term effects of Native American warfare, perhaps even medical illness—the fears took over Massachusetts society. Over 200 people were eventually accused of practicing witchcraft, and 20 people were executed after trials. The following document, taken from the court transcripts, shows how the trials proceeded. The person on trial in this case, Sarah Good, was one of the first people accused. Two young girls—Abigail Williams and Elizabeth Parris—accused Good and two other people of bewitching them, and the girls would dramatically convulse in their purported bewitched states. Susannah Sheldon, an eighteen-year-old girl whose family had been displaced during King Philip's War, was another of Good's accusers. This reading includes a description of Sheldon's accusation and the court's examination of Good. The court convicted Good and hanged her on July 29, 1692.

*(Susannah Sheldon v. Sarah Good)*

The Deposistion of Susannah Shelden agged about 18 years who testifieth and saith the sence I have ben affected I have very often ben most greviously tortured by Apperishtion of Sarah Good who has most dredfully affected me by biting pricking and pinching me and almost choaking me to death but on the 26.

---

*Source:* Paul Boyer and Stephen Nissenbaum, ed., *The Salem Witchcraft Papers, Volume II* (New York: Da Capo Press, 1977), 374–378.

June 1692 Sarah good most violently pulled down my head behind a Cheast and tyed my hands together with a whele band & allmost Choaked me to death: also william Battin and Thomas Buffington Juner ware forced to cutt the whele band from ofe my hands for they could not unty it

And farther s'd Sheldon upon giving in this testimony to the grand jury was seized with sundry fits w'ch. when she came to her self she told the s'd jury being aske that it was s'd. Good that afflicted her & a little after Mary Warren falling into a fit s'd. Sheldon affirmed to the Grand jury that she saw s'd Good upon her, & also a sauser being by invisible hands taken of from a Table & carried out of doors s'd. Sheldon affirmed she saw said Sarah Good carry it away & put it where it was found abroad.

Susanah Shelden: oned this har testimony to be the truth before the Juriars of Inquest on the oath which she had taken this. 28. of June 1692.

(Reverse) Susannah Sheldon Ag't Sarah Good

The deposition of Johanna Childun testifieth and saieth that upon 2d: of June: 1692: that the aparition of Sarah good and her least Child did apear to her : and the Child did tell its mother that she did murrder it : to which Sarah good replyed that she did it becaus that she Could not atend it and the Child tould its mother that she was A witch: and then Sarah good said she did give it to the divell

(*Henry Herrick and Jonathan Batchelor v. Sarah Good*)

The deposition of Henery Herrick aged About 21 years, this deponent testifieth & saith that in Last march was two yeare; Sarah Good came to his fathers house & desired to lodge there; & his father forbid it; & she went away Grumbling & my father bid us follow her & see that shee went away clear, lest she should lie in the barn: & by smoking of her pipe should fire the barn; & s'd deponent with Jonathan Batchelor seing her make a stop near the barne, bid her be gone; or he would set her farther of; to which she replied that then it should cost his father Zachariah Herick one; or two of the best Cowes which he had;—

And Jonathan Batchelor aged 14 year testifieth the same above-written; and doth farther testifie that about a weeke after two of his grandfathers: Master Catle were removed from their places: & other younger Catle put in their rooms & since that severall of their Catle have bene set Loose in a strange maner—

*Jurat in Curia*

(Reverse) H. Herrick   Sarah Good

(*Sarah Bibber v. Sarah Good*)

The Deposition of Sarah viber aged about 36 years who testifieth and saith that sence I have been afflected I have often seen the Apperishtion of Sarah Good but she did not hurt me tell the 2 day of May 1692 tho I saw hir Apperishtion most greviously tortor mercy lewes & Jno. Indian att Salem. on the 11th April 1692: but on the 2: may 1692 the Apperishtion of Sarah good did most greviously torment me by pressing my breath almost out of my body and also she did immediatly afflect my child by pinceing of it that I could hardly hold it and my husband seing of it took hold of the Child but it cried out and twisted so dreadfully by reson of the torture that the Apperishtion of Sarah Good did affect it with all that it gott out of its fathers Armes to:also several[ly] times sence the Apperishtion of Sarah Good has most greviously tormented me by beating and pinching me and almost Choaking me to death and pricking me with pinnes after a most dreadfull maner

Sarah viber ownid this har testimony to be the truth one the oath she had taken: be fore us the Juriars for Inquest: this: 28 dy of June 1692

*Sworne. in Court June 29th. 1692.*

And further Adds. that shee very beleives upon her Oath that Sarah Good had bewicthed her –

(Reverse) Sarah viber against Sarah good June 29, 1692

(*Mary Walcott v. Sarah Good*)

The Deposistion of Mary wolcott agged about 17 years who testifieth and saith that sence I have been afflected I have often see the Aperishtion of sarah good amongst the wicthes who has also afflected me and urged me writ in hir book

*The Mark of Mary Walcot*

Mary welcott ownid this har testimony to be the truth one har oath:before the Jurrars for Inqwest this 28.

of June 1692 also mary welcott testifieth that I have seen sarah good afflicting mercy lewes and Elizabeth Hubberd and Abigail Williams and I verily believe she bewicthed me

(Reverse) Mary Wallcott ag't Sarah Good

(*Death Warrant for Sarah Good, Rebecca Nurse, Susannah Martin, Elizabeth How, and Sarah Wilds*)

To Georg: Corwine Gent'n High Sheriff of the County of Essex Greeting Whereas Sarah Good Wife of William Good of Salem Village Rebecka Nurse wife of Francis Nurse of Salem Villiage Susanna Martin of Amesbury Widow Elizabeth How wif e of James How of Ipswich Sarah Wild Wife of John Wild of Topsfield all of the County of Essex in thier Maj'ts Province of the Massachusetts Bay in New England Att A Court of Oyer & Terminer held by Adjournment for Our Soveraign Lord & Lady King William & Queen Mary for the said County of Essex at Salem in the s'd County on the 29th day of June [torn] were Severaly arraigned on Several Indictments for the horrible Crime of Witchcraft by them practiced & Committed On Severall persons and pleading not guilty did for thier Tryall put themselves on God & Thier Countrey whereupon they were Each of themselves on God & Thier Countrey whereupon they were Each of them found & brought in Guilty by the Jury that passed On them according to thier respective Indictments and Sentence of death did then pass upon them as the Law directs Execution whereof yet remains to be done:

Those are Therefore in thier Maj'ties name William & Mary now King & Queen over England &ca:

to will & Comand you that upon Tuesday next being the 19th day of [torn] Instant July between the houres of Eight & [torn] in [torn] forenoon the same day you Safely conduct the s'd Sarah Good Rebecka Nurse Susanna Martin Elizabeth How & Sarah Wild From their Maj'ties Goal in Salem afores'd to the place of Execution & there Cause them & Every of them to be hanged by the Neck until they be dead and of the doings herein make return to the Clerke of the said Court & this precept and hereof you are not to fail at your peril and this Shall be your Sufficient Warrant Given under my hand & seale at Boston the 12'th day of July in the fourth year of the Reign of our Soveraigne Lord & Lady Wm & Mary King and Queen &ca:

*Wm Stoughton

Annoq Dom. 1692 –

(Reverse)

*Salem July 19th 1692*

I caused the within mentioned persons to be Executed according to the Tenour of the with[in] warrant
*George Corwin Sherif

### QUESTIONS TO CONSIDER

1. What kind of evidence did the Salem Witch Trials seek to uncover?
2. How would you describe the prosecution's questioning strategy?

# CHAPTER 5

# THE EIGHTEENTH-CENTURY WORLD, 1700–1775

## 5.1 EXCERPT FROM *A BRIEF ACCOUNT OF THE ESTABLISHMENT OF THE COLONY OF GEORGIA* (1735)

The British colony of Georgia was different than other British colonial experiments. In the late 1720s, British philanthropist James Oglethorpe (1696–1785) grew interested in sending British debtors to the New World, where, he hoped, they might both prosper and alleviate a burden on British society. He thought that debtors might form an ideal agrarian society, and he planned to limit urbanization and prohibit slavery in a proposed colony. Oglethorpe's group, the Trustees for Establishing the Colony of Georgia in America, issued the following document about their purposes. They received a royal charter, and Oglethorpe founded the colony in 1733. By the 1750s, colonists grew restless with the ban on slavery, however, and convinced both the Trustees and the British government to overturn it. Thereafter, Georgia became intricately tied to the global slave trade, which propelled that colony's plantation economy.

In *America* there are fertile lands sufficient to subsist all the useless Poor in *England*, and distressed Protestants in Europe ; yet Thousands starve for want of mere sustenance. The distance makes it difficult to get thither. The same want that renders men useless here, prevents their paying their passage ; and if others pay it for 'em, them become servants, or rather slaves for years to those who have defrayed the expense.

Therefore, money for passage is necessary, but is not the only want ; for if people were set down in America, and the land before them, they must cut down trees, build houses, fortify towns, dig and sow the land before they can get in a harvest ; and till then, they must be provided with food, and kept together, that they may be assistant to each other for their natural support and protection.

*Source: A Brief Account of the Establishment of the Colony of Georgia* (Washington, D.C.: Peter Force, 1835), 4–7. Retrieved from the Internet Archive website, https://archive.org/stream/briefaccountofes00geor/briefaccountofes00geor_djvu.txt (Accessed June 5, 2018).

The Romans esteemed the sending forth of Colonies, among their noblest works ; they observed that Rome, as she increased in power and empire, drew together such a conflux of people from all parts that she found herself over-burdened with their number, and the government brought under an incapacity to provide for them, or keep them in order. Necessity, the mother of invention, suggested to them an expedient, which at once gave ease to the capital, and increased the wealth and number of industrious citizens, by lessening the useless and unruly multitude ; and by planting them in colonies on the frontiers of their empire, gave a new strength to the whole ; and *This* they looked upon to be so considerable a service to the commonwealth, that they created peculiar officers for the establishment of such colonies, and the expence was defrayed out of the public treasury.

FROM THE CHARTER.—His Majesty having taken into his consideration, the miserable circumstances of many of his own poor subjects, ready to perish for want : as likewise the distresses of many poor foreigners, who would take refuge here from persecution ; and having a Princely regard to the great danger the southern frontiers of South Carolina are exposed to, by reason of the small number of white inhabitants there, hath, out of his Fatherly compassion towards his subjects, been graciously pleased to grant a charter for incorporating a number of gentlemen by the name of *The Trustees for establishing the Colony of Georgia in America.* They are impowered to collect benefactions ; and lay them out in cloathing. arming, sending over, and supporting colonies of the poor, whether subjects on foreigners, in Georgia. And his Majesty farther grants all his lands between the rivers *Savannah and Alatamaha*, which he erects into a Province by the name of GEORGIA, unto the Trustees, in trust for the poor, and for the better support of the Colony. At the desire of the Gentlemen, there are clauses in the Charter, restraining them and their successors from receiving any salary, fee, perquisite, or profit, whatsoever, by or from this undertaking; and also from receiving any grant of lands within the said district, to themselves, or in trust for them. There are farther clauses granting to the Trustees proper powers for establishing and governing the Colony, and liberty of conscience to all who shall settle there.

The Trustees intend to relieve such unfortunate persons as cannot subsist here, and establish them in an orderly manner, so as to form a well regulated town. As far as their fund goes, they will defray the charge of their passage to Georgia ; give them necessaries, cattle, land, and subsistence, till such time as they can build their houses and clear some of their land. They rely for success, first on the goodness of Providence, next on the compassionate disposition of the people of England ; and, they doubt not, that much will be spared from luxury, and superfluous expenses, by generous tempers, when such an opportunity is offered them by the giving of £10 to a child for ever.

In order to prevent the benefaction given to this purpose, from ever being misapplied ; and to keep up, as far as human Precaution can, a spirit of Disinterestedness, the Trustees have established the following method : That, each Benefactor may know what he has contributed is safely lodged, and justly accounted for, all money given will be deposited in the Bank of England ; and entries made of every benefaction, in a book to be kept for that purpose by the Trustees ; or, if concealed, the names of those, by whose hands they sent their money. There are to be annual accounts of all the money received, and how the same has been disposed of, laid before the Lord High Chancellor, the Lord Chief Justice of the King's Bench, the Master of the Rolls, the Lord Chief Justice of the Common Please, and the Lord Chief Baron of the Exchequer, or two them, will be transmitted to every considerable Benefactor.

By such a Colony, many families, who would otherwise starve, will be provided for, and made masters of houses and lands ; the people in Great Britain to whom these necessitous families were a burthen, will be relieved ; numbers of manufacturers will be here employed, for supplying them with clothes, working tools, and other necessaries; and by giving refuge to the distressed Saltzburghers, and other persecuted Protestants, the power of Britain, as a reward for its hospitality, will be increased by the addition of so many religious and industrious subjects.

The Colony of *Georgia* lying about the same latitude with part of *China, Persia, Palestine,* and the *Madeiras,* it is highly probable that when hereafter it shall be well-peopled and rightly cultivated, ENGLAND may be supplied from thence with raw Silk, Wine, Oil, Dyes, Drugs, and many other materials for manufactures, which she is obliged to purchase from Southern countries. As towns are established and grow populous along the rivers Savannah and Alatamaha, they will make such a barrier as will render the southern frontier of the British Colonies on the Continent of America, safe from Indian and other enemies.

All human affairs are so subject to chance, that there in no answering for events ; yet from reason and the nature of things, it may be concluded, that the riches and also the number of the inhabitants in *Great Britain* will be increased, by importing at a cheap rate from this new Colony, the materials requisite for carrying on in Britain several manufactures. For our Manufacturers will be encouraged to marry and multiply, when they find themselves in circumstances to provide for their families, which must necessarily be the happy effect of the increase and cheapness of our materials of those Manufactures, which at present we purchase with our money from foreign countries, at dear rates ; and also many people will find employment here, on account such farther demands by the people of this Colony, for those manufactures which are made for the produce of our own country ; and, as has been justly observed, the people will always abound where there is full employment for them.

CHRISTIANITY will be extended by the execution of this design ; since, the good discipline established by the Society, will reform the manners of those miserable objects, who shall be by them subsisted ; and the example of a whole Colony, who shall behave in a just, moral, and religious manner, will contribute greatly towards the conversion of the Indians, and taking off the prejudices received from the profligate lives of such who have scarce any thing of Christianity but the name.

The Trustees in their general meetings, will consider of the most prudent methods for effectually establishing a regular Colony ; and that it may be done, is demonstrable. Under what difficulties, was *Virginia* planted?—the coast and climate then unknown ; the Indians numerous, and at enmity with the first Planters, who were forced to fetch all provisions from England ; yet it is grown a mighty Province, and the Revenue receives £100,000 for duties upon the goods that they send yearly home. Within this 50 years, *Pennsylvania* was as much a forest as *Georgia* in now ; and in these few years, by the wise œconomy of William Penn, and those who assisted him, it now gives food to 80,000 inhabitants, and can boast of as fine a City as most in Europe.

This new Colony is more likely to succeed than either of the former were, since Carolina abounds with provisions, the climate is known, and there are men to instruct in the seasons and nature of cultivating the soil. There are but few *Indian* families within 400 miles ; and those, in perfect amity with the English :—*Port Royal* (the station of his Majesty's ships) is within 30, and *Charlestown* (a great mart) is within 120 miles. If the Colony is attacked, it may be relieved by sea, from Port Royal, or the Bahamas ; and the Militia of South Carolina is ready to support it, by land.

For the continuing the relief which is now given, there will be lands reserved in the Colony ; and the benefit arising from them is to go to the carrying on of the trust. So that, at the same time, the money by being laid out preserves the lives of the poor, and makes a comfortable provision for those whose expenses are by it defrayed ; their labor in improving their own lands, will make the adjoining reserved lands valuable ; and the rents of those reserved lands will be a perpetual fund for the relieving more poor people. So that instead of laying out the money upon lands, with the income thereof to support the poor, this is laying out money upon the poor ; and by relieving those who are now unfortunate, raises a fund for the perpetual relief of those who shall be so hereafter.

There is an occasion now offered for every one, to help forward this design ; the smallest benefaction will be received, and applied with the utmost care :—every little will do something ; and a great number of small benefactions will amount to a sum capable of doing a great deal of good.

If any person, moved with the calamities of the unfortunate, shall be inclined to contribute towards their relief, they are desired to pay their benefactions into the Bank of England, on account of the Trustees for establishing the Colony of Georgia in America ; or else, to any of the Trustees, who are, &c.

## QUESTIONS TO CONSIDER

1. What reasons did the Trustees give for establishing a colony?
2. What did the Trustees imagine that Georgia society might look like? How would it prosper?

# 5.2 BENJAMIN FRANKLIN DESCRIBES GEORGE WHITEFIELD (1739)

George Whitefield (1714–1770) was one of the first celebrities to come to North America. In 1740, Whitefield began a major tour of American cities, preaching at each stop to huge crowds. An immensely charismatic preacher, Whitefield had such a booming voice that he often spoke to crowds of 20,000 to 30,000 people, and perhaps as many as 50,000 people, without a microphone. For well over a year, Whitefield traveled up and down the eastern seaboard and became a major part of the religious revival known as the Great Awakening. For the next two decades, Whitefield would continue returning to preach in America. In this document, you will read Benjamin Franklin's reaction to Whitefield's travels. Franklin, though a relative skeptic on religious manners, became enamored of Whitefield's ministry and developed a close friendship with the English preacher. In this reading, taken from Franklin's autobiography, you can get a sense of Whitefield's enormous popular appeal.

In 1739 arriv'd among us from England the Rev. Mr. Whitefield, who had made himself remarkable there as an itinerant Preacher. He was at first permitted to preach in some of our Churches; but the Clergy taking a Dislike to him, soon refus'd him their Pulpits and he was oblig'd to preach in the Fields. The Multitudes of all Sects and Denominations that attended his Sermons were enormous and it was [a] matter of Speculation to me who was one of the Number, to observe the extraordinary Influence of his Oratory on his Hearers, and how much they admir'd and respected him, notwithstanding his common Abuse of them, by assuring them they were naturally *half Beasts and half Devils.* It was wonderful to see the Change soon made in the Manners [behavior] of our Inhabitants; from being thoughtless or indifferent about Religion, it seem'd as if all the World were growing Religious; so that one could not walk thro' the Town in an Evening without Hearing Psalms sung in different Families of every Street.

And it being found inconvenient to assemble in the open Air, subject to its Inclemencies, the Building of a House to meet in was no sooner propos'd and Persons appointed to receive Contributions, but sufficient Sums were soon receiv'd to procure the Ground and erect the Building, which was 100 feet long and 70 broad, about the Size of Westminster Hall, and the Work was carried on with such Spirit as to be finished in a much shorter time than could have been expected. Both House and Ground were vested in Trustees, expressly for the Use of any Preacher of any religious Persuasion who might desire to say something to the People of Philadelphia, the Design [purpose] in building not being to accommodate any particular Sect, but the Inhabitants in general, so that even if the Mufti of Constantinople were to send a Missionary to preach Mahometanism [Islam] to us, he would find a Pulpit at his Service.

Mr. Whitefield, in leaving us, went preaching all the Way thro' the Colonies to Georgia. The Settlement

*Source:* "Benjamin Franklin on Rev. George Whitefield, 1739," *National Humanities Center,* http://nationalhumanitiescenter.org/pds/becomingamer/ideas/text2/franklinwhitefield.pdf (Accessed June 5, 2018)

of that Province had lately been begun, but instead of being made with hardy industrious Husbandmen [farmers] accustomed to Labor, the only People fit for such an Enterprise, it was with Families of broken Shopkeepers and other insolvent Debtors, many of indolent and idle habits, taken out of the Jails, who being set down in the Woods, unqualified for clearing Land, and unable to endure the Hardships of a new Settlement, perished in Numbers, leaving many helpless Children unprovided for. The Sight of their miserable Situation inspired the benevolent Heart of Mr. Whitefield with the Idea of building an Orphan House there, in which they might be supported and educated. Returning northward, he preach'd up this Charity, and made large Collections; — for his Eloquence had a wonderful Power over the Hearts and Purses of his Hearers, of which I myself was an Instance [example]. I did not disapprove of the Design [plan], but as Georgia was then destitute of Materials & Workmen, and it was propos'd to send them from Philadelphia at a great Expense, I thought it would have been better to have built the House here [Philadelphia] and brought the Children to it. This I advis'd, but he was resolute in his first Project, and rejected my Counsel, and I thereupon refus'd to contribute.

I happened soon after to attend one of his Sermons, in the Course of which I perceived he intended to finish with a Collection, and I silently resolved he should get nothing from me. I had in my Pocket a Handful of Copper Money, three or four silver Dollars, and five Pistoles [Spanish coins] in Gold. As he proceeded I began to soften, and concluded to give the Coppers. Another Stroke of his Oratory made me asham'd of that, and determin'd me to give the Silver; and he finish'd so admirably, that I emptied my Pocket wholly into the Collector's Dish, Gold and all. At this Sermon there was also one of our Club [Junto literary club], who being of my Sentiments respecting [opinions concerning] the Building in Georgia, and suspecting a Collection might be intended, had by Precaution emptied his Pockets before he came from home; towards the Conclusion of the Discourse [sermon], however, he felt a strong Desire to give, and apply'd to a Neighbor who stood near him to borrow some Money for the Purpose. The Application was unfortunately to perhaps the only Man in the Company [audience] who

had the firmness not to be affected by the Preacher. His Answer was, *At any other time, Friend Hopkinson, I would lend to thee freely; but not now; for thee seems to be out of thy right Senses.*

Some of Mr. Whitefield's Enemies affected to suppose that he would apply these Collections to his own private Emolument [profit]; but I, who was intimately acquainted with him (being employ'd in printing his Sermons and Journals, etc.) never had the least Suspicion of his Integrity, but am to this day decidedly of Opinion that he was in all his Conduct a perfectly *honest Man.* And methinks my Testimony in his Favor ought to have the more Weight, as we had no religious Connection. He us'd indeed sometimes to pray for my Conversion, but never had the Satisfaction of believing that his Prayers were heard. Ours was a mere civil Friendship, sincere on both Sides, and lasted to his Death.

The following Instance will show something of the Terms on which we stood. Upon one of his Arrivals from England at Boston, he wrote to me that he should come soon to Philadelphia, but knew not where he could lodge when there, as he understood his old kind Host Mr. Benezet was remov'd to Germantown. My Answer was: ["]You know my House, if you can make shift with its scanty Accommodations you will be most heartily welcome." He replied, that if I made that kind Offer for Christ's sake, I should not miss of a Reward.—And I return'd, *Don't let me be mistaken; it was not for Christ's sake, but for your sake.* One of our common Acquaintance jocosely remark'd, that knowing it to be the Custom of the Saints, when they receiv'd any favor, to shift the Burden of the Obligation from off their own Shoulders and place it in Heaven, I had contriv'd to fix it on Earth.

The last time I saw Mr. Whitefield was in London, when he consulted me about his Orphan House Concern, and his Purpose of appropriating it to the Establishment of a College.

He had a loud and clear Voice, and articulated his Words and Sentences so perfectly that he might be heard and understood at a great Distance, especially as his Auditors [audience], however numerous, observ'd the most exact Silence. He preach'd one Evening from the Top of the Court House Steps, which are in the middle of Market Street, and on the West Side of Second Street which crosses it at right angles. Both Streets were fill'd with his Hearers to a considerable Distance. Being among the hindmost in Market Street, I had the Curiosity to learn how far he could be heard, by retiring backwards down the Street towards the River; and I found his Voice distinct till I came near Front Street, when some Noise in that Street, obscur'd it. Imagining then a Semicircle, of which my Distance should be the Radius, and that it were fill'd with Auditors, to each of whom I allow'd two square feet, I computed that he might well be heard by more than Thirty Thousand. This reconcil'd me to the Newspaper Accounts of his having preach'd to 25,000 People in the Fields, and to the ancient Histories of Generals haranguing whole Armies, of which I had sometimes doubted.

By hearing him often, I came to distinguish easily between Sermons newly compos'd, and those which he had often preach'd in the Course of his Travels. His Delivery of the latter was so improv'd by frequent Repetitions that every Accent, every Emphasis, every Modulation of Voice, was so perfectly well turn'd and well plac'd, that without being interested in the Subject, one could not help being pleas'd with the Discourse, a Pleasure of much the same kind with that receiv'd from an excellent Piece of Music. This is an Advantage itinerant Preachers have over those who are stationary:

as the latter cannot well improve their Delivery of a Sermon by so many Rehearsals.

His Writing and Printing from time to time gave great Advantage to his Enemies. Unguarded Expressions and even erroneous Opinions delivered in Preaching might have been afterwards explain'd, or qualify'd by supposing others that might have accompanied them; or they might have been denied; but litera scripta manet.* Critics attack'd his Writings violently, and with so much Appearance of Reason as to diminish the Number of his Votaries [adherents] and prevent their Increase; So that I am of Opinion, if he had never written anything he would have left behind him a much more numerous and important Sect. And his Reputation might in that case have been still growing, even after his Death; as there being nothing of his Writing on which to found a Censure and give him a lower Character [reputation], his Proselytes would be left at Liberty to feign for him as great a Variety of Excellencies [good features], as their enthusiastic Admiration might wish him to have Engraving by Elisha Gallaudet, 1774 possessed.

## QUESTIONS TO CONSIDER

1. Why was Franklin so attracted to Whitefield? What made Whitefield stand out?
2. What does Franklin's account reveal about the Great Awakening?

---

* "Vox audita perit, littera scripta manet": Latin, "The spoken word perishes, but the written word remains."

# 5.3 JONATHAN EDWARDS, "SINNERS IN THE HANDS OF AN ANGRY GOD" (1741)

Jonathan Edwards (1703–1758) was another major contributor to the Great Awakening. An American preacher and theologian, Edwards matriculated at Yale College at age 12 and became enamored with both science and theology. In 1729, Edwards became sole minister of the church at Northampton, a wealthy Puritan enclave in Massachusetts. As the Great Awakening swept through the colonies during the 1730s, Edwards increasingly began to study conversion, and he met George Whitefield (see Reading 5.2) in 1739. In 1741, Edwards preached "Sinners in the Hands of an Angry God," one of the most famous sermons in American history and from which the following document is taken. In the sermon, Edward logically outlined how his listeners were doomed without God. Edwards' words, while less emotional than Whitefield's, symbolize the main themes of the Great Awakening writ large: the absolute, immediate need for conversion and the horrors that would await the unconverted, most notably. After 1741, Edwards continued to preach about conversion, and he became President of the College of New Jersey (what would become Princeton University) shortly before his death in 1758.

DEUTERONOMY *xxxii. 35.—Their foot shall slide in due time.*

In this verse is threatened the vengeance of God on the wicked unbelieving Israelites, that were God's visible people, and lived under means of grace; and that notwithstanding all God's wonderful works that he had wrought towards that people, yet remained, as is expressed verse 28, void of counsel, having no understanding in them; and that, under all the cultivations of heaven, brought forth bitter and poisonous fruit; as in the two verses next preceding the text.

The expression that I have chosen for my text, *their foot shall slide in due time*, seems to imply the following things relating to the punishment and destruction that these wicked Israelites were exposed to.

1. That they were *always* exposed to destruction; as one that stands or walks in slippery places is always exposed to fall. This is implied in the manner of their destruction's coming upon them, being represented by their foot's sliding. The same is expressed, Psalm lxxiii. 18: "Surely thou didst set them in slippery places; thou castedst them down into destruction."

2. It implies that they were always exposed to *sudden*, unexpected destruction; as he that walks in slippery places is every moment liable to fall, he can't foresee one moment whether he shall stand or fall the next; and when he does fall, he falls at once, without warning, which is also expressed in that Psalm lxxiii. 18, 19: "Surely thou didst set them in slippery places: thou castedst them down into destruction. How are they brought into desolation, as *in a moment!*"

3. Another thing implied is, that they are liable to fall of *themselves*, without being thrown down by the hand of another; as he that stands or walks on slippery ground needs nothing but his own weight to throw him down.

4. That the reason why they are not fallen already, and don't fall now, is only that God's appointed time is not come. For it is said that when that due time, or appointed time comes, *their foot shall slide*. Then they

*Source:* H. Norman Gardiner, ed., *Selected Sermons of Jonathan Edwards* (New York: The MacMillan Company, 1904). Retrieved from the Project Gutenberg website, https://www.gutenberg.org/files/34632/34632-h/34632-h.htm (Accessed June 5, 2018).

shall be left to fall, as they are inclined by their own weight. God won't hold them up in these slippery places any longer, but will let them go; and then, at that very instant, they shall fall to destruction; as he that stands in such slippery declining ground on the edge of a pit that he can't stand alone, when he is let go he immediately falls and is lost.

The observation from the words that I would now insist upon is this,

*There is nothing that keeps wicked men at any one moment out of hell, but the mere pleasure of God. . . .*

## APPLICATION

The use may be of *awakening* to unconverted persons in this congregation. This that you have heard is the case of every one of you that are out of Christ. That world of misery, that lake of burning brimstone, is extended abroad under you. *There* is the dreadful pit of the glowing flames of the wrath of God; there is hell's wide gaping mouth open; and you have nothing to stand upon, nor any thing to take hold of. There is nothing between you and hell but the air; 'tis only the power and mere pleasure of God that holds you up.

You probably are not sensible of this; you find you are kept out of hell, but don't see the hand of God in it, but look at other things, as the good state of your bodily constitution, your care of your own life, and the means you use for your own preservation. But indeed these things are nothing; if God should withdraw his hand, they would avail no more to keep you from falling than the thin air to hold up a person that is suspended in it.

Your wickedness makes you as it were heavy as lead, and to tend downwards with great weight and pressure towards hell; and if God should let you go, you would immediately sink and swiftly descend and plunge into the bottomless gulf, and your healthy constitution, and your own care and prudence, and best contrivance, and all your righteousness, would have no more influence to uphold you and keep you out of hell than a spider's web would have to stop a falling rock. Were it not that so is the sovereign pleasure of God, the earth would not bear you one moment; for you are a burden to it; the creation groans with you; the creature is made subject to the bondage of your corruption, not willingly; the sun don't willingly shine upon you to give you

light to serve sin and Satan; the earth don't willingly yield her increase to satisfy your lusts; nor is it willingly a stage for your wickedness to be acted upon; the air don't willingly serve you for breath to maintain the flame of life in your vitals, while you spend your life in the service of God's enemies. God's creatures are good, and were made for men to serve God with, and don't willingly subserve to any other purpose, and groan when they are abused to purposes so directly contrary to their nature and end. And the world would spew you out, were it not for the sovereign hand of him who hath subjected it in hope. There are the black clouds of God's wrath now hanging directly over your heads, full of the dreadful storm, and big with thunder; and were it not for the restraining hand of God, it would immediately burst forth upon you. The sovereign pleasure of God, for the present, stays his rough wind; otherwise it would come with fury, and your destruction would come like a whirlwind, and you would be like the chaff of the summer threshing floor.

The wrath of God is like great waters that are dammed for the present; they increase more and more, and rise higher and higher, till an outlet is given; and the longer the stream is stopped, the more rapid and mighty is its course, when once it is let loose. 'Tis true, that judgment against your evil work has not been executed hitherto; the floods of God's vengeance have been withheld; but your guilt in the mean time is constantly increasing, and you are every day treasuring up more wrath; the waters are continually rising, and waxing more and more mighty; and there is nothing but the mere pleasure of God that holds the waters back, that are unwilling to be stopped, and press hard to go forward. If God should only withdraw his hand from the floodgate, it would immediately fly open, and the fiery floods of the fierceness and wrath of God would rush forth with inconceivable fury, and would come upon you with omnipotent power; and if your strength were ten thousand times greater than it is, yea, ten thousand times greater than the strength of the stoutest, sturdiest devil in hell, it would be nothing to withstand or endure it.

The bow of God's wrath is bent, and the arrow made ready on the string, and justice bends the arrow at your heart, and strains the bow, and it is nothing but the mere pleasure of God, and that of an angry God, without any promise or obligation at all, that keeps the arrow one moment from being made drunk with your blood.

Thus are all you that never passed under a great change of heart by the mighty power of the Spirit of God upon your souls; all that were never born again, and made new creatures, and raised from being dead in sin to a state of new and before altogether unexperienced light and life, (however you may have reformed your life in many things, and may have had religious affections, and may keep up a form of religion in your families and closets, and in the house of God, and may be strict in it), you are thus in the hands of an angry God; 'tis nothing but his mere pleasure that keeps you from being this moment swallowed up in everlasting destruction.

However unconvinced you may now be of the truth of what you hear, by and by you will be fully convinced of it. Those that are gone from being in the like circumstances with you see that it was so with them; for destruction came suddenly upon most of them; when they expected nothing of it, and while they were saying, Peace and safety: now they see, that those things that they depended on for peace and safety were nothing but thin air and empty shadows.

The God that holds you over the pit of hell, much as one holds a spider or some loathsome insect over the fire, abhors you, and is dreadfully provoked; his wrath towards you burns like fire; he looks upon you as worthy of nothing else, but to be cast into the fire; he is of purer eyes than to bear to have you in his sight; you are ten thousand times so abominable in his eyes, as the most hateful and venomous serpent is in ours. You have offended him infinitely more than ever a stubborn rebel did his prince: and yet it is nothing but his hand that holds you from falling into the fire every moment. 'Tis ascribed to nothing else, that you did not go to hell the last night; that you was suffered to awake again in this world after you closed your eyes to sleep; and there is no other reason to be given why you have not dropped into hell since you arose in the morning, but that God's hand has held you up. There is no other reason to be given why you han't gone to hell since you have sat here in the house of God, provoking his pure eyes by your sinful wicked manner of attending his solemn worship. Yea, there is nothing else that is to be given as a reason why you don't this very moment drop down into hell.

O sinner! consider the fearful danger you are in. 'Tis a great furnace of wrath, a wide and bottomless pit, full of the fire of wrath, that you are held over in the hand of that God whose wrath is provoked and incensed as much against you as against many of the damned in hell. You hang by a slender thread, with the flames of divine wrath flashing about it, and ready every moment to singe it and burn it asunder; and you have no interest in any Mediator, and nothing to lay hold of to save yourself, nothing to keep off the flames of wrath, nothing of your own, nothing that you ever have done, nothing that you can do, to induce God to spare you one moment. . . .

How dreadful is the state of those that are daily and hourly in danger of this great wrath and infinite misery! But this is the dismal case of every soul in this congregation that has not been born again, however moral and strict, sober and religious, they may otherwise be. Oh, that you would consider it, whether you be young or old! There is reason to think that there are many in this congregation now hearing this discourse, that will actually be the subjects of this very misery to all eternity. We know not who they are, or in what seats they sit, or what thoughts they now have. It may be they are now at ease, and hear all these things without much disturbance, and are now flattering themselves that they are not the persons, promising themselves that they shall escape. If we knew that there was one person, and but one, in the whole congregation, that was to be the subject of this misery, what an awful thing it would be to think of! If we knew who it was, what an awful sight would it be to see such a person! How might all the rest of the congregation lift up a lamentable and bitter cry over him! But alas! instead of one, how many is it likely will remember this discourse in hell! And it would be a wonder, if some that are now present should not be in hell in a very short time, before this year is out. And it would be no wonder if some persons that now sit here in some seats of this meeting-house in health, and quiet and secure, should be there before to-morrow morning. Those of you that finally continue in a natural condition, that shall keep out of hell longest, will be there in a little time! Your damnation don't slumber; it will come swiftly and, in all probability, very suddenly upon many of you. You have reason to wonder that you are not already in hell. 'Tis doubtless the case of some that heretofore you have seen and known, that never deserved hell more than you and that heretofore appeared as likely to have been now alive as you.

Their case is past all hope; they are crying in extreme misery and perfect despair. But here you are in the land of the living and in the house of God, and have an opportunity to obtain salvation. What would not those poor, damned, hopeless souls give for one day's such opportunity as you now enjoy!

And now you have an extraordinary opportunity, a day wherein Christ has flung the door of mercy wide open, and stands in the door calling and crying with a loud voice to poor sinners; a day wherein many are flocking to him and pressing into the Kingdom of God. Many are daily coming from the east, west, north and south; many that were very likely in the same miserable condition that you are in are in now a happy state, with their hearts filled with love to him that has loved them and washed them from their sins in his own blood, and rejoicing in hope of the glory of God. How awful is it to be left behind at such a day! To see so many others feasting, while you are pining and perishing! To see so many rejoicing and singing for joy of heart, while you have cause to mourn for sorrow of heart and howl for vexation of spirit! How can you rest for one moment in such a condition? Are not your souls as precious as the souls of the people at Suffield, where they are flocking from day to day to Christ?

Are there not many here that have lived long in the world that are not to this day born again, and so are aliens from the commonwealth of Israel and have done nothing ever since they have lived but treasure up wrath against the day of wrath? Oh, sirs, your case in an especial manner is extremely dangerous; your guilt and hardness of heart is extremely great. Don't you see how generally persons of your years are passed over and left in the present remarkable and wonderful dispensation of God's mercy? You had need to consider yourselves and wake thoroughly out of sleep; you cannot bear the fierceness and the wrath of the infinite God.

And you that are young men and young women, will you neglect this precious season that you now enjoy, when so many others of your age are renouncing all youthful vanities and flocking to Christ? You especially have now an extraordinary opportunity; but if you neglect it, it will soon be with you as it is with those persons that spent away all the precious days of youth in sin and are now come to such a dreadful pass in blindness and hardness.

And you children that are unconverted, don't you know that you are going down to hell to bear the dreadful wrath of that God that is now angry with you every day and every night? Will you be content to be the children of the devil, when so many other children in the land are converted and are become the holy and happy children of the King of kings?

And let every one that is yet out of Christ and hanging over the pit of hell, whether they be old men and women or middle-aged or young people or little children, now hearken to the loud calls of God's word and providence. This acceptable year of the Lord that is a day of such great favor to some will doubtless be a day of as remarkable vengeance to others. Men's hearts harden and their guilt increases apace at such a day as this, if they neglect their souls. And never was there so great danger of such persons being given up to hardness of heart and blindness of mind. God seems now to be hastily gathering in his elect in all parts of the land; and probably the bigger part of adult persons that ever shall be saved will be brought in now in a little time, and that it will be as it was on that great outpouring of the Spirit upon the Jews in the Apostles' days, the election will obtain and the rest will be blinded. If this should be the case with you, you will eternally curse this day, and will curse the day that ever you was born to see such a season of the pouring out of God's Spirit, and will wish that you had died and gone to hell before you had seen it. Now undoubtedly it is as it was in the days of John the Baptist, the axe is in an extraordinary manner laid at the root of the trees, that every tree that bringeth not forth good fruit may be hewn down and cast into the fire.

Therefore let every one that is out of Christ now awake and fly from the wrath to come. The wrath of Almighty God is now undoubtedly hanging over great part of this congregation. Let every one fly out of Sodom. *"Haste and escape for your lives, look not behind you, escape to the mountain, lest ye be consumed."*

### QUESTIONS TO CONSIDER

1. How does Edwards try to convince people to convert?

2. In what ways does God's all-encompassing power factor into Edwards' argument?

# 5.4 ADAM SMITH, EXCERPT FROM *THE WEALTH OF NATIONS* (1776)

The Scottish economist Adam Smith (1723–1790) in many ways founded the ideology of free market capitalism. His 1776 book *The Wealth of Nations,* from which the following document is excerpted, set out to describe how nations build wealth. *The Wealth of Nations* propagated the idea of an "invisible hand" that propels individual behavior in the marketplace. Smith also predicted, as you will read, the division of labor that would become increasingly important to the Industrial Revolution in the nineteenth century. While Smith's ideas were controversial in his own time, they are crucial to the modern field of economics, and *The Wealth of Nations* remains an essential text.

THE greatest improvement in the productive powers of labor, and the greater part of the skill, dexterity, and judgment with which it is anywhere directed, or applied, seem to have been the effects of the division of labor.

The effects of the division of labor, in the general business of society, will be more easily understood by considering in what manner it operates in some particular manufactures. It is commonly supposed to be carried furthest in some very trifling ones; not perhaps that it really is carried further in them than in others of more importance: but in those trifling manufactures which are destined to supply the small wants of but a small number of people, the whole number of workmen must necessarily be small; and those employed in every different branch of the work can often be collected into the same workhouse, and placed at once under the view of the spectator. In those great manufactures, on the contrary, which are destined to supply the great wants of the great body of the people, every different branch of the work employs so great a number of workmen, that it is impossible to collect them all into the same workhouse. We can seldom see more, at one time, than those employed in one single branch. Though in such manufactures, therefore, the work may really be divided into a much greater number of parts, than in those of a more trifling nature, the division is not near so obvious, and has accordingly been much less observed.

To take an example, therefore, from a very trifling manufacture; but one in which the division of labor has been very often taken notice of, the trade of the pin-maker; a workman not educated to this business (which the division of labor has rendered a district trade), nor acquainted with the use of the machinery employed in it (to the invention of which the same division of labor has probably given occasion), could scarce, perhaps, with his utmost industry, make one pin in a day, and certainly could not make twenty. But in the way in which this business is now carried on, not only the whole work is a peculiar trade, but it is divided into a number of branches, of which the greater part are likewise peculiar trades. One man draws out the wire, another straights its, a third cuts its, a fourth points its, a fifth grinds it at the top for receiving the head; to make the head requires two or three distinct operations; to put in on, is a peculiar business, to whiten the pins is another; it is even a trade by itself of put them into the paper; and the important business of making a pin is, in this manner, divided into about

*Source:* Adam Smith, *The Wealth of Nations* (New York: P.F. Collier & Son, 1911), 43–58. Retrieved from the Internet Archive website, https://ia802606.us.archive.org/25/items/wealthofnations00smituoft/wealthofnations00smituoft.pdf (Accessed June 5, 2018).

eighteen district operations, which, in some manu-factories, are all performed by distinct hands, though in others the same man will sometimes perform two or three of them. I have seen a small manufactory of this kind where ten men only were employed, and where some of them consequently performed two or three distinct operations. But though they were very poor, and therefore but indifferently accommodated with the necessary machinery, they could, when they exerted themselves, make among them about twelve pounds of pins in a day. There are in a pound upward of four thousand pins in a day. Each person, there-fore, making a tenth part of forty-eight thousand pins, might be considered as making four thousand eight hundred pins in a day. But if they had all wrought sep-arately and independently and without any of them having been educated to this peculiar business, they certainly could not each of them have made twenty, perhaps not one pin in a day; that is, certainly not the two hundred and fortieth, perhaps not the four thou-sand eight hundredth part of what they are at present capable of performing, in consequence of a proper di-vision and combination of their different operations.

In every other art and manufacture, the effects of the division of labor are similar to what they are in this very trifling one; though in many of them the labor can neither be so much subdivided, nor reduced to so great a simplicity of operation. The division of labor, however, so far as it can be introduced, occasions, in every art, a proportionable increase of the productive power of labor. . . .

This great increase in the quantity of work, which, in consequence of the division of labor, the same number of people are capable of performing, is owing to three different circumstances; first, to the increase of dexterity in every particular workman; secondly, to the saving of the time which is commonly lost in passing from one species of work to another; and lastly, to the invention of a great number of machines which facili-tate and abridge labor, and enable one man to do the work of many.

First, the improvement of the dexterity of the work-man necessarily increases the quantity of the work he can perform; and the division of labor, by reducing every man's business to some one simple operation, and by making this operation the sole employment of his life, necessarily increases very much the dexterity of the workman. A common smith, who, though ac-customed to handle the hammer, has never been used to make nails, if upon some particular occasion he is obliged to attempt it, will scarce, I am assured, be able to make above two or three hundred nails in a day, and those, too, very bad ones. A smith who has been accustomed make nails, but whose sole or principal business has not been that of a nailer, can seldom with his utmost diligence make more than eight hundred or a thousand nails in a day. I have seen several boys under twenty years of age who had never exercised any other trade but that of making nails, and who, when they exerted themselves, could make each of them upward of two thousand three hundred nails in a day. The making of a nail, however, is by no means one of the simplest operations. The same person blows the bellows, stirs or mends the fire as there is occasion, heats the iron, and forges every part of the nail: in forg-ing the head, too, he is obliged to change his tools. The different operations into which the making of a pin, or a metal button, is subdivided, are all of them much more simple, and the dexterity of the person whose whole life it has been the sole business to per-form them, is usually much greater. The rapidity with which some of the operations of those manufactures are performed, exceed what the human hand could, by those who had never seen them, be supposed capable of acquiring.

Secondly, the advantage which is gained by saving the time commonly lost in passing from one sort of work to another, is much greater than we should at first view be apt to imagine it. It is impos-sible to pass very quickly from one kind of work to another, that is carried on in a different place, and with quite different tools. A country weaver, who cul-tivates a small farm, must lose a good deal of time in passing from his loom to the field, and from the field to his loom. When the two trades can be car-ried on in the same workhouse, the loss of time is no doubt much less. It is even in this case, however, very considerable. A man commonly saunters a little in turning his hand from one sort of employment to another. When he first begins the new work he is seldom very keen and hearty; his mind, as they say, does go to it, and for some time he rather trifles than applies to good purpose. The habit of sauntering and of indolent careless application, which is naturally, or rather necessarily, acquired by every country workman who is obliged to change his work and his tools every half house and to apply his hand in twenty different ways almost every day of his life, renders him almost always slothful and lazy, and incapable of any vigorous application even on the most pressing occasion. Independent, therefore, of his deficiency in point of dexterity, this cause alone must always reduce considerably the quantity of work which he is capable of performing.

Thirdly, and lastly, everybody must be sensible how much labor is facilitated and abridged by the application of proper machinery. It is unnecessary to give any example. I shall only observe, therefore, that the invention of all those machines by which labor is so much facilitated and abridged, seems to have been originally owing to the division of labor. Men are much more likely to discover easier and readier methods of attaining any object, when the whole attention of their minds is directed toward that single object, than when it is dissipated among a great variety of things. But in consequence of the division of labor, the whole of every man's attention comes naturally to be directed toward some one very simple object. It is naturally to be expected, therefore, that some one or other of those who are employed in each particular branch of labor should soon find out easier and readier methods of performing their own particular work, wherever the nature of it admits of such improvement. A great part of the machines made use of in those manufactures in which labor is most subdivided, were originally the inventions of common workmen, who, being each of them employed in some very simple operation, naturally turned their thoughts toward finding out easier and readier methods of performing it. . . .

It is the great multiplication of the productions of all the different arts, in consequence of the division of labor, which occasions, in a well-governed society, that universal opulence which extends itself to the lowest ranks of the people. Every workman has a great quantity of his own work to dispose of beyond what he himself has occasion for; and every other workman being exactly in the same situation, he is enabled to exchange a great quantity of his own goods for a great quantity, or, what comes to the same thing, for the price of a great quantity of theirs. He supplies them abundantly with what they have occasion for, and they accommodate him as amply with what he has occasion for, and a general plenty diffuses itself through all the different ranks of the society.

Observe the accommodation of the most common artificer or day-laborer in a civilized and thriving country, and you will perceive that the number of people of whose industry a part, though but a small part, has been employed in procuring him this accommodation, exceeds all computation. The woolen coat, for example, which covers the day-laborer, as coarse and rough as it may appear, is the produce of the joint labor of a great multitude of workmen. The shepherd, the sorter of the wool, the wool-comber or carder, the dyer, the scribbler, the spinner, the weaver, the fuller, the dresser, with many others, must all join their different arts in order to complete even this homely production. How many merchants and carriers, besides, must have been employed in transporting the materials from some of those workmen to others who often live in a very distant part of the country! How much commerce and navigation in particular, how many shipbuilders, sailors, sailmakers, ropemakers, must have been employed in order to bring together the different drugs made use of by the dyer, which often come from the remotest corners of the world! What a variety of labor, too, is necessary in order to produce the tools of the meanest of those workmen! To say nothing of such complicated machines as the ship of the sailor, the mill of the fuller, or even the loom of the weaver, let us consider only what a variety of labor is requisite in order to form that very simple machine, the shears with which the shepherd clips the wool. The miner, the builder of the furnace for smelting the ore, the feller of the timber, the burner of the charcoal to be made use of in the smelting-house, the brickmaker, the bricklayer, the workmen who attend the furnace, the millwright, the forger, the smith, must all of them join their different arts in order or produce them. . . .

1. What is Smith's view of labor?
2. In Smith's mind, how does the division of labor spark economic growth?

# 5.5 THOMAS JEFFERSON, EXCERPT FROM *NOTES ON THE STATE OF VIRGINIA* (1783)

Thomas Jefferson was a true renaissance man. In addition to writing the Declaration of Independence, serving as the first Secretary of State, and being elected the third President of the United States, Jefferson tutored Meriwether Lewis on different scientific pursuits before the Lewis and Clark expedition, wrote widely on an array of topics, and even invented the swivel chair. In the centuries since his death, he has gained acclaim for his views on personal liberty and democracy. Jefferson's views on slavery, however, complicate such acclaim; Jefferson owned multiple plantations and over 600 slaves during his life. In 1781, he wrote *Notes on the State of Virginia*, a series of responses to questions sent to him by the Secretary of the French Delegation in Philadelphia, from which the following document is excerpted. The work as a whole contains observations about Virginia's resources, laws, and economy. In the two sections you will read, Jefferson ruminates on slavery and tries to square his personal views on it with his derogatory views of African Americans and their role in American society.

## QUERY XIV

THE ADMINISTRATION OF JUSTICE AND DESCRIPTION OF THE LAWS?

. . . Many of the laws which were in force during the monarchy being relative merely to that form of government, or inculcating principles inconsistent with Republicanism, the first assembly which met after the establishment of the Commonwealth, appointed a committee to revise the whole Code, to reduce it into proper form and volume, and report it to the assembly. This work has been executed by three gentlemen, and reported ; but probably will not be taken up till a restoration of peace shall leave to the Legislature leisure to go through such a work.

The plan of the revisal was this : The common law of England, by which is meant that part of the English law which was anterior to the date of the oldest statutes extant, is made the basis of the work. It was thought dangerous to attempt to reduce it to a text ; it was therefore left to be collected from the usual monuments of it. Necessary alternations in that, and so much of the whole body of the British statutes, and acts of assembly, as were thought proper to be retained, were digested into 126 new acts, in which simplicity of style was aimed at, as far as was safe. The following are the most remarkable alternations proposed :

To change the rules of descent, so as that the lands of any person dying intestate shall be divisible equally

*Source:* Thomas Jefferson, *Notes on the State of Virginia* (Richmond, VA: J.W. Randolph, 1853), 147–155, 173–175. Retrieved from the Internet Archive website, https://archive.org/details/notesonstateofvi01jeff (Accessed June 5, 2018).

among all his children, or other representatives, in equal degree :

To make slaves distributable among the next of kin, as other moveables :

To have all public expenses, whether of the general treasury, or of a parish or county, (as for the maintenance of the poor, building bridges, court houses, &c.,) supplied by assessments on the citizens, in proportion to their property :

To hire undertakers for keeping the public roads in repair, and indemnify individuals through whose lands new roads shall be opened :

To define with precision the rules whereby aliens should become citizens, and citizens make themselves aliens :

To establish religious freedom on the broadest bottom :

To emancipate all slaves born after passing the act. The bill reported by the revisors does not itself contain this proposition ; but an amendment containing it was prepared, to be offered to the Legislature whenever the bill should be taken up, and further directing that they should continue with their parents to a certain age, then be brought up at the public expense, to tillage, arts or sciences, according to their geniuses, till the females should be eighteen, and the males twenty-one years of age, when they should be colonized to such place as the circumstances of the time should render most proper, sending them out with arms, implements of household, and of the handicraft, seeds, pairs, of the useful domestic animals, &c., to declare them a free and independent people, and extend to them our alliance and protection, till they shall have acquired strength ; and to send vessels as the same time to other parts of the world for an equal number of white inhabitants; to induce whom to migrate hither, proper encouragements were to be proposed. It will probably be asked, Why not retain and incorporate the blacks into the State, and thus save the expense of supplying, by importation of white settlers, the vacancies they will leave? Deep-rooted prejudices entertained by the whites ; ten thousand recollections by the blacks of the injuries they have sustained ; new provocations ; the real distinctions which Nature has made ; and many other circumstances, will divide us into parties, and produce convulsions, which will probably never end but in the extermination of the one or the other race. To these objections, which are political, may be added others, which are physical and moral. The first difference which strikes us is that of color. Whether the black of the negro rides in the reticular membrane between the skin and scarf skin, or in the scarf skin itself ; whether it proceeds from the color of the blood, the color of the bile, or from that of some other secretion, the difference is fixed in Nature, and is as real as if its seat and cause were better known to us. And is this difference of no importance ? Is it not the foundation of a greater or less share of beauty in the two races ? Are not the fine mixtures of red and white, the expressions of every passion by greater or less suffusions of color in the one, preferable to that eternal monotony which reigns in the countenances, that immovable veil of black which covers all the emotions of the race ? Add to these flowing hair, a more elegant symmetry of form, their own judgment in favor of the whites, declared by their preference of them, as uniformly as is the preference of the Oranootan for the black women . . . Comparing them by their faculties of memory, reason, and imagination, it appears to me that in memory they are equal to the whites ; in reason much inferior, as I think one could scarcely be found capable of tracing and comprehending the investigations of Euclid ; and that in imagination they are dull, tasteless and anomalous. It would be unfair to follow them to Africa for this investigation. We will consider them here on the same stage with the whites, and where the facts are not apocryphal on which a judgment is to be formed. It will be right to make great allowances for the difference of condition, of education, of conversation, of the sphere in which they move. Many millions of them have been brought to, and born in America. Most of them, indeed, have been confined to tillage, to their own homes, and their own society ; yet many have been so situated, that they might have availed themselves of the conversation of their masters ; many have been brought up to the handicraft arts, and from that circumstance have always been associated with the whites. Some have been liberally educated, and all have lived in countries where the arts and sciences are cultivated to a considerable degree, and have had before their eyes samples of the best works from abroad. The Indians, with no advantages of this kind, will often carve figures on their pipes not destitute of design and merit. They will crayon out an animal, a plant, or a country, so as to prove the existence of a germ in their minds which only wants cultivation. They astonish you with strokes of the most sublime oratory ; such as prove their reason and sentiment strong, their imagination glowing and elevated. But never yet could I find that a black had uttered a thought above the level of pain narration ; never seen an elementary trait of painting or sculpture. In music they are more generally gifted than the whites with accurate ears for tune and time, and they have been found capable of imagining a small catch.* Whether they will be equal to the composition of a more extensive run of melody, or of complicated harmony, is yet to be proved. . . .

. . . This unfortunate difference of color, and perhaps of faculty, is a powerful obstacle to the emancipation of these people. Many of their advocates, while they wish to vindicate the liberty of human nature, are anxious also to preserve its dignity and beauty. Some of these, embarrassed by the question, "What further is to be done with them ?" join themselves in opposition with those who are actuated by sordid avarice only. Among the Romans emancipation required but one effort. The slave, when made free, might mix with, without staining the blood of his master. But with us a second is necessary, unknown to history. When freed, he is to be removed beyond the reach of mixture.

## QUERY XVII

THE PARTICULAR CUSTOMS AND MANNERS THAT MAY HAPPEN TO BE RECEIVED IN THAT STATE?

It is difficult to determine on the standard by which the manners of a nation may be tried, whether *catholic*, or *particular*. It is more difficult for a native to bring to that standard the manners of his own nation, familiarized to him by habit. There must, doubtless, be an unhappy influence on the manners of our people, produced by the existence of slavery among us. The whole commerce between master and slave is a perpetual exercise of the most boisterous passions, the most unremitting despotism on the one part, and degrading submissions on the other. Our children see this, and

learn to imitate it ; for man is an imitative animal. This quality is the germ of all education in him. From his cradle to his grave he is learning to do what he sees others do. If a parent could find no motive either in his philanthropy or his self-love for restraining the intemperance of passion towards his slave, it should always be a sufficient one that his child is present. But generally it is not sufficient. The parent storms, the child looks on, catches the lineaments of wrath, puts on the same airs in the circle of smaller slaves, gives a loose to his worst of passions, and thus nursed, educated, and daily exercised in tyranny, cannot but be stamped by it with odious peculiarities. The man must be a prodigy who can retain his manners and morals undepraved by such circumstances. And what execration should the statesman be loaded, who permitting one-half the citizens thus to trample on the right of the other, transforms those into despots, and these into enemies, destroys the morals of the one part, and the amor patriæ of the other. For if a slave can have a country in this world, it must be any other in preference to that in which he is born to live and labor for another ; in which he must lock up the faculties of his nature, contribute as far as depends on his individual endeavors to the evanishment of the human race, or entail his own miserable condition on the endless generations proceeding from him. With the morals of the people their industry also is destroyed. For in a warm climate no man will labor for himself who can make another labor for him. This is so true, that of the proprietors of slaves a very small proportion indeed are ever seen to labor. And can the liberties of a nation be thought secure when we have removed their only firm basis, a conviction in the minds of the people that these liberties are of the gift of God ? That they are not to be violated but with his wrath ? Indeed I tremble for my country when I reflect that God is just ; that his justice cannot sleep forever ; that considering numbers, nature and natural means only, a revolution of the wheel of fortune, an exchange of situation is among possible events ; that it may become probable by supernatural interference. The Almighty has no attribute which can take side with us in such a contest. But it is impossible

---

\* The instrument proper to them is the banjo, which they brought hither from Africa, and which is the original of the guitar, its chords being precisely the four lower chords of the guitar.

to be temperate, and to pursue this subject through the various considerations of policy, of morals, of history, natural and civil. We must be contented to hope they will force their way into every one's mind. I think a change already perceptible, since the origin of the present revolution. The spirit of the master is abating, that of the slave rising from the dust, his condition mollifying, the way I hope preparing, under the auspices of heaven, for a total emancipation, and that this is

disposed, in the order of events, to be with the consent of the masters, rather than by their extirpation.

### QUESTIONS TO CONSIDER

1. What did Jefferson propose to do about African American slavery?
2. On what basis did he defend this proposed strategy?

# 5.6 MERCY OTIS WARREN'S REVOLUTIONARY ERA LETTERS (1769–1772)

Mercy Otis Warren's letters provide crucial insight into the years preceding the American Revolution. Warren (1728–1814) was one of thirteen children born to James Otis, Sr., a Massachusetts farmer and attorney who opposed British rule, and Mary Allyne Otis. One of Warren's brothers, James Otis, Jr., coined the phrase "Taxation without representation is tyranny" and played a major role in the rhetoric surrounding the Revolution. Her husband, James Warren, was active in the revolutionary movement, and Mercy joined him in this endeavor. She corresponded via letter with large swaths of the elite class who supported the Revolution—Abigail and John Adams, Patrick Henry, and Thomas Jefferson among them. The three letters that follow show three different sides of Warren's life. The first letter, to her brother James, came after he was violently beaten by a British customs official. The second letter, to her husband James, informed him about daily events and her life while he was traveling. The last letter, to her son James, tried to keep him on the correct path in life. Collectively, the letters well illustrate how the elite class operated in early Revolutionary America.

## 1: TO JAMES OTIS, JR

Plymouth [c. September 10, 1769]

My dear Brother

You know not what I have suffered for you within the last twenty four hours—I saw you fallen—slain by the hands of merciless men.—I saw your wife a widow, your children orphans, your friends weeping round you, and your country in tears for the man who had sacrificed interest, health, and peace, for the public

weal,—but my distress was this evening alleviated by hearing that your life is now not despaired of.

I wish to know every circumstance of the guilty affair;—is it possible that we have men among us under the guise of officers of the Crown, who have become open assassins?—Have they with a band of ruffians at the heels, attacked a gentleman alone and unarmed with a design to take away his life? Thus it is reported:—and are these the *conservators* of peace?

*Source:* Jeffrey H. Richards and Sharon M. Harris, eds., *Mercy Otis Warren: Selected Letters* (Athens: The University of Georgia Press, 2009), 5–8.

We knew before that the business on which this armament was sent hither was detestable:—that it was abhorred by every one, who had any remains of integrity, humanity, or any ideas of freedom. Yet though we knew their errand was to uphold villany, and protect villains—I believe few expected they would carry their audacity so far as to stand by and [??] the miscreant, to spill the blood of citizens, who criminate the designs, and their measures.

Thanks to the unering hand which directs and overrules every event, the blow was not fatal, or to use one of their own expressions, the vilest of them can *go no further than the length of their tether*. When public affairs are in such a situation, how happy is it for the man of public avocations to have the answer of a good conscience?—This I trust you have—and though your conflicts are many[?] and severe yet I doubt not but in your calm moments you can retire into your own breast, and there find that principle of uprightness and benevolence, which ought to actuate, and which only can support you, and bear you above all opposition. You have long and painfully struggled to promote the interest of your country, thousands are thanking you therefor, and daily praying for the preservation of your life. To theirs let me add my most earnest solicitations that when you recover, you will never either give or receive a challenge from any man on earth, let his rank and character be what it may. This I urge for the sake of your lovely babes, for the sake of your worthy and venerable Father, for the sake of your many tender friends, and for that of this people who stand in need of your assistance.

Whatever may have been said of the laws of honour, false honour indeed—I am certain that the law of reason and the laws of God as well as man strictly forbid the practice of dueling. If assaulted it is your duty: and if on even ground you are able to defend yourself. I am not about to inform you, who have so much knowledge and understanding, what is legal, just, or rational, in any action;—but with a sisterly affection I must entreat that you would never let either public oppression or private wrongs, the injustice of a few in power, or the folly of the many that are out, ruffle and discompose a man, whose superior abilities are such that with a calm and steady mind, he is capable of promoting the greatest good to his fellow creatures—and in consequence thereof to secure to himself, eternal felicity.

You will excuse the freedom of my pen, when you consider it held by one who has your welfare more at heart, after a very few exceptions, than that of any other person in the world. I hope soon to hear that you are restored to perfect health and from your usual affection and attention. I expect this intelligence from your own hand as soon as you are able to write.

I now only add my fervent prayers for the most permanent happiness to you and yours. As ever I subscribe your most affectionate

*Sister, Mercy Warren*

## 2: TO JAMES WARREN

Plimouth April 22, 1772

The fond and affectionate friend of my heart tho absent but a day will doubtless think me inexcusable if I omit to let him know that I am as well as when he left me. All the pain I have suffer'd since that time is on his account. The impetuous Hurricane of yesterday shook my trembling heart when I considered one exposed to its pearcing Blasts whose health is precarious and yet all my earthly Happiness depending on the continuance of his life but I will hope you escaped every ill effect from this circumstance and that you will soon return Both well & happy.

My Family is greatly Lesson'd for besides the alteration of Teusday I've consented to let Henry go to Barnstable this morning with mr N. Winslow but do not [be] concerned about me. I find some of the ancients most exclent company, whilst others are holding up to view the wickedness of mankind in its Blackest array at the same time teaching the Vanity of all Human greatness.

And now I have got to the bottom of my page I shall conclude or follow my own inclination and fill another. If you will promise not to Laugh at the scribler (as you sometimes call her) I will go on to inform you (as the only peace of intelligence I can think of) that I had the agreeable company of miss P. Winslow last Night who proposes to continue this kindness through the week and Let me just observe that I think this is not a singular instance of a whig and a Tory Lodging in the same bed and believe there are very few instances where there is so great regard for Each other as between the parties above mention'd.

Gardning goes on finely to day under the direction and assistance of your industrious son who refused to go to Barnstable least he shou'd by it Loose the opportunity of going when his Aunt Otis comes. You know his great affection for that Lady to whom my best regards when you see her.

Thursday Evening. I suppose you are by this time much Engaged in politicks. Wishing you may help to stear the ship right I take Leave for the present only repeating that I am with the same respect & reason as usual your affectionate Wife

*Mercy Warren*

## 3. TO JAMES WARREN, JR

[Plymouth, September? 1772]

To a youth just entered Colledge

If my dear son was sensible her affection runs so great she never could forget him while she remembered any thing, he might be apt to suspect it from the late unusual silence of his mother; but a variety of cares united with an indifferent state of health since you last left me has prevented by renewed precepts to endeavor to fortify the mind of a youth who I flatter myself is well disposed against the snares of vice and the contagion of bad example, which like an army of scorpions lie in wait to destroy. I do not much fear that I shall ever be subjected to much disappointment or pain for any deviation in a son like yourself. Yet when I consider how easily the generality of youth are misled, either by novel opinions or unprincipled companions and how easily they often glide into the path of folly and how imperceptibly led into the mazes of error; I tremble for my children. Happy beyond expression will you be my son, if amidst the laudable pursuits of youth and its innocent amusement you ever keep that important period in view which must wind up this fleeting existence, and land as on the boundless shore, when the profligate can no longer sooth himself in the silken dream of pleasure, or the infidel entertain any farther doubts of the immortality of his deathless soul. May the Great Gaurdian of Virtue, the source, the fountain of everlasting truth watch over and ever preserve you from the baleful walks of vice, and the devious and not less baneful track of the bewildered sceptic. What vigilance is necessary when the solicitations of thoughtless companions on the one side, and the clamour of youthful passions on the other, plead for deviations and ever stand ready to excuse the highest instances of indulgence to depraved appetite. If you escape uncontaminated it must be in some measure by learning early to discriminate between the unoffending mirth of the generous and open hearted and the designed flighty vagaries of the virulent and narrow minded man.

My regards to your fellow student; tell him I feel interested in his welfare, not only as your companion, but from some partiality towards him. May you assist each other in your resolutions to repel every temptation to folly and while you are mutually aiding each other in your researches into the several branches of useful knowledge may you form a friendship founded on the most durable basis, a similitude of sentiment in your invariable adherence to every moral and religious obligation.

You will take the earliest opportunity to write to your affectionate mother.

*[no signature]*

## QUESTIONS TO CONSIDER

1. In the first letter, how does Warren express a pro-revolutionary sentiment?

2. What can you glean about Warren's life in the second and third letters?

# CHAPTER 6

# CONFLICT IN THE EMPIRE, 1713–1774

## 6.1 EXCERPT FROM THE MEMOIR OF LIEUTENANT JEAN-FRANCOIS-BENJAMIN DUMONT DE MONTIGNY (1747)

Jean-Francois-Benjamin Dumont de Montigny arrived in Louisiana in 1719. Over the next eighteen years, he carved out a crucial and varied role for himself in Louisiana society. He fought as a soldier for the royally chartered Mississippi Company (a trading company), owned a small plantation, and fought in the First Chickasaw War to prevent the Native American tribe from allying and trading with the British. Even with the help of the Choctaw tribe, the French never succeeded in subduing the Chickasaw, who would eventually prevail. This excerpt is taken from Dumont's personal memoirs and recounts Dumont's farming and his efforts fighting in the First Chickasaw War. He returned to France in 1738 and fought against the British to fend off an attack on Brittany, in northern France, in 1746. In many ways, then, he was intricately involved with European colonial efforts and the international battle to secure colonial properties.

As for me, I was with my companion at my second farm, where I made a rather good harvest of tobacco, cotton, and produce, since my wife had retrieved her male and female slaves from the hands of the Choctaws. When they refused to restore the slaves to the Company of the Indies unless paid for them in trade goods, the Company did so, and made payment to the owners of the slaves. Although she had kept the negroes working for her at her farm in order to make a double profit, it took a good deal of trouble to get them back to our property.[1]

Toward the month of September, 1732, I wanted to go to La Balize to sell my tobacco, which I had rolled into bundles called carrots, in order to obtain

*Source:* From THE MEMOIR OF LIEUTENANT DUMONT, 1715-1747: A SOJOURNER IN THE FRENCH ATLANTIC translated by Gordon M. Sayre, edited by Gordon M. Sayre and Carla Zecher. Published for the Omohundro Institute of Early American History and Culture. Copyright © 2012 by the University of North Carolina Press. Used by permission of the publisher. www.uncpress.org

1.  The crown agreed to pay the Company seven hundred livres for each slave when it took over the colony in 1731. Marie Baron Dumont appears to have avoided the exploitation that Dumont accused the Company of the Indies of perpetrating against the colonists.

other merchandise. I took one of my neighbors along to accompany me. We each had our pirogue. I arrived at the post and made a pretty good sale of my little crop of tobacco, and after we left and had traveled some four leagues, we entered a bayou, or little river. After covering another league and a half, we entered into some lakes of salt water, where we took in many beautiful oysters—enough to fill both our pirogues. Then we went ashore, set our negroes to opening the oysters, and packed and sealed them in ten or twelve jugs, each holding at least eight or ten quarts, after which we loaded up on oysters in their shells with the intention of carrying them to New Orleans and selling them. We paddled back up the bayou and arrived at the Saint Louis River, which we took back up toward my farm, where a great misfortune had occurred. And one misfortune is sometimes followed by another, as I experienced on this occasion. We had almost arrived at the port, being only three leagues away, and had put ashore to spend the night, as is the custom of all voyagers who ascend the Saint Louis or the rivers in canoes or pirogues, and often even those traveling at sea. In the morning, when I wanted to embark, I was quite surprised to find my pirogue sunk to the bottom of the river. All of what little I had amassed by the sweat and fatigue of my body was lost, having either floated away or sunk to the bottom of the river, for we were then on a bend where the water is at its deepest. It was only with great difficulty that we retrieved my boat from where it was resting and emptied it of water. My neighbor left first to get to New Orleans as soon as he could, to be able to earn something from the oysters in the shell that filled his pirogue.

I myself did not arrive at my farm until about three in the afternoon, where I found all the cabins of my negroes, with their cloths and belongings, burned by a fire, as well as my barn filled with unhusked rice, and next to that, a little study where I had my papers, my commissions, my writings. Everything was completely burned. My wife and two negro women she had with her just barely prevented the house where we were living from suffering the same fate, but by spreading water all around the house, they were able to save it. My wife and I had had a daughter a year earlier, and my wife was about ready to give birth again. What to do in this sad situation? I had nothing for my slaves to eat, since, in the granary in my house, I had only thirty quarts of rice and a few barrels of corn. Luckily, the potatoes had not yet been dug up from the ground. So I went to New Orleans to see whether the commandant would be willing to make me a loan of some quarts of rice from the royal plantation so that I might be able to continue to develop my lands and sustain my household. But the commandant was no longer that friend of the people, the courageous and charitable Périer. The men I saw would not hear my plea, would not listen to me at all, and even pretended not to recognize me. I told him I was an officer. He told me that he did not know me as one and that I would have to return home and make the best of it. I was therefore forced to abandoned my farm, just as many others were doing, and to sell one of my negroes and buy a house and a lot in the capital. I thus changed from a country dweller to a resident of the city. I had no sooner moved in than the commandant ordered me to report for a review of the guard in the status of a soldier of the militia, but I opposed this strongly and with justice on my side, and he could not force me.[2]

By the end of the month of February,[3] the companies had been formed and selected to pack up and go to war against the Chickasaws, who supported and took the side of the Natchez. Not wanting to get a reputation for staying at home like a coward while so many other honest men went to war, I voluntarily signed up as a cadet in the company of New Orleans militia under the Sr. Saint Martin, a former warehouse keeper who had retried to live off his wealth, and we embarked in a boat from the Bayou Saint John to report to Mobile,

---

2. Dumont's daughter, Marie-Françoise, was baptized November 28, 1731, and his son, Jean-François, was baptized January 2, 1733.

3. Index note: "1736".

which was the rendezvous point for the entire army.[4] We arrived there on March 7, along with almost all the other. We stayed for the remainder of that month, preparing what was needed for our voyage. Twenty-two large boats, fully loaded, and more than forty pirogues filled with troops, soldiers, civil militia, habitants, and negroes left the fort on the first of April, Easter Sunday, and we made just three leagues that day, ascending the river from Mobile. Our commandant general arrived there last, and as soon as he did, he gave orders laying out the route and the manner for travel on this river, based on his long experience at war. In the morning, at the first light of day, when the drumroll sounded, the men were to strike their tents. Each tent had seven or eight men in it, who each drew one unit of rations. We were at least a thousand to twelve hundred men, and it was a fine sight to see us all encamped or along the river as we rowed upstream one behind the other, both pirogues and flatboats.

Two hours after departing, the convoy was halted to take some time for breakfast and a smoke and then resumed its course until around noon, when we searched for a good place and pulled over to the shore. Everyone went ashore except the sentinels assigned to each boat. One man went looking for wood to heat the kettle; another went to walk around and gather, in lieu of vegetables, wild ginger leaves, some small wild onions, and the stems of grapevines that were just beginning to sprout. This is what we had to do in these immense forests, inhabited only by wild animals, with no human dwellings. When the kettle was ready, we dined as quickly as we could and then returned to the

boats. One boat always went a half league ahead of the other to serve as a vanguard, and, although they should not have been firing guns, they sometimes shot and killed bears, deer, buffalo or turkeys, even squirrels. At sunset, or rather a half hour before sunset, this first boat looked for a good spot to camp. Once the spot had been found, the engineer laid out the camp, and when the other boats arrived, each group pitched its tent. We ate dinner and went to bed, and during the night, sentinels were posted all around, both among the boats and in the depths of the forests.

Finally, on April 22, we arrived at Tombigbee. This is a place that had been chosen as a depot, and a fort was going to be built there, a wooden palisade made entirely of cedar wood: red, white, and multicolored. The fort was going to be erected on a rise, at the end of which was a handsome and spacious plain on which we pitched our tents. Our soldiers built, on the right side of the camp, several ovens in which bread was baked for the sustenance of the army, which was rather tired of eating only biscuits made from a mixture of half rice flour and half wheat flour from France and was surviving on husked rice, beans, swamp beans (or peas), and salt meat.[5]

When we arrived at that post, we met a detachment of sixty men, forty French and twenty Swiss, commanded by the Sr. de Lusser, who was their captain, with the Lieutenant Dutisnet, who had been rescued from his slavery among the Chickasaws. There was also a tent that served as a guardhouse, in which four prisoners were held in irons—a sergeant, a French soldier, and two Swiss—accused of conspiring to kill their

---

4. Dumont agreed to been a sublieutenant in the troops of the marines posted in Louisiana. This is the first on the two expeditions that Bienville organized to attack the Chickasaws. Since the destruction of Fort Rosalie at Natchez, the movement of essential supply boats up and down the Mississippi to the Illinois country had become endangered by raids that were attributed to Chickasaws. Bienville's initial goal was to exterminate the Natchez who had taken refuge among that nation. For a time in 1734–1735, Bienville hoped that he might persuade the Chickasaws themselves to deny such refuge or even to attack the Natchez. But Bienville then came fear that the English were courting the Chickasaws for an alliance and might arrange a peace between the Choctaws and the Chickasaws or even persuade the former to attack the French, in spite of the Choctaws' long-standing support for the French. See Jean-Baptiste Le Moyne de Bienville and Etienne Gatien Salmon to Maurepas, *MPA*, I, 274–276; Patricia Dillon Woods, *French-Indian Relations on the Southern Frontier, 1699–1762* (Ann Arbor, Mich., 1980), 119; Kathleen Duval, "Interconnected and Diversity in 'French Louisiana,'" in Gregory A. Waselkov, Peter H. Wood, and Tom Hatley, eds., *Powhatan's Mantle: Indians in the Colonial Southeast*, rev. ed. (Lincoln, Neb., 2006), 148–152.
5. Fort Tombecbé, or Tombigbee, was located near modern Epes, Alabama, on the Tombigbee River, through the side is now submerged beneath Demopolis Lake..

captain and seize their lieutenant and deliver him up to the Chickasaws, along with the entire Tombigbee post. And so, a week after our arrival, a council of war was held where they were condemned to have their heads broken (since no executioner was present). This sentence was carried out, more to give an example to the soldiers who were carrying arms than as a punishment for a crime that had been concocted under the influence of the fruit of the vine and revealed by a man drunk on the same beverage, who renounced it the next day, blaming it on the drink. But as the proverb says, "He who wishes to kill his dog claims that the dog is rabid." So these four soldiers had their heads smashed in, and when they were to be buried, it was necessary to carve out a grave in the rock, for although it was a pretty prairie where we were camped, there were only four inches of soil on top of it. Beneath that was rock and stone, although it was a stone soft enough that the Indian women ground it up to make very fine jugs or pots, and the name "Tombecbé" that is given to this place signifies, in the Choctaw language, "land of pottery."[6]

The first day of May, we were still in that place, and we erected a maypole in front of the general's and the officers' tents. We had continuous rain with sleet and snow for more than a week. The Choctaw Indians came to offer the calumet to our general, and they received from him a large quantity of presents to encourage them to come along and accompany us in our great enterprise that, according to the zealous declarations of everyone in the army, was going to completely exterminate the enemy. Already, men were planning to capture lots of slaves, and the officers were even bidding for them in advance from the soldiers, giving out money in return for a promise not to grant the slaves to others. A great presumption, and soon we shall see how well it succeeded.

Finally, on the fifth of May, the signal was given. The tents were taken down and stored in the boats, and we left that place. The Choctaws, to the number of more than five or six hundred, were going overland to protect our flank. It was forbidden to fire a gun, not even a single shot. At about three o'clock in the afternoon, the third day after we set out upriver, the sound of a gun startled us and set the convoy on alert. Every man grabbed his weapon and was therefore forced to let go of the oars; the boats were no longer being steered, and they drifted down into one another. It was the greatest confusion you could imagine. We believed that we had been not only discovered by the enemy but also attacked. In fact, it was nothing. It was an Indian, who, not knowing of the strict ban against shooting, had fired at a deer and killed it.

After this, the oars were taken up again, but out of fear of an actual attack, as we continued our voyage, half of the soldiers in each flatboat and pirogue kept their weapons ready for use, if needed. We passed by the base of some steep rocks, which was a very dangerous move for us because ten men on top of the rocks would have been able to damage or even destroy us without firing a single shot, using only stones, pushing them off the top into the river as we passed through the danger zone beneath the cliff. But our enemies were thinking only of meeting us face to face. The Choctaws, who, as I've said, were going with some Frenchmen by land alongside the river to protect our flank, had been forced to move inland away from the riverbank to avoid the dangers and precipices of these rocks. In the end, we were lucky to pass by the rocks without incident and reached the river landing closest to the enemy's territory. This was the twenty-fourth of May. We unloaded, set up the tents, and that same day began making the pilings or palisades for a fort in order to protect our belongings, our boats and pirogues, and for the sick and injured men. We went to sleep, without forgetting to place sentinels all around. The Choctaws, our friends and auxiliaries, had arrived there a day before us. . . .

The detachment where I was, in the company led by Sr. Saint Martin, who marched with us, was assigned its orders and began to set out from the place where the captain had received them. We did not receive a benediction from our chaplain, which we did not demand and he did not propose. The grenadiers' company marched in the van, and the Sr. Saint Pierre, its lieutenant, was like a lion roaring with anger as he

---

6. The difficulty in burying the executed soldiers expresses both the qualities of the soil and Dumont's sympathy for these men.

was the first to reach the plaza in front of the enemies' fort and to enter the first cabin, the door of which was open. He found there two Indians who were smoking a pipe and who apparently did not believe that we were going to come attack them so soon. They were holding a council or making plans, but the sight of our officer surprised them. They attempted to run for safety, but one of them paid with his life for coming there. The other reached the fort quickly.

Meanwhile, our detachment was still advancing toward the fort, flags flying in the wind, crying out, "Vive la France!" The Swiss soldiers were following after the grenadiers, then came the troops of the Company, then the habitants and militia. As we climbed up the butte, a soldier of the Company, named Tisbé, was killed. We reached the top, and as soon as all had gathered there, we began to set fire to the cabins on our left and right atop the butte. They were reduced to ashes by means of rockets with combustible materials in them. We approached closer still, and the habitants, myself among them, divided into two parties, one to the left and the other to the right of the enlisted troops, with the goal of reaching the pilings of the fort and setting fire to them. But in spite of our strong efforts, in the midst of our march, the Sr. Juzan, adjutant major, suddenly stopped us and forced us to retrace our steps. This maneuver slowed our enthusiasm. No doubt he only did this so that the regular soldiers would have the glory of being the first to breach the walls of the fort. But the gunfire from the Englishmen and the Indians had already killed or wounded a few of their men, as well as of ours—some in the feet, some in the arms— and this restrained, or rather warned, them not to expose themselves so much, for we were all more or less in the open. The Swiss advanced and retreated three times, and the French troops arranged themselves in a column, taking cover behind a round cabin that had not been burned and that served as a retrenchment.

_____

As the Sr. Juzan saw that the Swiss were retreating, he came up on their left flank close to where I was to encourage them to advance. But as he was trying to get them to put their hearts in it, as the saying goes, a shot fired from one of the stronghouses hit him between the shoulders. He staggered but did not fall. When he realized he was wounded, he redoubled his entreaties toward the Swiss, saying, "My friends, I am wounded. I'm going to return to camp, but before I die, at least let me learn that you have vanquished our enemies, and I will die contented." And he did die as soon as he arrived at camp. It was not long before at Mobile that he had married, and he left his wife pregnant. The Sr. de Lusser, captain commandant of Tombigbee, was also wounded and carried to camp, where he died. He said that he forgave his enemy because he was convinced that the ball that had hit him was not fired by the Indians but by one of the garrison's soldiers, who had avenged the death of his comrades who had had their heads smashed in, as I described above. One habitant who was a boat captain was also killed but could not return to camp, whereas the sergeant of the grenadiers and his captain, the Sr. Renaut, were wounded in the thigh and fell and had to be carried back behind the front lines.[7]

So in a word, those who attacked the fort all got what was coming to them, and even a little more. For, since the soldiers were lined up, as I've described, behind the round cabin, anyone who stuck his foot out a little more than his neighbor received a shot in the ankle. And the Sr. Grondel—a lieutenant in the Swiss regiment and the son of Grondel, the half-pay lieutenant for the Alsatian garrison at Port-Louis—this lieutenant, I say, in trying to encourage his company to follow his lead rather than retreat as they were doing, had set off running, along with the Sr. de Saint Pierre, to attack the walls of the fort, yelling, "Follow me, my friends!" The latter did not receive any wounds, even though his weapons, the brim of his hat, and the folds of his uniform were riddled with more than a dozen holes. But the former, the Swiss lieutenant, I mean, received two shots to his body out of four that brought him to the ground, and he was not able to rejoin the army. He dragged himself as best he could into a cabin that was nearby. M. Dupart, captain of the

_____

7.  Dumont's point here is that the militia helped the troops, but the troops did not reciprocate.

Swiss regiment, sent one of his soldiers to fetch him, which he did in the face of much gunfire. He carried his officer on his shoulders, much as Aeneas carried his father, Anchises, away from the walls of Troy. But there was this difference between the two: the latter was protected by a cloud that hid him from his enemies, whereas the Swiss soldier did not have this advantage when he carried his officer, and they were both hit by a single shot; that is to say, the ball hit the calf of the lieutenant, passed through his leg, and entered between the shoulders into the body of the valiant and generous soldier. It took several men to carry the two of them back to camp

As for me, I sought out an *antichon,* which is a house built upon four posts, with no enclosure or foundation, which one enters by climbing a ladder. I was there with the idea of firing at a loophole on the wall of the enemy fort from which constant fire had been coming. I wanted to try to hit the Indian behind it, but as I was aiming at him, a soldier asked me to step aside, saying he would not miss. As his gun was already loaded, I stepped back, gave him my place, and stood next to him. But just then, a ball entered the antichon through the bundles of canes that made up its roof; a gunshot was fired from two and a half feet above his head. The ball pierced his heart and came out at his knee. As I was right next to him, the sound rendered me deaf for nearly a quarter of an hour. I pushed the barrel of my gun up through the canes and I fired. The Indian who was up there quickly jumped down from the roof to escape, but some Swiss soldiers fired at him and made him plow the dirt with his nose. While I was reloading my gun, I was hit by a ball that passed through the tail of my vest, through my shirt in two places, stripped off the button from my breeches, and made me fall to the ground. But this was a very lucky shot for me, as it did not at all hurt me. As I got up, I was more embarrassed than hurt, for I held in one hand my gun and in my other hand my breeches and in this state ran to rejoin the Swiss soldiers, where I found the broken-off end of a bayonet to use as a button

The Swiss were deployed along a straight line, as were the troops of the Company, but had for cover only a pile of long, thick canes, such as were plentiful around there. The captain of the Swiss was in a pigsty, as if it were a little fort surrounded by palisades. As for our men, it was like a slaughterhouse: 37 men had been killed and 117 wounded, some in the feet, others in the thigh, arms, stomach, or shot through the body, the hand, etc. The Sr. de Noyan, who was then the commandant of the detachment, had given a wounded soldier one of those small bottles of spirits, the kind covered with woven basket-canes, that we called a pistol. The soldier had drunk some of it and then given the pistol back to the captain, who was going to put it in the pocket of his breeches, when a ball came that broke the bottle in half and penetrated the thigh of the commandant, who, having fallen to the ground, received an initial treatment for his wound along with the wound itself, for the brandy entered the wound, which could only be good for it. He had to be carried to camp, where the general was sitting on a crate, no doubt praying to God to give him the victory. When the general, I say, saw his nephew thus injured, he sounded the signal for retreat. But how to retreat? The army had no more powder, having used it all firing at the walls of the enemy fort. If the Indians had known of the practice of making sorties, a mere twenty men would have found us listless and would certainly have routed us. It was necessary to prepare a second detachment to rescue the first and to make our retreat possible. . . .

As for us, after staying for a while at Mobile, we embarked again and reached New Orleans. Each man went back home, counting himself lucky to have escaped and survived. Our general came home to his seat of government with the plan of returning another time to have his revenge on the Indians. We will see in what follows the progress and success of this plan. The rest of that year, nothing much happened, aside from learning of the continuing attacks made by our enemies. When they were able to find some of our men traveling, they did not spare them.

## QUESTIONS TO CONSIDER

1. What can you glean about Louisiana farming through Dumont's account?
2. How would you describe warfare during the First Chickasaw War?

# 6.2 TEXT FROM THE ALBANY PLAN OF UNION (1754)

In the midst of the Seven Years' War, Benjamin Franklin envisioned a strategy to ensure colonial unity. At the Albany Congress in 1754, convened by representatives from seven of the thirteen colonies to discuss common defense against a French attack from Canada, Franklin unveiled his plan in the following document, which called for a common government overseen by Parliament. Though most of the representatives at the Albany Congress supported Franklin's plan, colonial assemblies rejected it over fears of a centralized taxing body and government. Even so, Franklin's ideas would later influence the writers of the Articles of Confederation.

*[July 10, 1754]*

PLAN of a Proposed Union of the Several Colonies of Masachusets-bay, New Hampshire, Coneticut, Rhode Island, New York, New Jerseys, Pensilvania, Maryland, Virginia, North Carolina, and South Carolina, For their Mutual Defence and Security, and for Extending the British Settlements in North America.

THAT humble Application be made for an Act of the Parliament of Great Britain, by Virtue of which, one General Government may be formed in America, including all the said Colonies, within and under which Government, each Colony may retain its present Constitution, except in the Particulars wherein a Change may be directed by the said Act, as hereafter follows.

| President General | That the said General Government be administred by a President General, |
|---|---|
| Grand Council. | To be appointed and Supported by the Crown, and a Grand Council to be Chosen by the Representatives of the People of the Several Colonies, met in their respective Assemblies. |
| Election of Members. | That within Months after the passing of such Act, The House of Representatives in the Several Assemblies, that Happen to be Sitting within that time or that shall be Specially for that purpose Convened, may and Shall Choose Members for the Grand Council in the following Proportions, that is to say. |

| Masachusets-Bay | 7. |
| New Hampshire | 2. |
| Conecticut | 5. |
| Rhode-Island | 2. |
| New-York | 4. |
| New-Jerseys | 3. |
| Pensilvania | 6. |
| Maryland | 4. |
| Virginia | 7. |
| North-Carolina | 4. |
| South-Carolina | 4. |
| | 48. |

*Source:* "The Albany Plan of Union, 1754," https://founders.archives.gov/documents/Franklin/01-05-02-0104 (Accessed June 5, 2018).

| | |
|---|---|
| Place of first meeting. | Who shall meet for the first time at the City of Philadelphia, in Pensilvania, being called by the President General as soon as conveniently may be, after his Appointment. |
| New Election. | That there shall be a New Election of Members for the Grand Council every three years; And on the Death or Resignation of any Member his Place shall be Supplyed by a New Choice at the next Sitting of the Assembly of the Colony he represented. |
| Proportion of Members after first 3 years. | That after the first three years, when the Proportion of Money arising out of each Colony to the General Treasury can be known, The Number of Members to be Chosen, for each Colony shall from time to time in all ensuing Elections be regulated by that proportion (yet so as that the Number to be Chosen by any one Province be not more than Seven nor less than Two). |
| Meetings of Grand Council. Call. | That the Grand Council shall meet once in every Year, and oftner if Occasion require, at such Time and place as they shall adjourn to at the last preceeding meeting, or as they shall be called to meet at by the President General, on any Emergency, he having first obtained in Writing the Consent of seven of the Members to such call, and sent due and timely Notice to the whole. |
| Speaker. Continuance. | That the Grand Council have Power to Chuse their Speaker, and shall neither be Dissolved, prorogued nor Continue Sitting longer than Six Weeks at one Time without their own Consent, or the Special Command of the Crown. |
| Member's Allowance | That the Members of the Grand Council shall be Allowed for their Service ten shillings Sterling per Diem, during their Sessions or Journey to and from the Place of Meeting; Twenty miles to be reckoned a days Journey. |
| Assent of President General. His Duty. | That the Assent of the President General be requisite, to all Acts of the Grand Council, and that it be His Office, and Duty to cause them to be carried into Execution. |
| Power of President and Grand Council. Peace and War. Indian Purchases. New Settlements Laws to Govern them. | That the President General with the Advice of the Grand Council, hold or Direct all Indian Treaties in which the General Interest or Welfare of the Colony's may be Concerned; And make Peace or Declare War with the Indian Nations. That they make such Laws as they Judge Necessary for regulating all Indian Trade. That they make all Purchases from Indians for the Crown, of Lands not within the Bounds of Particular Colonies, or that shall not be within their Bounds when some of them are reduced to more Convenient Dimensions. That they make New Settlements on such Purchases, by Granting Lands in the Kings Name, reserving a Quit Rent to the Crown, for the use of the General Treasury. That they make Laws for regulating and Governing such new Settlements, till the Crown shall think fit to form them into Particular Governments. |

Raise Soldiers &c. Lakes.

Not to Impress

Power to make Laws
Duties &c.

Treasurer.

Money how to Issue.

That they raise and pay Soldiers, and build Forts for the Defence of any of the Colonies, and equip Vessels of Force to Guard the Coasts and Protect the Trade on the Ocean, Lakes, or Great Rivers; But they shall not Impress Men in any Colonies, without the Consent of its Legislature. That for these purposes they have Power to make Laws And lay and Levy such General Duties, Imposts, or Taxes, as to them shall appear most equal and Just, Considering the Ability and other Circumstances of the Inhabitants in the Several Colonies, and such as may be Collected with the least Inconvenience to the People, rather discouraging Luxury, than Loading Industry with unnecessary Burthens. That they may a General Treasurer and a Particular Treasurer in each Government, when Necessary, And from Time to Time may Order the Sums in the Treasuries of each Government, into the General Treasury, or draw on them for Special payments as they find most Convenient; Yet no money to Issue, but by joint Orders of the President General and Grand Council Except where Sums have been Appropriated to particular Purposes, And the President General is previously impowered By an Act to draw for such Sums.

Accounts.

That the General Accounts shall be yearly Settled and Reported to the Several Assembly's.

Quorum.

Laws to be Transmitted.

That a Quorum of the Grand Council impower'd to Act with the President General, do consist of Twenty-five Members, among whom there shall be one, or more from a Majority of the Colonies. That the Laws made by them for the Purposes aforesaid, shall not be repugnant but as near as may be agreeable to the Laws of England, and Shall be transmitted to the King in Council for Approbation, as Soon as may be after their Passing and if not disapproved within Three years after Presentation to remain in Force.

Death of President
General.

That in case of the Death of the President General T*he Speaker of the Grand Council for the Time Being shall Succeed, and be Vested with the Same Powers, and Authority, to Continue until the King's Pleasure be known.

Officers how Appointed.

That all Military Commission Officers Whether for Land or Sea Service, to Act under this General Constitution, shall be Nominated by the President General But the Approbation of the Grand Council, is to be Obtained before they receive their Commissions, And all Civil Officers are to be Nominated, by the Grand Council, and to receive the President General's Approbation, before they Officiate; But in Case of Vacancy by Death or removal of any Officer Civil or Military under this Constitution, The Governor of the Province, in which such Vacancy happens, may Appoint till the Pleasure of the President General and Grand Council can be known. That the Particular Military as well as Civil Establishments in each Colony remain in their present State, this General Constitution Notwithstanding. And that on Sudden Emergencies any Colony may Defend itself, and lay the Accounts of Expence thence Arisen, before the President General and Grand Council, who may allow and order payment of the same As far as they Judge such Accounts Just and reasonable.

## QUESTIONS TO CONSIDER

1. What powers in particular did Franklin wish to bestow on his Grand Council? Why were those powers important?

2. Is the Albany Plan of Union revolutionary?

# 6.3 THE DECLARATION OF RIGHTS OF THE STAMP ACT CONGRESS (1765) AND THE SUFFOLK RESOLVES TEXT (1774)

A decade after the Seven Years' War, colonial tensions began to grow more serious. First, colonial representatives convened in New York City in 1764 to oppose the Stamp Act, a new tax enforced by Parliament that required a special stamp on legal documents, newspapers, and other paper products. Colonial representatives argued that Parliament could not tax the colonies because the colonies did not have any representation in Parliament. As a result, they ratified the Declaration of Rights, the first document in this reading, which outlined their views. They also sent a list of their grievances to Parliament. Ten years later, on the eve of the Revolution, representatives from Suffolk County, Massachusetts, gathered to issue a declaration opposing the Intolerable Acts issued after the Boston Tea Party. The Suffolk Resolves, the second document, went a step further than the Declaration of Rights, however, by demanding a boycott of British goods, a refusal to pay taxes, and an independent Massachusetts government, among other things. Two years before the Declaration of Independence, the Suffolk Resolves illustrated the wave of revolutionary thought that pervaded the American northeast.

## DECLARATION OF RIGHTS

The members of this congress, sincerely devoted, with the warmest sentiments of affection and duty to his majesty's person and government, inviolably attached to the present happy establishment of the protestant succession, and with minds deeply impressed by a sense of the present and impending misfortunes of the British colonies on this continent ; having considered as maturely as time would permit, the circumstances of said colonies, esteem it our indispensable duty to make the following declarations, of our humble opinions, respecting the most essential rights and liberties of the colonists, and of the grievances under which they labor, by reason of several late acts of parliament.

1st. That his majesty's subjects in these colonies, owe the same allegiance to the crown of Great Britain, that is owing from his subjects born within the realm, and all due subordination to that august body, the parliament of Great Britain.

2d. That his majesty's liege subjects in these colonies are entitled to all the inherent rights and privileges of his natural born subjects within the kingdom of Great Britain,

*Source: Journal of the First Congress of the American Colonies in Opposition to The Tyrannical Acts of the British Parliament* (New York: E. Winchester, 1845), 27–34; "The Suffolk Resolves," https://www.nps.gov/mima/learn/education/upload/The%20 Suffolk%20Resolves.pdf (Accessed June 5, 2018).

3d. That it is inseparably essential to the freedom of a people, and the undoubted rights of Englishmen, that no taxes should be imposed on them, but with their own consent, given personally, or by their representatives.

4th. That the people of these colonies are not, and from their local circumstances, cannot be represented in the house of commons in Great Britain.

5th. That the only representatives of the people of these colonies, are persons chosen therein, by themselves ; and that no taxes ever have been, or can be constitutionally imposed on them, but by their respective legislatures.

6th. That all supplies to the crown, being free gifts of the people, it is unreasonable and inconsistent with the principles and spirit of the British constitution, for the people of Great Britain to grant to his majesty the property of the colonists.

7th. That trial by jury is the inherent and invaluable right of every British subject in these colonies.

8th. That the late act of parliament entitled, an act for granting and applying certain stamp duties, and other duties in the British colonies and plantations in America, &c, by imposing taxes on the inhabitants of these colonies, and the said act, and several other acts, by extending the jurisdiction of the courts of admiralty beyond its ancient limits, have a manifest tendency to subvert the rights and liberties *of* the colonists.

*9th.* That the duties imposed by several late acts of parliament, from the peculiar circumstances of these colonies, will be extremely buthensome and grievous, and from the scarcity of specie, the payment of them absolutely impracticable.

10th. That as the profits of the trade of these colonies ultimately centre in Great Britain, to pay for the manufactures which they are obliged to take from thence, they eventually contribute very largely to all supplies granted there to the crown.

11th. That the restrictions imposed by several late acts of parliament, on the trade of these colonies, will render them unable to purchase the manufactures of Great Britain.

12th. That the increase, prosperity, and happiness of these colonies, depend on the full and free enjoyment of their rights and liberties, and an intercourse, with Great Britain, mutually affectionate and advantageous.

*13th.* That it is the right of the British subjects in these colonies, to petition the king or either house of parliament.

Lastly, That it is the indispensable duty of these colonies to the best of sovereigns, to the mother country, and *to* themselves, to endeavor, by a loyal and dutiful address *to* his majesty, and humble application to both houses of parliament, to procure the repeal *of* the act for granting and applying certain stamp duties, of all clauses of any other acts of parliament, whereby the jurisdiction of the admiralty is extended as aforesaid, and of the other late acts for the restriction of the American commerce. . . .

*Tuesday, Oct. 22d, 1765, A. M.*—The congress met according to adjournment. The address to his majesty being engrossed, was read and compared, and is as follows, viz :

## TO THE KING'S MOST EXCELLENT MAJESTY

The petition of the Freeholders and other Inhabitants of the colonies of Massachusetts Bay, Rhode Island and Providence Plantations, New-York, New Jersey, Pennsylvania, the government of the counties of New Castle, Kent and Sussex, upon Delaware, and province of Maryland,

*Most humbly sheweth,*

That the inhabitants of these colonies, unanimously devoted with the warmest sentiments of duty and affection to your sacred person and government, and inviolably attached to the present happy establishment of the protestant succession in your illustrious house, and deeply sensible of your royal attention to their prosperity and happiness, humbly beg leave to approach the throne, by representing to your majesty, that these colonies were originally planted by subjects of the British crown, who, animated with the spirit of liberty, encouraged by your majesty's royal predecessors, and confiding in the public faith for the enjoyment of all the rights and liberties essential to freedom, emigrated from their native country to this continent, and, by their successful perseverance, in the midst of innumerable dangers and difficulties, together with a profusion of their blood and treasure, have happily added these vast and extensive dominions to the Empire of Great Britain.

That, for the enjoyment of these rights and liberties, several governments were early formed in the said colonies, with full power of legislation, agreeably to the principles of the English constitution ;—that, under these governments, these liberties, thus vested in their ancestors, and transmitted to their posterity, have been exercised and enjoyed, and by the inestimable blessings thereof, under the favor of Almighty God, the inhospitable deserts of America have been converted into flourishing counties ; science, humanity, and the knowledge of divine truths diffused through remote regions of ignorance, infidelity, and barbarism ; the number of British subjects wonderfully increased, and the wealth and power of Great Britain proportionably augmented.

That, by means of these settlements and the unparalleled success of your majesty's arms, a foundation is now laid for rendering the British empire the most extensive and powerful of any recorded in history ; our connection with this empire we esteem our greatest happiness and security, and humbly conceive it may now be so established by your royal wisdom, as to endure to the latest period of time ; this, with the most humble submission to your majesty, we apprehend will be most effectually accomplished by fixing the pillars thereof on liberty and justice, and securing the inherent rights and liberties of your subjects here, upon the principles of the English constitution. To this constitution, these two principles are essential ; the rights of your faithful subjects freely to grant to your majesty such aids as are required for the support of your government over them, and other public exigencies ; and trials by their peers. By the one they are secured from unreasonable impositions, and by the other from the arbitrary decisions of the executive power. The continuation of these liberties to the inhabitants of America, we ardently implore, as absolutely necessary to unite the several parts of your wide extended dominions, in that harmony so essential to the preservation and happiness of the whole. Protected in these liberties, the emoluments Great Britain receives from us, however great at present, are inconsiderable, compared with those she has the fairest prospect of acquiring. By this protection, she will for

ever secure to herself the advantages of conveying to all Europe, the merchandize which America furnishes, and for supplying, through the same channel, whatsoever is wanted from thence. Here opens a boundless source of wealth and naval strength. Yet these immense advantages, by the abridgement of those invaluable rights and liberties, by which our growth has been nourished, are in danger of being for ever lost, and our subordinate legislatures in effect rendered useless by the late acts of parliament imposing duties and taxes on these colonies, and extending the jurisdiction of the courts of admiralty here, beyond its ancient limits ; statutes by which your majesty's commons in Britain undertake absolutely to dispose of the property of their fellow-subjects in America without their consent, and for the enforcing whereof, they are subjected to the determination of a single judge, in a court unrestrained by the wise rules of the common law, the birthright of Englishmen, and the safeguard of their persons and properties.

The invaluable rights of taxing ourselves and trial by our peers, of which we implore your majesty's protection, are not, we most humbly conceive, unconstitutional, but confirmed by the Great Charter of English liberties. On the first of these rights the honorable house of commons found their practice of originating money, a right enjoyed by the kingdom of Ireland, by the clergy of England, until relinquished by themselves ; a right, in fine, which all other your majesty's English subjects, both within and without the realm, have hitherto enjoyed.

With hearts, therefore, impressed with the most indelible characters of gratitude to your majesty, and to the memory of the kings of your illustrious house, whose reigns have been signally distinguished by their auspicious influence on the prosperity of the British dominions ; and convinced by the most affecting proofs of your majesty's paternal love to all your people, however distant, and your unceasing and benevolent desires to promote their happiness ; we most humbly beseech your majesty that you will be graciously pleased to take into your royal consideration the distresses of your faithful subjects on this continent, and to lay the same before your majesty's parliament, and to afford them such relief as, in your royal wisdom, their unhappy circumstances shall be judged to require.

## THE SUFFOLK RESOLVES

At a meeting of the delegates of every town & district in the county of Suffolk, on Tuesday the 6th of September, at the house of Mr. Richard Woodward, of Deadham, & by adjournment, at the house of Mr. [Daniel] Vose, of Milton, on Friday the 9th instant, Joseph Palmer, esq. being chosen moderator, and William Thompson, esq. clerk, a committee was chosen to bring in a report to the convention, and the following being several times read, and put paragraph by paragraph, was unanimously voted, viz.

Whereas the power but not the justice, the vengeance but not the wisdom of Great-Britain, which of old persecuted, scourged, and exiled our fugitive parents from their native shores, now pursues us, their guiltless children, with unrelenting severity: And whereas, this, then savage and uncultivated desart, was purchased by the toil and treasure, or acquired by the blood and valor of those our venerable progenitors; to us they bequeathed the dearbought inheritance, to our care and protection they consigned it, and the most sacred obligations are upon us to transmit the glorious purchase, unfettered by power, unclogged with shackles, to our innocent and beloved offspring. On the fortitude, on the wisdom and on the exertions of this important day, is suspended the fate of this new world, and of unborn millions. If a boundless extent of continent, swarming with millions, will tamely submit to live, move and have their being at the arbitrary will of a licentious minister, they basely yield to voluntary slavery, and future generations shall load their memories with incessant execrations.—On the other hand, if we arrest the hand which would ransack our pockets, if we disarm the parricide which points the dagger to our bosoms, if we nobly defeat that fatal edict which proclaims a power to frame laws for us in all cases whatsoever, thereby entailing the endless and numberless curses of slavery upon us, our heirs and their heirs forever; if we successfully resist that unparalleled usurpation of unconstitutional power, whereby our capital is robbed of the means of life; whereby the streets of Boston are thronged with military executioners; whereby our coasts are lined and harbours crouded with ships of war; whereby the charter of the colony, that sacred barrier against the encroachments of tyranny, is mutilated and, in effect, annihilated; whereby

a murderous law is framed to shelter villains from the hands of justice; whereby the unalienable and inestimable inheritance, which we derived from nature, the constitution of Britain, and the privileges warranted to us in the charter of the province, is totally wrecked, annulled, and vacated, posterity will acknowledge that virtue which preserved them free and happy; and while we enjoy the rewards and blessings of the faithful, the torrent of panegyrists will roll our reputations to that latest period, when the streams of time shall be absorbed in the abyss of eternity.—Therefore, we have resolved, and do resolve,

1. That whereas his majesty, George the Third, is the rightful successor to the throne of Great-Britain, and justly entitled to the allegiance of the British realm, and agreeable to compact, of the English colonies in America—therefore, we, the heirs and successors of the first planters of this colony, do cheerfully acknowledge the said George the Third to be our rightful sovereign, and that said covenant is the tenure and claim on which are founded our allegiance and submission.

2. That it is an indispensable duty which we owe to God, our country, ourselves and posterity, by all lawful ways and means in our power to maintain, defend and preserve those civil and religious rights and liberties, for which many of our fathers fought, bled and died, and to hand them down entire to future generations.

3. That the late acts of the British parliament for blocking up the harbour of Boston, for altering the established form of government in this colony, and for screening the most flagitious violators of the laws of the province from a legal trial, are gross infractions of those rights to which we are justly entitled by the laws of nature, the British constitution, and the charter of the province.

4. That no obedience is due from this province to either or any part of the acts abovementioned, but that they be rejected as the attempts of a wicked administration to enslave America.

5. That so long as the justices of our superior court of judicature, court of assize, &c. and inferior court of common pleas in this county are appointed, or hold their places, by any other tenure than that which the charter and the laws of the province direct, they must be considered as under undue influence, and are therefore unconstitutional officers, and, as such, no regard ought to be paid to them by the people of this county.

6. That if the justices of the superior court of judicature, assize, &c. justices of the court of common pleas, or of the general sessions of the peace, shall sit and act during their present disqualified state, this county will support, and bear harmless, all sheriffs and their deputies, constables, jurors and other officers who shall refuse to carry into execution the orders of said courts; and, as far as possible, to prevent the many inconveniencies which must be occasioned by a suspension of the courts of justice, we do most earnestly recommend it to all creditors, that they shew all reasonable and even generous forbearance to their debtors; and to all debtors, to pay their just debts with all possible speed, and if any disputes relative to debts or trespasses shall arise, which cannot be settled by the parties, we recommend it to them to submit all such causes to arbitration; and it is our opinion that the contending parties or either of them, who shall refuse so to do, onght to be considered as co-operating with the enemies of this country.

7. That it be recommended to the collectors of taxes, constables and all other officers, who have public monies in their hands, to retain the same, and not to make any payment thereof to the provincial county treasurer until the civil government of the province is placed upon a constitutional foundation, or until it shall otherwise be ordered by the proposed provincial Congress.

8. That the persons who have accepted seats at the council board, by virtue of a mandamus from the King, in conformity to the late act of the British parliament, entitled, an act for the regulating the government of the Massachusetts-Bay, have acted in direct violation of the duty they owe to their country, and have thereby given great and just offence to this people; therefore, resolved, that this county do recommend it to all persons, who have so highly offended by accepting said departments, and have not already publicly resigned their seats at the council board, to make public resignations of their places at said board, on or before the 20th day of this instant, September; and that all persons refusing so to do, shall, from and after said day, be considered by this county as obstinate and incorrigible enemies to this country.

9. That the fortifications begun and now carrying on upon Boston Neck, are justly alarming to this county, and gives us reason to apprehend some hostile intention against that town, more especially as the commander in chief has, in a very extraordinary manner, removed the powder from the magazine at Charlestown, and has also forbidden the keeper of the magazine at Boston, to deliver out to the owners, the powder, which they had lodged in said magazine.

10. That the late act of parliament for establishing the Roman Catholic religion and the French laws in that extensive country, now called Canada, is dangerous in an extreme degree to the Protestant religion and to the civil rights and liberties of all America; and, therefore, as men and Protestant Christians, we are indispensubly obliged to take all proper measures for our security.

11. That whereas our enemies have flattered themselves that they shall make an easy prey of this numerous, brave and hardy people, from an apprehension that they are unacquainted with military discipline; we, therefore, for the honour, defence and security of this county and province, advise, as it has been recommended to take away all commissions from the officers of the militia, that those who now hold commissions, or such other persons, be elected in each town as officers in the militia, as shall be judged of sufficient capacity for that purpose, and who have evidenced themselves the inflexible friends to the rights of the people; and that the inhabitants of those towns and districts, who are qualified, do use their utmost diligence to acquaint themselves with the art of war as soon as possible, and do, for that purpose, appear under arms at least once every week.

12. That during the present hostile appearances on the part of Great-Britain, notwithstanding the many insults and oppressions which we most sensibly resent, yet, nevertheless, from our affection to his majesty, which we have at all times evidenced, we are determined to act merely upon the defensive, so long as such conduct may be vindicated by reason and the principles of self-preservation, but no longer.

13. That, as we understand it has been in contemplation to apprehend sundry persons of this county, who have rendered themselves conspicuous in contending for the violated rights and liberties of their countrymen; we do recommend, should such an audacious measure be put in practice, to seize and keep

in safe custody, every servant of the present tyrannical and unconstitutional government throughout the county and province, until the persons so apprehended be liberated from the bands of our adversaries, and restored safe and uninjured to their respective friends and families.

14. That until our rights are fully restored to us, we will, to the utmost of our power, and we recommend the same to the other counties, to withhold all commercial intercourse with Great-Britain, Ireland, and the West-Indies, and abstain from the consumption of British merchandise and manufactures, and especially of East-Indies, and piece goods, with such additions, alterations, and exceptions only, as the General Congress of the colonies may agree to.

15. That under our present circumstances, it is incumbent on us to encourage arts and manufactures amongst us, by all means in our power, and that be and are hereby appointed a committee, to consider of the best ways and means to promote and establish the same, and to report to this convention as soon as may be.

16. That the exigencies of our public affairs, demand that a provincial Congress be called to consult such measures as may be adopted, and vigorously executed by the whole people; and we do recommend it to the several towns in this county, to chuse members for such a provincial Congress, to be holden at Concord, on the second Tuesday of October, next ensuing.

17. That this county, confiding in the wisdom and integrity of the continental Congress, now sitting at Philadelphia, pay all due respect and submission to such measures as may be recommended by them to the colonies, for the restoration and establishment of our just rights, civil and religious, and for renewing that harmony and union between Great-Britain and the colonies, so earnestly wished for by all good men.

18. That whereas the universal uneasiness which prevails among all orders of men, arising from the wicked and oppressive measures of the present administration, may influence some unthinking persons to commit outrage upon private property; we would heartily recommend to all persons of this community, not to engage in any routs, riots, or licentious attacks upon the properties of any person whatsoever, as being subversive of all order and government; but, by a steady, manly, uniform, and persevering opposition, to convince our enemies, that in a contest so important, in a cause so solemn, our conduct shall be such as to merit the approbation of the wise, and the admiration of the brave and free of every age and of every country.

19. That should our enemies, by any sudden manoeuvres, render it necessary to ask the aid and assistance of our brethren in the country, some one of the committee of correspondence, or a select man of such town, or the town adjoining, where such hostilities shall commence, or shall be expected to commence, shall despatch couriers with written messages to the select men, or committees of correspondence, of the several towns in the vicinity, with a written account of such matter, who shall despatch others to committees more remote, until proper and sufficient assistance be obtained, and that the expense of said couriers be defrayed by the county, until proper and sufficient assistance be obtained, and that the expense of said couriers be defrayed by the county, until it shall be otherwise ordered by the provincial Congress.

## QUESTIONS TO CONSIDER

1. How did the Stamp Act Congress try to convince Parliament of their case?
2. How revolutionary were the Suffolk Resolves?

# 6.4 GEORGE ROBERT TWELVE HEWES, EXCERPT FROM *TRAITS OF THE TEA PARTY* (1835)

George Robert Twelve Hewes, a Boston shoemaker, gained some acclaim in the early nineteenth century as one of the last survivors of the Boston Tea Party and the Boston Massacre. As a result, authors published several works about him, one of which, *Traits of the Tea Party*, is excerpted here. In *Traits of the Tea Party*, the author, Benjamin Bussey Thatcher, interviewed Hewes for his memories and interspersed the recollections with Thatcher's own views. The excerpt contains Hewes' remembrances of the Tea Party: he was on one of the three boats that boarded the tea-carrying *Dartmouth*, and he fully participated in the events of that night. Hewes later fought in the Revolution as a member of the Connecticut militia. He died in 1840 at the age of 98. *Traits of the Tea Party* is notable for its illustration of an ordinary person's experiences in the months preceding the outbreak of war.

There was not a *crowd*, Mr. Hewes says, on the wharf when he reached there, and that was just in season; there were *"considerable many."* The moon shone bright, and they saw their position clearly, and went to work, from 100 to 150, he thinks, being more or less actively engaged. Instead of finishing the ship first, he states that the whole company was divided into three divisions, intended to be about equal. A commander and a boatswain were chosen for each. Pierce was in the party which boarded the ship. Hewes went on board one of the brigs, with a company as fantastically arrayed in old frocks, red woolen caps, gowns, and all manner of like devices, as need be seen. Lendall Pitts, a well-known Whig, led this party; and Hewes, whose whistling talent was a manner of public notoriety, acted as a boatswain.

One of Pitt's first movements in office, was to send a man to the mate, who was on board, in his cabin, with a message, politely requesting the use of a few lights, and the brig's *Keys*—so that as little damage as possible might be done to the vessel;—and such was the case. The mate acted the part of a gentleman altogether. He handed over the keys without hesitation and without saying a single word, and sent his cabin-boy for a bunch of candles, to be immediately put in use; all which agrees with the newspaper statement respecting the "masters." The three parties finished their respective tasks pretty nearly at the same time, and that without unnecessary delay, as may be inferred from the amount of labor accomplished in three hours. A considerable number of sailors, and some others, joined them from time to time, and aided in hoisting the chests from the hold.

One of the persons alluded to by the papers as having been roughly handled, was a man named Charles O'Conner—probably a foreigner—well known to Hewes. He pretended at one period to be particularly zealous in the good work. Hewes, however, rather suspected him, and watching him slily, noticed a gratuitous manœuvre of his hands, now and then, up and down his pantaloons, and along the lining of his coat. He informed Pitts. O'Conner took the hint, and moved off. They raised the cry of an *"East Indian!"* and Hewes pursued him, caught him (a great, lusty, long-legged fellow) by the skirts of his frock, and pulled him back from the wharf's

*Source:* B. B. Thatcher, *Traits of the Tea Party: Being a Memoir of George R. T. Hewes* (New York: Harper & Brothers, 1835), 180–195. Retrieved from the Internet Archive website, https://archive.org/details/traitsteapartyb00thatgoog (Accessed June 5, 2018).

edge, aboard the brig, where he floundered about till a few of them had pretty essentially relieved him of his cargo, as well as of the obnoxious apparel which contained it; and then, with an application or two in the rear, to hasten his flight, they discharged him from farther discussion. He turned out to be an old fellow-apprentice of Hewes—having once lived with him at Downing's. They recognized each other in the course of the scuffle, and O'Connor, calling him by name, threatened to "Complain to the Governor," "You had better make your *will* first!" quoth Hewes, doubling his fist expressively—but he fled, without a waiting the result of the argument.

When all was done, the whole company rallied together on the wharf, which was now covered with people. Here an old gentleman was detected with a quantity of tea in his coat pocket, which was stripped off with little ceremony, without doing him much other harm. A fresh inspection was then instituted, and all the tea-men were ordered to take their shoes off and empty them, which was supposed to be done. Pitts, who was quite a military man, as well as a mighty son of Liberty, was appointed commander-in-chief of the forces then and there assembled; they were formed in rank and file by his direction, with the aid of Barber, Proctor, and some others; and "Shouldering" their arms, such as they had—tomahawks included—they marched up the wharf to the music of a fife, to what is now the termination of pearl Street, back into town, and there separated in a short time, and went quietly home.

It is remarkable, that all this transaction was carried through in plain sight (and by a fine moonlight too) of the British squadron, which partly lay perhaps less than a quarter of a mile distant from the scene, and at hours when those who belonged to it must have been generally both aboard and awake. The Admiral, indeed, is believed to have witnessed most of the affair at a much more convenient point, and even to have come ashore for the purpose. When the people marched off, according to Hewes, he shewed himself at the house of a Tory, named Coffin, who lived at the head of the wharf, running up the window, where he sat as they came along, and crying out, "Well, boys,

you have had a fine pleasant evening for your Indian caper—havn't you? But mind, you have got to pay the fiddler yet!"

"Oh, never mind!" shouted Pitts, "never mind, 'squire! Just come out here, if you please, and we'll settle bill in two minutes!"

This raised a shout—the fifer struck up a lively air—the Admiral put the window down in a hurry—and the company marched on.

Hewes went home by way of his brother's, in Oliver Street, entered the room where the women were, gravely enquired if Solomon Hewes was about, and getting no satisfaction, walked off again, with his blanket and dirty face, leaving them to this day, we suppose,—if any of them still remain,—not a whit wiser than they were before; from which we infer that the *disguise* answered its purpose pretty well. . . .

It was rumored, a day or two after, that part of a chest has gone ashore at South Boston. A detachment of Whigs went over there, and looked up the fellow who had taken it in charge. Finding he had sold some of the tea, they made him give up the money, took possession of the residue of the chest, marched in triumphal procession back to the Common, and there set it off to the best advantage in a bonfire, just in front of Mr. Hancock's house, who (as Hewes says,) came to his front door to see it. The money went for what was popularly called "*ok-kuppee,*" just then the Indian translation of *grog*.

The inspection was rather close, indeed, for a long time. A January paper says—"Thursday last, several casks of tea, supposed to be *damaged*, were taken from Tileston's wharf, South End, and carried on a sled into King Street, where it was committed to the flames. . . ."

It was therefore, on the whole, and on all sides, a remarkably popular movement . . .

### QUESTIONS TO CONSIDER

1. How would you describe the Tea Party after reading Hewes' account?
2. Do you agree with Thatcher that the Tea Party was "a remarkably popular movement"? Why or why not?

# CHAPTER 7

# CREATING A NEW NATION, 1775–1788

## 7.1 FIRST CONTINENTAL CONGRESS, NEGOTIATIONS WITH GEORGE III (1775–1776)

The Declaration of Independence did not emerge from a vacuum. Instead, it came at the end of the First Continental Congress' negotiations with George III, as you will read in the following documents. In July 1775—a little over two months after the battles at Lexington and Concord—the First Continental Congress sent a petition to George III, often known as the "Olive Branch Petition," as an attempt to fend off war between the colonies and Britain. In response, George III issued a brief proclamation that declared the colonies to be in "open and avowed rebellion." After George's response, the Continental Congress began to formally consider declaring independence, and a committee eventually chose Thomas Jefferson to write the document. Jefferson's draft was debated and revised by the body for a two-week period and eventually passed on July 4, 1776.

### OLIVE BRANCH PETITION

MOST GRACIOUS SOVEREIGN,

We, your Majesty's faithful subjects of the colonies new Hampshire, Massachusetts bay, Rhode island and Providence Plantations, Connecticut, New York, New Jersey, Pennsylvania, the counties of New Castle, Kent, and Sussex, on Delaware, Maryland, Virginia, North Carolina, and South Carolina, in behalf of ourselves, and the inhabitants of these colonies, who have deputed us to represent them in general Congress, entreat your Majesty's gracious attention to this our humble petition.

The union between our Mother country and these colonies, and the energy of mild and just government, produced benefits so remarkably important, and afforded such an assurance of their permanency and increase, that the wonder and envy of other Nations were excited, while they beheld Great Britain riseing to a power the most extraordinary the world had ever known.

*Sources:* "Journals of the Continental Congress—Petition to the King; July 8, 1775," http://avalon.law.yale.edu/18th_century/contcong_07-08-75.asp (Accessed June 6, 2018); "By the King, A Proclamation, For Suppressing Rebellion and Sedition," https://www.archives.gov/historical-docs/todays-doc/?dod-date=823 (Accessed June 6, 2018); Julian P. Boyd, ed., *The Papers of Thomas Jefferson, Volume 1: 1760–1776* (Princeton: Princeton University Press, 1950), 423–427.

Her rivals, observing that there was no probability of this happy connexion being broken by civil dissensions, and apprehending its future effects, if left any longer undisturbed, resolved to prevent her receiving such continual and formidable accessions of wealth and strength, by checking the growth of these settlements from which they were to be derived.

In the prosecution of this attempt, events so unfavourable to the design took place, that every friend to the interests of Great Britain and these colonies, entertained pleasing and reasonable expectations of seeing an additional force and extension immediately given to the operations of the union hitherto experienced, by an enlargement of the dominions of the Crown, and the removal of ancient and warlike enemies to a greater distance.

At the conclusion, therefore, of the late war, the most glorious and advantageous that ever had been carried on by British arms, your loyal colonists having contributed to its success, by such repeated and strenuous exertions, as frequently procured them the distinguished approbation of your Majesty, of the late king, and of parliament, doubted not but that they should be permitted, with the rest of the empire, to share in the blessings of peace, and the emoluments of victory and conquest. While these recent and honorable acknowledgments of their merits remained on record in the journals and acts of that august legislature, the Parliament, undefaced by the imputation or even the suspicion of any offense, they were alarmed by a new system of statutes and regulations adopted for the administration of the colonies, that filled their minds with the most painful fears and jealousies; and, to their inexpressible astonishment, perceived the dangers of a foreign quarrel quickly succeeded by domestic dangers, in their judgment, of a more dreadful kind.

Nor were their anxieties alleviated by any tendency in this system to promote the welfare of the Mother country. For tho' its effects were more immediately felt by them, yet its influence appeared to be injurious to the commerce and prosperity of Great Britain.

We shall decline the ungrateful task of describing the irksome variety of artifices, practiced by many of your Majesty's Ministers, the delusive presences, fruitless terrors, and unavailing severities, that have, from time to time, been dealt out by them, in their attempts to execute this impolitic plan, or of traceing, thro'a series of years past, the progress of the unhappy differences between Great Britain and these colonies, which have flowed from this fatal source.

Your Majesty's Ministers, persevering in their measures, and proceeding to open hostilities for enforcing them, have compelled us to arm in our own defence, and have engaged us in a controversy so peculiarly abhorrent to the affections of your still faithful colonists, that when we consider whom we must oppose in this contest, and if it continues, what may be the consequences, our own particular misfortunes are accounted by us only as parts of our distress.

Knowing to what violent resentments and incurable animosities, civil discords are apt to exasperate and inflame the contending parties, we think ourselves required by indispensable obligations to Almighty God, to your Majesty, to our fellow subjects, and to ourselves, immediately to use all the means in our power, not incompatible with our safety, for stopping the further effusion of blood, and for averting the impending calamities that threaten the British Empire.

Thus called upon to address your Majesty on affairs of such moment to America, and probably to all your dominions, we are earnestly desirous of performing this office, with the utmost deference for your Majesty; and we therefore pray, that your royal magnanimity and benevolence may make the most favourable construction of our expressions on so uncommon an occasion. Could represent in their full force, the sentiments that agitate the minds of us your dutiful subjects, we are persuaded your Majesty would ascribe any seeming deviation from reverence in our language, and even in our conduct, not to any reprehensible intention, but to the impossibility of reconciling the usual appearances of respect, with a just attention to our own preservation against those artful and cruel enemies, who abuse your royal confidence and authority, for the purpose of effecting our destruction.

Attached to your Majesty's person, family, and government, with all devotion that principle and affection can inspire, connected with Great Britain by the strongest ties that can unite societies, and deploring every event that tends in any degree to weaken them, we solemnly assure your Majesty, that we not only most ardently desire the former harmony between her and these colonies may be restored, but that a concord may be established between them upon so firm a basis as to perpetuate its blessings, uninterrupted by any future dissensions, to succeeding generations in both countries, and to transmit your Majesty's Name to posterity, adorned with that signal and lasting glory, that has attended the memory of those illustrious personages, whose virtues and abilities have extricated states from dangerous convulsions, and, by securing happiness to others, have erected the most noble and durable monuments to their own fame.

We beg leave further to assure your Majesty, that notwithstanding the sufferings of your loyal colonists, during the course of the present controversy, our breasts retain too tender a regard for the kingdom from which we derive our origin, to request such a reconciliation as might in any manner be inconsistent with her dignity or her welfare. These, related as we are to her, honor and duty, as well as inclination, induce us to support and advance; and the apprehensions that now oppress our hearts with unspeakable grief, being once removed, your Majesty will find your faithful subjects on this continent ready and willing at all times, as they ever have been, with their lives and fortunes, to assert and maintain the rights and interests of your Majesty, and of our Mother country.

We, therefore, beseech your Majesty, that your royal authority and influence may be graciously interposed to procure us relief from our afflicting fears and jealousies, occasioned by the system before mentioned, and to settle peace through every part of your dominions, with all humility submitting to your Majesty's wise consideration whether it may not be expedient for facilitating those important purposes, that your Majesty be pleased to direct some mode, by which the united applications of your faithful colonists to the throne, in pursuance of their common councils, may be improved into a happy and permanent reconciliation; and that, in the mean time, measures may be taken for preventing the further destruction of the lives of your Majesty's subjects; and that such statutes as more immediately distress any of your Majesty's colonies may be repealed.

For by such arrangements as your Majesty's wisdom can form, for collecting the united sense of your American people, we are convinced your Majesty would receive such satisfactory proofs of the disposition of the colonists towards their sovereign and parent state, that the wished for opportunity would soon be restored to them, of evincing the sincerity of their professions, by every testimony of devotion becoming the most dutiful subjects, and the most affectionate colonists.

That your Majesty may enjoy a long and prosperous reign, and that your descendants may govern your dominions with honor to themselves and happiness to their subjects, is our sincere and fervent prayer.

## A ROYAL PROCLAMATION

WHEREAS many of Our Subjects in divers Parts of Our Colonies and Plantations in *North America*, milled by dangerous and ill-designing Men, and forgetting the Allegiance which they owe to the Power that has protected and sustained them, after various disorderly Acts committed in Disturbance of the Publick Peace, to the Obstruction of lawful Commerce, and to the Oppression of Our loyal subjects carrying on the fame, have at length proceeded to an open and avowed Rebellion, by arraying themselves in hostile Manner to withstand the Execution of the Law, and traitorously preparing, ordering, and levying War against Us. And whereas there is Reason to apprehend that such Rebellion hath been much promoted and encouraged by the traitorous Correspondence, Counseils, and Comfort of divers wicked and operate Persons within this Realm : To the End therefore that none of Our Subjects may neglect or violate their Duty through Ignorance thereof, or through any Doubt of the Protection which the Law will afford to their Loyalty and zeal ; We have thought fit, by and with the Advice of Our Privy Council, to issue this Our Royal Proclamation, hereby declaring that not only all Our Officers Civil and Military are obliged to exert their utmost Endeavours to suppress such Rebellion, and to being the Traitors to Justice ; but that all Our Subjects of this Realm and the Dominions thereunto belonging are bound by Law to be aiding and assisting in the Suppression of such Rebellion, and to disclose and make known all traitorous Conspiracies and Attempts against Us, Our Crown and Dignity ; And We do accordingly strictly charge and command all Our Officers as well Civil as Military, and all other Our obedient and loyal Subjects, to use their utmost Endeavours to withstand and suppress such Rebellion, and to disclose and make known all Treasons and traitorous Conspiracies which they shall know to be against Us, Our Crown and Dignity ; and for the purpose, that they transmit to One of Our Principal Secretaries of State, or other proper Officer, due and full Information of all Persons who shall be found carrying on Correspondence with, or in any Manner or Degree aiding or abetting the persons now in open Arms and Rebellion against Our Government within any of Our Colonies and Plantations in *North America*, is order to bring to condign Punishment to Authors, Perpetrators, and Abettors of such traitorous Designs.

## DECLARATION OF INDEPENDENCE

A Declaration of the Representatives of the United States of America, in General Congress assembled.

When in the course of human events it becomes necessary for a people to advance from that subordination in which they have hitherto remained, & to assume among the powers of the earth the equal & independent station to which the laws of nature & of nature's god entitle them, a decent respect to the opinions of mankind requires that they should declare the causes which impel them to the change.

We hold these truths to be sacred & undeniable; that all men are created equal & independant, that from that equal creation they derive rights inherent & inalienable, among which are the preservation of life, & liberty, & the pursuit of happiness; that to secure these ends, government shall become destructive of these ends, it is the right of the people to alter or to abolish it, & to institute new government, laying it's foundation on such principles & organizing it's powers in such form, as to them shall seem most likely to effect their safety & happiness. Prudence indeed will dictate that mankind are more disposed to suffer while evils are sufferable, than to right themselves by abolishing the forms to which they are accustomed. But when a long train of abuses & usurpations, begun at a distinguished period, & pursuing invariably the same object, evinces a design to subject them to arbitrary power, it is their right, it is their duty, to throw off such government & to provide new guards for their future security. such has been the patient sufferance of these

colonies; & such is now the necessity which constrains them to expunge their former systems of government. The history of his present majesty, is a history of unremitting injuries and usurpations, among which no one fact stands single or solitary to contradict the uniform tenor of the rest, all of which have in direct object the establishment of the absolute tyranny over these states. To prove this, let facts be submitted to a candid world, for the truth of which we pledge a faith yet unsullied by falsehood.

- He has refused his assent to laws the most wholesome and necessary for the public good:
- He has forbidden his governors to pass laws of immediate & pressing importance, unless suspended in their operation till his assent should be obtained; and when so suspended, he has neglected utterly to attend to them.
- He has refused to pass other laws for the accomodation of large districts of people unless those people would relinquish the right of representation, a right inestimable to them, & formidable to tyrants alone:
- He has dissolved Representative houses repeatedly & continually, for opposing with manly firmness his invasions on the rights of the people:
- He has refused for a long space of time to cause others to be elected, whereby the legislative powers, incapable of annihilation, have returned to the people at large for their exercise, the state remaining in the mean time exposed to all the dangers of invasion from without, & convulsions within:
- He has endeavored to prevent the population of these states; for that purpose obstructing the laws for naturalization of foreigners; refusing to pass others to encourage their migrations hither; & raising the conditions of new appropriations of lands:
- He has suffered the administration of justice totally to cease in some of these colonies, refusing his assent to laws for establishing judiciary powers:
- He has made our judges dependant on his will alone, for the tenure of their offices, and amount of their salaries:
- He has erected a multitude of new offices by a self-assumed power, & sent hither swarms of officers to harass our people & eat out their substance:

- He has kept among us in times of peace standing armies & superior to the civil power:
- He has combined with others to subject us to a jurisdiction foreign to our constitutions and unacknowledged by our laws; giving his assent to their pretended acts of legislation, for quartering large bodies of armed troops among us;
  - For protecting them by a mock-trial from punishment for any murders they should commit on the inhabitants of these states;
  - For cutting off our trade with all parts of the world;
  - For imposing taxes on us without our consent;
  - For depriving us of the benefits of trial by jury;
  - For transporting us beyond seas to be tried for pretended offences:
  - For taking away our charters, & altering fundamentally the forms of our governments;
  - For suspending our own legislatures & declaring themselves invested with power to legislate for us in all cases whatsoever:
- He has abdicated government here, withdrawing his governors, & declaring us out of his allegiance & protection:
- He has plundered our seas, ravaged our coasts, burnt our towns & destroyed the lives of our people:
- He is at this time transporting large armies of foreign mercenaries to compleat the works of death, desolation & tyranny, already begun with circumstances of cruelty & perfidy unworthy the head of a civilized nation:
- He has endeavored to bring on the inhabitants of our frontiers the merciless Indian savages, whose known rule of warfare is an undistinguished destruction of all ages, sexes, & conditions of existence:
- He has incited treasonable insurrections in our fellow-subjects, with the allurements of forfeiture & confiscation of our property:
- He has waged cruel war against human nature itself, violating it's most sacred rights of life & liberty in the persons of a distant people who never offended him, captivating & carrying them into slavery in another hemisphere, or to incur miserable death in their transportation thither. This piratical warfare, the opprobrium of *infidel* powers, is the warfare of the CHRISTIAN king of Great Britain. Determined to keep open a market where

MEN should be bought & sold, he has prostituted his negative for suppressing every legislative attempt to prohibit or to restrain this execrable commerce: and that this assemblage of horrors might want no fact of distinguished die, he is now exciting those very people to rise in arms among us, and to purchase that liberty of which *he* has deprived them, by murdering the people upon whom *he* also obtruded them; thus paying off former crimes committed against the *liberties* of one people, with crimes which he urges them to commit against the *lives* of another.

In every stage of these oppressions we have petitioned for redress in the most humble terms; our repeated petitions have been answered by repeated injury. A prince whose characters is thus marked by every act which may define a tyrant, is unfit to be the ruler of a people who mean to be free. Future ages will scarce believe that the hardiness of one man, adventured within the short compass of 12 years only, on so many acts of tyranny without a mask, over a people fostered & fixed in principles of liberty.

Nor have we been wanting in attentions to our British brethren. We have warned them from time to time of attempts by their legislature to extend a jurisdiction over these our states. We have reminded them of the circumstances of our emigration & settlement here, no one of which could warrant so strange a pretension: that these were effected at the expence of our own blood & treasure, unassisted by the wealth or the strength of Great Britain: That in constituting indeed our several forms of government, we had adopted one common king, thereby laying a foundation for perpetual league & amity with them: But that submission to their parliament was no part of our constitution, nor ever in idea, if history may be credited: And we appealed to their native justice & magnanimity, as well as to the ties of our common kindred to disavow these usurpations which were likely to interrupt our correspondence & connection. They too have been deaf to the voice of justice & of consanguinity, & when occasions have been given them, by the regular course of their laws, of removing from their councils the disturbers of our harmony, they have by their free election re-established them in power. At this very time too they are permitting their chief magistrate to send over not only soldiers of our common blood, but Scotch & foreign mercenaries to invade & deluge us in blood. These facts have given the last stab to agonizing affection, and manly spirit bids us to renounce for ever these unfeeling brethren. We must endeavor to forget our former love for them, and to hold them as we hold the rest of mankind, enemies in war, in peace friends. We might have been a free & a great people together; but a communication of grandeur & of freedom it seems is below their dignity. Be it so, since they will have it: the road to glory & happiness is open to us too; we will climb it in a separate state, and acquiesce in the necessity which pronounces our everlasting Adieu!

We therefore the representatives of the United States of America in General Congress assembled do, in the name & by authority of the good people of these states, reject and renounce all allegiance & subjection to the kings of Great Britain & all others who may hereafter claim by, through, or under them; we utterly dissolve & break off all political connection which may have heretofore subsisted between us & the people or parliament of Great Britain; and finally we do assert and declare these colonies to be free and independent states, and that as free & independent states they shall hereafter have power to levy war, conclude peace, contract alliances, establish commerce, & to do all other acts and things which independent states may of right do. And for the support of this declaration we mutually pledge to each other our lives, our futures, & our sacred honour.

**QUESTIONS TO CONSIDER**

1. How did the Olive Branch Petition differ from the Declaration of Independence in tone?
2. Does Jefferson's draft contain any statements that surprise you? If so, which ones?

# 7.2 CONTINENTAL CONGRESS, TORY ACT (1776)

Even before Jefferson began writing the Declaration of Independence, the First Continental Congress grew concerned with the "Tories" or loyalists, those Americans who supported the British crown, in their midst. The "Tory Act," passed on January 2, 1776, sought to codify measures to limit loyalist influence. The Tory Act, as you will read, also contained sections on British mistreatment of the American colonies and called for unity among the colonies themselves. Facing increasing abuse, loyalists left America in large numbers during the war. Some 60,000 to 70,000 free loyalists fled the colonies, primarily to Canada.

Whereas it has been represented to this Congress, that divers honest and well meaning, but uninformed people in these colonies, have by the art and address of ministerial agents, been deceived and drawn into erroneous opinions, respecting the American cause, and the probable issue of the present contest.

*Resolved*, That it be recommended to the several Committees, and other friends to American liberty in the said colonies, to treat all such persons with kindness and attention, to consider them as the inhabitants of a country determined to be free, and to view their errors as proceeding rather from want of information,

*Source:* "The Tory Act," https://www.loc.gov/item/90898112 (Accessed June 6, 2018).

than want of virtue or public spirit, to explain to them the origin, nature and extent of the present controversy, to acquaint them with the fate of the numerous petitions presented to his Majesty, as well by Assemblies as by Congress, humbly requesting the single favour of being heard, like all the others has proved unsuccessful; to unfold to them the various arts of administration to ensnare and enslave us, and the manner in which we have been cruelly driven to defend by arms those very rights, liberties and estates which we and our forefathers had so long enjoyed unmolested in the reigns of his present Majesty¢s predecessors. And it is hereby recommended to all Conventions and Assemblies in these colonies liberally to distribute among the people the Proceedings of this and the former Congress, the late speeches of the great patriots in bothe houses of parliament relative to American grievances, and such other pamphlets and papers as tend to elucidate the merits of the American cause. The Congress being fully persuaded that the more our right to the enjoyment of our antient liberties and privileges is examined, the more just and necessary our present opposition to ministerial tyranny will appear.

And with respect to all such unworthy Americans, as regardless of their duty to their creator, their country, and their posterity, have taken part with our oppressors, and influenced by the hope or possession of ignominious rewards, strive to recommend themselves to the bounty of administration by misrepresenting and traducing the conduct and principles to the friends of American liberty, and opposing every measure formed for its preservation and security.

*Resolved,* that it be recommended to the different Assemblies, convention, and committees or Councils of Safety in the United Colonies, by the most speedy and effectual measures to frustrate the mischievous machinations, and restrain the wicked practices of these men. And it is the opinion of this congress that they ought to be disarmed, and the more dangerous among them either kept in safe custody, or bound with sufficient sureties to their good behavior.

And in order that the said Assemblies, Conventions, Committees or councils of Safety may be enabled with greater ease and facility to carry this Resolution into execution, *Resolved,* That they be authorized to call to their aid whatever Continental troops stationed in or

near their respective colonies, may be conveniently spared from their more immediate duty; and the commanding officers of such troops are hereby directed to afford the said Assemblies, Conventions, committees or Councils of Safety, all such assistance in executing this resolution as they may require, and which, consistent with the good of the service, may be supplied.

*Resolved,* That all detachments of Continental troops which may be ordered on the business in the a foregoing resolution mentioned, be, while so employed, under the direction and control of the Assemblies Conventions, Committees, or Councils of Safety aforesaid.

*Resolved,* That it be recommended to all the United Colonies to aid each other (on request from their respective Assemblies Convention Committees or Councils of Safety, and county committees) on every emergency, and to cultivate, cherish and increase the present happy and necessary union, by a continual interchange of mutual good offices.

And whereas the execrable barbarity with which this unhappy war has been conducted on the part of our enemies, such as burning our defenseless towns and villages, exposing their inhabitants, without regard to sex or age, to all the miseries which loss of property, the rigour of the season, and inhuman devastation can inflict, exciting domestic insurrection and murders, bribing the Savages to desolate our frontiers, and casting such of us, as the fortune of war has put into their power, into gaols there to languish in irons and want; compelling the inhabitants of Boston, in violation of the treaty, to remain confined within the town, exposed to the insolence of the soldiery, and other enormities, as the mention of which decency and humanity will forever blush, may justly provoke the inhabitants of these colonies to retaliation.

*Resolved.* That it be recommended to them to continue mindful that humanity ought to distinguish the cruelty should find no admission among a free people, and to take care that no page in the annals of America be stained by a recital of any action which justice or christianity may condemn, and to rest assured that whenever retaliation may be necessary or tend to their security, this Congress will undertake the disagreeable task.

*Resolved,* That the Assemblies, Conventions, or Committees or Councils of safety be requested forthwith to transmit to this Congress copies of all the petitions, memorials, and remonstrances which have been by their respective Colonies presented to the Throne, or either house of Parliament, since the year 1762, and that they also inform this Congress whether any and what answers were given to them.

# 7.3 "THE SENTIMENTS OF AN AMERICAN WOMAN" (1780)

As the American Revolution progressed, the Continental Army encountered severe supply shortages. In response, different private organizations tried to answer the call and support the army. Esther de Berdt Reed led one such effort in Philadelphia. The wife of well-known lawyer Joseph Reed and a member of the Philadelphia elite, she formed the Ladies Association of Philadelphia as a fundraising vehicle for the army. Reed found great success in doing so—her group raised thousands of dollars by going door-to-door to ask for donations. "The Sentiments of an American Woman," probably written by Reed, aimed to help the fundraising effort. In it, the author places the women's effort in a historical context of female activism, argues for the need to help the army, and sets out a series of steps to be taken to do so. Though Reed died in 1780 at age 34, her organization would continue to raise funds during the remainder of the war.

ON the commencement of actual war, the Women of America manifested a firm resolution to contribute as much as could depend on them, to the deliverance of their country. Animated by the purest patriotism, they are sensible of sorrow at this day, in not offering more than barren wishes for the success of so glorious a revolution. They aspire to render themselves more really useful; and this sentiment is universal from the north to the south of the Thirteen United States. Our ambition is kindled by the same of those heroines of antiquity, who have rendered their sex illustrious, and have proved to the universe, that, if the weakness of our Constitution, if opinion and manners did not forbid us to march to glory by the same paths as the Men, we should at least equal, and sometimes surpass them in our love for the public good. I glory in all that which my sex has done great and commendable. I call to mind with enthusiasm and with admiration, all those acts of courage, of constancy and patriotism, which history has transmitted to us: The people favoured by Heaven, preserved from destruction by the virtues, the zeal and the resolution of Deborah, of Judith, of Esther! The fortitude of the mother of the Massachabees, in giving up her sons to die before her eyes: Rome saved from the fury of a victorious enemy by the efforts of Volumnia, and other Roman Ladies: So many famous sieges where the Women have been seen forgetting the weakness of their sex, building new walls, digging trenches with their feeble hands, furnishing arms to their defenders, they themselves darting the missile weapons on the enemy, resigning the ornaments of their apparel, and

*Source:* "The Sentiments of an American Woman," https://www.loc.gov/resource/rbpe.14600300/ (Accessed June 6, 2018).

their fortune, to fill the public treasury, and to hasten the deliverance of their country; burying themselves under its ruins, throwing themselves into the flames rather than submit to the disgrace of humiliation before a proud enemy.

Born for liberty, disdaining to bear the irons of a tyrannic Government, we associate ourselves to the grandeur to those Sovereigns, cherished and revered, who have held with so much splendour the scepter of the greatest Sates, The Batildas, the Elizabeths, the Maries, the Catharines, who have extended the empire of liberty, and contented to reign by sweetness and justice, have broken the chains of slavery, forged by tyrants in the times of ignorance and barbarity. The Spanish Women, do they not make, at this moment, the most patriotic sacrifices, to increase the means of victory in the hands of their Sovereign. He is a friend to the French Nation. They are our allies. We call to mind, doubly interested, that it was a French Maid who kindled up amongst her fellow-citizens, the flame of patriotism buried under long misfurtunes: It was the Maid of Orleans who drove from the kingdom of France the ancestors of those same British, whose odious yoke we have just shaken off; and whom it is necessary that we drive from these Continent.

But I must limit myself to the recollection of this small number of achievements. Who knows if persons disposed to censure, and sometimes too severely with regard to us, may not disapprove our appearing acquainted even with the actions of which our sex boasts? We are at least certain, that he cannot be a good citizen who will not applaud our efforts for the relief of the armies which defend our lives, our possessions, our liberty? The situation of our soldiery has been represented to me; the evils inseparable from war, and the firm and generous spirit which has enabled them to support these. But it has been said, that they may apprehend, that, in the course of a long war, the view of their distresses may be lost, and their services be forgotten. Forgotten! Never; I can answer in the name of all my sex. Brave Americans, your disinterestedness, your courage, and your constancy will always be dear to America, as long as she shall preserve her virtue.

We know that at a distance from the theatre of war, if we enjoy tranquility, it is the fruit of your watchings, your labours, your dangers. If I live happy in the midst of my family; if my husband cultivates his field, and reaps his harvest in peace; if, surrounded with my children, I myself nourish the youngest, and press it to my bosom, without being afraid of seeing myself separated from it, by a ferocious enemy; if the house in which we dwell; if our barns, our orchards are safe at the present time from the hands of those incendiaries, it is to you that we owe it. And shall we hesitate to evidence to you our gratitude? Shall we hesitate to wear a cloathing more simple; hair dressed less elegant, while at the price of this small privation, we shall deserve your benedictions. Who, amongst us, will not renounce with the highest pleasure, those vain ornaments, when she shall consider that the valiant defenders of America will be able to draw some advantage from the money which she may have laid out in these; that they will be better defended from the rigours of the seasons, that after their painful toils, they will receive some extraordinary and unexpected relief; that these presents will perhaps be valued by them at a greater price, when they will have it in their power to say: *This is the offering of the Ladies.* The time is arrived to display the same sentiments which animated us at the beginning of the revolution, when we renounced the use of teas, however agreeable to our taste, rather than receive them from our persecutors; when we made it appear to them that we placed former necessaries in the rank of superfluities, when our liberty was interested; when our republican and laborious hands spun the flax, prepared the linen intended for the use of our soldiers; when exiles and fugitives we supported with courage all the evils which are the concomitants of war. Let us not lose a moment; let us be engaged to offer the homage of our gratitude at the altar of military valour, and you, our brave deliverers, while mercenary slaves combat to cause you to share with them, the irons with which they are loaded, receive with a free hand our offering, the purest which can be presented to your virtue.

*By An AMERICAN WOMAN.*

*IDEAS, relative to the manner of forwarding to the American Soldiers, the presents of the American Women.*

ALL plans are eligible, when doing good is the object; there is however one more preferable; and when the operation is extensive, we cannot give it too much uniformity. On the other side, the wants of our army do not permit the slowness of an ordinary path. It is not in one month, nor in eight days, that we would relieve our soldiery. It is immediately, and our impatience does not permit us to proceed by the long circuitry of collectors, receivers and treasurers. As my idea with regard to this, have been approved by some Ladies of my friends, I will explain them here; every other person will not be less at liberty to prepare and to adopt a different plan.

1st. All Women and Girls will be received without exception, to present their patriotic offering; and, as it is absolutely voluntary, every one will regulate it according to her ability, and her disposition. The shilling offered by the Widow of the young girl, will be received as well as the most considerable sums presented by the Women who have the happiness to join to their patriotism, greater means to be useful.

2d. A Lady chosen by the others in each county, shall be the Treasuress; and to render her task more simple, and more easy, she will not receive but determinate sums, in a round number, from twenty hard dollars to any greater sum. The exchange forty dollars in paper for one dollar in specie.

It is hoped that here will not be one Woman who will not with pleasure charge herself with the embarrassment which will attend so honorable an operation.

3d. The Women who shall not be in a condition to send twenty dollars in specie, or above, will join in as great a number as will be necessary to make this or any greater sum, and one amongst them will carry it, or cause it to be sent to the Treasuress.

4th. The Treasuress of the county will receive the money, and will keep a register, writing the sums in her book, and causing it to be signed at the side of the whole by the person who has presented it.

5th. When several Women shall join together to make a total sum of twenty dollars or more, she amongst them who shall have the charge to carry it to the Treasuress, will make mention of all their names on the register, if her associates shall have so directed her; those whose choice it shall be, will have the liberty to remain unknown.

6th. As soon as the Treasuress of the county shall judge, that the sums which she shall have received, deserve to be sent to their destination, she will cause them to be presented with the lists, to the wife of the Governor or President of the State, who will be the Treasuress-General of the State; and she will cause it to be set down

in her register, and have it sent to Mistress Washington. If the Governor or President are unmarried, all will address themselves to the wife of the Vice-President, if there is one, or of the Chief-justice, &c.

7th. Women settled in the distant parts of the country, and not chusing for any particular reason as for the sake of greater expedition, to remit their Capital to the Treasuress, may send it directly to the wife of the Governor, or President, &c, or to Mistress Washington, who, if she shall judge necessary, will in a short answer to the sender, acquaint her with the reception of it.

8th. As Mrs. Washington may be absent from the camp when the greater part of the banks shall be sent there the American Women considering, that General Washington is the Father and Friend of the Soldiery; that he is himself, the first Soldier of the Republic, and that their offering will be received at its destination, as soon as it shall come to his hands, they will pray him, to take the charge of receiving it, in the absence of Mrs. Washington.

9th. General Washington will dispose of this fund in the manner that he shall judge most advantageous to the Soldiery. The American Women desire only that it may not be considered as to be employed, to procure to the army, the objects of subsistence, arms or clothing, which are due to them by the Continent. It is an extraordinary bounty intended to render the condition of the Soldier more pleasant, and not to hold place of the things which they ought to receive from the Congress, or from the States.

10th. If the General judges necessary, he will publish at the end of a certain time, an amount of that which shall have been received from each particular State.

11th. The Women who shall send their offerings, will have in their choice to conceal or to give their names; and if it shall be thought proper, on a fit occasion, to publish one day the lists, they only, who Shall consent, shall be named; when with regard to the sums sent, there will be no mention made, if they so desire it.

### QUESTIONS TO CONSIDER

1. Why did Reed use historical examples at the beginning of the document?
2. How does the author make her case for the need to support the army? Is it persuasive? Is the document revolutionary?

# 7.4 THOMAS JEFFERSON AND GEORGE WASHINGTON ON SHAYS' REBELLION (1787)

Shays' Rebellion was the first test of the nascent American republic and its governing document: the Articles of Confederation. During 1786 and 1787, Daniel Shays, a Revolutionary War veteran, amassed a militia of thousands of farmers in western Massachusetts. Enraged by policies that forced farmers to repay debts in scarce hard currency, which led to property seizures, Shays' army attacked a U.S. armory at Springfield, Massachusetts, in 1787, in an attempt to take the weapons stored there. Though the attack was unsuccessful, Shays' Rebellion profoundly worried colonial leaders. Because the Articles of Confederation did not allow a centralized monetary policy or a centralized army for common defense, the rebellion spurred colonial leaders to rethink their strategy and eventually ratify the significantly stronger U.S. Constitution. The following letters come from two colonial leaders, Thomas Jefferson and George Washington, who had different reactions to Shays' Rebellion. In Jefferson's letter, he speculates on the beneficial effects of the rebellion and then discusses the need for the United States to contest Spanish influence in the Southeast. In Washington's letter, he laments the effects of the rebellion. Pay careful attention to those differences.

## FROM THOMAS JEFFERSON TO JAMES MADISON, 30 JANUARY 1787

DEAR SIR

My last to you was of the 16th of Dec. since which I have received yours of Nov. 25. and Dec. 4. which afforded me, as your letters always do, a treat on matters public, individual and oeconomical. I am impatient to learn your sentiments on the late troubles in the Eastern states. So far as I have yet seen, they do not appear to threaten serious consequences. Those states have suffered by the stoppage of the channels of their commerce, which have not yet found other issues. This must render money scarce, and make the people uneasy. This uneasiness has produced acts absolutely unjustifiable: but I hope they will provoke no severities from their governments. A consciousness of those in power that their administration of the public affairs has been honest, may perhaps produce too great a degree of indignation: and those characters wherein fear predominates over hope may apprehend too much from these instances of irregularity. They may conclude too hastily that nature has formed man insusceptible of any other government but that of force, a conclusion not founded in truth, nor experience. Societies exist under three forms sufficiently distinguishable. 1. Without government, as among our Indians. 2. Under governments wherein the will of every one has a just influence, as is the case in England in a slight degree, and in our states in a great one. 3. Under governments of force: as is the case in all other monarchies and in most of the other republics. To have an idea of the curse of existence under these last, they must be seen. It is a government of wolves over sheep. It is a problem, not clear in my mind, that the 1st. condition is not the best. But I believe it to be inconsistent with any great degree of population. The second state has a great deal of good in it. The mass of mankind under that enjoys a precious degree of liberty and happiness. It has it's evils too: the principal of which is the turbulence to which

*Sources:* "Thomas Jefferson to James Madison, 30 January 1787," https://founders.archives.gov/documents/Jefferson/01-11-02-0095 (Accessed June 6, 2018); George Washington to Henry Lee, Jr., 31 October 1786," https://founders.archives.gov/documents/Washington/04-04-02-0286 (Accessed June 6, 2018).

it is subject. But weigh this against the oppressions of monarchy, and it becomes nothing. Malo periculosam, libertatem quam quietam servitutem. Even this evil is productive of good. It prevents the degeneracy of government, and nourishes a general attention to the public affairs. I hold it that a little rebellion now and then is a good thing, and as necessary in the political world as storms in the physical. Unsuccesful rebellions indeed generally establish the incroachments on the rights of the people which have produced them. An observation of this truth should render honest republican governors so mild in their punishment of rebellions, as not to discourage them too much. It is a medecine necessary for the sound health of government. If these transactions give me no uneasiness, I feel very differently at another peice of intelligence, to wit, the possibility that the navigation of the Missisipi may be abandoned to Spain. I never had any interest Westward of the Alleghaney; and I never will have any. But I have had great opportunities of knowing the character of the people who inhabit that country. And I will venture to say that the act which abandons the navigation of the Missisipi is an act of separation between the Eastern and Western country. It is a relinquishment of five parts out of eight of the territory of the United States, an abandonment of the fairest subject for the paiment of our public debts, and the chaining those debts on our own necks in perpetuum. I have the utmost confidence in the honest intentions of those who concur in this measure; but I lament their want of acquaintance with the character and physical advantages of the people who, right or wrong, will suppose their interests sacrificed on this occasion to the contrary interests of that part of the confederacy in possession of present power. If they declare themselves a separate people, we are incapable of a single effort to retain them. Our citizens can never be induced, either as militia or as souldiers, to go there to cut the throats of their own brothers and sons, or rather to be themselves the subjects instead of the perpetrators of the parricide. Nor would that country quit the cost of being retained against the will of it's inhabitants, could it be done. But it cannot be done. They are able already to rescue the navigation of the Missisipi out of the hands of Spain, and to add New Orleans to their own territory. They will be joined by the inhabitants of Louisiana. This will bring on a war between them and Spain; and that will produce

the question with us whether it will not be worth our while to become parties with them in the war, in order to reunite them with us, and thus correct our error? And were I to permit my forebodings to go one step further, I should predict that the inhabitants of the U.S. would force their rulers to take the affirmative of that question. I wish I may be mistaken in all these opinions. . . .

### FROM GEORGE WASHINGTON TO HENRY LEE, JR., 31 OCTOBER 1786

Dear Sir,

I am indebted to you for your several favors of the 1st 11th & 17th instt, and shall reply to them in the order of their dates: But first let me thank you for the interesting communications imparted in them.

The picture which you have drawn, & the accts which are published, of the commotions & temper of numerous bodies in the Eastern States, are equally to be lamented and deprecated. They exhibit a melancholy proof of what our trans atlantic foe have predicted; and of another thing perhaps, which is still more to be regretted, and is yet more unaccountable; that mankind left to themselves are unfit for their own government. I am mortified beyond expression whenever I view the clouds which have spread over the brightest morn that ever dawned upon any Country. In a word, I am lost in amazement, when I behold what intriegueing; the interested views of desperate characters; Jealousy; & ignorance of the Minor part, are capable of effecting as a scurge on the major part of our fellow citizens of the Union: for it is hardly to be imagined that the great body of the people tho' they will not act can be so enveloped in darkness, or short sighted as not to see the rays of a distant sun through all this mist of intoxication & folly.

You talk, my good Sir, of employing influence to appease the tumults in Massachusetts—I know not where that influence is to be found; and if attainable, that it would be a proper remedy for the disorders. Influence is no government. Let us have one by which our lives, liberties, and properties will be secured, or let us know the worst at once. Under these impressions, my humble opinion is, that there is a call for decision. Know precisely what the Insurgents aim at. If they have real grievances, redress them, *if possible,* or acknowledge the justice of their complaints and your inability of doing it, in the present moment. If they have not, employ the force of government against them at once. If this is inadequate, *all* will be convinced that the superstructure is bad, or wants support. To be more exposed in the eyes of the world & more contemptible than we already are, is hardly possible. To delay one of the other of these, is to exasperate in one case, and to give confidence in the other; and will add to their numbers; for like Snow-balls, such bodies encrease by every movement, unless there is something in the way to obstruct, & crumble them before the weight is too great & irrisistable.

These are my sentiments. Precedents are dangerous things. Let the reins of government then be braced in time & held with a steady hand; & every violation of the constitution be reprehended. If defective, let it be amended, but not suffered to be trampled on whilst it has an existence. . . .

**QUESTIONS TO CONSIDER**

1. How does each man support his case?
2. Which case is more persuasive to you?

# 7.5 JAMES MADISON, EXCERPT FROM "FEDERALIST 10" (1787)

In September 1787, the Constitutional Convention ratified the U.S. Constitution and sent it to the states for their ratification. Legislatures in nine states needed to approve the document for it to become law. New York, formerly a hotbed of loyalist activity, seemed to be a crucial state from which to secure ratification. Anti-Federalists, those who opposed ratification, thus broadcast a series of letters and articles denouncing the document. In response, Alexander Hamilton recruited two other Federalists, John Jay and James Madison, to write a series of eight-five public essays supporting the document. While Hamilton wrote fifty-one of the articles, Madison's essay 'Federalist 10," published on November 23, 1787, remains the best known. In it, Madison defended the Constitution as a means to guard against harmful "factions." New York eventually ratified the Constitution on July 26, 1788.

To the People of the State of New York:

AMONG the numerous advantages promised by a well constructed Union, none deserves to be more accurately developed than its tendency to break and control the violence of faction. The friend of popular governments never finds himself so much alarmed for their character and fate, as when he contemplates their propensity to this dangerous vice. He will not fail, therefore, to set a due value on any plan which, without violating the principles to which he is attached, provides a proper cure for it. The instability, injustice, and confusion introduced into the public councils, have, in truth, been the mortal diseases under which popular governments have everywhere perished; as they continue to be the favorite and fruitful topics from which the adversaries to liberty derive their most specious declamations. The valuable improvements made by the American constitutions on the popular models, both ancient and modern, cannot certainly be too much admired; but it would be an unwarrantable partiality, to contend that they have as effectually obviated the danger on this side, as was wished and expected. Complaints are everywhere heard

*Source:* Alexander Hamilton, John Jay, and James Madison, *The Federalist Papers* (Urbana Champaign: Project Gutenberg, 2009).

from our most considerate and virtuous citizens, equally the friends of public and private faith, and of public and personal liberty, that our governments are too unstable, that the public good is disregarded in the conflicts of rival parties, and that measures are too often decided, not according to the rules of justice and the rights of the minor party, but by the superior force of an interested and overbearing majority. However anxiously we may wish that these complaints had no foundation, the evidence, of known facts will not permit us to deny that they are in some degree true. It will be found, indeed, on a candid review of our situation, that some of the distresses under which we labor have been erroneously charged on the operation of our governments; but it will be found, at the same time, that other causes will not alone account for many of our heaviest misfortunes; and, particularly, for that prevailing and increasing distrust of public engagements, and alarm for private rights, which are echoed from one end of the continent to the other. These must be chiefly, if not wholly, effects of the unsteadiness and injustice with which a factious spirit has tainted our public administrations.

By a faction, I understand a number of citizens, whether amounting to a majority or a minority of the whole, who are united and actuated by some common impulse of passion, or of interest, adversed to the rights of other citizens, or to the permanent and aggregate interests of the community.

There are two methods of curing the mischiefs of faction: the one, by removing its causes; the other, by controlling its effects.

There are again two methods of removing the causes of faction: the one, by destroying the liberty which is essential to its existence; the other, by giving to every citizen the same opinions, the same passions, and the same interests.

It could never be more truly said than of the first remedy, that it was worse than the disease. Liberty is to faction what air is to fire, an aliment without which it instantly expires. But it could not be less folly to abolish liberty, which is essential to political life, because it nourishes faction, than it would be to wish the annihilation of air, which is essential to animal life, because it imparts to fire its destructive agency.

The second expedient is as impracticable as the first would be unwise. As long as the reason of man continues fallible, and he is at liberty to exercise it, different opinions will be formed. As long as the connection subsists between his reason and his self-love, his opinions and his passions will have a reciprocal influence on each other; and the former will be objects to which the latter will attach themselves. The diversity in the faculties of men, from which the rights of property originate, is not less an insuperable obstacle to a uniformity of interests. The protection of these faculties is the first object of government. From the protection of different and unequal faculties of acquiring property, the possession of different degrees and kinds of property immediately results; and from the influence of these on the sentiments and views of the respective proprietors, ensues a division of the society into different interests and parties.

The latent causes of faction are thus sown in the nature of man; and we see them everywhere brought into different degrees of activity, according to the different circumstances of civil society. A zeal for different opinions concerning religion, concerning government, and many other points, as well of speculation as of practice; an attachment to different leaders ambitiously contending for pre-eminence and power; or to persons of other descriptions whose fortunes have been interesting to the human passions, have, in turn, divided mankind into parties, inflamed them with mutual animosity, and rendered them much more disposed to vex and oppress each other than to co-operate for their common good. So strong is this propensity of mankind to fall into mutual animosities, that where no substantial occasion presents itself, the most frivolous and fanciful distinctions have been sufficient to kindle their unfriendly passions and excite their most violent conflicts. But the most common and durable source of factions has been the various and unequal distribution of property. Those who hold and those who are without property have ever formed distinct interests in society. Those who are creditors, and those who are debtors, fall under a like discrimination. A landed interest, a manufacturing interest, a mercantile interest, a moneyed interest, with many lesser interests, grow up of necessity in civilized nations, and divide them into different classes, actuated by different sentiments and views. The regulation of these various and interfering interests forms the principal task of modern legislation, and involves the spirit of party and faction in the necessary and ordinary operations of the government.

No man is allowed to be a judge in his own cause, because his interest would certainly bias his judgment, and, not improbably, corrupt his integrity. With equal, nay with greater reason, a body of men are unfit to be both judges and parties at the same time; yet what are many of the most important acts of legislation, but so many judicial determinations, not indeed concerning the rights of single persons, but concerning the rights of large bodies of citizens? And what are the different classes of legislators but advocates and parties to the causes which they determine? Is a law proposed concerning private debts? It is a question to which the creditors are parties on one side and the debtors on the other. Justice ought to hold the balance between them. Yet the parties are, and must be, themselves the judges; and the most numerous party, or, in other words, the most powerful faction must be expected to prevail. Shall domestic manufactures be encouraged, and in what degree, by restrictions on foreign manufactures? are questions which would be differently decided by the landed and the manufacturing classes, and probably by neither with a sole regard to justice and the public good. The apportionment of taxes on the various descriptions of property is an act which seems to require the most exact impartiality; yet there is, perhaps, no legislative act in which greater opportunity and temptation are given to a predominant party to trample on the rules of justice. Every shilling with which they overburden the inferior number, is a shilling saved to their own pockets.

It is in vain to say that enlightened statesmen will be able to adjust these clashing interests, and render them all subservient to the public good. Enlightened statesmen will not always be at the helm. Nor, in many cases, can such an adjustment be made at all without taking into view indirect and remote considerations, which will rarely prevail over the immediate interest which one party may find in disregarding the rights of another or the good of the whole.

The inference to which we are brought is, that the CAUSES of faction cannot be removed, and that relief is only to be sought in the means of controlling its EFFECTS.

If a faction consists of less than a majority, relief is supplied by the republican principle, which enables the majority to defeat its sinister views by regular vote. It may clog the administration, it may convulse the society; but it will be unable to execute and mask its violence under the forms of the Constitution. When a majority is included in a faction, the form of popular government, on the other hand, enables it to sacrifice

to its ruling passion or interest both the public good and the rights of other citizens. To secure the public good and private rights against the danger of such a faction, and at the same time to preserve the spirit and the form of popular government, is then the great object to which our inquiries are directed. Let me add that it is the great desideratum by which this form of government can be rescued from the opprobrium under which it has so long labored, and be recommended to the esteem and adoption of mankind.

By what means is this object attainable? Evidently by one of two only. Either the existence of the same passion or interest in a majority at the same time must be prevented, or the majority, having such coexistent passion or interest, must be rendered, by their number and local situation, unable to concert and carry into effect schemes of oppression. If the impulse and the opportunity be suffered to coincide, we well know that neither moral nor religious motives can be relied on as an adequate control. They are not found to be such on the injustice and violence of individuals, and lose their efficacy in proportion to the number combined together, that is, in proportion as their efficacy becomes needful.

From this view of the subject it may be concluded that a pure democracy, by which I mean a society consisting of a small number of citizens, who assemble and administer the government in person, can admit of no cure for the mischiefs of faction. A common passion or interest will, in almost every case, be felt by a majority of the whole; a communication and concert result from the form of government itself; and there is nothing to check the inducements to sacrifice the weaker party or an obnoxious individual. Hence it is that such democracies have ever been spectacles of turbulence and contention; have ever been found incompatible with personal security or the rights of property; and have in general been as short in their lives as they have been violent in their deaths. Theoretic politicians, who have patronized this species of government, have erroneously supposed that by reducing mankind to a perfect equality in their political rights, they would, at the same time, be perfectly equalized and assimilated in their possessions, their opinions, and their passions.

A republic, by which I mean a government in which the scheme of representation takes place, opens a different prospect, and promises the cure for which we are seeking. Let us examine the points in which it varies from pure democracy, and we shall comprehend both the nature of the cure and the efficacy which it must derive from the Union.

The two great points of difference between a democracy and a republic are: first, the delegation of the government, in the latter, to a small number of citizens elected by the rest; secondly, the greater number of citizens, and greater sphere of country, over which the latter may be extended.

The effect of the first difference is, on the one hand, to refine and enlarge the public views, by passing them through the medium of a chosen body of citizens, whose wisdom may best discern the true interest of their country, and whose patriotism and love of justice will be least likely to sacrifice it to temporary or partial considerations. Under such a regulation, it may well happen that the public voice, pronounced by the representatives of the people, will be more consonant to the public good than if pronounced by the people themselves, convened for the purpose. On the other hand, the effect may be inverted. Men of factious tempers, of local prejudices, or of sinister designs, may, by intrigue, by corruption, or by other means, first obtain the suffrages, and then betray the interests, of the people. The question resulting is, whether small or extensive republics are more favorable to the election of proper guardians of the public weal; and it is clearly decided in favor of the latter by two obvious considerations:

In the first place, it is to be remarked that, however small the republic may be, the representatives must be raised to a certain number, in order to guard against the cabals of a few; and that, however large it may be, they must be limited to a certain number, in order to guard against the confusion of a multitude. Hence, the number of representatives in the two cases not being in proportion to that of the two constituents, and being proportionally greater in the small republic, it follows that, if the proportion of fit characters be not less in the large than in the small republic, the former will present a greater option, and consequently a greater probability of a fit choice.

In the next place, as each representative will be chosen by a greater number of citizens in the large than in the small republic, it will be more difficult for unworthy candidates to practice with success the vicious arts by which elections are too often carried; and the suffrages of the people being more free, will be more likely to centre in men who possess the most attractive merit and the most diffusive and established characters.

It must be confessed that in this, as in most other cases, there is a mean, on both sides of which inconveniences will be found to lie. By enlarging too much the number of electors, you render the representatives too little acquainted with all their local circumstances and lesser interests; as by reducing it too much, you render him unduly attached to these, and too little fit to comprehend and pursue great and national objects. The federal Constitution forms a happy combination in this respect; the great and aggregate interests being referred to the national, the local and particular to the State legislatures.

The other point of difference is, the greater number of citizens and extent of territory which may be brought within the compass of republican than of democratic government; and it is this circumstance principally which renders factious combinations less to be dreaded in the former than in the latter. The smaller the society, the fewer probably will be the distinct parties and interests composing it; the fewer the distinct parties and interests, the more frequently will a majority be found of the same party; and the smaller the number of individuals composing a majority, and the smaller the compass within which they are placed, the more easily will they concert and execute their plans of oppression. Extend the sphere, and you take in a greater variety of parties and interests; you make it less probable that a majority of the whole will have a common motive to invade the rights of other citizens; or if such a common motive exists, it will be more difficult for all who feel it to discover their own strength, and to act in unison with each other. Besides other impediments, it may be remarked that, where there is a consciousness of unjust or dishonorable purposes, communication is always checked by distrust in proportion to the number whose concurrence is necessary.

Hence, it clearly appears, that the same advantage which a republic has over a democracy, in controlling the effects of faction, is enjoyed by a large over a small republic,—is enjoyed by the Union over the States composing it. Does the advantage consist in the substitution of representatives whose enlightened views and virtuous sentiments render them superior to local prejudices and schemes of injustice? It will not be denied that the representation of the Union will be most likely to possess these requisite endowments. Does it consist in the greater security afforded by a greater variety of parties, against the event of any one party being able to outnumber and oppress the rest? In an equal degree does the increased variety of parties comprised within the Union, increase this security. Does it, in fine, consist in the greater obstacles opposed to the concert and accomplishment of the secret wishes of an unjust and interested majority? Here, again, the extent of the Union gives it the most palpable advantage.

The influence of factious leaders may kindle a flame within their particular States, but will be unable to spread a general conflagration through the other States. A religious sect may degenerate into a political faction in a part of the Confederacy; but the variety of sects dispersed over the entire face of it must secure the national councils against any danger from that source. A rage for paper money, for an abolition of debts, for an equal division of property, or for any other improper or wicked project, will be less apt to pervade the whole body of the Union than a particular member of it; in the same proportion as such a malady is more likely to taint a particular county or district, than an entire State.

In the extent and proper structure of the Union, therefore, we behold a republican remedy for the diseases most incident to republican government. And according to the degree of pleasure and pride we feel in being republicans, ought to be our zeal in cherishing the spirit and supporting the character of Federalists.

### QUESTIONS TO CONSIDER

1. How does Madison define a "faction"?
2. How, in Madison's argument, would the Constitution guard against the influence of factions? Do you find the argument convincing?

# 7.6 JOSEPH PLUMB MARTIN, EXCERPT FROM *A NARRATIVE OF SOME OF THE ADVENTURES, DANGERS AND SUFFERINGS OF A REVOLUTIONARY SOLDIER* (1830)

The American Revolution was a difficult experience for many of the common soldiers who fought in it. They had to contend with brutal cold, limited supplies, and generally poor conditions. Joseph Plumb Martin's account vividly illustrates the travails of a Continental Army soldier. Martin, who joined the army at the age of 15, wrote a memoir in the 1820s that mainly focused on his day-to-day life. In the following excerpt, Martin describes his life in camp and the experience of being under artillery bombardment while defending a fort.

Our batteries were nothing more than old spars and timber laid up in parallel lines and filled between with mud and dirt. The British batteries in the course of the day would nearly level our works, and we were, like the beaver, obliged to repair our dams in the night. During the whole night, at intervals of a quarter or half an hour, the enemy would let off all their pieces, and although we had sentinels to watch them and at every flash of their guns to cry, "a shot," upon hearing which everyone endeavored to take care of himself, yet they would ever and anon, in spite of our precaution, cut up some of us . . .

It was utterly impossible to lie down to get any rest or sleep on account of the mud, if the enemy's shot

*Source:* Joseph Plumb Martin, *A Narrative of Some of the Adventures, Dangers and Sufferings of a Revolutionary Soldier; Interspersed with Anecdotes of Incidents that Occurred within His Own Observation* (Hallowell, ME: Glazier, Masters & Co., 1830), pp. 165–175, http://www.urhistory.org/march/other/martindiary.htm (Accessed **June 6, 2018**).

would have suffered [allowed] us to do so. Sometime some of the men, when overcome with fatigue and want of sleep, would slip away into the barracks to catch a nap of sleep, but it seldom happened that they all came out again alive. I was in this place a fortnight and can say in sincerity that I never lay down to sleep a minute in all that time. . . . What little provisions we had was cooked by the invalids in our camp and brought to the island in old flour barrels; it was mostly corned beef and hard bread, but it was not much trouble to cook or fetch what we had.

We continued here, suffering cold, hunger and other miseries, till the fourteenth day of November. On that day, at the dawn, we discovered six ships of the line . . . within pistol shot of the fort, on the western side . . . The soldiers were all ordered to take their posts at the palisades, which they were ordered to defend to the last extremity, as it was expected the British would land under the fire of their cannon and attempt to storm the fort. The cannonade was server, as well it might be, six sixty-four-gun-ships, a thirty-six-gun frigate, a twenty-gun ship, a galley and a sloop of six guns, together with six batteries of six guns each and a bomb battery of three mortars, all playing at once upon our poor little fort, if fort it might be called.

Some of our officers endeavored to ascertain how many guns were fired in a minute by the enemy, but it was impossible, the fire was incessant. In the height of the cannonade it was desirable to hoist a signal flag for some of our galleys that were laying above us to come down to our assistance. The officers inquired who would undertake it. As none appeared willing for some time, I was about to offer my services. I considered it no more exposure of my life than it was to remain where I was. The flagstaff was of easy ascent, being an old ship's mast, having shrouds to the ground, and the round top still remaining. While I was still hesitating, a sergeant of the artillery offered himself. He accordingly ascended to the round top, pulled down the flag to affix the signal flag to the halyard, upon which the enemy, thinking we had struck, [surrendered] ceased firing in every direction and cheered. "Up with the flag!" was the cry of our officers in every part of the fort. The flags were accordingly hoisted, and the firing was immediately renewed. The sergeant then came down and had not gone half a rod from the foot of the staff when he was cut in two by a cannon shot.

This caused me some serious reflection at the time. He was killed! Had I been at the same business I might have been killed, but it might have been otherwise ordered by Divine Providence, we might have both lived. I a not predestination enough to determine it. The enemy's shot cut us up. I saw five artillerists belonging to one gun cut down by a single shot, and I saw men who were stooping to be protected by the works; but not stooping low enough, split like fish to be broiled. . . .

The cannonade continued, directed mostly at the fort, till the dusk of the evening. As soon as it was dark we began to make preparations for evacuation the fort and endeavoring to escape to the Jersey shore. When the firing had in some measure subsided and I could look about me, I found the fort exhibited a picture of desolation. The whole area of the fort was completely ploughed as a field. The buildings of every kind hanging in broken fragments, and the guns all dismounted, and how many of the garrison sent to the world of spirits, I knew not. If ever destruction was complete, it was here. The surviving part of the garrison were now drawn off and such of the stores as could conveniently be taken away were carried to the Jersey shore.

[ . . . After evacuating the fort,] we marched a little back into some pitch-pine woods, where we found the rest of the troops that had arrived before us. They had made up some comfortable fires and were enjoying the warmth, and that was all the comfort they had to partake of, except rest, for victuals was out of the question. I wrapped myself up in my blanket and lay down upon the leaves and soon fell asleep and continued so till past noon, when I awoke from the first sound sleep I had for a fortnight. Indeed, I had not laid down in all that time. The little sleep I had obtained was in cat naps, sitting up and leaning against the wall, and I thought myself fortunate if I could do that much. When I awoke I was as crazy as a goose shot through the head.

We left our flag flying when we left the island, and the enemy did not take possession of the fort till late in the morning after we left it.

## QUESTIONS TO CONSIDER

1. How would you describe warfare at the time?
2. Does this change the way you think about the American Revolution? Why or why not?

# CHAPTER 8

# CONTESTED REPUBLIC, 1789–1800

## 8.1 CONNECTICUT SLAVES' PETITION FOR FREEDOM (1779) AND MASSACHUSETTS SLAVES' ANTI-TAXATION PETITION (1780)

The rhetoric behind the American Revolution spread faster and to more populations than American leaders had likely intended. Two striking examples of this change are the following documents from African Americans in Connecticut and Massachusetts. The first petition—brought by two slaves, Prime and Prince, to the Connecticut legislature—attempted to convince that legislature to abolish slavery. The second petition—brought by seven African Americans to the Massachusetts legislature in 1780—argued for voting rights for freed African Americans. While the Connecticut legislature denied the first petition—Connecticut did not fully abolish slavery until 1848—a 1783 court case ruled in favor of the Massachusetts petitioners and gave African Americans subject to taxation the right to vote in the state.

### CONNECTICUT SLAVES' PETITION FOR FREEDOM

To the Honbl. General Assembly of the State of Connecticut to be held at Hartford on the Second Thursday of Instant May. [1779]—The Petition of the Negroes in the Towns of Stratford and Fairfield in the County of Fairfield who are held in a State of Slavery humbly sheweth—

That many of your Petitioners, were (as they verily believe) most unjustly torn, from the Bosom of their dear Parents, and Friends, and without any Crime, by

them committed, doomed, and bound down, to perpetual Slavery; and as if the Perpetrators of this horrid Wickedness, were conscious (that we poor Ignorant Africans, upon the least Glimering Sight, derived from a Knowledge of the Sense and Practice of civilized Nations) should Convince them of their Sin, they have added another dreadful Evil, that of holding us in gross Ignorance, so as to render Our Subjection more easy and tolerable. may it please your Honours, we are most grievously affected, under the Consideration of the flagrant Injustice; Your Honours who are nobly

*Source:* Herbert Aptheker ed., *A Documentary History of The Negro People in the United States* (New York: The Citadel Press, 1968), 10–16.

contending, in the Cause of Liberty, whose Conduct excites the Admiration, and Reverence, of all the great Empires of the World; will not resent, our thus freely animadverting, on this detestable Practice; although our Skins are different in Colour, from those whom we serve, Yet Reason & Revelation join to declare, that we are the Creatures of that God, who made of one Blood, and Kindred, all the Nations of the Earth; we perceive by our own Reflection, that we are endowed with the same Faculties with our masters, and there is nothing that leads us to a Belief, or Suspicion, that we are any more obliged to serve them, than they us, and the more we Consider of this matter, the more we are Convinced of our Right (by the Laws of Nature and by the whole Tenor of the Christian Religion, so far as we have been taught) to be free; we have endeavoured rightly to understand what is our Right, and what is our Duty, and can never be convinced that we were made to be Slaves. Altho God almighty may justly lay this, and more upon us, yet we deserve it not, from the hands of Men. We are impatient under the grievous Yoke, but our Reason teaches us that it is not best for us to use violent measures, to cast it off; we are also convinced, that we are unable to extricate ourselves from our abject State; but we think we may with the greatest Propriety look up to your Honours, (who are the fathers of the People) for Relief. And we not only groan under our own burden, but with concern, & Horror, look forward, & contemplate, the miserable Condition of our Children, who are training up, and kept in Preparation, for a like State of Bondage, and Servitude. We beg leave to submit, to your Honours serious Consideration, whether it is consistent with the present Claims, of the united States, to hold so many Thousands, of the Race of Adam, our Common Father, in perpetual Slavery. Can human Nature endure the Shocking Idea? Can your Honours any longer Suffer this great Evil to prevail under your Government: we entreat your Honours, let no considerations of Publick Inconvenience deter your Honours from interposing in behalf of your Petitioners; we ask for nothing, but what we are fully persuaded is ours to Claim. We beseech your Honours to weigh this matter in the Scale of Justice, and in your great Wisdom and goodness, apply such Remedy as the Evil does Require; and let your Petitioners rejoice with your Honours in the Participation with your Honours of that inestimable Blessing, *Freedom* and your Humble Petitioners, as in Duty bound shall ever pray &c.

Dated in Fairfield the
11th Day of May A D 1779–

*Prime a Negro man servant to Mr. Vam A. Sturge of Fairfield his Prince X a Negro man mark Servant of Capt. Stephen Jenings of Farifield— in Behalf of themselves and the other Petitioners*

*Signed in Presence of*
*Jonth Sturges*

## MASSACHUSETTS SLAVES' ANTI-TAXATION PETITION

To The Honouerable Councel and House of Representatives in General Court assembled for the State of the Massachusetts Bay in New England—March 14th A D 1780—

The petition of several poor Negroes & molattoes who are Inhabitant of the Town of Dartmouth Humbly Sheweth—That we being Chiefly of the African Extract and by Reason of Long Bondag and hard Slavery we have been deprived of Injoying the Profits of our Labouer or the advantage of Inheriting Estates from our Parents as our Neighbouers the white peopel do having some of us not long Injoyed our own freedom & yet of late, Contrary to the invariable Custom & Practice of the Country we have been & now are Taxed both in our Polls and that small Pittance of Estate which through much hard Labour & Industry we have got together to Sustain our selves & families withal— We apprehend it therefore to be hard usag and [one word is illegible here—ed.] doubtless (if Continued will) Reduce us to a State of Beggary whereby we shall become a Berthan to others if not timely prevented by the Interposition of your Justice & power & yor Petitioners farther sheweth that we apprehend ourselves to be Aggreeved, in that while we are not allowed the Privilage of freemen of the State having no vote or Influence in the Election of those that Tax us yet many of our Colour (as is well known) have cheerfully Entered the field of Battle in the defence of the Common Cause and that (as we conceive) against a similar Exertion of

Power (in Regard to taxation) too well Known to need a recital in this place—

That these the Most honouerable Court we Humbley Beseech they would to take this into Considerration and Let us aside from Paying tax or taxes or cause us to Be Cleaired for we ever have Been a people that was fair from all these thing ever since the days of our four fathers and therefore we take it as aheard ship that we should be so delt By now in these Difficulty times for their is not to exceed more then five or six that hath a cow in this town and theirfore in our Distress we send unto the peaceableness of thee people and the mercy of God that we may be Releaved for we are not alowed in voating in the town meating in nur to chuse an officer Neither their was not one ever heard in the active Court of the General Assembly the poor Dispised miserable Black people, & we have not an equal chance with white people neither by Sea nur by Land therefore we take it as a heard ship that poor old Negroes should be Rated which have been in Bondage some thirty some forty and some fifty years and now just got their Liberty some by going into the serviese and some by going to Sea and others by good fortan and also poor Distressed mungrels which have no larning and no land and also no [one word illegible—ed.] Neither where to put their head but some shelter them selves into an old rotten hut which thy dogs would not lay in[.]

Therefore we pray that these may give no offence at all By no means But that thee most Honouerable Court will take it in to consideration as if it were their own case for we think it as to be a heard ship that we should be assessed and not be a lowed as we may say to Eat Bread therefore we Humbley Beg and pray thee to plead our Case for us with thy people O God; that those who have the rule in their hands may be mercyfull unto the poor and needy give unto those who ask of thee and he that would Borrow of thee turn not away empty: O God be mercyfull unto the poor and give unto those who give ought unto the poor therefore we return unto thee again: most honouerable Court that thou wouldst Consider us in these Difficut times for we send in nur come unto thee not with false words Neither with lieing Lips therefore we think that we may be clear from being called tories tho some few of our Colour hath Rebelled and Done Wickedly however we think that there is more of our Collour gone into the wars according to the Number of them into the Respepiktive towns then any other nation here and [one word illegible—ed.] therefore We most humbley Request therefore that you would take our unhappy Case into your serious Consideration and in your wisdom and Power grant us Relief from Taxation while under our Present depressed Circumstances and your poor Petioners as in duty bound shall ever pray &c[.]

### QUESTIONS TO CONSIDER

1. How does each document use the rhetoric behind the American Revolution to make its case?
2. To what degree, then, was the American Revolution radical?

# 8.2 HECTOR ST. JOHN DE CRÈVECŒUR, EXCERPT FROM *LETTERS FROM AN AMERICAN FARMER* (1782)

Hector St. John de Crèvecœur (1735–1813) was probably the first American author to have success abroad. Born in Normandy, France, Crèvecœur moved to New France at the age of 20 and fought in the Seven Years' War on the French side. During the American Revolution, Crèvecœur moved back to France to live with his ailing father. In 1782, he published *Letters from an American Farmer,* an immediately popular series of essays primarily written to provide information about America and Americans to Europeans. In these essays, Crèvecœur generally lauded American society and upheld the opportunities Europeans might find there. In the following excerpt, from "Letter III: What Is an American," Crèvecœur describes American diversity, democracy, and equality. After publishing *Letters from an American Farmer,* Crèvecœur moved back to the United States and spent much of the rest of his life in New York City.

I wish I could be acquainted with the feelings and thoughts which must agitate the heart and present themselves to the mind of an enlightened Englishman, when he first lands on this continent. He must greatly rejoice that he lived at a time to see this fair country discovered and settled; he must necessarily feel a share of national pride, when he views the chain of settlements which embellishes these extended shores. When he says to himself, this is the work of my countrymen, who, when convulsed by factions, afflicted by a variety of miseries and wants, restless and impatient, took refuge here. They brought along with them their national genius, to which they principally owe what liberty they enjoy, and what substance they possess. Here he sees the industry of his native country displayed in a new manner, and traces in their works the embrios of all the arts, sciences, and ingenuity which flourish in Europe. Here he beholds fair cities, substantial villages, extensive fields, an immense country filled with decent houses, good roads, orchards, meadows, and bridges, where an hundred years ago all was wild, woody and uncultivated! What a train of pleasing ideas this fair spectacle must suggest; it is a prospect which must inspire a good citizen with the most heartfelt pleasure. The difficulty consists in the manner of viewing so extensive a scene. He is arrived on a new continent; a modern society offers itself to his contemplation, different from what he had hitherto seen. It is not composed, as in Europe, of great lords who possess every thing, and of a herd of people who have nothing. Here are no aristocratical families, no courts, no kings, no bishops, no ecclesiastical dominion, no invisible power giving to a few a very visible one; no great manufacturers employing thousands, no great refinements of luxury. The rich and the poor are not so far removed from each other as they are in Europe. Some few towns excepted, we are all tillers of the earth, from Nova Scotia to West Florida. We are a people of cultivators, scattered over an immense territory, communicating with each other by means of good roads and navigable

*Source:* Hector St. John de Crèvecœur, *Letters from an American Farmer* (New York: Fox, Duffield & Company, 1904), 48–53, 74–78. Retrieved from the Internet Archive website, https://archive.org/stream/lettersfromameri00stjo/lettersfromameri00stjo_djvu.txt (Accessed June 6, 2018).

rivers, united by the silken bands of mild government, all respecting the laws, without dreading their power, because they are equitable. We are all animated with the spirit of an industry which is unfettered and unrestrained, because each person works for himself. If he travels through our rural districts he views not the hostile castle, and the haughty mansion, contrasted with the clay-built hut and miserable cabin, where cattle and men help to keep each other warm, and dwell in meanness, smoke, and indigence. A pleasing uniformity of decent competence appears throughout our habitations. The meanest of our log-houses is a dry and comfortable habitation. Lawyer or merchant are the fairest titles our towns afford; that of a farmer is the only appellation of the rural inhabitants of our country. It must take some time ere he can reconcile himself to our dictionary, which is but short in words of dignity, and names of honour. There, on a Sunday, he sees a congregation of respectable farmers and their wives, all clad in neat homespun, well mounted, or riding in their own humble wagons. There is not among them an esquire, saving the unlettered magistrate. There he sees a parson as simple as his flock, a farmer who does not riot on the labour of others. We have no princes, for whom we toil, starve, and bleed: we are the most perfect society now existing in the world. Here man is free as he ought to be; nor is this pleasing equality so transitory as many others are. Many ages will not see the shores of our great lakes replenished with inland nation, nor the unknown bounds of North America entirely peopled. Who can tell how far it extends? Who can tell the millions of men whom it will feed and contain? for no European foot has as yet travelled half the extent of this mighty content! . . .

In this great American asylum, the poor of Europe have by some means met together, and in consequence of various causes; to what purpose should they ask one and other what countrymen they are? Alas, two thirds of them had no country. Can a wretch who wanders about, who works and starves, whose life is a continual scene of sore affliction or pinching penury; can that man call England or any other kingdom his country? A country that had no bread for him, whose fields procured him no harvest, who met with nothing but the frowns of the rich, the severity of the laws, with jails and punishments; who

owned not a single foot of the extensive surface of this planet? No! urged by a variety of motives, here they came. Every thing has tended to regenerate them; new laws, a new mode of living, a new social system; here they are become men: in Europe they were as so many useless plants, wanting vegetative mould, and refreshing showers; they withered, and were mowed down by want, hunger, and war; but now by the power of transplantation, like all other plants they have taken root and flourished! . . .

There is no wonder that this country has so many charms, and presents to Europeans so many temptations to remain in it. A traveler in Europe becomes a stranger as soon as he quits his own kingdom; but it is otherwise here. We know, properly speaking, no strangers; this is every person's country; the variety of our soils, situations, climates, governments, and produce, hath something which must please every body. No sooner does an European arrive, no matter of what condition, than his eyes are opened upon the fair prospect; he hears his language spoke, he retraces many of his own country manners, he perpetually hears the names of families and towns with which he is acquainted; he sees happiness and prosperity in all places disseminated; he meets with hospitality, kindness, and plenty every where; he beholds hardly any poor, he seldom hears of punishments and executions; and he wonders at the elegance of our towns, those miracles of industry and freedom. He cannot admire enough our rural districts, our convenient roads, good taverns, and our many accommodations; he involuntarily loves a country where every thing is so lovely. When in England, he was a mere Englishman; here he stands on a larger portion of the globe, not less than its fourth part, and may see the productions of the north, in iron and naval stores; the provisions of Ireland, the grain of Egypt, the indigo the rice of China. He does not find, as in Europe, a clouded society, where every place is over-stocked; he does not feel that perpetual collision of parties, that difficulty of beginning, that contention which oversets so many. There is room for every body in America; has he any particular talent, or industry? he exerts it in order to procure a livelihood, and it succeeds. Is he a merchant? the avenues of trade are infinite; is he eminent in any respect? he will be employed and respected. Does he love a country life? pleasant farms present themselves; he may purchase what he wants, and thereby become an American farmer. Is he a laborer, sober and industrious? he need not go many miles, nor receive many informations before he will be hired, will fed at the table of his employer, and paid four or five times more than he can get in Europe. Does he want uncultivated lands? thousands of acres present themselves, which he may purchase cheap. Whatever be his talents or inclinations, if they are moderate, he may satisfy them. I do not mean that every one who comes will grow rich in a little time; no, but he may procure an easy, decent maintenance, by his industry. Instead of starving he will be fed, instead of being idle he will have employment; and these are riches enough for such men as come over here. The rich stay in Europe, it is only the middling and the poor that emigrate. Would you wish to travel in independent idleness, from north to south, you will find easy access, and the most cheerful reception at every house; society without ostentation, good cheer without pride, and every decent diversion which the country affords, with little expense. It is no wonder that the European who has lived here a few years, is desirous to remain; Europe with all its pomp, is not to be compared to this continent, for men of middle stations, or labourers.

An European, when he first arrives, seems limited in his intentions, as well as in his views; but he very suddenly alters his scale; two hundred miles formerly appeared a very great distance, it is now but a trifle; he no sooner breathes our air than he forms schemes, and embarks in designs he never would have thought of in his own country. There the plenitude of society confines many useful ideas, and often extinguishes the most laudable schemes which here ripen into maturity. Thus Europeans become Americans.

But how is this accomplished in that croud of low, indigent people, who flock here every year from all parts of Europe? I will tell you; they no sooner arrive than they immediately feel the good effects of that plenty of provisions we possess: they fare on our best food, and the[y] are kindly entertained; their talents, character, and peculiar industry are immediately inquired into; they find countrymen every where disseminated, let them come from whatever part of Europe. Let me select one as an epitome of the rest he is hired, he goes to work, and works moderately; instead of being employed by a haughty person, he finds himself with his equal, placed at the substantial table of the farmer, or else at an inferior one as good; his wages are high, his bed is not like that bed of sorrow on which he used to lie: if he behaves with propriety, and is faithful, he is caressed, and becomes as it were a member of the family. He begins to feel the effects of a sort of resurrection ; hitherto he had not lived, but simply vegetated; he now feels himself a man, because he is treated as such; the laws of his own country had overlooked him in hid insignificancy; the laws of this cover him with their man; he begins to forget his former servitude and dependence, his heart involuntarily swells and glows; this first swell inspires him with those new thoughts which constitute an American. What love can he entertain for a country where his existence was a burthen to him; if he is a generous good man, the love of this new adoptive parent will sink deep into his heart. . . .

### QUESTIONS TO CONSIDER

1. What did Crèvecœur find especially laudable about America?
2. Would you have wanted to move to America after reading *Letters from an American Farmer*?

# 8.3 ALEXANDER HAMILTON, EXCERPT FROM HIS OPINION ON THE FIRST NATIONAL BANK (1791), AND THOMAS JEFFERSON, EXCERPT FROM HIS OPINION ON THE FIRST NATIONAL BANK (1791)

As a part of his financial plan for the United States, Treasury Secretary Alexander Hamilton championed a new institution in 1791. The First Bank of the United States would, if created, hold U.S. deposits and issue stock. These measures would allow the Bank to fulfill its primary purpose, which in Hamilton's mind was to distribute credit to private institutions and the Federal government in order to spur economic development via infrastructure improvements and other projects. More broadly, the Bank would help to establish financial order in the United States. Hamilton's idea was certainly controversial at the time. In the following documents, you will read Hamilton's defense of the plan and Thomas Jefferson's argument against it. Each man used the newly ratified U.S. Constitution to support his argument. In the end, Hamilton prevailed. President George Washington signed the bank bill, which gave the intrusion a twenty-year charter, on February 25, 1791.

## ALEXANDER HAMILTON, EXCERPT FROM HIS OPINION ON THE FIRST NATIONAL BANK

The said Secretary further respectfully reports

That from a conviction (as suggested in his report No. 1 herewith presented) That a National Bank is an Institution of primary importance to the prosperous administration of the Finances, and would be of the greatest utility in the operations connected with the support of the Public Credit, his attention has been drawn to devising the plan of such an institution, upon a scale, which will intitle it to the confidence, and be likely to render it equal to the exigencies of the Public.

Previously to entering upon the detail of this plan, he entreats the indulgence of the House, towards some preliminary reflections naturally arising out of the subject, which he hopes will be deemed, neither useless, nor out of place. Public opinion being the ultimate arbiter of every measure of Government, it can scarcely appear improper, in deference to that, to accompany the origination of any new proposition with explanations, which the superior information of those, to whom it is immediately addressed, would render superfluous.

It is a fact well understood, that public Banks have found admission and patronage among the principal and most enlightened commercial nations. They have successively obtained in Italy, Germany, Holland, England and France, as well as in the United States. And it is a circumstance, which cannot but have considerable weight, in a candid estimate of their tendency, that

*Sources:* "Final Version of the Second Report on the Further Provision Necessary for Establishing Public Credit (Report on a National Bank), 13 December 1790," https://founders.archives.gov/documents/Hamilton/01-07-02-0229-0003 (Accessed June 6, 2018); "Opinion on the Constitutionality of the Bill for Establishing a National Bank, 15 February 1791," https://founders.archives.gov/documents/Jefferson/01-19-02-0051 (Accessed June 6, 2018).

after an experience of centuries, there exists not a question about their util[ity] in the countries in which they have been so long established. Theorists and men of business unite in the acknowlegment of it.

Trade and industry, wherever they have been tried, have been indebted to them for important aid. And Government has been repeatedly under the greatest obligations to them, in dangerous and distressing emergencies. That of the United States, as well in some of the most critical conjunctures of the late war, as since the peace, has received assistance from those established among us, with which it could not have dispensed.

With this two fold evidence before us, it might be expected, that there would be a perfect union of opinions in their favour. Yet doubts have been entertained; jealousies and prejudices have circulated: and though the experiment is every day dissipating them, within the spheres in which effects are best known; yet there are still persons by whom they have not been intirely renounced. To give a full and accurate view of the subject would be to make a Treatise of a report; but there are certain aspects in which it may be cursorily exhibited, which may perhaps conduce to a just impression of its merits. These will involve a comparison of the advantages, with the disadvantages, real or supposed, of such institutions.

The following are among the principal advantages of a Bank.

First. The augmentation of the active or productive capital of a country. Gold and Silver, when they are employed merely as the instruments of exchange and alienation, have been not improperly denominated dead Stock; but when deposited in Banks, to become the basis of a paper circulation, which takes their character and place, as the signs or representatives of value, they then acquire life, or, in other words, an active and productive quality. This idea, which appears rather subtil and abstract, in a general form, may be made obvious and palpable, by entering into a few particulars. It is evident, for instance, that the money, which a merchant keeps in his chest, waiting for a favourable opportunity to employ it, produces nothing 'till that opportunity arrives. But if instead of locking it up in this manner, he either deposits it in a Bank, or invests it in the Stock of a Bank, it yields a profit, during the interval; in which he partakes, or not, according to the choice he may have made of being a depositor or a proprietor; and when any advantageous speculation offers, in order to be able to embrace it, he has only to withdraw his money, if a depositor, or if a proprietor to obtain a loan from the Bank, or to dispose of his Stock; an alternative seldom or never attended with difficulty, when the affairs of the institution are in a prosperous train. His money thus deposited or invested, is a fund, upon which himself and others can borrow to a much larger amount. It is a well established fact, that Banks in good credit can circulate a far greater sum than the actual quantum of their capital in Gold & Silver. The extent of the possible excess seems indeterminate; though it has been conjecturally stated at the proportions of two and three to one. This faculty is produced in various ways. First. A great proportion of the notes, which are issued and pass current as Cash, are indefinitely suspended in circulation, from the confidence which each holder has, that he can at any moment turn them into gold and silver. Secondly, Every loan, which a Bank makes is, in its first shape, a credit given to the borrower on its books, the amount of which it stands ready to pay, either in its own notes, or in gold or silver, at his option. But, in a great number of cases, no actual payment is made in either. The Borrower frequently, by a check or order, transfers his credit to some other person, to whom he has a payment to make; who, in his turn, is as often content with a similar credit, because he is satisfied, that he can, whenever he pleases, either convert it into cash, or pass it to some other hand, as an equivalent for it. And in this manner the credit keeps circulating, performing in every stage the office of money, till it is extinguished by a discount with some person, who has a payment to make to the Bank, to an equal or greater amount. Thus large sums are lent and paid, frequently through a variety of hands, without the intervention of a single piece of coin. Thirdly, There is always a large quantity of gold and silver in the repositories of the Bank, besides its own Stock, which is placed there, with a view partly to its safe keeping and partly to the accommodation of an institution, which is itself a source of general accommodation. These deposits are of immense consequence in the operations of a Bank. Though liable to be redrawn at any moment, experience proves, that the money so much oftener changes proprietors than place, and that what is drawn out is generally so speedily replaced, as to authorise the counting upon the sums deposited, as an *effective fund*; which, concurring with the Stock of the Bank, enables it to extend its loans, and to answer all the demands for coin, whether in consequence of those loans, or arising from the occasional return of its notes.

These different circumstances explain the manner, in which the ability of a bank to circulate a greater sum, than its actual capital in coin, is acquired. This however must be gradual; and must be preceded by a firm establishment of confidence; a confidence which may be bestowed on the most rational grounds; since the excess in question will always be bottomed on good security of one kind or another. This, every well conducted Bank carefully requires, before it will consent to advance either its money or its credit; and where there is an auxiliary capital (as will be the case in the plan hereafter submitted) which, together with the capital in coin, define the boundary, that shall not be exceeded by the engagements of the Bank, the security may, consistently with all the maxims of a reasonable circumspection be regarded as complete.

The same circumstances illustrate the truth of the position, that it is one of the properties of Banks to increase the active capital of a country. This, in other words is the sum of them. The money of one individual, while he is waiting for an opportunity to employ it, by being either deposited in the Bank for safe keeping, or invested in its Stock, is in a condition to administer to the wants of others, without being put out of his own reach, when occasion presents. This yields an extra profit, arising from what is paid for the use of his money by others, when he could not himself make use of it; and keeps the money itself in a state of incessant activity. In the almost infinite vicissitudes and competitions of mercantile enterprise, there never can be danger of an intermission of demand, or that the money will remain for a moment idle in the vaults of the Bank. This additional employment given to money, and the faculty of a bank to lend and circulate a greater sum than the amount of its stock in coin are to all the purposes of trade and industry an absolute increase of capital. Purchases and undertakings, in general, can be carried on by any given sum of bank paper or credit, as

effectually as by an equal sum of gold and silver. And thus by contributing to enlarge the mass of industrious and commercial enterprise, banks become nurseries of national wealth: a consequence, as satisfactorily verified by experience, as it is clearly deducible in theory.

Secondly. Greater facility to the Government in obtaining pecuniary aids, especially in sudden emergencies. This is another and an undisputed advantage of public banks: one, which as already remarked, has been realised in signal instances, among ourselves. The reason is obvious: The capitals of a great number of individuals are, by this operation, collected to a point, and placed under one direction. The mass, formed by this union, is in a certain sense magnified by the credit attached to it: And while this mass is always ready, and can at once be put in motion, in aid of the Government, the interest of the bank to afford that aid, independent of regard to the public safety and welfare, is a sure pledge for its disposition to go as far in its compliances, as can in prudence be desired. There is in the nature of things, as will be more particularly noticed in another place, an intimate connection of interest between the government and the Bank of a Nation.

Thirdly. The facilitating of the payment of taxes. This advantage is produced in two ways. Those who are in a situation to have access to the Bank can have the assistance of loans to answer with punctuality the public calls upon them. This accommodation has been sensibly felt in the payment of the duties heretofore laid, by those who reside where establishments of this nature exist. This however, though an extensive, is not an universal benefit. The other way, in which the effect here contemplated is produced, and in which the benefit is general, is the encreasing of the quantity of circulating medium and the quickening of circulation. The manner in which the first happens has already been traced. The last may require some illustration. When payments are to be made between different places, having an intercourse of business with each other, if there happen to be no private bills, at market, and there are no Bank notes, which have a currency in both, the consequence is, that coin must be remitted. This is attended with trouble, delay, expence and risk. If on the contrary, there are bank notes current in both places, the transmission of these by the post, or any other speedy, or convenient conveyance answers the purpose; and these again, in the alternations of demand, are frequently returned, very soon after, to the place from whence they were first sent: Whence the transportation and retransportation of the metals are obviated; and a more convenient and more expeditious medium of payment is substituted. Nor is this all. The metals, instead of being suspended from their usual functions, during this process of vibration from place to place, continue in activity, and administer still to the ordinary circulation; which of course is prevented from suffering either diminution or stagnation. These circumstances are additional causes of what, in a practical sense, or to the purposes of business, may be called greater plenty of money. And it is evident, that whatever enhances the quantity of circulating money adds to the ease, with which every industrious member of the community may acquire that portion of it, of which he stands in need; and enables him the better to pay his taxes, as well as to supply his other wants. Even where the circulation of the bank paper is not general, it must still have the same effect, though in a less degree. For whatever furnishes additional supplies to the channels of circulation, in one quarter, naturally contributes to keep the streams fuller elsewhere. This last view of the subject serves both to illustrate the position, that Banks tend to facilitate the payment of taxes; and to exemplify their utility to business of every kind, in which money is an agent. . . .

There is nothing in the Acts of Congress, which imply an exclusive right in the institution, to which they relate, except during the term of the war. There is therefore nothing, if the public good require it, which prevents the establishment of another . . . This is a strong argument for a new institution, or for a renovation of the old, to restore it to the situation in which it originally stood, in the view of the United States. . . .

## THOMAS JEFFERSON, EXCERPT FROM HIS OPINION ON THE FIRST NATIONAL BANK

The bill for establishing a National Bank undertakes, among other things

1.  to form the subscribers into a Corporation.
2.  to enable them, in their corporate capacities to receive grants of land; and so far is against the laws of *Mortmain*.

3.  to make *alien* subscribers capable of holding lands, and so far is against the laws of *Alienage*.
4.  to transmit these lands, on the death of a proprietor, to a certain line of successors: and so far changes the course of *Descents*.
5.  to put the lands out of the reach of forfeiture or escheat and so far is against the laws of *Forfeiture and Escheat*.
6.  to transmit personal chattels to successors in a certain line: and so far is against the laws of *Distribution*.
7.  to give them the sole and exclusive right of banking under the national authority: and so far is against the laws of *Monopoly*.
8.  to communicate to them a power to make laws paramount to the laws of the states: for so they must be construed, to protect the institution from the controul of the state legislatures; and so, probably they will be construed.

I consider the foundation of the Constitution as laid on this ground that 'all powers not delegated to the U.S. by the Constitution, not prohibited by it to the states, are reserved to the states or to the people' [XIIth. Amendmt.]. To take a single step beyond the boundaries thus specially drawn around the powers of Congress, is to take possession of a boundless feild of power, no longer susceptible of any definition.

The incorporation of a bank, and other powers assumed by this bill have not, in my opinion, been delegated to the U.S. by the Constitution.

I. They are not among the powers specially enumerated, for these are

1. A power to *lay taxes* for the purpose of paying the debts of the U.S. But no debt is paid by this bill, nor any tax laid. Were it a bill to raise money, it's origination in the Senate would con demn it by the constitution.

2. 'to borrow money'. But this bill neither borrows money, nor ensures the borrowing it. The proprietors of the bank will be just as free as any other money holders, to lend or not to lend their money to the public. The operation proposed in the bill, first to lend them two millions, and then borrow them back again, cannot change the nature of the latter act, which will still be a payment, and not a loan, call it by what name you please.

3. 'to regulate commerce with foreign nations, and among the states, and with the Indian tribes'. To erect

a bank, and to regulate commerce, are very different acts. He who erects a bank creates a subject of commerce in it's bills: so does he who makes a bushel of wheat, or digs a dollar out of the mines. Yet neither of these persons regulates commerce thereby. To erect a thing which may be bought and sold, is not to prescribe regulations for buying and selling. Besides; if this was an exercise of the power of regulating commerce, it would be void, as extending as much to the internal commerce of every state, as to it's external. For the power given to Congress by the Constitution, does not extend to the internal regulation of the commerce of a state (that is to say of the commerce between citizen and citizen) which remains exclusively with it's own legislature; but to it's external commerce only, that is to say, it's commerce with another state, or with foreign nations or with the Indian tribes. Accordingly the bill does not propose the measure as a 'regulation of trade,' but as 'productive of considerable advantage to trade.'

Still less are these powers covered by any other of the special enumerations.

II. Nor are they within either of the general phrases, which are the two following.

1. 'To lay taxes to provide for the general welfare of the U.S.' that is to say 'to lay taxes *for the purpose* of providing for the general welfare.' For the laying of taxes is the *power* and the general welfare the *purpose* for which the power is to be exercised. They are not to lay taxes ad libitum *for any purpose they please;* but only to *pay the debts or provide for the welfare of the Union.* In like manner they are not *to do anything they please* to provide for the general welfare, but only *to lay taxes* for that purpose. To consider the latter phrase, not as describing the purpose of the first, but as giving a distinct and independent power to do any act they please, which might be for the good of the Union, would render all the preceding and subsequent enumerations of power completely useless. It would reduce the whole instrument to a single phrase, that of instituting a Congress with power to do whatever would be for the good of the U.S. and as they would be the sole judges of the good or evil, it would be also a power to do whatever evil they pleased. It is an established rule of construction, where a phrase will bear either of two meanings, to give it that which will allow some meaning to the other parts of the instrument, and not that which

would render all the others useless. Certainly no such universal power was meant to be given them. It was intended to lace them up straitly within the enumerated powers, and those without which, as means, these powers could not be be carried into effect. It is known that the very power now proposed *as a means*, was rejected *as an end*, by the Convention which formed the constitution. A proposition was made to them to authorize Congress to open canals, and an amendatory one to empower them to incorporate. But the whole was rejected, and one of the reasons of rejection urged in debate was that then they would have a power to erect a bank, which would render the great cities, where there were prejudices and jealousies on that subject adverse to the reception of the constitution.

2. The second general phrase is 'to make all laws *necessary* and proper for carrying into execution the enumerated powers.' But they can all be carried into execution without a bank. A bank therefore is not *necessary*, and consequently not authorised by this phrase.

It has been much urged that a bank will give great facility, or convenience in the collection of taxes. Suppose this were true: yet the constitution allows only the means which are 'necessary' not those which are merely 'convenient' for effecting the enumerated powers. If such a latitude of construction be allowed to this phrase as to give any non-enumerated power, it will go to every one, for these is no one which ingenuity may not torture into a *convenience, in some way or other*, to *some one* of so long a list of enumerated powers. It would swallow up all the delegated powers, and reduce the whole to one phrase as before observed. Therefore it was that the constitution restrained them to the *necessary* means, that is to say, to those means without which the grant of the power would be nugatory. . . .

It may be said that a bank, whose bills would have a currency all over the states, would be more convenient than one whose currency is limited to a single state. So it would be still more convenient that there should be a bank whose bills should have a currency all over the world. But it does not follow from this superior conveniency that there exists anywhere a power to establish such a bank; or that the world may not go on very well without it.

Can it be thought that the Constitution intended that for a shade or two of *convenience*, more or less, Congress should be authorised to break down the most antient and fundamental laws of the several states, such as those against Mortmain, the laws of alienage, the rules of descent, the acts of distribution, the laws of escheat and forfeiture, the laws of monopoly? Nothing but a necessity invincible by any other means, can justify such a prostration of laws which constitute the pillars of our whole system of jurisprudence. Will Congress be too strait-laced to carry the constitution into honest effect, unless they may pass over the foundation-laws of the state-governments for the slightest convenience to theirs?

The Negative of the President is the shield provided by the constitution to protect against the invasions of the legislature 1. the rights of the Executive 2. of the Judiciary 3. of the states and state legislatures. The present is the case of a right remaining exclusively with the states and is consequently one of those intended by the constitution to be placed under his protection.

It must be added however, that unless the President's mind on a view of every thing which is urged for and against this bill, is tolerably clear that it is unauthorised by the constitution, if the pro and the con hang so even as to balance his judgment, a just respect for the wisdom of the legislature would naturally decide the balance in favour of their opinion. It is chiefly for cases where they are clearly misled by error, ambition, or interest, that the constitution has placed a check in the negative of the President.

**QUESTIONS TO CONSIDER**

1. How does each man use the Constitution to defend his position?
2. Which position do you find more convincing?

# 8.4 TRANSLATED TEXT OF HAITIAN DECLARATION OF INDEPENDENCE (1804)

The Haitian Revolution, though less well-known than the American Revolution, was just as dramatic, if not more so. Haiti, one of the world's largest suppliers of sugar, was a jewel of the French colonial system, and the French enforced a brutal system of slavery on the island. Death rates hovered around fifty percent just in the first year following a slave's arrival on the island. Haiti contained a fairly large free African population, but slaves outnumbered all others on the island by about ten to one. In 1791, probably sparked in part by the French Revolution of 1789, a massive group of slaves some 100,000 strong in northern Haiti rose up against the French colonial plantation system. The French abolished slavery in their colonies in 1793, but the revolution continued. For the next decade, revolutionary forces fought off both French and British forces. Haiti gained its independence in 1804. In the United States, the Haitian Revolution set off a major debate about slavery and its future. The following document illustrates some of the rhetoric behind the Haitian Revolution.

*Source:* Laurent Dubois and John D. Garrigus, eds., *Slave Revolution in the Caribbean, 1789–1804: A Brief History with Documents* (New York: Bedford/St. Martin's, 2006), 188–191.

## THE COMMANDER IN CHIEF TO THE PEOPLE OF HAITI

Citizens:

It is not enough to have expelled the barbarians who have bloodied our land for two centuries; it is not enough to have restrained those ever-evolving factions that one after another mocked the specter of liberty that France dangled before you. We must, with the last act of national authority, forever ensure liberty's reign in the country of our birth; we must take any hope of re-enslaving us away from the inhumane government that for so long kept us in the most humiliating stagnation. In the end we must live independent or die.

Independence or death . . . let these sacred words unite us and be the signal of battle and of our reunion.

Citizens, my countrymen, on this solemn day I have brought together those courageous soldiers who, as liberty lay dying, spilled their blood to save it: these generals who have guided your efforts against tyranny have not yet done enough for your happiness; the French name still haunts our land.

Everything revives the memories of the cruelties of this barbarous people: our laws, our habits, our towns, everything still carries the stamp of the French. Indeed! There are still French in our island, and you believe yourself free and independent of that republic, which it is true, has fought all the nations, but which has never defeated those who wanted to be free.

What! Victims of our [own] credulity and indulgence for fourteen years; defeated not by French armies, but by the pathetic eloquence of their agents' proclamations; when will we tire of breathing the air that they breathe? What do we have in common with this nation of executioners? The difference between its cruelty and our patient moderation, its color and ours, the great seas that separate us, our avenging climate, all tell us plainly that they are not our brothers, that they never will be, and that if they find refuge among us, they will plot again to trouble and divide us.

Native citizens, men, women, girls, and children, let your gaze extend on all parts of this island: look there for your spouses, your husbands, your brothers, your sisters, Indeed! Look there for your children, your suckling infants, what have they become? . . . I shudder to say it . . . the prey of these vultures.

Instead of these dear victims, your alarmed gaze will see only their assassins, these tigers still dripping with their blood, whose terrible presence indicts your lack of feeling and your guilty slowness in avenging them. What are you waiting for before appeasing their spirits? Remember that you had wanted your remains to rest next to those of your fathers after you defeated tyranny; will you descend into their tombs without having avenged them? No! Their bones would reject yours.

And you, precious men, intrepid generals, who, without concern for your own pain, have revived liberty by shedding all our blood, know that you have done nothing if you do not give the nations a terrible, but just example of the vengeance that must be wrought by a people proud to have recovered its liberty and jealous to maintain it. Let us frighten all those who would dare try to take it from us again; let us begin with the French. Let them tremble when they approach our coast, if not from the memory of those cruelties they perpetrated here, then from the terrible resolution that we will have made to put to death anyone born French whose profane foot soils the land of liberty.

We have dared to be free, let us be thus by ourselves and for ourselves. Let us imitate the grown child: his own weight breaks the boundary that has become an obstacle to him. What people fought for us? What people wanted to gather the fruits of our labor? And what dishonorable absurdity to conquer in order to be enslaved. Enslaved? . . . Let us leave this description for the French; they have conquered but are no longer free.

Let us walk down another path: let us imitate those people who, extending their concern into the future and dreading to leave an example of cowardice for posterity, preferred to be exterminated rather than lose their place as one of the world's free peoples.

Let us ensure, however, that a missionary spirit does not destroy our work; let us allow our neighbors to breathe in peace; may they live quietly under the laws that they have made for themselves, and let us not, as revolutionary firebrands, declare ourselves the lawgivers of the Caribbean, nor let our glory consist in troubling the peace of the neighboring islands. Unlike that which we inhabit, theirs has not been drenched in the innocent blood of its inhabitants; they have no vengeance to claim from the authority that protects them.

Fortunate to have never known the ideals that have destroyed us, they can only have good wishes for our prosperity.

Peace to our neighbors; but let this be our city: "Anathema to the French name! Eternal hatred of France!"

Natives of Haiti! My happy fate was to be one day the sentinel who would watch over the idol to which you sacrifice; I have watched, sometimes fighting alone, and if I have been so fortunate as to return to your hands the sacred trust you confided to me, know that it is now your task to preserve it. In fighting for your liberty, I was working for my own happiness. Before consolidating it with laws that will guarantee your free individuality, your leaders, who I have assembled here, and I, owe you the final proof of our devotion.

Generals and you, leaders, collected here close to me for the good of our land, the day has come, the day which must make our glory, our independence, eternal.

If there could exist among us a lukewarm heart, let him distance himself and tremble to take the oath which must unite us. Let us vow to ourselves, to posterity, to the entire universe, to forever renounce France, and to die rather than live under its domination: to fight until our last breath for the independence of our country.

And you, a people so long without good fortune, witness to the oath we take, remember that I counted on your constancy and courage when I threw myself into the career of liberty to fight the despotism and tyranny you had struggled against for fourteen years. Remember that I sacrificed everything to rally to your defense; family, children, fortune, and now I am rich only with your liberty; my name has become a horror to all those who want slavery. Despots and tyrants curse the day that I was born. If ever you refused or grumbled while receiving those laws that the spirit guarding your fate dictates to me for your own good, you would deserve the fate of an ungrateful people. But I reject that awful idea; you will sustain the liberty that you cherish and support the leader who commands you. Therefore, vow before me to live free and independent and to prefer death to anything that will try to place you back in chains. Swear, finally, to pursue forever the traitors and enemies of your independence.

Done at the headquarters of Gonaives, the first day of January 1804, the first year of independence.

## QUESTIONS TO CONSIDER

1. What differences and/or similarities do you see between this document and the American Declaration of Independence?

2. Which document do you find more rhetorically effective?

# 8.5 JAMES FENIMORE COOPER, EXCERPT FROM *THE PIONEERS* (1823)

American novelist James Fenimore Cooper (1789—1851) is best known for his *Leatherstocking* series of five novels set on the New York frontier before and after the American Revolution. *The Last of the Mohicans*, which takes place in 1757, is the second book in the series. Cooper spent his childhood in upstate New York. His father, the merchant and developer William Cooper, founded Cooperstown, New York, on a vast tract of land he had purchased and settled his family there. The *Leatherstocking* series features Natty Bumppo, a white frontiersman who spent his childhood with the Delaware tribe, and illustrates the changes that took place on the frontier during the eighteenth century. The following excerpt comes from *The Pioneers*, the first book in the series, which takes place in 1793, a decade after the conclusion of the American Revolution. In the excerpt, taken from the first chapter of the novel, Cooper introduces the reader to Bumppo, Judge Temple (a fictionalized version of Cooper's father), and Temple's daughter Elizabeth (Bess).

Near the centre of the State of New York lies an extensive district of country whose surface is a succession of hills and dales, or, to speak with greater deference to geographical definitions, of mountains and valleys. It is among these hills that the Delaware takes its rise; and flowing from the limpid lakes and thousand springs of this region the numerous sources of the Susquehanna meander through the valleys until, uniting their streams, they form one of the proudest rivers of the United States. The mountains are generally arable to the tops, although instances are not wanting where the sides are jutted with rocks that aid greatly in giving to the country that romantic and picturesque character which it so eminently possesses. The vales are narrow, rich, and cultivated, with a stream uniformly winding through each. Beautiful and thriving villages are found interspersed along the margins of the small lakes, or situated at those points of the streams which are favorable for manufacturing; and neat and comfortable farms, with every indication of wealth about them, are scattered profusely through the vales, and even to the mountain tops. Roads diverge in every direction from the even and graceful bottoms of the valleys to the most rugged and intricate passes of the hills. Academies and minor edifices of learning meet the eye of the stranger at every few miles as he winds his way through this uneven territory, and places for the worship of God abound with that frequency which characterize a moral and reflecting people, and with that variety of exterior and canonical government which flows from unfettered liberty of conscience. In short, the whole district is hourly exhibiting how much can be done, in even a rugged country and with a severe climate, under the dominion of mild laws, and where every man feels a direct interest in the prosperity of a commonwealth of which he knows himself to form a part. The expedients of the pioneers who first broke ground in the settlement of this country are succeeded by the permanent improvements of the yeoman who intends to leave his remains to moulder under the sod which he tills, or perhaps of the son, who, born in the land, piously wishes to linger around the grave of his father. Only forty years have passed since this territory was a wilderness.

Very soon after the establishment of the independence of the States by the peace of 1783, the enterprise

*Source:* James Fenimore Cooper, *The Pioneers* (Urbana Champaign: Project Gutenberg, 2000).

of their citizens was directed to a development of the natural advantages of their widely extended dominions. Before the war of the Revolution, the inhabited parts of the colony of New York were limited to less than a tenth of its possessions, A narrow belt of country, extending for a short distance on either side of the Hudson, with a similar occupation of fifty miles on the banks of the Mohawk, together with the islands of Nassau and Staten, and a few insulated settlements on chosen land along the margins of streams, composed the country, which was then inhabited by less than two hundred thousand souls. Within the short period we have mentioned, the population has spread itself over five degrees of latitude and seven of longitude, and has swelled to a million and a half of inhabitants, who are maintained in abundance, and can look forward to ages before the evil day must arrive when their possessions shall become unequal to their wants.

It was near the setting of the sun, on a clear, cold day in December, when a sleigh was moving slowly up one of the mountains in the district we have described. The day had been fine for the season, and but two or three large clouds, whose color seemed brightened by the light reflected from the mass of snow that covered the earth, floated in a sky of the purest blue. The road wound along the brow of a precipice, and on one side was upheld by a foundation of logs piled one upon the other, while a narrow excavation in the mountain in the opposite direction had made a passage of sufficient width for the ordinary travelling of that day. But logs, excavation, and every thing that did not reach several feet above the earth lay alike buried beneath the snow. A single track, barely wide enough to receive the sleigh, denoted the route of the highway, and this was sunk nearly two feet below the surrounding surface.

In the vale, which lay at a distance of several hundred feet lower, there was what, in the language of the country, was called a clearing, and all the usual improvements of a new settlement; these even extended up the hill to the point where the road turned short and ran across the level land, which lay on the summit of the mountain; but the summit itself remained in the forest . . . Huge saddles, studded with nails and fitted with cloth that served as blankets to the shoulders of the cattle, supported four high, square-topped turrets, through which the stout reins led from the mouths of the horses to the hands of the driver, who was a negro,

of apparently twenty years of age. His face, which nature had colored with a glistening black, was now mottled with the cold, and his large shining eyes filled with tears; a tribute to its power that the keen frosts of those regions always extracted from one of his African origin. Still, there was a smiling expression of good-humor in his happy countenance, that was created by the thoughts of home and a Christmas fireside, with its Christmas frolics. The sleigh was one of those large, comfortable, old-fashioned conveyances, which would admit a whole family within its bosom, but which now contained only two passengers besides the driver . . .

Both the father and daughter (for such was the connection between the two travellers) were too much occupied with their reflections to break a stillness that derived little or no interruption from the easy gliding of the sleigh by the sound of their voices. The former was thinking of the wife that had held this their only child to her bosom, when, four years before, she had reluctantly consented to relinquish the society of her daughter in order that the latter might enjoy the advantages of an education which the city of New York could only offer at that period. A few months afterward death had deprived him of the remaining companion of his solitude; but still he had enough real regard for his child not to bring her into the comparative wilderness in which he dwelt, until the full period had expired to which he had limited her juvenile labors. The reflections of the daughter were less melancholy, and mingled with a pleased astonishment at the novel scenery she met at every turn in the road.

The mountain on which they were journeying was covered with pines that rose without a branch some seventy or eighty feet, and which frequently doubled that height by the addition of the tops. Through the innumerable vistas that opened beneath the lofty trees, the eye could penetrate until it was met by a distant inequality in the ground, or was stopped by a view of the summit of the mountain which lay on the opposite side of the valley to which they were hastening. The dark trunks of the trees rose from the pure white of the snow in regularly formed shafts, until, at a great height, their branches shot forth horizontal limbs, that were covered with the meagre foliage of an evergreen, affording a melancholy contrast to the torpor of nature below. To the travellers there seemed to be no wind; but these pines waved majestically at their topmost boughs, sending forth a dull, plaintive sound that was quite in consonance with the rest of the melancholy scene.

The sleigh had glided for some distance along the even surface, and the gaze of the female was bent in inquisitive and, perhaps, timid glances into the recesses of the forest, when a loud and continued howling was heard, pealing under the long arches of the woods like the cry of a numerous pack of hounds. The instant the sounds reached the ear of the gentleman he cried aloud to the black:

"Hol up, Aggy; there is old Hector; I should know his bay among ten thousand! The Leather-Stocking has put his hounds into the hills this clear day, and they have started their game. There is a deer-track a few rods ahead; and now, Bess, if thou canst muster courage enough to stand fire, I will give thee a saddle for thy Christmas dinner."

The black drew up, with a cheerful grin upon his chilled features, and began thrashing his arms together in order to restore the circulation of his fingers, while the speaker stood erect and, throwing aside his outer covering, stepped from the sleigh upon a bank of snow which sustained his weight without yielding.

In a few moments the speaker succeeded in extricating a double-barrelled fowling-piece from among a multitude of trunks and bandboxes. After throwing aside the thick mittens which had encased his hands, there now appeared a pair of leather gloves tipped with fur; he examined his priming, and was about to move forward, when the light bounding noise of an animal plunging through the woods was heard, and a fine buck darted into the path a short distance ahead of him. The appearance of the animal was sudden, and his flight inconceivably rapid; but the traveller appeared to be too keen a sportsman to be disconcerted by either. As it came first into view he raised the fowling-piece to his shoulder and, with a practised eye and steady hand, drew a trigger. The deer dashed forward undaunted, and apparently unhurt. Without lowering his piece, the traveller turned its muzzle toward his victim, and fired again. Neither discharge, however, seemed to have taken effect.

The whole scene had passed with a rapidity that confused the female, who was unconsciously rejoicing in the escape of the buck, as he rather darted like a meteor than ran across the road, when a sharp, quick sound struck her ear, quite different from the full, round reports of her father's gun, but still sufficiently distinct to be known as the concussion produced by firearms. At the same instant that she heard this unexpected report, the buck sprang from the snow to a great height in the air, and directly a second discharge, similar in sound to the first, followed, when the animal came to the earth, falling head long and rolling over on the crust with its own velocity. A loud shout was given by the unseen marksman, and a couple of men instantly appeared from behind the trunks of two of the pines, where they had evidently placed them selves in expectation of the passage of the deer.

"Ha! Natty, had I known you were in ambush, I should not have fired," cried the traveller, moving toward the spot where the deer lay—near to which he was followed by the delighted black, with his sleigh; "but the sound of old Hector was too exhilarating to be quiet; though I hardly think I struck him, either."

"No—no——Judge," returned the hunter, with an inward chuckle, and with that look of exultation that indicates a consciousness of superior skill, "you burnt your powder only to warm your nose this cold evening. Did ye think to stop a full-grown buck, with Hector and the slut open upon him within sound, with that popgun in your hand! There's plenty of pheasants among the swamps; and the snow-birds are flying round your own door, where you may feed them with crumbs, and shoot them at pleasure, any day; but if you're for a buck, or a little bear's meat, Judge, you'll have to take the long rifle, with a greased wadding, or you'll waste more powder than you'll fill stomachs, I'm thinking."

As the speaker concluded he drew his bare hand across the bottom of his nose, and again opened his enormous mouth with a kind of inward laugh.

"The gun scatters well, Natty, And it has killed a deer before now," said the traveller, smiling good-humoredly. "One barrel was charged with buckshot, but the other was loaded for birds only. Here are two hurts; one through the neck, and the other directly through the heart. It is by no means certain, Natty, but I gave him one of the two."

"Let who will kill him." said the hunter, rather surily.

"I suppose the creature is to be eaten." So saying, he drew a large knife from a leathern sheath, which was stuck through his girdle, or sash, and cut the throat of the animal, "If there are two balls through the deer, I would ask if there weren't two rifles fired—besides, who ever saw such a ragged hole from a smooth-bore as this through the neck? And you will own yourself, Judge, that the buck fell at the last shot, which was sent from a truer and a younger hand than your'n or mine either; but, for my part, although I am a poor man I can live without the venison, but I don't love to give up my lawful dues in a free country. Though, for the matter of that, might often makes right here, as well as in the old country, for what I can see."

An air of sullen dissatisfaction pervaded the manner of the hunter during the whole of his speech; yet he thought it prudent to utter the close of the sentence in such an undertone as to leave nothing audible but the grumbling sounds of his voice.

"Nay, Natty," rejoined the traveller, with undisturbed good-humor, "it is for the honor that I contend. A few dollars will pay for the venison; but what will requite me for the lost honor of a buck's tail in my cap? Think, Natty, how I should triumph over that quizzing dog, Dick Jones, who has failed seven times already this season, and has only brought in one woodchuck and a few gray squirrels."

"Ah! The game is becoming hard to find, indeed, Judge, with your clearings and betterments," said the old hunter, with a kind of compelled resignation. "The time has been when I have shot thirteen deer without counting the fa'ns standing in the door of my own hut; and for bear's meat, if one wanted a ham or so, he had only to watch a-nights, and he could shoot one by moonlight, through the cracks of the logs, no fear of his oversleeping himself neither, for the howling of the wolves was sartin to keep his eyes open. There's old Hector"—patting with affection a tall hound of black and yellow spots, with white belly and legs, that just then came in on the scent, accompanied by the slut he had mentioned; "see where the wolves bit his throat, the night I druv them from the venison that was smoking on the chimney top—that dog is more to be trusted than many a Christian man; for he never forgets a friend, and loves the hand that gives him bread."

There was a peculiarity in the manner of the hunter that attracted the notice of the young female, who had been a close and interested observer of his appearance and equipments, from the moment he came into view.

He was tall, and so meagre as to make him seem above even the six feet that he actually stood in his stockings. On his head, which was thinly covered with lank, sandy hair, he wore a cap made of fox-skin, resembling in shape the one we have already described, although much inferior in finish and ornaments. His face was skinny and thin almost to emaciation; but yet it bore no signs of disease—on the contrary, it had every indication of the most robust and enduring health. The cold and exposure had, together, given it a color of uniform red. His gray eyes were glancing under a pair of shaggy brows, that over hung them in long hairs of gray mingled with their natural hue; his scraggy neck was bare, and burnt to the same tint with his face; though a small part of a shirt-collar, made of the country check, was to be seen above the overdress he wore. A kind of coat, made of dressed deer-skin, with the hair on, was belted close to his lank body by a girdle of colored worsted. On his feet were deer-skin moccasins, ornamented with porcupines' quills, after the manner of the Indians, and his limbs were guarded with long leggings of the same material as the moccasins, which, gartering over the knees of his tarnished buckskin breeches, had obtained for him among the settlers the nickname of Leather-Stocking. Over his left shoulder was slung a belt of deer-skin, from which depended an enormous ox-horn, so thinly scraped as to discover the powder it contained. The larger end was fitted ingeniously and securely with a wooden bottom, and the other was stopped tight by a little plug. A leathern pouch hung before him, from which, as he concluded his last speech, he took a small measure, and, filling it accurately with powder, he commenced reloading the rifle, which as its butt rested on the snow before him reached nearly to the top of his fox-skin cap.

The traveller had been closely examining the wounds during these movements, and now, without heeding the ill-humor of the hunter's manner, he exclaimed:

"I would fain establish a right, Natty, to the honor of this death; and surely if the hit in the neck be mine it is enough; for the shot in the heart was unnecessary—what we call an act of supererogation, Leather-Stocking."

"You may call it by what larned name you please, Judge," said the hunter, throwing his rifle across his left arm, and knocking up a brass lid in the breech, from which he took a small piece of greased leather and, wrapping a bail in it, forced them down by main strength on the powder, where he continued to pound them while speaking. "It's far easier to call names than to shoot a buck on the spring; but the creatur came by his end from a younger hand than either your'n or mine, as I said before."

"What say you, my friend," cried the traveller, turning pleasantly to Natty's companion; "shall we toss up this dollar for the honor, and you keep the silver if you lose; what say you, friend?"

"That I killed the deer," answered the young man, with a little haughtiness, as he leaned on another long rifle similar to that of Natty.

"Here are two to one, indeed," replied the Judge with a smile; "I am outvoted—overruled, as we say on the bench. There is Aggy, he can't vote, being a slave; and Bess is a minor—so I must even make the best of it. But you'll send me the venison; and the deuce is in it, but I make a good story about its death."

"The meat is none of mine to sell," said Leather-Stocking, adopting a little of his companion's hauteur; "for my part, I have known animals travel days with shots in the neck, and I'm none of them who'll rob a man of his rightful dues."

"You are tenacious of your rights, this cold evening, Natty," returned the Judge with unconquerable good-nature; "but what say you, young man; will three dollars pay you for the buck?"

"First let us determine the question of right to the satisfaction of us both," said the youth firmly but respectfully, and with a pronunciation and language vastly superior to his appearance: "with how many shot did you load your gun?"

"With five, sir," said the Judge, a little struck with the other's manner; "are they not enough to slay a buck like this?"

"One would do it; but," moving to the tree from behind which he had appeared, "you know, sir, you fired in this direction—here are four of the bullets in the tree."

The Judge examined the fresh marks in the bark of the pine, and, shaking his head, said with a laugh:

"You are making out the case against yourself, my young advocate; where is the fifth?"

"Here," said the youth, throwing aside the rough over coat that he wore, and exhibiting a hole in his under-garment, through which large drops of blood were oozing.

"Good God!" exclaimed the Judge, with horror; "have I been trifling here about an empty distinction, and a fellow-creature suffering from my hands without a murmur? But hasten—quick—get into my sleigh—it is but a mile to the village, where surgical aid can be obtained—all shall be done at my expense, and thou shalt live with me until thy wound is healed, ay, and forever afterward."

"I thank you for your good intention, but I must decline your offer. I have a friend who would be uneasy were he to hear that I am hurt and away from him. The injury is but slight, and the bullet has missed the bones; but I believe, sir, you will now admit me title to the venison."

"Admit it!" repeated the agitated Judge; "I here give thee a right to shoot deer, or bears, or anything thou pleasest in my woods, forever. Leather-Stocking is the only other man that I have granted the same privilege to; and the time is coming when it will be of value."

## QUESTIONS TO CONSIDER

1. What changes in New York are revealed through Bumppo and Temple's conversation? How do they see the world differently?
2. Who would you say Cooper sympathizes with, and why do you think that?

# CHAPTER 9

# A REPUBLIC IN TRANSITION, 1800–1819

## 9.1 GEORGE GLEIG, EXCERPT FROM *A BRITISH ACCOUNT OF THE BURNING OF WASHINGTON* (1814)

The War of 1812 is sometimes called "America's Second War of Independence." In many ways, the United States fought the war to secure some of the gains the country had made in the Treaty of Paris. In the early 1800s, Britain began infringing on American trading ships and supporting Native American raids in the American Midwest. U.S. politicians began to call for military action to secure American economic independence. Some Americans also wished to conquer British Canada. On June 1, 1812, President James Madison asked Congress to approve a set of grievances against the British. Congress then ratified a declaration of war in a close vote. Though confident at the beginning of the war, U.S. forces failed to conquer Canadian territory, however, and British forces made gains in the Midwest and Northeast. In August 1814, a British force of 2,500 soldiers landed in the Chesapeake Bay and attacked Washington, D.C. After the British easily took the city, they burned many of its public buildings. George R. Gleig was one of the British soldiers who attacked Washington. Gleig's account, published in his 1821 memoir, gives an enlightening viewpoint about America from a different perspective. Though the United States and Britain eventually fought to a stalemate, and both sides agreed to end the war in December 1814, the burning of Washington remained a stark example of the new republic's fragility.

As it was not the intention of the British Government to attempt permanent conquests in this part of America ; and as the General was well aware that, with a handful of men, he could not pretend to establish himself, for any length of time, in an enemy's capital, he determined to lay it under

Source: George R. Gleig, *The Campaigns of the British Army at Washington and New Orleans in the Years 1814–1815* (London: John Murray, 1827), 128–135. Retrieved from the Internet Archive website, https://archive.org/details/campaignsofbriti00inglei (Accessed June 6, 2018).

contribution, and to return quietly to the shipping. Nor was there any thing unworthy of the character of a British officer, in this determination. By all the customs of war, whatever public property may chance to be in a captured town, becomes, confessedly, the just spoil of the conqueror ; and in thus proposing to accept a certain sum of money in lieu of that property, he was showing mercy, rather than severity, to the vanquished. It is true, that if they chose to reject his terms, he and his army would be deprived of their booty, because, without some more convenient mode of transporting it than we possessed, even the portable part of the property itself could not be removed. But, on the other hand, there was no difficulty in destroying it ; and thus, though we should gain nothing, the American Government would lose probably to a much greater amount than if they had agreed to purchase its preservation by the money demanded.

Such being the intention of General Ross, he did not march the troops immediately into the city, but halted them upon a plain in its immediate vicinity, whilst a flag of truce was sent forward with terms. But whatever his proposal might have been, it was not so much as heard ; for scarcely had the party bearing the flag entered the street, when it was fired upon from the windows of one of the houses, and the horse of the General himself, who accompanied it, killed. The indignation excited by this act throughout all ranks and classes of men in the army, was such as the nature of the case could not fail to occasion. Every thought of accommodation was instantly laid aside ; the troops advanced forthwith into the town, and having first put to the sword all who were found in the house form which the shots were fired, and reduced it to ashes, they proceeded, without a moment's delay, to burn and destroy every thing in the most distant degree connected with Government. In this general devastation were included the Senate-house, the President's palace, and extensive dock-yard and arsenal, barracks for two or three thousand men, several large store-houses filled with navel and military stores, some hundreds of cannon of different descriptions, and nearly twenty thousand stand of small arms. There were also two or three public rope-works which shared the same fate, a fine frigate pierced for sixty guns, and just ready to be launched, several gun brigs and armed schooners, with a variety of gun boats and small craft. The powder magazines were set on fire, and exploded with a tremendous crash, throwing down many houses in their vicinity, partly by pieces of the walls striking them, and partly by the concussion of the air ; whilst quantities of shot, shell, and hand grenades, which could not otherwise be rendered useless, were cast into the river. In destroying the cannon, a method was adopted, which I had never before witnessed, and which, as it was both effectual and expeditious, I cannot avoid relation. One gun of rather a small caliber, was pitched upon as the executioner of the rest ; and being loaded with ball, and turned to the muzzles of the others, it was fired, and thus beat out their breechings. Many, however, not being mounted, could not be thus dealt with ; these were spiked, and having their grunions knocked off, were afterwards cast into the bed of the river.

All this was as it should be, and had the arm of vengeance been extended no farther, there would not have been room given for so much as a shipper of disapprobation. But, unfortunately, it did not stop here ; a noble library, several printing offices, and all the national archives were likewise committed to the flames, which, though no doubt the property of Government, might better have been spared. It is not, however, my intentions join the outcry, which was raised at the time against what the Americans and their admirers were pleased to term a line of conduct at once barbarous and unprofitable. Far from it ; on the contrary, I cannot help admiring the forbearance and humanity of the British troops, who, irritated as they had every right to be, spared as far as was possible, all private property, neither plundering nor destroying a single house in the place, except that from which the General's horse had been killed. . . .

I need scarcely observe, that the consternation of the inhabitants was complete, and that to them this was a night of terror. So confident had they been of the success of their troops, that few of them had dreamt of quitting their houses, or abandoning the city ; nor was it till the fugitives from the battle began to rush in, filling every place as they came with dismay, that the President himself thought of providing for his safety. That gentleman, as I was credibly informed, had gone forth in the morning with the army, and had continued among his troops till the British forces began to make their appearance. Whether the sight of his enemies cooled his courage or not, I cannot say, but, according to my informant, no sooner was the glittering of our arms discernible, than he began to discover that his presence was more wanted in the senate that in the field; and having ridden through the ranks, and exhorted every man to do his duty, he hurried back to his own house, that he might prepare a feast for the entertainment of his officers, when they should return victorious. For the truth of these details, I will not be answerable ; but this much I know, that the feast was actually prepared, though, instead of being devoured by American officers, it went to satisfy the less delicate appetites of a party of English soldiers. When the detachment, sent out to destroy Mr. Madison's house, entered his dining parlour, they found a dinner table spread, and covers laid for forty guests. Several kinds of wine, in handsome cut-glass decanters, were cooling on the sideboard ; plate-holders stood by the fire-place, filled with dishes and plates ; knives, forks and spoons, were arranged for immediate use ; every thing in short was ready for the entertainment of a ceremonious party. Such were the arrangements in the dining-room, whilst in the kitchen were others

answerable to them in every respect. Spits, loaded with joints of various sorts, turned before the fire ; pots, saucepans, and other culinary utensils, stood upon the grate ; and all the other requisites for an elegant and substantial repast, were in the exact state which indicated that they had been lately and precipitately abandoned.

The reader will easily believe, that these preparations were beheld, by a party of hungry soldiers, with no indifferent eye. An elegant dinner, even though considerably over-dressed ; was a luxury to which few of them, at least for some time back, had been accustomed ; and which, after the dangers and fatigues of the day, appeared peculiarly inviting. They sat down to it, therefore, not indeed in the most orderly manner, but with countenances which would not have disgraced a party of aldermen at a civic feast ; and having satisfied their appetites with fewer complaints than would have probably escaped their rival *gourmands*, and partaken pretty freely of the wines, they finished by setting fire to the house which had so liberally entertained them. . . .

**QUESTIONS TO CONSIDER**

1. What did Gleig think about Americans?
2. Do you find his defense of British actions persuasive?

# 9.2 JOHN MARSHALL, MAJORITY OPINION IN *GIBBONS V. OGDEN* (1824)

John Marshall (1755–1835) is perhaps the most important Chief Justice in the history of the U.S. Supreme Court. A Federalist from Virginia, Marshall was appointed to the Court by John Adams in 1801 and set about issuing opinions that established the Court's power. In 1803's *Marbury v. Madison,* the Court under Marshall essentially created the doctrine of judicial review, which allowed the Court to rule laws unconstitutional. In *McCulloch v. Maryland* (1819), the Court ruled that states could not impede the work of the Second Bank of the United States. In the following document, the majority opinion in 1824's *Gibbons v. Ogden* hinged on the ability of the Federal government to regulate interstate commerce. The New York legislature had given a steamship monopoly to certain companies operating routes between New York and New Jersey. Competitors who opposed the monopoly asked the Court to overturn such monopolies on the basis that they violated the commerce clause of the Constitution, giving Congress the power "to regulate Commerce with foreign Nations, and among the several States." In a carefully argued opinion, Marshall overturned the monopolies and again reinforced Federal power.

Mr. Chief Justice MARSHALL delivered the opinion of the Court, and, after stating the case, proceeded as follows:

The appellant contends that this decree is erroneous because the laws which purport to give the exclusive privilege it sustains are repugnant to the Constitution and laws of the United States. They are said to be repugnant: first, to that clause in the Constitution which authorizes Congress to regulate commerce; second, to that which authorizes Congress to promote the progress of science and useful arts.

As preliminary to the very able discussions of the Constitution which we have heard from the bar, and as having some influence on its construction, reference has been made to the political situation of these states, anterior to its formation. It has been said that they were sovereign, were completely independent, and were connected with each other only by a league. This is true. But, when these allied sovereigns converted their league into a government, when they converted their congress of ambassadors, deputed to deliberate on their common concerns, and to recommend measures of general utility, into a legislature, empowered to enact laws on the most interesting subjects, the whole character in which the states appear underwent a change, the extent of which must be determined by a fair consideration of the instrument by which that change was effected.

This instrument contains an enumeration of powers expressly granted by the people to their government. It has been said that these powers ought to be construed strictly. But why ought they to be so construed? Is there one sentence in the Constitution which gives countenance to this rule? In the last of the enumerated powers, that which grants, expressly, the means for carrying all others into execution, Congress

*Source:* "Transcript of Gibbons v. Ogden (1824)," https://www.ourdocuments.gov/doc.php?flash=false&doc=24&page=transcript (Accessed June 6, 2018).

is authorized *to make all laws which shall be necessary and proper* for the purpose. But this limitation on the means which may be used is not extended to the powers which are conferred; nor is there one sentence in the Constitution, which has been pointed out by the gentlemen of the bar, or which we have been able to discern, that prescribes this rule. We do not, therefore, think ourselves justified in adopting it.

What do gentlemen mean by a strict construction? If they contend only against that enlarged construction which would extend words beyond their natural and obvious import, we might question the application of the term, but should not controvert the principle. If they contend for that narrow construction which, in support of some theory not to be found in the Constitution, would deny to the government those powers which the words of the grant, as usually understood, import, and which are consistent with the general views and objects of the instrument; for that narrow construction, which would cripple the government, and render it unequal to the objects for which it is declared to be instituted, and to which the powers given, as fairly understood, render it competent; then we cannot perceive the propriety of this strict construction, nor adopt it as the rule by which the Constitution is to be expounded. As men whose intentions require no concealment generally employ the words which most directly and aptly express the ideas they in tend to convey, the enlightened patriots who framed our Constitution, and the people who adopted it, must be understood to have employed words in their natural sense, and to have intended what they have said.

If, from the imperfection of human language, there should be serious doubts respecting the extent of any given power, it is a well-settled rule that the objects for which it was given, especially when those objects are expressed in the instrument itself, should have great influence in the construction. We know of no reason for excluding this rule from the present case. The grant does not convey power which might be beneficial to the grantor, if retained by himself, or which can inure solely to the benefit of the grantee, but is an investment of power for the general advantage in the hands of agents selected for that purpose; which power can never be exercised by the people

themselves, but must be placed in the hands of agents, or lie dormant. We know of no rule for construing the extent of such powers other than is given by the language of the instrument which confers them, taken in connection with the purposes for which they were conferred.

The words are: *Congress shall have power to regulate commerce with foreign nations, and among the several states, and with the Indian tribes.* The subject to be regulated is commerce; and our Constitution being, as was aptly said at the bar, one of enumeration and not of definition, to as certain the extent of the power it becomes necessary to settle the meaning of the word.

Commerce, undoubtedly, is traffic, but it is something more—it is intercourse. It describes the commercial intercourse between nations, and parts of nations, in all its branches, and is regulated by prescribing rules for carrying on that intercourse. The mind can scarcely conceive a system for regulating commerce between nations which shall exclude all laws concerning navigation, which shall be silent on the admission of the vessels of the one nation into the ports of the other, and be confined to prescribing rules for the conduct of individuals in the actual employment of buying and selling or of barter. If commerce does not include navigation, the government of the Union has no direct power over that subject, and can make no law prescribing what shall constitute American vessels, or requiring that they shall be navigated by American seamen.

Yet this power has been exercised from the commencement of the government, has been exercised with the consent of all, and. has been understood by all to be a commercial regulation. All America understands, and has uniformly understood, the word *commerce* to comprehend navigation.

The word used in the Constitution, then, comprehends, and has been always understood to comprehend, navigation within its meaning; and a power to regulate navigation is as expressly granted as if that term had been added to the word *commerce*. To what commerce does this power extend? The Constitution informs us to commerce *with foreign nations, and among the several states, and with the Indian tribes.* It has, we believe, been universally admitted that these words comprehend every species of commercial intercourse between the United States and foreign nations. No sort of trade can be carried on between this country and any other to which this power does not extend. It has been truly said that commerce, as the word is used in the Constitution, is a unit, every part of which is indicated by the term. If this be the admitted meaning of the word in its application to foreign nations, it must carry the same meaning throughout the sentence and remain a unit, unless there be some plain intelligible cause which alters it.

The subject to which the power is next applied is to commerce *among the several states.* The word *among* means intermingled with. A thing which is among others is intermingled with them. Commerce among the states cannot stop at the external boundary line of each state, but may be introduced into the interior. It is not intended to say that these words comprehend that commerce which is completely internal, which is carried on between man and man in a state, or between different parts of the same state, and which does not extend to or affect other states. Such a power would be inconvenient and is certainly unnecessary. Comprehensive as the word *among* is, it may very properly be restricted to that commerce which concerns more states than one. The phrase is not one which would probably have been selected to indicate the completely interior traffic of a state, because it is not an apt phrase for that purpose; and the enumeration of the particular classes of commerce to which the power was to be extended would not have been made had the intention been to extend the power to every description. The enumeration presupposes something not enumerated; and that something, if we regard the language or the subject of the sentence, must be the exclusively internal commerce of a state.

The genius and character of the whole government seem to be that its action is to be applied to all the external concerns of the nation and to those internal concerns which affect the states generally; but not to those which are completely within a particular state, which do not affect other states, and with which it is not necessary to interfere for the purpose of executing some of the general powers of the government. The completely internal commerce of a state, then, may be considered as reserved for the state itself.

But, in regulating commerce with foreign nations, the power of Congress does not stop at the jurisdictional lines of the several states. It would be a very useless power if it could not pass those lines. The commerce of the United States with foreign nations is that of the whole United States. Every district has a right to participate in it. The deep streams which penetrate our country in every direction pass through the interior of almost every state in the Union, and furnish the means of exercising this right. If Congress has the power to regulate it, that power must be exercised whenever the subject exists. If it exists within the states, if a foreign voyage may commence or terminate at a port within a state, then the power of Congress may be exercised within a state.

This principle is, if possible, still more clear, when applied to commerce *among the several states.* They either join each other, in which case they are separated by a mathematical line, or they are remote from each other, in which case other states lie between them. What is commerce *among* them, and how is it to be conducted? Can a trading expedition between two adjoining states commence and terminate outside of each? And if the trading intercourse be between two states remote from each other, must it not commence in one, terminate in the other, and probably pass through a third? Commerce among the states must, of necessity, be commerce with the states. In the regulation of trade with the Indian tribes, the action of the law, especially, when the Constitution was made, was chiefly within a state.

The power of Congress, then, whatever it may be, must be exercised within the territorial jurisdiction of the several states. The sense of the nation on this subject is unequivocally manifested by the provisions made in the laws for transporting goods by land between Baltimore and Providence, between New York and Philadelphia, and between Philadelphia and Baltimore. . . .

In one case and the other the acts of New York must yield to the law of Congress; and the decision sustaining the privilege they confer against a right given by a law of the Union must be erroneous. This opinion has been frequently expressed in this court, and is founded as well on the nature of the government as on the words of the Constitution. In argument, however, it has been contended that, if a law passed by a state in the exercise of its acknowledged sovereignty comes into conflict with a law passed by Congress in pursuance of the Constitution, they affect the subject and each other like equal opposing powers.

But the framers of our Constitution foresaw this state of things and provided for it by declaring the supremacy not only of itself but of the laws made in pursuance of it. The nullity of any act inconsistent with the Constitution is produced by the declaration that the Constitution is supreme law. The appropriate application of that part of the clause which confers the same supremacy on laws and treaties is to such acts of the state legislatures as do not transcend their powers, but though enacted in the execution of acknowledged state powers, interfere with, or are contrary to, the laws of Congress, made in pursuance of the Constitution or some treaty made under the authority of the United States. In every such case, the act of Congress or the treaty is supreme; and the law of the state, though enacted in the exercise of powers not controverted, must yield to it.

**DECREE**

This court is of opinion that so much of the several laws of the state of New York as prohibits vessels, licensed according to the laws of the United States, from navigating the waters of the state of New York, by means of fire or steam, is repugnant to the said Constitution and void. This court is, therefore, of opinion that the decree of the court of New York for the trial of impeachments and the correction of errors, affirming the decree of the chancellor of that state is erroneous and ought to be reversed, and the same is hereby reversed and annulled. And this court doth further direct, order, and decree that the bill of the said Aaron Ogden be dismissed, and the same is hereby dismissed accordingly.

**QUESTIONS TO CONSIDER**

1. How did Marshall support the decision?
2. Do you find the decision to be persuasive?

# 9.3 NATHANIEL HAWTHORNE, EXCERPT FROM "THE CANAL BOAT" (1835)

American author Nathaniel Hawthorne (1804–1864) is probably best known for his 1850 novel *The Scarlet Letter,* set in seventeenth-century Puritan Massachusetts. In 1835, however, he published a more modern short story, "The Canal Boat." Hawthorne set the story on the Erie Canal, which ran between Albany and Buffalo, New York, and connected the Great Lakes to the Atlantic Ocean. Built between 1817 and 1825, the Canal quickly became an enormously successful venture. Originally derided as "Clinton's Folly," after New York Governor Dewitt Clinton, who had supported the project, the Canal cut transport costs by ninety-five percent and helped to develop western New York. Hawthorne's story provides a whimsical look at the changing geography of New York State.

I was inclined to be poetical about the Grand Canal. In my imagination, DeWitt Clinton was an enchanter, who had waved his magic wand from the Hudson to lake Erie, and united them by a watery highway crowded with the commerce of two worlds, till then inaccessible to each other. This simple and might conception had conferred inestimable value on spots which nature seemed to have thrown carelessly

*Source:* Roger W. Hecht, ed., *The Erie Canal Reader, 1790–1950* (Syracuse: Syracuse University Press, 2003), 78–85.

into the great body of the earth, without foreseeing that they could ever attain importance. I pictured the surprise of the sleepy Dutchmen when the new river first glittered by their doors, bringing them hard cash or foreign commodities, in exchange for their hitherto unmarketable produce. Surely, the water of this canal must be the most fertilizing of all fluids; for it causes towns—with their masses of brick and stone, their churches and theatres, their business and hubbub, their luxury and refinement, their gay dames and polished citizens—to spring up, till, in time, the wondrous stream may flow between two continuous lines of buildings, through one thronged street, from Buffalo to Albany. I embarked about thirty miles below Utica, determining to voyage along the whole extent of the canal, at least twice in the course of the summer.

Behold us, then, fairly afloat, with three horses harnessed to our vessel, like the steeds of Neptune to a huge scallop-shell, in mythological pictures. Bound to a distant port, we had neither chart nor compass, nor cared about the wind, nor felt the heaving of a billow, nor dreaded shipwreck, however fierce the tempest, in our adventurous navigation of an interminable mud-puddle—for a mud-puddle it seemed, and as dark and turbid as if every kennel in the land paid contribution to it. With an imperceptible current, it holds its drowsy way through all the dismal swamps and unimpressive scenery, that could be found between the great lakes and sea-coast. yet there is variety enough, both on the surface of the canal and along its banks, to amuse the traveler, if an overpowering tedium did not deaden his perceptions.

Sometimes we met a black and rusty-looking vessel, laden with lumber, salt from Syracuse, or Genessee [*sic*] flour, and shaped at both ends like a square-toed boot, as if it had two sterns, and were fated always to advance backward. On its deck would be a square hut, and a woman seen through the window at her house-hold work, with a little tribe of children, who perhaps had been born in this strange dwelling and knew no other home. Thus, while the husband smoked his pipe at the helm, and the eldest son rode one of their horses, on went the family, traveling hundreds of miles in their own house, and carrying their fireside with them. The most frequent species of crafter were the 'line boats,' which had a cabin at each end, and a great bulk of barrels, bales, and boxes in the midst; or light packets, like our own, decked all over, with a row of curtained windows from stem to stern, and a drowsy face at every one. Once, we encountered a boat, of rude construction, painted all in gloomy black, and manned by three Indians, who gazed at us in silence and with a singular fixedness of eye. Perhaps these three alone, among the ancient possessors of the land, had attempted to derive benefit from the white man's mighty projects, and float along the current of his enterprise. Not long after, in the midst of a swamp and beneath a clouded sky, we overtook a vessel that seemed full of mirth and sunshine. It contained a little colony of Swiss, on their way to Michigan, clad in garments of strange fashion and gay colors, scarlet, yellow and bright blue, singing, laughing, and making merry, in odd tones and a babble of outlandish words. One pretty damsel with a beautiful pair of naked white arms, addressed a mirthful remark to me; she spoke in her native tongue, and I retorted in good English, both of us laughing heartily at each other's unintelligible wit. I cannot describe how pleasantly this incident affected me. These honest Swiss were an itinerant community of jest and fun, journeying through a gloomy land and among a dull race of money-getting drudges, meeting none to understand their mirth and only one to sympathize with it, yet still retaining the happy lightness of their own spirit. . . .

. . . A lantern was burning at each end of the boat, and one of the crew was stationed at the bows, keeping watch, as mariners do on the ocean. Though the rain had ceased, the sky was all one cloud, and the darkness so intense, that there seemed to be no world, except the little space on which our lanterns glimmered. Yet, it was an impressive scene.

We were traversing the "long level," a dead flat between Utica and Syracuse, where the canal has not rise or fall enough to require a lock for nearly seventy miles. There can hardly be a more dismal tract of country. The forest which covers it, consisting chiefly of white cedar, black ash, and other trees that live in excessive moisture, is now decayed and death-struck, by the partial draining of the swamp into the great ditch of the canal. Sometimes, indeed, our lights were reflected from pools of stagnant water, which stretched far in among the trunks of the trees, beneath dense masses of dark foliage. But generally, the tall stems and intermingled branches were naked, and brought into strong relief, amid the surrounding gloom, by the whiteness of their decay. Often, we beheld the prostrate form of some old sylvan giant, which had fallen, and crushed down smaller trees under its immense ruin. In spots, where destruction had been riotous, the lanterns showed perhaps a hundred trunks, erect, half overthrown, extended along the ground, resting on their shattered limbs, or tossing them desperately into the darkness, but all of one ashy-white, all naked together, in desolate confusion. Thus growing out of the night as we drew nigh, and vanishing as we glided on, based on obscurity, and overhung and bounded by it, the scene was ghost-like—the very land of unsubstantial things, whither dreams might betake themselves, when they quit the slumberer's brain.

My fancy found another emblem. The wild Nature of America had been driven to this desert-place by the encroachments of civilized man. And even here, where the savage queen was throned on the ruins of her empire, did we penetrate, a vulgar and worldly throng, intruding on her latest solitude. In other lands, Decay sits among fallen palaces; but here, her home is in the forests.

Looking ahead, I discerned a distant light, announcing the approach of another boat, which soon passed us, and proved to be a rusty old scow—just such a craft as the "Flying Dutchman" would navigate on the canal. Perhaps it was that celebrated personage himself, whom I imperfectly distinguished at the helm, in a glazed hat and rough greatcoat, with a pipe in his mouth, leaving the fumes of tobacco a hundred yards behind. Shortly after, our boatman blew a horn, sending a long and melancholy note through the forest-avenue, as a signal for some watcher in the wilderness to be ready with a change of horses. We had proceeded a mile or two with our fresh team, when the tow-rope got entangled in a fallen branch on the edge of the canal, and caused a momentary delay, during which I went to examine the phosphoric light of an old tree, a little within the forest. It was not the first delusive radiance that I had followed.

The tree lay along the ground, and was wholly converted into a mass of diseased splendor, which threw a ghastliness around. Being full of conceits that night, I called it a frigid fire; a funeral light, illumining decay and death; an emblem of fame, that gleams around the dead man without warming him; or of genius, when it owes its brilliancy to moral rottenness; and was thinking that such ghost-like torches were just fit to light up this dead forest, or to blaze coldly in tombs, when, starting from my abstraction, I looked up the canal. I recollected myself, and discovered the lanterns glimmering far away.

"Boat ahoy!" shouted I, making a trumpet of my closed fists.

Though the cry must have rung for miles along that hollow passage of the woods, it produced no effect. These packet-boats make up for their snail-like pace by never loitering day nor night, especially for those who have paid their fare. Indeed, the captain had an interest in getting rid of me, for I was his creditor for a breakfast.

"They are gone! Heaven be praised!" ejaculated I, "for I cannot possibly overtake them! Here I am, on the 'long level,' at midnight, with the comfortable prospect of a walk to Syracuse, where my baggage will be left: and now to find a house or shed, wherein to pass the night." So thinking aloud, I took a flambeau from the old tree, burning, but consuming not, to light my steps withal, and, like a Jack-o'-the-lantern, set out on my midnight tour.

## QUESTIONS TO CONSIDER

1. Does Hawthorne portray the Canal in a positive or negative light?
2. What do you make of the end of the story? Does it change how Hawthorne portrays the Canal?

# 9.4 HARRIET HANSON ROBINSON, "CHARACTERISTICS OF THE EARLY FACTORY GIRLS" (1898)

In 1813, an entrepreneur named Francis Cabot Lowell built a textile mill in Waltham, Massachusetts. Over the next three decades, additional mills were built, and Lowell came to be known as the "City of Spindles." Largely, the Lowell Mills depended on the labor of young, working-class women. These "factory girls" simultaneously labored in a large-scale industrial experiment and lived in single-sex dormitories meant to uplift them. Women worked an average of seventy-three hours per week in the mills, but the boarding houses offered a relatively intellectual culture. The Lowell Mills, therefore, were meant to combine the benefits of the large-scale British industrial system while avoiding the deleterious effects on worker populations. Harriet Hanson Robinson (1825–1911) began working at the Lowell Mills at age 10. Her 1898 memoir *Loom and Spindle, or Life among the Early Mills Girls*, from which the following reading is taken, gives wonderful detail as to life at the mills. In the reading, Robinson describes the worker population and then narrates an 1836 strike carried out in response to the Lowell Board of Directors' decision to raise rents.

## CHAPTER IV. THE CHARACTERISTICS OF THE EARLY FACTORY GIRLS.

WHEN I look back into the factory life of fifty or sixty years ago, I do not see what is called "a class" of young men and women going to and from their daily work, like so many ants that cannot be distinguished one from another ; I see them as individuals, with personalities of their own. This one has about her the atmosphere of her early home. That one is impelled by a strong and noble purpose. The other,—what she is, has been an influence for good to me and to all womankind.

Yet they were a class of factory operatives, and were spoken of (as the same class in spoken of now) as a set of persons who earned their daily bread, whose condition was fixed, and who must continue to spin and to weave to the end of their natural existence. Nothing but this was expected of them, and they were not supposed to be capable of social or mental improvement. That they could be educated and developed into something more than mere work-people, was an idea that had not yet entered the public mind. So little does one class of persons really know about the thoughts and aspirations of another! It was the good fortune of these early mill-girls to teach the people of that time that this sort of labor is not degrading ; that the operative is not only "capable of virtue," but also capable of self-cultivation.

At the time the Lowell cotton-mills were started, the factory girl was the lowest among women. In England, and in France particularly, great injustice had been done to her real character ; she was represented as subjected to influences that could not fail to destroy her purity and self-respect. In the eyes of her overseer she was but a brute, a slave, to be beaten, pinched, and pushed about. It was to overcome this prejudice that

*Source:* Harriet Hanson Robinson, *Loom and Spindle, or Life among the Early Mill Girls* (New York: Thomas Y. Crowell & Company, 1898), 60–64, 83–85. Retrieved from the Internet Archive website, https://archive.org/details/loomspindleorlif00robiuoft (Accessed June 6, 2018).

such high wages had been offered to women that they might be induced to become mill-girls, in spite of the opprobrium that still clung to this "degrading occupation." At first only a few came ; for, though tempted by the high wages to be regularly paid in "cash," there were many who still preferred to go on working at some more *genteel* employment at seventy five cents a week and their board.

But in a short time the prejudice against factory labor wore away, and the Lowell mills became filled with blooming and energetic New England women. They were naturally intelligent, had mother-wit, and fell easily into the ways of their new life. They soon began to associate with those who formed the community in which they had come to live, and were invited to their houses. They went to the same church, and sometimes married into some of the best families. Or if they returned to their secluded homes again, instead of being looked down upon as "factory girls" by the squire's or the lawyer's family, they were more often welcomed as coming from the metropolis, bringing new fashions, new books, and new ideas with them.

In 1831 Lowell was little more than a factory village. Several corporations were started, and the cotton-mills belonging to them were building. Help was in great demand ; and stories were told all over the country of the new factory town, and the high wages that were offered to all classes of work-people,—stories that reached the ears of mechanics' and farmers' sons, and gave new life to lonely and dependent women in distant towns and farmhouses. Into this Yankee El Dorado, these needy people began to pour by the various modes of travel known to those slow old days. The stage-coach and the canal-boat came every day, always filled with new recruits for this army of useful people. The mechanic and machinist came, each with his home-made chest of tools, and oftentimes his wife and little ones. The widow came with her little flock and her scanty housekeeping goods to open a boarding-house or variety store, and so provided a home for her fatherless children. Many farmers' daughters came to earn money to complete their wedding outfit, or but the bride's share of housekeeping articles.

Women with past histories came, to hide their griefs and their identity, and to earn an honest living in the "sweat of their brow." Single young men came, full of hope and life, to get money for an education, or to lift the mortgage from the home-farm. Troops of young girls came by stages and baggage-wagons, men often being employed to go to other States and to Canada, to collect them at so much a head, and deliver them at the factories.

A very curious sight these country girls presented to young eyes accustomed to a more modern style of things. When the large covered baggage-wagon arrived in front of a block-on the corporation, they would descend from it, dressed in various and outlandish fashions, and with their arms brimful of bandboxes containing all their worldly goods. On each of these was sewed a card, on which one could read the old-fashioned New England name of the owner. And sorrowful enough they looked, even to the fun-loving child who has lived to tell the story ; for they had all left their pleasant country homes to try their fortunes in a great manufacturing town, and they were homesick even before they landed at the doors of their even they landed at the doors of their boarding-houses. Years after, this scene dwelt in my memory ; and whenever anyone said anything about being homesick, there rose before me the picture of a young girl with a sorrowful face and a big tear in each eye, clambering down the steps at the rear of a great covered wagon, holding fast to a cloth-covered bandbox, drawn up at the top with a string, on which was sewed a paper bearing the name of Plumy Clay! . . .

### CHAPTER V. CHARACTERISTICS (CONTINUED).

One of the first strikes of cotton-factory operatives that ever took place in this country was that in Lowell, in October, 1836. When it was announced that the wages were to be cut down. Great indignation was felt, and it was decided to strike, *en masse*. This was done. The mills were shut down, and the girls went in procession from their several corporations to the "grove" on Chapel Hill, and listened to "incendiary" speeches from early labor reformers.

One of the girls stood on a pump, and gave vent to the feelings of her companions in a neat speech, declaring that it was their duty to resist all attempts at cutting down the wages. This was the first time a woman had spoken in public in Lowell, and the event caused surprise and consternation among her audience.

Cutting down the wages was not their only grievance, nor the only cause of this strike. Hitherto the corporations had paid twenty-five cents a week towards the board of each operative, and now it was their purpose to have the girls pay the sum ; and this, in addition to the cut in the wages, would make a difference of at least one dollar a week. It was estimated that as many as twelve or fifteen hundred girls turned out, and walked in procession through the streets. They had neither flags nor music, but sang songs, a favorite (but rather inappropriate) one being a parody on "I won't be a nun."

> "Oh ! isn't it a pity, such a pretty girl as I—
> Should be sent to the factory to pine away and
>     die?
> Oh ! I cannot be a slave,
> I will not be a slave,
> For I'm so fond of liberty
> That I cannot be a slave."

My own recollection of this first strike (or "turn out" as it was called) is very vivid. I worked in a lower room, where I had heard the proposed strike fully, if not vehemently, discussed ; I had been an ardent listener to what was said against this attempt at "oppression" on the part of the corporation, and naturally I took sides with the strikers. When the day came on which the girls were to turn out, those in the upper rooms started first, and so many of them left that our mill was at once shut down. Then, when the girls in my room stood irresolute, uncertain what to do, asking each other, "Would you?" or "Shall we turn out?" and not one of them having the courage to lead off, I, who began to think they would not go out, after all their talk, became impatient, and started on ahead, saying, with childish bravado, "I don't care what you do, I am going to turn out, whether any one else does or not ;" and I marched out, and was followed by the others.

As I looked back at the long line that followed me, I was more proud than I have ever been since at any success I may have achieved, and more proud than I shall ever be again until my own beloved State gives to its women citizens the right of suffrage. . . .

## QUESTIONS TO CONSIDER

1. Does Robinson view the Lowell Mills as a positive place for women? Do you agree?
2. Do you think the strike was a transformative moment for Robinson and for women's rights at Lowell more broadly?

# CHAPTER 10

# JACKSONIAN DEMOCRACY, 1820–1840

## 10.1 JAMES MONROE, "SEVENTH ANNUAL MESSAGE" (MONROE DOCTRINE) (1823)

James Monroe (1758–1831) was the fifth President of the United States. A Revolutionary War veteran, Monroe served as a U.S. Senator, Governor of Virginia, and Secretary of State before becoming President in 1817. Monroe is probably best known for his "Monroe Doctrine," which he formulated in his 1823 State of the Union Address, the following document. In it, Monroe tried to combat European encroachment into the Americas. The doctrine was also part of a broader effort to remove the United States from its isolationist, parochial roots. Under Monroe, the United States created a colony for freed slaves in Africa, Liberia; secured land and fishing rights in the American west; and purchased Florida. Notably, Monroe issued his proclamation in the midst of widespread independence movements throughout Latin America. During the centuries ahead, Americans politicians would continue to return to the Monroe Doctrine as a basis for foreign policies toward Central and South America.

Many important subjects will claim your attention during the present session, of which I shall endeavor to give, in aid of your deliberations, a just idea in this communication. I undertake this duty with diffidence, from the vast extent of the interests on which I have to treat and of their great importance to every portion of our Union. I enter on it with zeal from a thorough conviction that there never was a period since the establishment of our Revolution when, regarding the condition of the civilized world and its bearing on us, there was greater necessity for devotion in the public servants to their respective duties, or for virtue, patriotism, and union in our constituents.

Meeting in you a new Congress, I deem it proper to present this view of public affairs in greater detail than might otherwise be necessary. I do it, however, with peculiar satisfaction, from a knowledge that in this respect I shall comply more fully with the sound principles of our Government.

The people being with us exclusively the sovereign, it is indispensable that full information be laid before them on all important subjects, to enable them to

*Source:* "James Monroe: Seventh Annual Message," http://www.presidency.ucsb.edu/ws/index.php?pid=29465 (Accessed June 6, 2018).

exercise that high power with complete effect. If kept in the dark, they must be incompetent to it. We are all liable to error, and those who are engaged in the management of public affairs are more subject to excitement and to be led astray by their particular interests and passions than the great body of our constituents, who, living at home in the pursuit of their ordinary avocations, are calm but deeply interested spectators of events and of the conduct of those who are parties to them.

To the people every department of the Government and every individual in each are responsible, and the more full their information the better they can judge of the wisdom of the policy pursued and of the conduct of each in regard to it. From their dispassionate judgment much aid may always be obtained, while their approbation will form the greatest incentive and most gratifying reward for virtuous actions, and the dread of their censure the best security against the abuse of their confidence. Their interests in all vital questions are the same, and the bond, by sentiment as well as by interest, will be proportionably strengthened as they are better informed of the real state of public affairs, especially in difficult conjunctures. It is by such knowledge that local prejudices and jealousies are surmounted, and that a national policy extending its fostering care and protection to all the great interests of our Union, is formed and steadily adhered to.

A precise knowledge of our relations with foreign powers as respects our negotiations and transactions with each is thought to be particularly necessary. Equally necessary is it that we should for a just estimate of our resources, revenue, and progress in every kind of improvement connected with the national prosperity and public defense. It is by rendering justice to other nations that we may expect it from them. It is by our ability to resent injuries and redress wrongs that we may avoid them. . . .

At the commencement of the recent war between France and Spain it was declared by the French Government that it would grant no commissions to privateers, and that neither the commerce of Spain herself nor of neutral nations should be molested by the naval force of France, except in the breach of a lawful blockade. This declaration, which appears to have been faithfully carried into effect, concurring with

principles proclaimed and cherished by the United States from the first establishment of their independence, suggested the hope that the time had arrived when the proposal for adopting it as a permanent and invariable rule in all future maritime wars might meet the favorable consideration of the great European powers. Instructions have accordingly been given to our ministers with France, Russia, and Great Britain to make those proposals to their respective Governments, and when the friends of humanity reflect on the essential amelioration to the condition of the human race which would result from the abolition of private war on the sea and on the great facility by which it might be accomplished, requiring only the consent of a few sovereigns, an earnest hope is indulged that these overtures will meet with an attention animated by the spirit in which they were made, and that they will ultimately be successful. . . .

It was stated at the commencement of the last session that a great effort was then making in Spain and Portugal to improve the condition of the people of those countries, and that it appeared to be conducted with extraordinary moderation. It need scarcely be remarked that the result has been so far very different from what was then anticipated. Of events in that quarter of the globe, with which we have so much intercourse and from which we derive our origin, we have always been anxious and interested spectators.

The citizens of the United States cherish sentiments the most friendly in favor of the liberty and happiness of their fellow men on that side of the Atlantic. In the wars of the European powers in matters relating to themselves we have never taken any part, nor does it comport with our policy so to do.

It is only when our rights are invaded or seriously menaced that we resent injuries or make preparation for our defense. With the movements in this hemisphere we are of necessity more immediately connected, and by causes which must be obvious to all enlightened and impartial observers.

The political system of the allied powers is essentially different in this respect from that of America. This difference proceeds from that which exists in their respective Governments; and to the defense of our own, which has been achieved by the loss of so much blood and treasure, and matured by the wisdom of their most enlightened citizens, and under which we have enjoyed unexampled felicity, this whole nation is devoted.

We owe it, therefore, to candor and to the amicable relations existing between the United States and those powers to declare that we should consider any attempt on their part to extend their system to any portion of this hemisphere as dangerous to our peace and safety. With the existing colonies or dependencies of any European power we have not interfered and shall not interfere, but with the Governments who have declared their independence and maintained it, and whose independence we have, on great consideration and on just principles, acknowledged, we could not view any interposition for the purpose of oppressing them, or controlling in any other manner their destiny, by any European power in any other light than as the manifestation of an unfriendly disposition toward the United States.

In the war between those new Governments and Spain we declared our neutrality at the time of their recognition, and to this we have adhered, and shall continue to adhere, provided no change shall occur which, in the judgment of the competent authorities of this Government, shall make a corresponding change on the part of the United States indispensable to their security.

The late events in Spain and Portugal shew that Europe is still unsettled. Of this important fact no stronger proof can be adduced than that the allied powers should have thought it proper, on any principle satisfactory to themselves, to have interposed by force in the internal concerns of Spain. To what extent such interposition may be carried, on the same principle, is a question in which all independent powers whose governments differ from theirs are interested, even those most remote, and surely none more so than the United States.

Our policy in regard to Europe, which was adopted at an early stage of the wars which have so long agitated that quarter of the globe, nevertheless remains the same, which is, not to interfere in the internal concerns of any of its powers; to consider the government de facto as the legitimate government for us; to cultivate friendly relations with it, and to preserve those relations by a frank, firm, and manly policy, meeting in all instances the just claims of every power, submitting to injuries from none.

But in regard to those continents circumstances are eminently and conspicuously different. It is impossible that the allied powers should extend their political system to any portion of either continent without endangering our peace and happiness; nor can anyone believe that our southern brethren, if left to themselves, would adopt it of their own accord. It is equally impossible, therefore, that we should behold such interposition in any form with indifference. If we look to the comparative strength and resources of Spain and those new Governments, and their distance from each other, it must be obvious that she can never subdue them. It is still the true policy of the United States to leave the parties to themselves, in the hope that other powers will pursue the same course.

If we compare the present condition of our Union with its actual state at the close of our Revolution, the history of the world furnishes no example of a progress in improvement in all the important circumstances which constitute the happiness of a nation which bears any resemblance to it. At the first epoch our population did not exceed 3,000,000. By the last census it amounted to about 10,000,000, and, what is more extraordinary, it is almost altogether native, for the immigration from other countries has been inconsiderable.

At the first epoch half the territory within our acknowledged limits was uninhabited and a wilderness. Since then new territory has been acquired of vast extent, comprising within it many rivers, particularly the Mississippi, the navigation of which to the ocean was of the highest importance to the original States. Over this territory our population has expanded in every direction, and new States have been established almost equal in number to those which formed the first bond of our Union. This expansion of our population and accession of new States to our Union have had the happiest effect on all its highest interests.

That it has eminently augmented our resources and added to our strength and respectability as a power is admitted by all, but it is not in these important circumstances only that this happy effect is felt. It is manifest that by enlarging the basis of our system and increasing the number of States the system itself has been greatly strengthened in both its branches. Consolidation and disunion have thereby been rendered equally impracticable.

Each Government, confiding in its own strength, has less to apprehend from the other, and in consequence each, enjoying a greater freedom of action, is rendered more efficient for all the purposes for which it was instituted.

It is unnecessary to treat here of the vast improvement made in the system itself by the adoption of this Constitution and of its happy effect in elevating the character and in protecting the rights of the nation as well as individuals. To what, then, do we owe these blessings? It is known to all that we derive them from the excellence of our institutions. Ought we not, then, to adopt every measure which may be necessary to perpetuate them?

**QUESTIONS TO CONSIDER**

1. How does Monroe make his case for the Monroe Doctrine?

2. If you were running a European power at the time, would you have found his case convincing?

# 10.2 ELIAS BOUDINOT, "AN ADDRESS TO THE WHITES" (1826)

In the eighteenth century, the Cherokee Nation occupied a large tract of land in northern Georgia and eastern Alabama. One of the "Five Civilized Tribes," the Cherokee increasingly submitted to Federal demands to assimilate into white society during the late eighteenth and early nineteenth centuries. They abandoned traditional hunting practices, created a court system, and implemented a republican form of government. One Cherokee, Sequoyah, even created a Cherokee syllabary that allowed them to write in the traditionally spoken Cherokee language. During the first decades of the nineteenth century, however, whites increasingly moved in close proximity to Cherokee land and began urging their political leaders to move the Cherokee farther west. The potential for their removal led to a split amongst Cherokee power brokers. On the one side were men such as Elias Boudinot (1802–1839), who believed that removal was inevitable. On the other side were men such as John Ross (see Reading 10.5), who wanted to fight removal. In 1826, Boudinot gave the following fundraising speech to a Presbyterian Church in Philadelphia. In it, he compared white society to Cherokee society and argued for a greater understanding and acceptance of Cherokee culture. In 1835, Boudinot and other accommodationists signed the Treaty of New Echota, which ceded all Cherokee land in exchange for land farther west. Though the Cherokee Nation did not approve the treaty, the U.S. Senate ratified it and began removing the tribe. In 1839, Boudinot was among a group of three treaty-signers assassinated by a group of enraged Cherokee who blamed them for removal.

*Source:* Elias Boudinot, *An Address to the Whites* (Philadelphia: William F. Geddes, 1826), 3–14. Retrieved from the Internet Archive website, https://archive.org/details/addressto00boud (Accessed June 6, 2018).

To those who are unacquainted with the manners, habits, and improvements of the Aborigines of this country, the term *Indian* in pregnant with ideas the most repelling and degrading. But such impressions, originating as they frequently do, from infant prejudices, although they hold too true when applied to some, do great injustice to many of this race of beings.

Some there are, perhaps even in this enlightened assembly, who at the bare sight of an Indian, or at the mention of the name, would throw back their imaginations to ancient times, to the ravages of savage warfare, to the yells pronounced over the mangled bodies of women and children, thus creating an opinion, inapplicable and highly injurious to those for whose temporal interest and eternal welfare, I come to plead.

What is an Indian? Is he not formed of the same materials with yourself? For "of one blood God created all the nations that dwell on the face of the earth." Though it be true that he is ignorant, that he is a heathen, that he is a savage ; yet he is no more than all others have been under similar circumstances. Eighteen centuries ago what were the inhabitants of Great Britain?

You here behold an *Indian*, my kindred are *Indians*, and my fathers sleeping in the wilderness grave—they too were *Indians*. But I am not as my fathers were—broader means and nobler influences have fallen upon me. Yet I was not born as thousands are, in a stately dome and amid the congratulations of the great, for on a little hill, in a lonely cabin, overspread by the forest oak, I first drew my breath ; and in a language unknown to learned and polished nations, I learnt to lisp my fond mother's name. In after days, I have had greater advantages than most of my race ; and I now stand before you delegated by my native country to seek her interest, to labour for her respectability, and by my public efforts to assist in raising her to an equal standing with other nations of the earth.

The time has arrived when speculations and conjectures as to the practicability of civilizing the Indians must forever cease. A period is fast approaching when the stale remark—"Do what you will, an Indian will still be an Indian," must be placed no more in speech. With whatever plausibility this popular objection may have heretofore been made, every candid mind must now be sensible that it can no longer be uttered, except by those who are uninformed with respect to us, who are strongly prejudiced against us, or who are filled with vindictive feelings towards us ; for the present history of the Indians, particularly of that nation to which I belong, most incontrovertibly establishes the fallacy of this remark. I am aware of the difficulties which have ever existed to Indian civilization, I do not deny the almost insurmountable obstacles which we ourselves have thrown in the way of this improvement, nor do I say that difficulties no longer remain ; but facts will permit me to declare that there are none which may not easily be overcome, by strong and continued exertions. It needs not abstract reasoning to prove this position. It needs not the display of language to prove to the minds of good men, that Indians are susceptible of attainments necessary to the formation of polished society. It needs not the power of argument on the nature of man, to silence forever the remark that "it is the purpose of the Almighty that the Indians should be exterminated." It needs only that the world should know what we have done in the few last years, to foresee what yet we may do with the assistance of our white brethren, and that of the common Parent of us all . . . .

The Cherokee nation lies within the chartered limits of the states of Georgia, Tennessee, and Alabama. Its extent as defined by treaties is about 200 miles in length from East to West, and about 120 in breadth. This country which is supposed to contain about 10,000,000 of acres exhibits great varieties of surface, the most part being hilly and mountaneous, affording soil of no value. The vallies, however, are well watered and afford excellent land, in many parts particularly on the large streams, that of the first quality. The climate is temperate and healthy, indeed I would not be guilty of exaggeration were I to say, that the advantages which this country possesses to render it salubrious, are many and superior. Those lofty and barren mountains, defying the labour and ingenuity of man, and supposed by some as placed there only to exhibit omnipotence, contribute to the healthiness and beauty of the surrounding plains, and give to us that free air and pure water which distinguish our country. These advantages, calculated to make the inhabitants healthy, vigorous, and intelligent, cannot fail to cause this country to become interesting. And there can be no doubt that the Cherokee Nation, however obscure and trifling it may now appear, will finally become, if not under its present occupants, one of the Garden spots of America. And here, let me be indulged in the fond wish, that she may thus become under those who now possess her ; and ever be fostered, regulated and protected by the generous government of the United States.

The population of the Cherokee Nation increased from the year 1810 to that of 1824, 2000 exclusive of those who emigrated in 1818 and 19 to the west of the Mississippi—of those who reside on the Arkansas the number is supposed to be about 5000.

The rise of these people in their movement towards civilization, may be traced as far back as the relinquishment of their towns ; when game became incompetent to their support, by reason of the surrounding white population. They then betook themselves to the woods, commenced the opening of small clearings, and the raising of stock ; still however following the chase. Game has since become so scarce that little dependence for subsistence can be placed upon it. They have gradually and I could almost say universally forsaken their ancient employment. In fact, there is not a single family in the nation, that can be said to subsist on the slender support which the wilderness would afford. The love and the practice of hunting are not now carried to a higher degree, than among all frontier people whether white or red. It cannot be doubted, however, that there are many who have commenced a life of agricultural labour from mere necessity, and if they could, would gladly resume their former course of living. But these are individual failings and ought to be passed over.

On the other hand it cannot be doubted that the nation is improving, rapidly improving in all those particulars which must finally constitute the inhabitants an industrious and intelligent people.

It is a matter of surprise to me, and must be to all those who are properly acquainted with the condition of the Aborigines of this country, that the Cherokees have advanced so far and so rapidly in civilization. But there are yet powerful obstacles, both within and without, to be surmounted in the march of improvement. The prejudices in regard to them in the general community are strong and lasting. The evil effects of

their intercourse with their immediate white neighbours, who differ from them chiefly in name, are easily to be seen, and it is evident that from this intercourse proceed those demoralizing practices which in order to surmount, peculiar and unremitting efforts are necessary. In defiance, however, of these obstacles the Cherokees have improved and are still rapidly improving. . . .

There are three things of late occurance, which must certainly place the Cherokee Nation in a fair light, and act as a powerful argument in favor of Indian improvement.

First. The invention of letters.

Second. The translation of the New Testament into Cherokee.

And third. The organization of a Government.

The Cherokee mode of writing lately invented by George Guest, who could not read any language nor speak any other than his own, consists of eighty-six characters, principally syllabic, the combinations of which form all the words of the language. Their terms may be greatly simplified, yet they answer all the purposes of writing, and already many natives use them.

The translation of the New Testament, together with Guest's mode of writing, has swept away that barrier which has long existed, and opened a spacious channel for the instruction of adult Cherokees. Persons of all ages and classes may now read the precepts of the Almighty in their own language. Before it is long, there will scarcely be an individual in the nation who can say, "I know not God neither understand I what thou sayest," for all shall know him from the greatest to the least. The aged warrior over whom has rolled three score and ten years of savage life, will grace the temple of God with his hoary head ; and the little child yet on the breast of its pious mother shall learn to lisp its Maker's name.

The shrill sound of the Savage yell shall die away as the roaring of far distant thunder ; and Heaven wrought music will gladden the affrighted wilderness. "The solitary places will be glad for them, and the desert shall rejoice and blossom as a rose." Already do we see the morning star, forerunner of approaching dawn, rising over the tops of those deep forests in which for ages have echoed the warrior's whoop. But has not God said it, and will he not do it? The Almighty decrees his purposes, and man cannot with all his ingenuity and device countervail them. They are more fixed in their course than the rolling sun—more durable than the everlasting mountains.

The Government, though defective in many respects, is well suited to the condition of the inhabitants. As they rise in information and refinement, changes in it must follow, until they arrive at that state of advancement, when I trust they will be admitted into all the privileges of the American family.

The Cherokee Nation is divided into right districts, in each of which are established courts of justice, where all disputed cases are decided by a Jury, under the direction of a circuit Judge, who has jurisdiction over two districts. Sheriffs and other publice officers are appointed to execute the decisions of the courts, collect debts, and arrest thieves and other criminals. Appeals may be taken to the Superior Court, held annually at the seat of Government. The Legislative authority is vested in a General Court, which consists of the National Committee and Council. The National Committee consists of thirteen members, who are generally men of sound sense and fine talents. The National Council consists of thirty-two members, beside the speaker, who act as the representatives of the people. Every bill passing these two bodies, becomes the law of the land. Clerks are appointed to do the writings, and record the proceedings of the Council. The executive power is vested in two principal chiefs, who hold their office during good behavior, and sanction all the decisions of the legislative council. Many of the laws display some degree of civilization, and establish the respectability of the nation.

Polygamy is abolished. Female chastity and honor are protected by law. The Sabbath is respected by the Council during session. Mechanics are encouraged by law. The practice of putting aged persons to death for witchcraft is abolished and murder has now become a governmental crime. . . .

When before did a nation of Indians step forward and ask for the means of civilization? The Cherokee authorities have adopted the measures already stated, with a sincere desire to make their nation an intelligent and a virtuous people, and with a full hope that those who have already pointed out to them the road of happiness, will now assist them to pursue it. With that assistance, what are the prospects of the Cherokees? Are they not indeed glorious, compared to that deep darkness in which the nobler qualities of their souls have slept. Yes, methinks I can view my native country, rising from the ashes of her degradation, wearing her purified and beautiful garments, and taking her seat with the nations of the earth. I can behold her sons bursting the fetters of ignorance and unshackling her from the vices of heathenism. She is at this instant, risen like the first morning sun, which grows brighter and brighter, until it reaches its fullness of glory.

She will become not a great, but a faithful ally of the United States. In times of peace she will plead the common liberties of America. In times of war her intrepid sons will sacrifice their lives in your defence. And because she will be useful to you in coming time, she asks you to assist her in her present struggles. She asks not for greatness ; she seeks not wealth ; she pleads only for assistance to become respectable as a nation, to enlighten and ennoble her sons, and to ornament her daughters with modesty and virtue. She pleads for this assistance, too, because on her destiny hangs that of many nations. If she complete her civilization— then may we hope that all our nations will—then, indeed, may true patriots be encouraged in their efforts to make this world of the West, one continuous abode of enlightened, free, and happy people.

**QUESTIONS TO CONSIDER**

1. How does Boudinot make his case for Cherokee civilization?

2. What do you think of Boudinot's assimilationist strategy?

# 10.3 "ADDRESS OF THE CHEROKEE NATION TO THE PEOPLE OF THE UNITED STATES" (1830)

In the 1820s, the idea of Cherokee removal took greater hold in the Federal government. One of the main supporters of removal was President Andrew Jackson (1767–1845), a southerner who had gained fame for his exploits during the War of 1812. As President, Jackson sympathized with white agrarian landholders, and he viewed Cherokee removal as a crucial step toward opening up more land for such people. On May 28, 1830, Jackson signed the Indian Removal Act into law, which opened the door for Federal action to remove the "Five Civilized Tribes" from the American southeast. Cherokees who resisted removal then issued the following document, the "Address of the Cherokee Nation to the People of the United States," in response to Jackson's policies. In the document, they recounted recent political events, summarized the history of Cherokee relations with the Federal government, and made a final plea for being allowed to stay on their land.

Address of the "Committee and Council of the Cherokee Nation in General Council convened" to the people of the United States.

Some months ago a delegation was appointed by the constituted authorities of the Cherokee Nation, to repair to the City of Washington, and, in behalf of this Nation to lay before the Government of the United States such representations as should seem most likely to secure to us as a people that protection, aid, and good neighborhood, which had been so often promised to us, and of which we stand in great need. Soon after their arrival in the City they presented to Congress a petition from our National Council, asking for the interposition of that body in our behalf, especially with reference to the laws of Georgia, which were suspended in a most terrifying manner over a large part of our population, and protesting in the most decided terms against the operation of these laws. In the course of the winter they presented petitions to Congress signed by more than four thousand of our citizens, including probably more than nineteen twentieths, and for ought we can tell ninety nine hundredths of the adult males of the nation (our whole population being about sixteen thousand,) pleading with the assembled representatives of the American people, that the solemn engagements between their fathers and our fathers may be preserved, as they have been till recently in full force and continued operation; asking, in a word, for protection against threatened usurpation, and for a faithful execution of a guaranty, which is perfectly plain in its meaning has been repeatedly and rigidly enforced in our favor, and has received the sanction of the government of the United States for nearly forty years.

More than a year ago we were officially given to understand by the Secretary of War that the President could not protect us against the laws of Georgia. This information was entirely unexpected; as it went upon the principle that treaties made between the United States and the Cherokee Nation have no power to withstand the legislation of separate States; and of course that they have not efficacy whatever,

*Source:* Lewis Ross et al., "Appeal of the Cherokee Nation (1830)," https://liberalarts.utexas.edu/coretexts/_files/resources/texts/1830CherokeeAppeal.pdf (Accessed June 6, 2018).

but leave our people to the mercy of the neighboring whites, whose supposed interests would be promoted by our expulsion or extermination. It would be impossible to describe the sorrow which effected our minds on learning that the Chief magistrate of the United States had come to this conclusion, that all his illustrious predecessors had held intercourse with us on principles which could not be sustained; that they had made promises of vital importance to us, which could not be fulfilled—promises made hundreds of times, in almost every conceivable manner—often in the form of solemn treaties, sometimes in letters written by the Chief magistrate with his own hand, very often in letters written by the Secretary of War under his direction, sometimes orally by the President and the Secretary to our chiefs, and frequently, and always both orally and in writing for the Agent of the United States residing among us, whose most important business it was to see the guaranty of the United States faithfully executed.

Soon after the War of the Revolution, as we have learned from our fathers, the Cherokees looked upon the promises of the whites with great distrust and suspicion; but the frank and magnanimous conduct of General Washington did much to allay these feelings. The perseverance of successive Presidents, and especially of Mr. Jefferson in the same course of policy, and in the constant assurance that our country should remain inviolate, except so far as we voluntarily ceded it nearly perished anxiety in regard to encroachments from the whites. To this result the aid which we received from the United States in the attempts of our people to become civilized, and the kind efforts of benevolent societies have greatly contributed. Of late years, however, much solicitude was occasioned among our people by the claims of Georgia. This solicitude arose from an apprehension that by extreme importunity, threats, and other undue influence, a treaty would be made, which should cede the territory and thus compel the inhabitants to remove. But it never occurred to us for a moment, that without any new treaty, without any assent of our rulers and people, without even a pretended compact, and against our vehement and unanimous protestations, we should be delivered over to the discretion of those, who had declared by a legislative act, that they wanted the Cherokee lands and would have them.

Finding that relief could not be obtained from the Chief Magistrate, and not doubting that our claim to protection was just, we made our application to Congress. During four long months our delegation waited at the doors of the national Legislature of the United States, and the people at home, in the most painful suspense, to learn in what manner our application would be answered; & now that Congress has adjourned, on the very day before the date fixed by Georgia for the extension of her oppressive laws over the greater part of our country, the distressing intelligence has been received that we have received no answer at all; and no department of the Government has assured us, that we are to receive the desired protection. But just at the close of the session, an act was passed, by which half a million of dollars was appropriated towards effecting a removal of Indians; and we have great reason to fear that the influence of this act, will be brought to bear most injuriously upon us. The passage of this act is certainly understood by the representatives of Georgia as abandoning us to the oppressive and cruel measures of the State, and is sustaining the opinion that treaties with Indians do not restrain State Legislation. We are informed by those who are competent to judge that the [p]resent act does not admit of such construction; but that the passage of it under the actual circumstances of the controversy, will be considered as sanctioning the pretensions of Georgia, there is too much reason to fear.

Thus have we realized with heavy hearts, that our supplication has not been heard; that the protection heretofore experienced is now to be withheld; that the guaranty in consequence of which our fathers laid aside their arms and ceded the best portion of our country means nothing and that was must either emigrate to an unknown region and leave the pleasant land to which we have the strongest attachments, or submit to the legislation of a State, which has already made our people outlaws and enacted that any Cherokee, who shall endeavor to prevent the selling of his country shall be imprisoned in the Penitentiary of Georgia not less than four years. To our countrymen, this has been melancholy intelligence and with the most bitter disappointment has it been received. . . .

We are aware, that some persons suppose it will be for our advantage to remove beyond the Mississippi.

We think otherwise. Our people universally think otherwise. Thinking that it would be fatal to their interests, they have almost to a man sent their memorial to Congress, deprecating the necessity of a removal. This question was distinctly before their minds when they signed their memorial. Not an adult person can be found, who has not an opinion on the subject, and if the people were to understand distinctly, that they could be protected against the laws of the neighboring States, there is probably not an adult person in the nation who would think it best to remove; though possibly a few might emigrate individually. There are doubtless many, who would flee to an unknown country, however, beset with dangers, privations and sufferings, rather than be sentenced to spend six years in a Georgia prison for advising one of their neighbors not to betray his country. And there are others who could not think of living as outlaws in their native land, exposed to numberless vexations, and excluded from being parties of witnesses in a court of justice. It is incredible that Georgia should ever have enacted the oppressive laws, to which reference is here made, unless she had supposed that something extremely terrific in its character was necessary in order to make the Cherokees willing to remove. We are not willing to remove; and if we could be brought to this extremity, it would be not by argument, not because our judgment was satisfied, not because our condition will be improved; but only because we cannot endure to be deprived of our national and individual rights and subjected to a process of intolerable oppression.

We wish to remain on the land of our fathers. We have a perfect & original right to claim without interruption or molestation. The treaties with us, and laws of the United States made in pursuance of treaties, guaranty our residence, and our privileges and secure us against intruders. Our only request is, that these treaties may be fulfilled, and these laws executed.

But if we are compelled to leave our country, we see nothing but ruin before us. The country west of the Arkansas territory is unknown to us. From what we can learn of it, we have no prepossessions in its favor. All the inviting parts of it, as we believe, are preoccupied by various Indian nations, to which it has become assigned. They would regard us as intruders, and look upon us with an evil eye. The far greater part of that region is, beyond all controversy, badly supplied with wood and water; and no Indian tribe can live as agriculturists with these articles. All our neighbors in case of our removal though crowded into our near vicinity, would speak a language totally different from ours and practice different customs[.] The original possessors of that region are now wandering savages, lurking for prey in the neighborhood. They have always been at war, and would be easily tempted to turn their arms against peaceful emigrants. Were the country to which we are urged much better than it is represented to be, and were it free from objections which we have made to it, still it is not the land of our birth, nor of our affections. It contains neither the scenes of our childhood, nor the graves of our fathers.

The removal of families to a new country, even under the most favorable auspices, and when the spirits are sustained by pleasing visions of the future, is attended with much depression of mind and sinking of heart. This is the case, when the removal is a matter of decided preference, and when the persons concerned are in early youth or vigorous manhood. Judge, then, what must be the circumstances of a removal, when a whole community, embracing persons of all classes and every description, from the infant to the man of extreme old age, the sick, the blind, the lame,—the improvident, the reckless, the desperate, as well as the prudent—the considerate, the industrious, are compelled to remove by odious and intolerable vexations and persecutions, brought upon them in the forms of law, when all will agree only in this, that they have been cruelly robbed of their country, in violation of the most solemn compacts which it is possible for communities to form with each other; and that if they should make themselves comfortable in their residence, they have nothing to expect hereafter but to be the victims of a future legalized robbery!

Such we deem, and are absolutely certain, will be the feelings of the whole Cherokee people, if they are forcibly compelled by the laws of Georgia to remove; and with these feelings, how is it possible that we should pursue our present course of improvement, or avoid sinking into utter despondency? We have been called a poor, ignorant, and degraded people. We certainly are not rich; nor have we ever boosted of our knowledge of our moral or intellectual elevation. But there is not a man within our limits so ignorant as not to know that he has a right to live on the land of his fathers, in the possession of his immemorial privileges, and that this right has been acknowledged and guaranteed by the United States; nor is there a man so degraded as not to feel a keen sense of injury, on being deprived of this right and driven into exile.

It is under a sense of the most pungent feelings that we make this, perhaps our last appeal to the good people of the United States. It cannot be that the community we are addressing, remarkable for its intelligence and religious sensibilities, and prominent for its devotion to the rights of man, will lay aside this appeal, without considering that we stand in need of its sympathy and commiseration. We know that to the Christian and Philanthropist the voice of our multiplied sorrows and fiery trials will not appear as an idle tale in our own land, on our own soil, and in our own dwellings, which were reared for our wives, and for our little ones when there was peace on our mountains and in our valleys, we are encountering troubles which cannot but try our very souls. But shall we on account of these troubles, forsake our beloved country? Shall we, be compelled by a civilized and Christian people, with whom we have lived in perfect peace for the last forty years, and for whom we have willingly bled in war, to bid a final adieu to our homes, our farms, our streams, and our beautiful forests? No. We are still firm. We intend still to cling with our wonted affection to the land which gave us birth and which every day of our lives brings to us new and stronger ties of attachment. We appeal to the judge of all the earth who will fairly award us justice, and to the good sense of the American people, whether we are intruding upon the land of others. Our consciences bear us witness that we are the invaders of no man's rights—we have robbed no man of his territory—we have usurped no man's

authority, nor have we deprived anyone of his unalienable privileges. How then shall we indirectly confess the right of another people to our land by leaving if forever? On the soil which contains the ashes of our beloved men we wish to live—on this soil we wish to die.

We entreat those to whom the preceding paragraphs are addressed to remember the great law of love, "Do to others as ye would that others should do to you"—Let them remember that of all nations on the earth, they are under the greatest obligations to obey this law. We pray them to remember that, for the sake of our people, their forefathers were compelled to leave, therefore driven from the old world, and that the winds of persecution wafted them over the great waters and landed them on the shores of the new world, when the Indian was the sole lord and proprietor of these extensive domains.—Let them remember in what way they were received by the savage of America, when power was in his hand, and his ferocity could not be restrained by any human arm. We urge them to bear in mind, that those who would now ask of them a cup of cold water, and a spot of earth, a portion of their own patrimonial possessions on which to live and die in peace, are the descendants of those, whose origin as inhabitants of North America history and tradition are alike insufficient to reveal. Let them bring to remembrance all these facts, and they cannot, and we are sure they will not, fail to remember, and sympathize with us in these our trials and sufferings.

### QUESTIONS TO CONSIDER

1. What rhetorical strategies did the Cherokee Nation use to appeal to the "People of the United States"?

2. How effective are those rhetorical strategies, in your mind?

# 10.4 JOHN C. CALHOUN, "EXPOSITION AND PROTEST" (1828)

In many ways, John C. Calhoun is the originator of southern secessionist ideology. Throughout his career as a South Carolina politician, Calhoun (1782—1850) propagated a political ideology in support of slavery and states' rights. In 1828, Calhoun formally theorized a constitutional basis for such an ideology in the anonymously published "Exposition and Protest," written in response to the Tariff of 1828, which was designed to protect northern industry by placing duties on imported goods that were also manufactured in the north. The Tariff, then, would make prices higher for southern consumers. In "Exposition and Protest," Calhoun laid out a theory of "nullification," the idea that any state could invalidate any Federal law it viewed as unconstitutional. In 1832, the South Carolina legislature took up Calhoun's theory and tried to nullify a new Federal tariff. In response, President Andrew Jackson, a southerner but also a believer in Federal power, sent the U.S. Navy to South Carolina. Congress subsequently gave Jackson the power to enforce Federal laws through the U.S. Military, and South Carolina backed down. Calhoun remained a prominent political figure until his death in 1850, and his ideologies would live on in the debates over secession. Until the end of his life, Jackson regretted not executing Calhoun for treason.

The Committee of the whole, to whom were referred the Governor's Message and various memorials on the subject of the Tariff, having reported, and the House having adopted the following resolution, viz:

"*Resolved*, That it is expedient to protest against the unconstitutionality and oppressive operation of the system of protecting duties, and to have such protest entered on the Journals of the Senate of the United States—Also, to make a public exposition of our wrongs and of the remedies within our power, to be communicated to our sister states, with a request that they will co-operate with this state in procuring a repeal of the Tariff for protection, and an abandonment of the principle; and if the repeal be not procured, that they will co-operate in such measures as may be necessary for arresting the evil."

"*Resolved*, That a committee of seven be raised to carry the foregoing resolution into effect:" which was decided in the affirmative, and the following gentlemen appointed on the committee, viz—JAMES GREGG, D. L. WARDLAW, HUGH S. LEGARE, ARTHUR P. HAYNE, WM. C. PRESTON, WILLIAM ELLIOTT, and R. BARNWELL SMITH.

*The special Committee to whom the above Resolution was referred, beg leave to Report the following Exposition and Protest—*

## EXPOSITION

THE Committee have bestowed on the subject referred to them, the deliberate attention which its importance merits; and the result, on full investigation is, and unanimous opinion, that the Act of Congress of the last session, with the whole system of legislation imposing duties on imports, not for revenue, but for the protection of one branch of industry, at the expense of others, is unconstitutional, unequal and oppressive; calculated to corrupt the public morals, and to destroy

*Source:* "Exposition and Protest Reported by the Special Committee of the House of Representatives on the Tariff," https://dc.statelibrary.sc.gov/handle/10827/21911 (Accessed June 6, 2018).

the liberty of the country. These propositions they propose to consider in the order stated, and then conclude their report, with the consideration of the important question of the remedy.

The Committee do not propose to enter into an elaborate, or refined argument on the question of the constitutionality of the Tariff system.

The general government is one of specific powers, and it can rightfully exercise only the powers expressly granted, and those that may be "necessary and proper" to carry them into effect; all others being reserved expressly to the states, or to the people. It results necessarily, that those who claim to exercise a power under the constitution, are bound to shew, that it is expressly granted, or that it is necessary and proper, as a means to some of the granted powers. The advocates of the Tariff have offered no such proof. It is true, that the third section of the first article of the constitution of the United States authorizes Congress to lay and collect an impost duty, but it is granted as a tax power, for the sole purpose of revenue; a power in its nature essentially different from that of imposing protective or prohibitory duties. The two are incompatable; for the prohibitory system must end in destroying the revenue from impost. It has been said that the system is a violation of the spirit and not the letter of the constitution. The distinction is not material. The constitution may be as grossly violated by acting against its meaning as against its letter; but it may be proper to dwell a moment on the point, in order to understand more fully the real character of the acts, under which the interest of this, and other states similarly situated, has been sacrificed. The facts are few and simple. The constitution grants to Congress the power of imposing a duty on imports for revenue; which power is abused by being converted into an instrument for rearing up the industry of one section of the country on the ruins of another. The violation then consists in using a power, granted for one object, to advance another, and that by the sacrifice of the original object. It is, in a word, *a violation of perversion*, the most dangerous of all, because the most insidious, and difficult to resist. Others cannot be perpetrated without the aid of the judiciary; this may be, by the executive and legislative alone. The courts by their own decisions cannot look into the motives of legislators—they are obliged to take acts by their titles and professed objects, and

if *they* be constitutional they cannot interpose their power, however grossly the acts may violate the constitution. The proceedings of the last session sufficiently prove, that the House of Representatives are aware of the distinction, and determined to avail themselves of the advantage.

In the absence of arguments drawn from the constitution itself, the advocates of the power have attempted to call in the aid of precedent. The committee will not waste their time in examining the instances quoted. If they were strictly in point they would be entitled to little weight. Ours is not a government of precedents, nor can they be admitted, except to a very limited extent, and with great caution, in the interpretation of the constitution, without changing in time the entire character of the instrument. The only safe rule is the constitution itself, or, if that be doubtful, the history of times. In this case, if doubts existed, the journals of the convention would remove them. It was moved in that body to confer on Congress, the very power in question; to encourage manufactures, but it was deliberately withheld, except to the extent of granting patent rights for new and useful inventions. Instead of granting the power to Congress, permission was given to the states to impose duties, with consent of that body, to encourage their own manufactures; and thus in the true spirit of justice, imposing the burden on those, who were to be benefited. But giving to precedents, whatever weight may be claimed, the committee feel confident, that in this case there are none in point, previous to the adoption of the present Tariff system. Every instance which has been cited, may fairly be referred to the legitimate power of Congress to impose duties on imports for revenue. It is a necessary incident of such duties to act as an encouragement to manufactures, whenever imposed on articles, which may be manufactured in our own country. In this incidental manner Congress has the power of encouraging manufactures; and the committee readily concede, that in the passage of an impost bill, that body may, in modifying the details, so arrange the provisions of the bill, as far as it may be done consistently with its proper object, as to aid manufactures. To this extent Congress may constitutionally go, and has gone from the commencement of the government, which will fully explain the precedents cited from the early stages of its operation. Beyond this, *they* never advanced until the commencement of the present system, the inequality and oppression of which, your committee will next proceed to consider.

The committee feel, on entering upon this branch of the subject, the painful character of the duty they must perform. They would desire never to speak of our country, as far as the action of the general government is concerned, but as one great whole, having a common interest, which all its parts ought zealously to promote. Previously to the adoption of the Tariff system, such was the unanimous feeling of this state; but in speaking of its operation it will be impossible to avoid the discussion of sectional interest, and the use of sectional language. On its authors, however, and not on us, who are compelled to adopt this course in self-defence by the injustice and oppression of their measures—be the censure. So partial are the effects of the system, that its burdens are exclusively on one side and its benefits on the other. It imposes on the agricultural interest of the South, including the South West, and that portion of our commerce and navigation engaged in foreign trade, the burden, not only of sustaining the system itself, but that also of sustaining government. In stating the case thus strongly, it is not the intention of the committee to exaggerate. If exaggeration were not unworthy of the gravity of the subject, the reality is such as to render it unnecessary. . . .

## PROTEST

*The Senate and House of Representatives of South Carolina, now met and sitting in general assembly, through the Honorable Wm. Smith and the Hon. Robert Y. Hayne, their Representatives in the Senate of the United States, do in the name and on behalf of the good people of the said Commonwealth, solemnly protest against the system of protecting duties, lately adopted by the Federal Government, for the following reasons.*

1st. Because the good people of this Commonwealth believe, that the powers of Congress were delegated to it, in trust for the accomplishment of certain specified objects which limit and control them, and that every exercise of them, for any other purposes, is a violation of the Constitution as unwarrantable as the undisguised assumption of substantive, independent powers not granted or expressly withheld.

2nd. Because the power to lay duties on imports is and in its very nature can be only a means of effecting objects specified by the Constitution; since no free government and least of all a government of enumerated powers, can of right impose any tax, any more than a penalty which is not at once justified by public necessity and clearly within the scope and purview of the social compact, and since the right of confining appropriations of the public money, to such legitimate and constitutional objects, as is essential to the liberties of the people, as their unquestionable privilege to be taxed only by their own consent.

3rd. Because they believe that the Tariff Law passed by Congress at its last session, and all other acts of which the principal object is the protection of manufactures, or any other branch of domestic industry, if they be considered as the exercise of a supposed power in Congress to tax the people at its own good will and pleasure, and to apply the money raised to objects not specified in the Constitution, is a violation of these fundamental principles, a breach of a well defined trust and a perversion of the high powers vested in the Federal Government for federal purposes only.

4th. Because such acts considered in the light of a regulation of commerce, are equally liable to objection—since although the power to regulate commerce, may like other powers be exercised so as to protect domestic manufactures, yet it is clearly distinguishable from a power to do so *co nomine* both in the nature of the thing and in the common acceptation of the terms; and because the confounding of them would lead to the most extravagant results, since the encouragement of domestic industry implies an absolute controul over all the interests, resources and pursuits of a people, and is inconsistent with the idea of any other than a simple, consolidated government.

5th. Because from the contemporaneous exposition of the Constitution in the numbers of the Federalist, (which is cited only because the Supreme Court has recognized its authority,) it is clear that the power to regulate commerce was considered by the Convention as only incidentally connected with the encouragement of agriculture and manufactures; and because the power of laying imposts and duties on imports, was not understood to justify in any case a prohibition of foreign commodities, except as a means of extending commerce, by coercing foreign nations to a fair reciprocity in their intercourse with us, or for some other bona fide commercial purpose.

6th. Because whilst the powers to protect manufactures, is no where expressly granted to Congress, nor can be considered as necessary and proper to carry into effect any specified power, it seems to be expressly reserved to the states, by the tenth section of the first article of the Constitution.

7th. Because even admitting Congress to have a constitutional right to protect manufactures by the imposition of duties or by regulations of commerce, designed principally for that purpose, yet a Tariff of which the operation is grossly unequal and oppressive is such an abuse of power, as is incompatible with the principles of a free government and the great ends of civil society, justice, and equality of rights and protection.

8th. Finally, because South Carolina from her climate, situation, and peculiar institutions, is, and must ever continue to be, wholly dependent upon agriculture and commerce, not only for her prosperity, but for her very existence as a state—because the valuable products of her soil—the blessings by which Divine Providence seems to have designed to compensate for the great disadvantages under which she suffers in other respects—are among the very few that can be cultivated with any profit by slave labor—and if by the loss of her foreign commerce, these products should be confined to an inadequate market, the fate of this fertile state would be poverty, and utter desolation; her citizens in despair would emigrate to more fortunate regions, and the whole frame and constitution of her civil polity, be impaired and deranged if not dissolved entirely.

Deeply impressed with these considerations, the Representatives of the good people of this Commonwealth, anxiously desiring to live in peace with their fellow citizens, and to do all that in them lies to preserve and perpetuate the Union of the States and the liberties of which it is the surest pledge, but feeling it to be their bounden duty to expose and resist all encroachments upon the true spirit of the Constitution, lest an apparent acquiescence in the system of protecting duties should be drawn into precedent, do in the name of the Commonwealth of South Carolina, claim to enter upon the Journals of the Senate, their protest against it as unconstitutional, oppressive, and unjust.

*Which Exposition and Protest are respectfully submitted.*

*J. GREGG, Chairman.*

### QUESTIONS TO CONSIDER

1. How did Calhoun make his case? How persuasive was it?
2. Should states be allowed to nullify Federal law?

# 10.5 JOHN MARSHALL, MAJORITY OPINION IN *WORCESTER V. GEORGIA* (1832)

As a last, desperate effort, the Cherokee Nation began a legal campaign to resist removal (see Readings 10.2 and 10.3). Chief John Ross (1790—1866) led the initiative, and two separate cases reached the U.S. Supreme Court. Chief Justice John Marshall wrote the majority opinion in both cases. In the first, *Cherokee Nation v. Georgia*, the Court ruled that the Cherokees lacked a basis to sue as a "foreign nation" because the tribe, in Marshall's ruling, was a "domestic dependent nation." Two years later, in *Worcester v. Georgia*, the Court ruled more in favor of the Cherokee Nation. In the end, however, the ruling had little effect. The Court did not order the Federal Government to enforce the ruling, and Cherokee removal continued throughout the 1830s. The final step, termed the "Trail of Tears," involved the removal of around 13,000 Cherokee to Oklahoma in 1838 at the hands of the U.S. Army. Around 4,000 Cherokee died during the forced 1,000-mile march.

*Source:* "Worcester v. Georgia," https://cdn.loc.gov/service/ll/usrep/usrep031/usrep031515/usrep031515.pdf (Accessed June 6, 2018).

Mr Chief Justice MARSHALL delivered the opinion of the Court.

This cause, in every point of view in which it can be placed, is of the deepest interest.

The defendant is a state, a member of the union, which has exercised the powers of government over a people who deny its jurisdiction, and are under the protection of the United States.

The plaintiff is a citizen of the state of Vermont, condemned to hard labour for four years in the penitentiary of Georgia; under colour of an act which he alleges to be repugnant to the constitution, laws, and treaties of the United States.

The legislative power of a state, the controlling power of the constitution and laws of the United States, the rights, if they have any, the political existence of a once numerous and powerful people, the personal liberty of a citizen, are all involved in the subject now to be considered.

It behoves this court, in every case, more especially in this, to examine into its jurisdiction with scrutinizing eyes; before it proceeds to the exercise of a power which is controverted. . .

. . . From the commencement of our government, congress has passed acts to regulate trade and intercourse with the Indians; which treat them as nations, respect their rights, and manifest a firm purpose to afford that protection which treaties stipulate. All these acts, and especially that of 1802, which is still in force, manifestly consider the several Indian nations as distinct political communities, having territorial boundaries, within which their authority is exclusive, and having a right to all the lands within those boundaries, which is not only acknowledged, but guarantied by the United States.

In 1819, congress passed an act for promoting those humane designs of civilizing the neighbouring Indians, which had long been cherished by the executive. It enacts, "that, for the purpose of providing against the further decline and final extinction of the Indian tribes adjoining to the frontier settlements of the United States, and for introducing among them the habits and arts of civilization, the president of the United States shall be, and he is hereby authorized, in every case where he shall judge improvement in the habits and condition of such Indians practicable, and that the means of instruction can be introduced *with*

*their own consent,* to employ capable persons, of good moral character, to instruct them in the mode of agriculture suited to their situation; and for teaching their children in reading, writing and arithmetic; and for performing such other duties as may be enjoined, according to such instructions and rules as the president may give and prescribe for the regulation of their conduct in the discharge of their duties."

This act avowedly contemplates the preservation of the Indian nations as an object sought by the United States, and proposes to effect this object by civilizing and converting them from hunters into agriculturists. Though the Cherokees had already made considerable progress in this improvement, it cannot be doubted that the general words of the act comprehend them. Their advance in the "habits and arts of civilization," rather encouraged perseverance in the laudable exertions still farther to meliorate their condition. This act furnishes strong additional evidence of a settled purpose to fix the Indians in their country by giving them security at home.

The treaties and laws of the United States contemplate the Indian territory as completely separated from that of the states; and provide that all intercourse with them shall be carried on exclusively by the government of the union.

Is this the rightful exercise of power, or is it usurpation?

While these states were colonies, this power, in its utmost extent, was admitted to reside in the crown. When our revolutionary struggle commenced, congress was composed of an assemblage of deputies acting under specific powers granted by the legislatures, or conventions of the several colonies. It was a great popular movement, not perfectly organized; nor were the respective powers of those who were entrusted with the management of affairs accurately defined. The necessities of our situation produced a general conviction that those measures which concerned all, must be transacted by a body in which the representatives of all were assembled, and which could command the confidence of all: congress, therefore, was considered as invested with all the powers of war and peace, and congress dissolved our connexion with the mother country, and declared these United Colonies to be independent states. Without any written definition of powers, they employed diplomatic agents to represent the United States at the several courts of Europe; offered to negotiate treaties with them, and did actually negotiate treaties with France. From the same necessity, and on the same principles, congress assumed the management of Indian affairs; first in the name of these United Colonies; and, afterwards, in the name of the United States. Early attempts were made at negotiation, and to regulate trade with them. These not proving successful, war was carried on under the direction, and with the forces of the United States, and the efforts to make peace, by treaty, were earnest and incessant. The confederation found congress in the exercise of the same powers of peace and war, in our relations with Indian nations, as with those of Europe.

Such was the state of things when the confederation was adopted. That instrument surrendered the powers of peace and war to congress, and prohibited them to the states, respectively, unless a state be actually invaded, "or shall have received certain advice of a resolution being formed by some nation of Indians to invade such state, and the danger is so imminent as not to admit of delay till the United States in congress assembled can be consulted." This instrument also gave the United States in congress assembled the sole and exclusive right of "regulating the trade and managing all the affairs with the Indians, not members of any of the states: provided, that the legislative power of any state within its own limits be not infringed or violated."

The ambiguous phrases which follow the grant of power to the United States, were so construed by the states of North Carolina and Georgia as to annul the power itself. The discontents and confusion resulting from these conflicting claims, produced representations to congress, which were referred to a committee, who made their report in 1787. The report does not assent to the construction of the two states, but recommends an accommodation, by liberal cessions of territory, or by an admission, on their part, of the powers claimed by congress. The correct exposition of this article is rendered unnecessary by the adoption of our existing constitution. That instrument confers on congress the powers of war and peace; of making treaties, and of regulating commerce with foreign nations, and among the several states, and *with the Indian tribes.* These powers comprehend all that is required for the

regulation of our intercourse with the Indians. They are not limited by any restrictions on their free actions. The shackles imposed on this power, in the confederation, are discarded.

The Indian nations had always been considered as distinct, independent political communities, retaining their original natural rights, as the undisputed possessors of the soil, from time immemorial, with the single exception of that imposed by irresistible power, which excluded them from intercourse with any other European potentate than the first discoverer of the coast of the particular region claimed: and this was a restriction which those European potentates imposed on themselves, as well as on the Indians. The very term "nation," so generally applied to them, means "a people distinct from others." The constitution, by declaring treaties already made, as well as those to be made, to be the supreme law of the land, has adopted and sanctioned the previous treaties with the Indian nations, and consequently admits their rank among those powers who are capable of making treaties. The words "treaty" and "nation" are words of our own language, selected in our diplomatic and legislative proceedings, by ourselves, having each a definite and well understood meaning. We have applied them to Indians, as we have applied them to the other nations of the earth. They are applied to all in the same sense.

Georgia, herself, has furnished conclusive evidence that her former opinions on this subject concurred with those entertained by her sister states, and by the government of the United States. Various acts of her legislature have been cited in the argument, including the contract of cession made in the year 1802, all tending to prove her acquiescence in the universal conviction that the Indian nations possessed a full right to the lands they occupied, until that right should be extinguished by the United States, with their consent: that their territory was separated from that of any state within whose chartered limits they might reside, by a boundary line, established by treaties: within their boundary, they possessed rights with which no state could interfere: and that the whole power of regulating the intercourse with them, was vested in the United States. A review of these acts, on the part of Georgia, would occupy too much time, and is the less necessary, because they have been accurately detailed in the argument at the bar. Her new series of laws, manifesting her abandonment of these opinions, appears to have commenced in December 1828.

In opposition to this original right, possessed by the undisputed occupants of every country; to this recognition of that right, which is evidenced by our history, in every change through which we have passed; is placed the charters granted by the monarch of a distant and distinct region, parceling out a territory in possession of others whom he could not remove and did not attempt to remove, and the cession made of his claims by the treaty of peace.

The actual state of things at the time, and all history since, explain these charters; and the king of Great Britain, at the treaty of peace, could cede only what belonged to his crown. These newly asserted titles can derive no aid from the articles so often repeated in Indian treaties; extending to them, first, the protection of Great Britain, and afterwards that of the United States. These articles are associated with others, recognizing their title to self government. The very fact of repeated treaties with them recognizes it; and the settled doctrine of the law of nations is, that a weaker power does not surrender its independence—its right to self government, by associating with a stronger, and taking its protection. A weak state, in order to provide for its safety, may place itself under the protection of one more powerful, without stripping itself of the right of government, and ceasing to be a state. Examples of this kind are not wanting in Europe. "Tributary and feudatory states," says Vattel, "do not thereby cease to be sovereign and independent states, so long as self government and sovereign and independent authority are left in the administration of the state." At the present day, more than one state may be considered as holding its right of self government under the guarantee and protection of one or more allies.

The Cherokee nation, then, is a distinct community occupying its own territory, with boundaries accurately described, in which the laws of Georgia can have no force, and which the citizens of Georgia have no right to enter, but with the assent of the Cherokees themselves, or in conformity with treaties, and with the acts of congress. The whole intercourse between the United States and this nation, is, by our constitution and laws, vested in the government of the United States.

The act of the state of Georgia, under which the plaintiff in error was prosecuted, is consequently void, and the judgement a nullity. Can this court revise, and reverse it?

If the objection of Georgia, in relation to the Cherokee nation, was confined to its extra-territorial operation, the objection, though complete, so far as respected mere right, would give this court no power over the subject. But it goes much further. If the review which has been taken be correct, and we think it is, the acts of Georgia are repugnant to the constitution, laws, and treaties of the United States.

They interfere forcibly with the relations established between the United States and the Cherokee nation, the regulation of which, according to the settled principles of our constitution, are committed exclusively to the government of the union.

They are in direct hostility with treaties, repeated in a succession of years, which mark out the boundary that separates the Cherokee country from Georgia; guaranty to them all the land within their boundary; solemnly pledge the faith of the United States to restrain their citizens from trespassing on it; and recognize the pre-existing power of the nation to govern itself.

They are in equal hostility with the acts of congress for regulating this intercourse, and giving effect to the treaties.

The forcible seizure and abduction of the plaintiff in error, who was residing in the nation with its permission, and by authority of the president of the United States, is also a violation of the acts which authorize the chief magistrate to exercise this authority.

Will these powerful considerations avail the plaintiff in error? We think they will. He was seized, and forcibly carried away, while under guardianship of treaties guarantying the country in which he resided, and taking it under the protection of the United States. He was seized while performing, under the sanction of the chief magistrate of the union, those duties which the humane policy adopted by congress had recommended. He was apprehended, tried, and condemned, under colour of a law which has been shown to be repugnant to the constitution, laws, and treaties of the United States. Had a judgment, liable to the same objections, been rendered for property, none would question the jurisdiction of this court. It cannot be less clear when the judgment affects personal liberty, and inflicts disgraceful punishment, if punishment could disgrace when inflicted on innocence. The plaintiff in error is not less interested in the operation of this unconstitutional law than if it affected his property. He is not less entitled to the protection of the constitution, laws, and treaties of his country.

This point has been elaborately argued and, after deliberate consideration, decided, in the case of Cohens v. The Commonwealth of Virginia, 6 Wheat. 264.

It is the opinion of this court that the judgment of the superior court for the county of Gwinnett, in the state of Georgia, condemning Samuel A. Worcester to hard labour, in the penitentiary of the state of Georgia, for four years, was pronounced by that court under colour of a law which is void, as being repugnant to the constitution, treaties, and laws of the United States, and ought, therefore, to be reversed and annulled.

**QUESTIONS TO CONSIDER**

1. What did the Court rule, and how did Marshall support this ruling?

2. Do you find the ruling convincing? Should the U.S. Government have been allowed to remove the Cherokee?

# 10.6 HARRIET JACOBS, EXCERPT FROM *INCIDENTS IN THE LIFE OF A SLAVE GIRL* (1861)

Harriet Jacobs' autobiographical *Incidents in the Life of a Slave Girl* provides an illustrative, brutal look at the experience of slavery. Jacobs (1813–1897) was born into slavery in North Carolina. Her owner sexually assaulted Jacobs beginning in her childhood, and the abuse only ended when Jacobs escaped in 1835. She lived in the tiny attic of her grandmother's shack in North Carolina for seven years, until she was eventually able to escape to Philadelphia. During the Civil War, Jacobs ran a school for African American children in Virginia and became active in the African American suffrage movement. *Incidents in the Life of a Slave Girl,* published under a pseudonym in 1861, has come to be a foundational text for the study of the experience of slavery.

## I. CHILDHOOD

I was born a slave; but I never knew it till six years of happy childhood had passed away. My father was a carpenter, and considered so intelligent and skilful in his trade, that, when buildings out of the common line were to be erected, he was sent for from long distances, to be head workman. On condition of paying his mistress two hundred dollars a year, and supporting himself, he was allowed to work at his trade, and manage his own affairs. His strongest wish was to purchase his children; but, though he several times offered his hard earnings for that purpose, he never succeeded. In complexion my parents were a light shade of brownish yellow, and were termed mulattoes. They lived together in a comfortable home; and, though we were all slaves, I was so fondly shielded that I never dreamed I was a piece of merchandise, trusted to them for safe keeping, and liable to be demanded of them at any moment. I had one brother, William, who was two years younger than myself—a bright, affectionate child. I had also a

*Source:* Harriet Jacobs, *Incidents in the Life of a Slave Girl, Written by Herself* (Urbana-Champaign, IL: Project Gutenberg, 2004).

great treasure in my maternal grandmother, who was a remarkable woman in many respects. She was the daughter of a planter in South Carolina, who, at his death, left her mother and his three children free, with money to go to St. Augustine, where they had relatives. It was during the Revolutionary War; and they were captured on their passage, carried back, and sold to different purchasers. Such was the story my grandmother used to tell me; but I do not remember all the particulars. She was a little girl when she was captured and sold to the keeper of a large hotel. I have often heard her tell how hard she fared during childhood. But as she grew older she evinced so much intelligence, and was so faithful, that her master and mistress could not help seeing it was for their interest to take care of such a valuable piece of property. She became an indispensable personage in the household, officiating in all capacities, from cook and wet nurse to seamstress. She was much praised for her cooking; and her nice crackers became so famous in the neighborhood that many people were desirous of obtaining them. In consequence of numerous requests of this kind, she asked permission of her mistress to bake crackers at night, after all the household work was done; and she obtained leave to do it, provided she would clothe herself and her children from the profits. Upon these terms, after working hard all day for her mistress, she began her midnight bakings, assisted by her two oldest children. The business proved profitable; and each year she laid by a little, which was saved for a fund to purchase her children. Her master died, and the property was divided among his heirs. The widow had her dower in the hotel which she continued to keep open. My grandmother remained in her service as a slave; but her children were divided among her master's children. As she had five, Benjamin, the youngest one, was sold, in order that each heir might have an equal portion of dollars and cents. There was so little difference in our ages that he seemed more like my brother than my uncle. He was a bright, handsome lad, nearly white; for he inherited the complexion my grandmother had derived from Anglo-Saxon ancestors. Though only ten years old, seven hundred and twenty dollars were paid for him. His sale was a terrible blow to my grandmother, but she was naturally hopeful, and she went to work with renewed energy, trusting in time to be able to purchase some of her children. She had laid up three hundred dollars, which her mistress one day begged as a loan, promising to pay her soon. The reader probably knows that no promise or writing given to a slave is legally binding; for, according to Southern laws, a slave, *being* property, can *hold* no property. When my grandmother lent her hard earnings to her mistress, she trusted solely to her honor. The honor of a slaveholder to a slave!

To this good grandmother I was indebted for many comforts. My brother Willie and I often received portions of the crackers, cakes, and preserves, she made to sell; and after we ceased to be children we were indebted to her for many more important services.

Such were the unusually fortunate circumstances of my early childhood. When I was six years old, my mother died; and then, for the first time, I learned, by the talk around me, that I was a slave. My mother's mistress was the daughter of my grandmother's mistress. She was the foster sister of my mother; they were both nourished at my grandmother's breast. In fact, my mother had been weaned at three months old, that the babe of the mistress might obtain sufficient food. They played together as children; and, when they became women, my mother was a most faithful servant to her whiter foster sister. On her death-bed her mistress promised that her children should never suffer for any thing; and during her lifetime she kept her word. They all spoke kindly of my dead mother, who had been a slave merely in name, but in nature was noble and womanly. I grieved for her, and my young mind was troubled with the thought who would now take care of me and my little brother. I was told that my home was now to be with her mistress; and I found it a happy one. No toilsome or disagreeable duties were imposed on me. My mistress was so kind to me that I was always glad to do her bidding, and proud to labor for her as much as my young years would permit. I would sit by her side for hours, sewing diligently, with a heart as free from care as that of any free-born white child. When she thought I was tired, she would send me out to run and jump; and away I bounded, to gather berries or flowers to decorate her room. Those were happy days—too happy to last. The slave child had no thought for the morrow; but there came that blight, which too surely waits on every human being born to be a chattel.

When I was nearly twelve years old, my kind mistress sickened and died. As I saw the cheek grow paler, and the eye more glassy, how earnestly I prayed in my heart that she might live! I loved her; for she had been almost like a mother to me. My prayers were not answered. She died, and they buried her in the little churchyard, where, day after day, my tears fell upon her grave.

I was sent to spend a week with my grandmother. I was now old enough to begin to think of the future; and again and again I asked myself what they would do with me. I felt sure I should never find another mistress so kind as the one who was gone. She had promised my dying mother that her children should never suffer for any thing; and when I remembered that, and recalled her many proofs of attachment to me, I could not help having some hopes that she had left me free. My friends were almost certain it would be so. They thought she would be sure to do it, on account of my mother's love and faithful service. But, alas! we all know that the memory of a faithful slave does not avail much to save her children from the auction block.

After a brief period of suspense, the will of my mistress was read, and we learned that she had bequeathed me to her sister's daughter, a child of five years old. So vanished our hopes. My mistress had taught me the precepts of God's Word: "Thou shalt love thy neighbor as thyself." "Whatsoever ye would that men should do unto you, do ye even so unto them." But I was her slave, and I suppose she did not recognize me as her neighbor. I would give much to blot out from my memory that one great wrong. As a child, I loved my mistress; and, looking back on the happy days I spent with her, I try to think with less bitterness of this act of injustice. While I was with her, she taught me to read and spell; and for this privilege, which so rarely falls to the lot of a slave, I bless her memory.

She possessed but few slaves; and at her death those were all distributed among her relatives. Five of them were my grandmother's children, and had shared the same milk that nourished her mother's children. Notwithstanding my grandmother's long and faithful service to her owners, not one of her children escaped the auction block. These God-breathing machines are no more, in the sight of their masters, than the cotton they plant, or the horses they tend.

## II. THE NEW MASTER AND MISTRESS

Dr. Flint, a physician in the neighborhood, had married the sister of my mistress, and I was now the property of their little daughter. . . .

## V. THE TRIALS OF GIRLHOOD

During the first years of my service in Dr. Flint's family, I was accustomed to share some indulgences with the children of my mistress. Though this seemed to me no more than right, I was grateful for it, and tried to merit the kindness by the faithful discharge of my duties. But I now entered on my fifteenth year—a sad epoch in the life of a slave girl. My master began to whisper foul words in my ear. Young as I was, I could not remain ignorant of their import. I tried to treat them with indifference or contempt. The master's age, my extreme youth, and the fear that his conduct would be reported to my grandmother, made him bear this treatment for many months. He was a crafty man, and resorted to many means to accomplish his purposes. Sometimes he had stormy, terrific ways, that made his victims tremble; sometimes he assumed a gentleness that he thought must surely subdue. Of the two, I preferred his stormy moods, although they left me trembling. He tried his utmost to corrupt the pure principles my grandmother had instilled. He peopled my young mind with unclean images, such as only a vile monster could think of. I turned from him with disgust and hatred. But he was my master. I was compelled to live under the same roof with him—where I saw a man forty years my senior daily violating the most sacred commandments of nature. He told me I was his property; that I must be subject to his will in all things. My soul revolted against the mean tyranny. But where could I turn for protection? No matter whether the slave girl be as black as ebony or as fair as her mistress. In either case, there is no shadow of law to protect her from insult, from violence, or even from death; all these are inflicted by fiends who bear the shape of men. The mistress, who ought to protect the helpless victim, has no other feelings towards her but those of jealousy and rage. The degradation, the wrongs, the vices, that grow out of slavery, are more than I can describe. They are greater than you would willingly believe. Surely, if you credited one half the truths that are told you concerning the helpless millions suffering in this cruel bondage, you at the north would not help to tighten the yoke. You surely would refuse to do for the master, on your own soil, the mean and cruel work which trained bloodhounds and the lowest class of whites do for him at the south.

Every where the years bring to all enough of sin and sorrow; but in slavery the very dawn of life is darkened by these shadows. Even the little child, who is accustomed to wait on her mistress and her children, will learn, before she is twelve years old, why it is that her mistress hates such and such a one among the slaves. Perhaps the child's own mother is among those hated ones. She listens to violent outbreaks of jealous passion, and cannot help understanding what is the cause. She will become prematurely knowing in evil things. Soon she will learn to tremble when she hears her master's footfall. She will be compelled to realize that she is no longer a child. If God has bestowed beauty upon her, it will prove her greatest curse. That which commands admiration in the white woman only hastens the degradation of the female slave. I know that some are too much brutalized by slavery to feel the humiliation of their position; but many slaves feel it most acutely, and shrink from the memory of it. I cannot tell how much I suffered in the presence of these wrongs, nor how I am still pained by the retrospect. My master met me at every turn, reminding me that I belonged to him, and swearing by heaven and earth that he would compel me to submit to him. If I went out for a breath of fresh air, after a day of unwearied toil, his footsteps dogged me. If I knelt by my mother's grave, his dark shadow fell on me even there. The light heart which nature had given me became heavy with sad forebodings. The other slaves in my master's house noticed the change. Many of them pitied me; but none dared to ask the cause. They had no need to inquire. They knew too well the guilty practices under that roof; and they were aware that to speak of them was an offence that never went unpunished.

I longed for some one to confide in. I would have given the world to have laid my head on my grandmother's faithful bosom, and told her all my troubles. But Dr. Flint swore he would kill me, if I was not as silent as the grave. Then, although my grandmother was all in all to me, I feared her as well as loved her. I had been accustomed to look up to her with a respect bordering upon awe. I was very young, and felt shamefaced about telling her such impure things, especially as I knew her to be very strict on such subjects. Moreover, she was a woman of a high spirit. She was usually very quiet in her demeanor; but if her indignation was once roused, it was not very easily quelled. I had been told that she once chased a white gentleman with a loaded pistol, because he insulted one of her daughters. I dreaded the consequences of a violent outbreak; and both pride and fear kept me silent. But though I did not confide in my grandmother, and even evaded her vigilant watchfulness and inquiry, her presence in the neighborhood was some protection to me. Though she had been a slave, Dr. Flint was afraid of her. He dreaded her scorching rebukes. Moreover, she was known and patronized by many people; and he did not wish to have his villany made public. It was lucky for me that I did not live on a distant plantation, but in a town not so large that the inhabitants were ignorant of each other's affairs. Bad as are the laws and customs in a slaveholding community, the doctor, as a professional man, deemed it prudent to keep up some outward show of decency.

O, what days and nights of fear and sorrow that man caused me! Reader, it is not to awaken sympathy for myself that I am telling you truthfully what I suffered in slavery. I do it to kindle a flame of compassion in your hearts for my sisters who are still in bondage, suffering as I once suffered.

I once saw two beautiful children playing together. One was a fair white child; the other was her slave, and also her sister. When I saw them embracing each other, and heard their joyous laughter, I turned sadly away from the lovely sight. I foresaw the inevitable blight that would fall on the little slave's heart. I knew how soon her laughter would be changed to sighs. The fair child grew up to be a still fairer woman. From childhood to womanhood her pathway was blooming with flowers, and overarched by a sunny sky. Scarcely one day of her life had been clouded when the sun rose on her happy bridal morning.

How had those years dealt with her slave sister, the little playmate of her childhood? She, also, was very beautiful; but the flowers and sunshine of love were not for her. She drank the cup of sin, and shame, and misery, whereof her persecuted race are compelled to drink.

In view of these things, why are ye silent, ye free men and women of the north? Why do your tongues falter in maintenance of the right? Would that I had more ability! But my heart is so full, and my pen is so weak! There are noble men and women who plead for us, striving to help those who cannot help themselves. God bless them! God give them strength and courage to go on! God bless those, every where, who are laboring to advance the cause of humanity!

## QUESTIONS TO CONSIDER

1. What can you glean about the experience of slavery from Jacobs' account?
2. What does Jacobs identify as the worst aspects of her life as a slave?

# CHAPTER 11

# REFORM AND CONFLICT, 1820–1848

## 11.1 ROBERT OWEN, *AN ADDRESS TO THE INHABITANTS OF NEW LANARK* (1816)

Robert Owen (1771–1858) was a Welsh industrialist who became interested in trying to tie manufacturing to utopian social communities. In 1799, Owen purchased a textile mill in New Lanark, Scotland. He set about trying to both produce goods efficiently and uplift his 2,000 factory workers. He instituted an eight-hour work day and implemented education programs in the mill's boarding houses. In the following speech from 1816, Owen sets out to define the problems of contemporary capitalist society and his strategy to remedy them. The next year, Owen began to more fully embrace socialism. In 1825, he founded a communal utopian community at New Harmony, Indiana. Though the community lasted only two years, Owen's ideas lived on in many other American utopian communities. More broadly, throughout his life Owen helped to improve workers' rights, establish public libraries, and support labor unions.

We have met to-day for the purpose of opening this Institution ; and it is my intention to explain to you the objects for which it has been founded.

These objects are most important.

The first relates to the immediate comfort and benefit of all the inhabitants of this village ;

The second, to the welfare and advantage of the neighbourhood ;

The third, to extensive ameliorations throughout the British Dominions ;

And the last, to the gradual improvement of every nation in the world.

I will briefly explain how this Institution is to contribute towards producing these effects.

Long before I came to reside among you, it had been my chief study to discover the extent, causes, and remedy, of the inconveniences and miseries which were perpetually recurring to every class in society.

The history of man informed me, that innumerable attempts had been made through every age to lessen these evils ; and experience convinced me that the present generation, stimulated by an accession of knowledge derived from past times, was eagerly engaged in the same pursuit. My mind at a very early

*Source:* Robert Owen, *An Address Delivered to the Inhabitants of New Lanark* (London, 1817), 5–7, 13–18, 32–34. Retrieved from the Hathi Trust website, https://catalog.hathitrust.org/Record/001746286 (Accessed June 6, 2018).

period took a similar direction ; and I became ardently desirous of investigating to its source a subject which involved the happiness of every human being.

It soon appeared to me, that the only path to knowledge on this subject had been neglected ; that one leading in an opposite direction had alone been followed ; that while causes existed to compel mankind to pursue such direction, it was idle to expect any successful result : and experience proves how vain their pursuit has been.

In this inquiry, men have hitherto been directed by their inventive faculties, and have almost entirely disregarded the only guide that can lead to true knowledge on any subject experience. They have been governed, in the most important concerns of life, by mere illusions of the imagination, in direct opposition to existing facts. Having satisfied myself beyond doubt with regard to this fundamental error ; having traced the ignorance and misery which it has inflicted on man, by a calm and patient investigation of the causes which have continued this evil, without any intermission, from one generation to another ; and having also maturely reflected on the obstacles to be overcome before a new direction could be given to the human mind :—I was induced to form the resolution of devoting my life to relieve mankind from this mental disease, and all its miseries.

It was evident to me that the evil was universal ; that in practice none were in the right path—no, not one ;—and that in order to remedy the evil a different one must be pursued. That the whole man must be re-formed on fundamental principles, the very reverse of those in which he had hitherto been trained ; in short, that the minds of all men must be born again, and their knowledge and practice commence on a new foundation. . . .

This Institution, when all its parts shall be completed, is intended to produce permanently beneficial effects ; and instead of longer applying temporary expedients for correcting some of your most prominent external habits, to effect a complete and thorough improvement in the *internal* as well as *external* character of the whole village. For this purpose the Institution has been devised to afford the means of receiving your children at an early age, as soon almost as they can walk. By this means, many of you, mothers of families, will be enabled to earn

a better maintenance or support for your children ; you will have less care and anxiety about them ; while the children will be prevented from acquiring any bad habits and gradually prepared to learn the best.

The middle room of the story below will be appropriated to their accommodation ; and in this, their chief occupation will be to play and amuse themselves in severe weather : at other times they will be permitted to occupy the inclosed area before the building ; for, to give children a vigorous constitution they ought to be kept as much as possible in the open air. As they advance in years they will be taken into the rooms on the right and left, where they will be regularly instructed in the rudiments of common learning ; which, before they shall be six years old, they may be taught in a superior manner. These states may be called the 1st and 2d preparatory schools; and when your children shall have passed through them, they will be admitted into this place, which with the adjoining apartment is to be the general school-room for reading, writing, arithmetic, sewing, and knitting ; all which, on the plan to be pursued, will be accomplished to a considerable extent by the time the children are ten years old ; before which age none of them will be permitted to enter the works. For the benefit of the health and spirits of the children, both boys and girls will be taught to dance, and the boys will be instructed in military exercises : those of each sex who may have good voices will be taught to sing, and those among the boys who have a taste for music will be taught to play upon some instrument ; for it is intended to give them as much diversified innocent amusement as the local circumstances of the establishment will admit.

The rooms to the east and west on the story below will also be appropriated in bad weather for relaxation and exercise during some part of the day, to the children who, in the regular hours of teaching, are to be instructed in these apartments.

In this manner is the Institution to be occupied during the day in winter. In summer it is intended that they shall derive knowledge from a personal examination of the works of nature and of art, by going out frequently with some of their masters into the neighbourhood and country around.

After the instruction of the children who are too young to attend the works shall have been finished for the day, the apartments shall be cleaned, ventilated, and in winter lighted and heated, and in all respects made comfortable, for the reception of other classes of the population. The apartments on this floor are then to be appropriated for the use of the children and youth of both sexes who have been employed at work during the day, and who may wish still further to improve themselves in reading, writing, arithmetic, sewing, or knitting ; or to learn any of the useful arts ; to instruct them in which, proper masters and mistresses who are appointed will attend for two hours every evening. The three lower rooms, which in winter will also be well lighted and properly heated, will be thrown open for the use of the adult part of the population, who are to be provided with every accommodation requisite to enable them to read, write, account, sew, or play, converse, or walk about. But strict order and attention to the happiness of every one of the party will be enforced, until such habits shall be acquired as will render any formal restriction unnecessary ; and the measures thus adopted will soon remove such necessity. Two evenings in the week will be appropriated to dancing and music ; but on these occasions every accommodation will be prepared for those who prefer to study or follow any of the occupations pursued on the other evenings. One of the apartments will also be occasionally appropriated for the purpose of giving useful instruction to the older class of the inhabitants. For, believe me, my friends, you are yet very deficient with regard to the best modes of training your children, or of arranging your domestic concerns ; as well as in that wisdom which is requisite to direct your conduct towards each other, so as to enable you to become greatly more happy than you have ever yet been. There will be no difficulty in teaching you what is right and proper ; your own interests will afford ample stimulus for that purpose ; but the real and only difficulty will be to unlearn those pernicious habits and sentiments which an infinite variety of causes, existing through all past ages, have combined to impress upon your minds and bodies, so as to make you imagine that they are inseparable from your nature. It shall however, ere along be proved to you, that in this respect as well as in many others, you and all mankind are mistaken. Yet, think not from what I have said that I mean to infringe, even in the most slight degree, on the liberty of private

judgement or religious opinions. No! They have hitherto been unrestrained ; and the most effectual measures have been adopted by all the parties interested in the concern, to secure to you these most invaluable privileges. And here I now publicly declare (and while I make the declaration I wish my voice could extend to the ear, and make its due impression on the mind, of every one of our fellow-creatures), "That the individual who first placed restraint on private judgement and religious opinions was the author of hypocrisy, and the origin of innumerable evils which mankind through every past age have experienced." The right, however, of private judgement and of real religious liberty is no where yet enjoyed. It is not possessed by any nation in the world ; and thence the unnecessary ignorance as well as endless misery of all. Nor can this right be enjoyed until the principle whence opinions originate be universally known and acknowledged.

The chief object of my existence will be to make this knowledge universal, and thence to bring the right of private judgement into general practice ; to show the infinitely beneficial consequences that will result to mankind from its adoption.—To effect this important purpose is a part, and an essential part, of that system which is about to be introduced. . . .

Every society which exists at present, as well as every society which history records, has been formed and governed on a belief in the following notions, assumed as *first principles*.

1st. That it is in the power of every individual to form his own character.

Hence the various systems called by the name of religion, codes of law, and punishments. Hence also the angry passions entertained by individuals and nations towards each other.

2nd. That the affections are at the command of the individual.

Hence insincerity and degradation of character.

Hence the miseries of domestic life, and more than one-half of all the crimes of mankind.

3rd. That it is necessary a large portion of mankind should exist in ignorance and poverty, in order to secure to the remaining part such a degree of happiness as they now enjoy.

Hence a system of counteraction in the pursuits of men, a general opposition among individuals to the interests of each other, and the necessary effects of such a system—ignorance, poverty, and vice.

Facts prove, however,

1st. That character is universally formed *for* and not *by* the individual.

2nd. That *any* habits and sentiments may be given to mankind.

3rd. That the affections are *not* under the control of the individual.

4th. That every individual may be trained to produce far more than he can consume, while there is a sufficiency of soil left for him to cultivate.

5th. That nature has provided means by which population may be at all times maintained in the proper state to give the greatest happiness to every individual, without one check of vice or misery.

6th. That any community may be arranged on a due combination of the foregoing principles, in such a manner as not only to withdraw vice, poverty, and in a great degree misery, from the world, but also to place

*every* individual under circumstances in which he shall enjoy more permanent happiness than can be given to *any* individual under the principles which have hitherto regulated society.

7th. That all the assumed fundamental principles on which society has hitherto been founded are erroneous, and may be demonstrated to be contrary to fact.

And last. That the change which would follow the abandonment of those erroneous maxims which bring misery into the world, and the adoption of principles of truth, unfolding a system which shall remove and for ever exclude that misery, may be effected without the slightest injury to any human being. . . .

### QUESTIONS TO CONSIDER

1. What did Owen view as the problems of modern society? How did he seek to address them?
2. Would you have wanted to work at New Lanark?

# 11.2 WILLIAM LLOYD GARRISON, "TO THE PUBLIC" (1831)

William Lloyd Garrison (1805–1879) was one of the most prominent abolitionists in nineteenth-century America. Born in Massachusetts, Garrison worked in the newspaper industry during the 1820s. At the time, many anti-slavery Americans supported moderate positions: either for colonizing freed slaves in Africa or slowly emancipating slaves. Garrison rejected such moderation and became a strong proponent of immediate abolitionism. In 1832, he founded *The Liberator*, an abolitionist newspaper. In the following article, from the first edition of *The Liberator*, Garrison summarized his viewpoints in a forceful tone. Garrison would publish the newspaper until the end of the Civil War in 1865.

### THE LIBERATOR

"To The Public"

In the month of August, I issued proposals for the publishing 'The Liberator' in Washington city; but the enterprise, though hailed in different sections of the country, was palsied by public indifference. Since that time, the removal of the Genius of Universal Emancipation to the Seat of Government has rendered less

---

*Source:* William Lloyd Garrison, "To the Public," *The Liberator,* January 1, 1831.

imperious the establishment of a similar periodical in that quarter.

During my recent tour for the purpose of exciting the minds of the people by a series of discourses on the subject of slavery, every place that I visited gave fresh evidence of the fact, that a greater revolution in public sentiment was to be effected in the free states—*and particularly in New-England*—than at the south. I found contempt more bitter, opposition more active, detraction more relentless, prejudice more stubborn, and apathy more frozen, than among slave owners themselves. Of course, there were individual exceptions to the contrary. This state of things afflicted, but did not dishearten me. I determined, at every hazard, to lift up the standard of emancipation in the eyes of the nation, *within sight of Bunker Hill and in the birth place of liberty*. That standard is now unfurled; and long may it float, unhurt by the spoliations of time or the missiles of a desperate foe—yea, till every chain be broken, and every bondman set free! Let southern oppressors tremble—let their northern apologists tremble—let all the enemies of the persecuted blacks tremble.

I deem the publication of my original Prospectus* unnecessary, as it has obtained a wide circulation. The principles therein inculcated will be steadily pursued in this paper, excepting that I shall not array myself as the political partisan of any man. In defending the great cause of human rights, I wish to derive the assistance of all religions and of all parties.

Assenting to the 'self-evident truth' maintained in the American Declaration of Independence, 'that all men are created equal, and endowed by their Creator with certain inalienable rights—among which are life, liberty and the pursuit of happiness,' I shall strenuously contend for the immediate enfranchisement of our slave population. In Park-street Church, on the Fourth of July, 1829, in an address on slavery, I unreflectingly assented to the popular but pernicious doctrine of *gradual* abolition. I seize this opportunity to make a full and unequivocal recantation, and thus publicly to ask pardon of my God, of my country, and of my brethren the poor slaves, for having uttered a

sentiment so full of timidity, injustice and absurdity. A similar recantation, from my pen, was published in the Genius of Universal Emancipation at Baltimore, in September, 1829. My conscience is now satisfied.

I am aware, that many object to the severity of my language; but is there not cause for severity? I *will be* as harsh as truth, and as uncompromising as justice. On this subject, I do not wish to think, or speak, or write, with moderation. No! no! Tell a man whose house is on fire, to give a moderate alarm; tell him to moderately rescue his wife from the hands of the ravisher; tell the mother to gradually extricate her babe from the fire into which it has fallen;—but urge me not to use moderation in a cause like the present. I am in earnest—I will not equivocate—I will not excuse—I will not retreat a single inch—AND I WILL BE HEARD. The apathy of the people is enough to make every statue leap from its pedestal, and to hasten the resurrection of the dead.

It is pretended, that I am retarding the cause of emancipation by the coarseness of my invective, and the precipitancy of my measures. *The charge is not true.* On this question my influence,—humble as it is,—is felt at this moment to a considerable extent, and shall be felt in coming years—not perniciously, but beneficially— not as a curse, but as a blessing; and posterity will bear testimony that I was right. I desire to thank God, that he enables me to disregard 'the fear of man which bringeth a snare,' and to speak his truth in its simplicity and power. And here I close with this fresh dedication:

'Oppression! I have seen thee, face to face,
And met thy cruel eye and cloudy brow;
But thy soul-withering glance I fear not now—
For dread to prouder feelings doth give place
Of deep abhorrence! Scorning the disgrace
Of slavish knees that at thy footstool bow,
I also kneel—but with far other vow
Do hail thee and thy herd of hirelings base :—
I swear, while life-blood warms my throbbings
    veins,
Still to oppose and thwart, with heart and hand,
Thy brutalizing swar—till Afric's chains

---

* I would here offer my grateful acknowledgment to these editors who so promptly and generously inserted my Proposals. They must give me an available opportunity to repay their liberality.

Are burst, and Freedom rules the rescued land,—
Trampling Oppression and his iron rod:
*Such is the cow I take*—SO HELP ME GOD!'

*William Lloyd Garrison.*
*Boston, January 1, 1831*

**QUESTIONS TO CONSIDER**

1. How does Garrison support his abolitionism?
2. Do you think his passionate tone helps or hinders his argument?

# 11.3 SENECA FALLS CONVENTION, MINUTES AND DECLARATION OF SENTIMENTS (1848)

In July, 1848, around 300 people gathered together in Seneca Falls, a small town in upstate New York, to discuss the growing movement for women's suffrage. Suffrage advocates, including Elizabeth Cady Stanton and Lucretia Mott, planned the gathering to spread news about their movement and to collectively discuss strategies that might gain the movement broader traction. On the second morning, those gathered discussed the "Declaration of Sentiments," a document modeled on the Declaration of Independence that Stanton had written before convention. In the end, 100 people—68 women and 32 men—signed, and it became a founding document of the women's suffrage movement. The territory of Wyoming gave women the right to vote in 1869, but women did not receive the franchise on a national level until the ratification of the Nineteenth Amendment in 1920.

. . . In the afternoon, the meeting assembled according to adjournment, and was opened by reading the minutes of the morning session. E. C. Stanton then addressed the meeting, and was followed by Lucretia Mott. The reading of the Declaration was called for, an addition having been inserted since the morning session. A vote taken upon the amendment was carried, and papers circulated to obtain signatures. The following resolutions were then read:

Whereas, the great precept of nature is conceded to be, "that man shall pursue his own true and substantial happiness," Blackstone, in his Commentaries, remarks, that this law of Nature being coeval with mankind, and dictated by God himself, is of course superior in obligation to any other. It is binding over all the globe, in all countries, and at all times; no human laws are of any validity if contrary to this, and such of

them as are valid, derive all their force, and all their validity, and all their authority, mediately and immediately, from this original; Therefore,

Resolved, That such laws as conflict, in any way, with the true and substantial happiness of woman, are contrary to the great precept of nature, and of no validity; for this is "superior in obligation to any other."

Resolved, That all laws which prevent woman from occupying such a station in society as her conscience shall dictate, or which place her in a position inferior to that of man, are contrary to the great precept of nature, and therefore of no force or authority.

Resolved, That woman is man's equal—was intended to be so by the Creator, and the highest good of the race demands that she should be recognized as such.

Resolved, That the women of this country ought to be enlightened in regard to the laws under which

*Source:* Ann D. Gordon ed., *The Selected Papers of Elizabeth Cady Stanton and Susan B. Anthony, Volume I* (New Brunswick: Rutgers University Press, 1997), 76–81.

they live, that they may no longer publish their degradation, by declaring themselves satisfied with their present position, nor their ignorance, by asserting that they have all the rights they want.

Resolved, That inasmuch as man, while claiming for himself intellectual superiority, does accord to woman moral superiority, it is preeminently his duty to encourage her to speak, and teach, as she has an opportunity, in all religious assemblies.

Resolved, That the same amount of virtue, delicacy, and refinement of behavior, that is required of woman in the social state, should also be required of man, and the same transgressions should be visited with equal severity on both man and woman.

Resolved, That the objection of indelicacy and impropriety, which is so often brought against woman when she addresses a public audience, comes with a very ill grace from those who encourage, by their attendance, her appearance on the stage, in the concert, or in the feats of the circus.

Resolve, That woman has too long rested satisfied in the circumscribed limits which corrupt customs and a perverted application of the Scriptures have marked out for her, and that it is time she should move in the enlarged sphere which her great Creator has assigned her.

Resolved, That it is the duty of the women of this country to secure to themselves their sacred right to the elective franchise.

Resolved, That the equality of human rights results necessarily from the fact of the identity of the race in capabilities and responsibilities.

Resolved, therefore, That, being invested by the Creator with the same capabilities, and the same consciousness of responsibility for their exercise, it is demonstrably the right and duty of woman, equally with man, to promote every righteous cause, by every righteous means; and especially in regard to the great subjects of morals and religion, it is self-evidently her right to participate with her brother in teaching them, both in private and in public, by writing and by speaking, by any instrumentalities proper to be used, and in any assemblies proper to be held; and this being a self-evident truth, growing out of the divinely implanted principles of human nature, any custom or authority adverse to it, whether modern or wearing the hoary

sanction of antiquity, is to be regarded as self-evident falsehood, and at war with the interests of mankind...

## ... THURSDAY MORNING

The Convention assembled at the hour appointed, James Mott, of Philadelphia, in the Chair. The minutes of the previous day having been read, E. C. Stanton again read the Declaration of Sentiments, which was freely discussed by Lucretia Mott, Ansel Bascom, S. E. Woodworth, Thomas and Mary Ann M'Clintock, Frederick Douglass, Amy Post, Catharine Stebbins, and Elizabeth C. Stanton, and was unanimously adopted, as follows:

## DECLARATION OF SENTIMENTS

When, in the course of human events, it becomes necessary for one portion of the family of man to assume among the people of the earth a position different from that which they have hitherto occupied, but one to which the laws of nature and of nature's God entitled them, a decent respect to the opinions of mankind requires that they should declare the causes that impel them to such a course.

We hold these truths to be self-evident: that all men and women are created equal; that they are endowed by their Creator with certain inalienable rights; that among these are life, liberty, and the pursuit of happiness; that to secure these rights governments are instituted, deriving their just powers from the consent of the governed. Whenever any form of Government becomes destructive of these ends, it is the right of those who suffer from it to refuse allegiance to it, and to insist upon the institution of a new government, laying its foundation on such principles, and organizing its powers in such form as to them shall seem most likely to effect their safety and happiness. Prudence, indeed, will dictate that governments long established should not be changed for light and transient causes; and accordingly, all experience hath shown that mankind are more disposed to suffer, while evils are sufferable, than to right themselves by abolishing the forms to which they are accustomed. But when a long train of abuses and usurpations, pursuing invariably the same object, evinces a design to reduce them under absolute despotism, it is their duty to throw off such government, and to provide new guards for their future security. Such has been the patient sufferance of the women under this government, and such is now the necessity which constrains them to demand the equal station to which they are entitled.

The history of mankind is a history of repeated injuries and usurpations on the part of man toward woman, having in direct object the establishment of an absolute tyranny over her. To prove this, let facts be submitted to a candid world.

He has never permitted her to exercise her inalienable right to the elective franchise.

He has compelled her to submit to laws, in the formation of which she had no voice.

He has withheld from her rights which are given to the most ignorant and degraded men—both natives and foreigners.

Having deprived her of this first right of a citizen, the elective franchise, thereby leaving her without representation in the halls of legislation, he has oppressed her on all sides.

He has made her, if married, in the eye of the law, civilly dead.

He has taken from her all right in property, even to the wages she earns.

He has made her, morally, an irresponsible being, as she can commit many crimes with impunity, provided they be done in the presence of her husband. In the covenant of marriage, she is compelled to promise obedience to her husband, he becoming, to all intents and purposes, her master—the law giving him power to deprive her of her liberty, and to administer chastisement.

He is so framed the laws of divorce, as to what shall be the proper causes of divorce; in case of separation, to whom the guardianship of the children shall be given; as to be wholly regardless of the happiness of women—the law, in all cases, going upon the false supposition of the supremacy of man, and giving all power into his hands.

After depriving her of all rights as a married woman, if single and the owner of property, he has taxed her to support a government which recognizes her only when her property can be made profitable to it.

He has monopolized nearly all the profitable employments, and from those she is permitted to follow, she receives but a scanty remuneration.

He closes against her all the avenues to wealth and distinction, which he considers most honorable to himself. As a teach of theology, medicine, or law, she is not known.

He has denied her the facilities for obtaining a thorough education—all colleges being closed against her.

He allows her in Church as well as State, but a subordinate position, claiming Apostolic authority for her exclusion from the ministry, and, with some exceptions, from any public participation in the affairs of the Church.

He has created a false public sentiment, by giving to the world a different code of morals for men and women, by which moral delinquencies which exclude women from society, are not only tolerated but deemed of little account in man.

He has usurped the prerogative of Jehovah himself, claiming it as his right to assign for her a sphere of action, when that belongs to her conscience and her God.

He has endeavored, in every way that he could to destroy her confidence in her own powers, to lessen her self-respect, and to make her willing to lead a dependant and abject life.

Now, in view of this entire disfranchisement of one-half the people of this country, their social and religious degradation,—in view of the unjust laws above mentioned, and because women do feel themselves aggrieved, oppressed, and fraudulently deprived of their most sacred rights, we insist that they have immediate admission to all the rights and privileges which belong to them as citizens of these United States.

In entering upon the great work before us, we anticipate no small amount of misconception, misrepresentation, and ridicule; but we shall use every instrumentality within our power to effect our object. We shall employ agents, circulate tracts, petition the State and national Legislatures, and endeavor to enlist the pulpit and the press in our behalf. We hope this Convention will be followed by a series of Conventions, embracing every part of the country.

**QUESTIONS TO CONSIDER**

1. What did the Convention most cite as grievances?
2. Do you find the Declaration of Sentiments to be rhetorically effective?

# 11.4 CHARLES FINNEY, EXCERPT FROM *LECTURES ON REVIVALS OF RELIGION* (1853)

In the late eighteenth and early nineteenth centuries, a series of religious revivals swept through America, especially through western New York, the American West, and the American South. These revivals were termed the "Second Great Awakening," after the religious revivals of the 1730s and 1740s, which featured, among many other preachers, George Whitefield and Jonathan Edwards (see Chapter 5). In western New York, preacher Charles Grandison Finney (1792–1875) held sway. Finney moved with his family to New York at a young age and then studied to be a lawyer. In the mid-1820s, Finney became interested in religious revivals. He preached the importance of conversion, repentance, and a close, personal relationship with god. The following excerpt, from Finney's 1835 *Lectures on Revivals of Religion*, encapsulates his ideas about how to promote a revival. After the Second Great Awakening, Finney taught at and then served as the President of Oberlin University in Ohio, where he was active in the women's suffrage and abolitionist movements.

A revival consists of two parts ; as it respects the church, and as it respects the ungodly. I shall speak to-night of a revival in the church. Fallow ground is ground which has once been tilled, but which now lies waste, and needs to be broken up and mellowed, before it is suited to receive grain. I shall show, as it respects a revival in the church,

1. What it is to break up the fallow ground, in the sense of the text.
2. How it is to be performed.

## I. WHAT IS IT TO BREAK UP THE FALLOW GROUND?

To break up the fallow ground, is to break up your hearts—to prepare your minds to bring forth fruit unto God. The mind of man is often compared in the Bible to ground, and the word of God to seed sown in it, and the fruit represents the actions and affections of those who receive it. To break up the fallow ground, therefore, is to bring the mind into such a state, that it is fitted to receive the word of God. Sometime your

hearts get matted down hard and dry, and all run to waste, till there is no such thing as getting fruit from them till they are all broken up, and mellowed down, and fitted to receive the word of God. It is this softening of the hear, so as to make it feel the truth, which the prophet calls breaking up your fallow ground.

## II. HOW IS THE FALLOW GROUND TO BE BROKEN UP?

*1. It is not by any direct efforts to feel.* People run into a mistake on this subject, from not making the laws of mind the object of thought. There are great errors on the subject of the laws which govern the mind. People talk about religious feeling, as if they thought they could, by direct effort, call forth religious affection. But this is not the way, merely by acts. No man can make himself feel in this way, merely by *trying* to feel. The feelings of the mind are not *directly* under our control. We cannot by willing, or by direct volition, call forth religious feelings. We might as well think to call spirits up from the deep. They are purely involuntary states

*Source:* Charles G. Finney, *Lectures on Revivals of Religion* (New York: Fleming H. Revell, 1868), 35–47. Retrieved from the Internet Archive website, https://archive.org/details/lecturesonreviva00finn (Accessed June 6, 2018).

of mind. They naturally and necessarily exist in the mind under certain circumstances calculated to excite them. But they can be controlled *indirectly*. Otherwise there would be no moral character in our feelings, if there were not a way to control them. We cannot say, "Now I will feel so and so to wards such an object." But we can command our *attention* to it, and look at it intently, till the involuntary affections arise. Let a man who is away from his family, bring them up before his mind, and will he not feel? But it is not by saying to himself, "Now I will feel deeply for my family." A man can direct his attention to any object, about which he ought to feel and wishes to feel, and in that way he will call into existence the proper emotions. Let a man call up his enemy before his mind, and his feelings of enmity will rise. So if a man thinks of God, and fastens his mind on any parts of God's character, he will feel—emotions will come up, by the very laws of mind. If he is a friend of God, let him contemplate God as a gracious and holy being, and he will have emotions of friendship kindled up in his mind. If he is an enemy of God, only let him get the true character of God before his mind, and look at it, and fasten his attention on it, and his enmity will rise against God, or he will break down and give his heart to God.

If you wish to break up the fallow ground of your hearts, and make your minds feel on the subject of religion, you must go to work just as you would to feel on any other subject. Instead of keeping your thoughts on every thing else, and then imagine that by going to a few meetings you will get your feelings enlisted, go the common sense way to work, as you would on any other subject. It is just as easy to make your minds feel on the subject of religion as it is on any other subject. God has put these states of mind under your control. If people were as unphilosophical about moving their limbs, as they are about regulating their emotions, you would never have got here to meetings to-night.

If you mean to break the fallow ground of your hearts, you must begin by looking at your hearts–examine and note the state of your minds, and see where you are. Many never seem to think about this. They pay no attention to their own hearts, and never known whether they are doing well in religion or not—whether they are gaining ground or going back—whether they are fruitful, or lying waste like the fallow

ground. Now you must draw off your attention from other things, and look into this. Make a business of it. Do not be in a hurry. Examine thoroughly the state of your hearts, and see where you are—whether you are walking with God every day, or walking with the devil—whether you are serving God or serving the devil most—whether you are under the dominion of the prince of darkness, or of the Lord Jesus Christ.

To do all this, you must set yourselves at work to consider your sins. You must examine yourselves. And by this I do not mean, that you must stop and look directly within to see what is the present state of your feelings. That is the very way to put a stop to all feeling. This is just as absurd as it would be for a man to shut his eyes on the lamp, and try to turn his eyes inward to find out whether there was any image painted on the retina. The man complains that does not see anything! And why? Because he has turned his eyes away from the objects of sight. The truth is, our moral feelings are as much an object of consciousness as our sensations. And the way to excite them is to go on acting, and employing our minds. Then we can tell our moral feelings by consciousness, just as I could tell my natural feelings by considering your actions, if I should put my hand in the fire.

Self-examination consists in looking at your lives, in considering your actions, in calling up the past, and learning its true character. Look back over your past history. Take up your individual sins one by one, and look at them. I do not mean that you should just cast a glance at your past life, and see that it has been full of sins, and then go to God and make a sort of general confession, and ask for pardon. That is not the way. Your must take them up one by one. It will be a good thing to take a pen and paper, as you go over them, and write them down as they occur to you. Go over them as carefully as a merchant goes over his books ; and as often as a sin comes before your memory, add it to the list. General confessions of sin will never do. Your sins were committed *one by one* ; and as far as you can come at them, they ought to be reviewed and repented of one by one. . . .

Go thoroughly to work in all this. Go *now*. Don't put it off ; that will only make the matter worse. Confess to God those sins that have been committed against God, and to man those sins that have been committed against man. Don't think of getting off by going round the stumbling blocks. Take them up out of the way. In breaking up your fallow ground, you must remove every obstruction. Things may be left that you may think little things, and you may wonder why you do not feel as you wish to in religion, when the reason is that your proud and carnal mind has covered up something which God required you to confess and remove. Break up all the ground and turn it over. Do not balk it, as the farmers say ; do not turn aside for little difficulties ; drive the plow right through them, beam deep, and turn the ground all up, so that it may all be mellow and soft, and fit to receive the speed and bear fruit a hundred fold.

When you have gone over your whole history in this way thoroughly, if you will go over the ground the second time and give your solemn and fixed attention to it, you will find that the things you have put down will suggest other things of which you have been guilty, connected with them or near them. Then go over it a third time, and you will recollect other things connected with these. And you will find in the end that you can remember an amount of your history, and particular actions, even in this life, which you did not think you should remember in eternity. Unless you do take up your sins in this way, and consider them in detail, one by one, you can form no idea of the amount of your sins. You should go over it as thoroughly and as carefully, and as solemnly, as you would if you were just preparing yourself for the judgment.

As you go over the catalogue of your sins, be sure to resolve upon present and entire reformation. Wherever you find any thing wrong, resolve at once, in the strength of God, to sin no more in that way. It will be of no benefit to examine yourself, unless you determine to amend in *every particular* that you find wrong in heart, temper, or conduct.

If you find, as you go on with this duty, that your mind is still all dark, cast about you, and you will find there is some reason for the Spirit of God to depart from you. You have not been faithful and thorough. In the progress of such a work you have got to do violence to yourself, and bring yourself as a rational being up to this work, with the Bible before you, and try your heart till you do feel. You need not expect that God will work a miracle for you to break up your fallow ground.

It is to be done by means. Fasten your attention to the subject of your sins. You cannot look at your sins log and thoroughly, and see how bad they are, without feelings, and feeling deeply. Experience abundantly proves the benefit of going over our history in this way. Set yourself to the work now ; resolve that you never will stop till you find you can *pray*. You never will have the spirit of prayer, till you examine yourself, and confess your sins, and break up your fallow ground. You never will have the Spirit of God dwelling in you, till you have unraveled this whole mystery of iniquity, and spread out your sins before God. Let there be this deep work of repentance, and full confession, this breaking down before God, and you will have as much of the spirit of prayer as your body can bear up under. The reason why so few Christians know any thing about the spirit of prayer, is because they never would take the pains to examine themselves properly, and so never knew what it was to have their hearts all broken up in this way.

Your see I have only begun to lay open this subject to-night, I want to lay it out before you, in the course of these lectures, so that if you will begin and go on to do as I say, the results will be just as certain as they are when the farmer breaks a fallow field, and mellows it and sows his grain. It will be so, if you will only begin in this way, and hold on till all your hardened and callous hearts break up.

### REMARKS

1. It will do no good to preach to you while your hearts are in this hardened, and waste, and fallow state. The farmer might just as well sow his grain on the rock. It will bring forth no fruit. This is the reason why there are so many fruitless professors in the church, and why there are so much outside machinery, and so little deep-toned feeling in the church. Look at the Sabbath-School for instance, and see how much machinery there is, and how little of the power of godliness. If you go on in this way, the word of God will continue to harden you, and you will grow worse and worse, just as the rain and snow on an old fallow field makes the turf thicker, and the clods stronger.

2. See why so much preaching is wasted, and worse than wasted. It is because the church will not break

up their fallow ground. A preacher may wear out his life, and do very little good, while there are so many stony-ground hearers, who have converted, and their religion is rather a change of opinion than a change of the feeling of their hearts. There is mechanical religion enough, but very little that looks like deep heart work.

3. Professors of religion should never satisfy themselves, or expect a revival, just by starting out of their slumbers, and blustering about, and making a noise, and talking to sinners. They must get their fallow ground broken up. It is utterly philosophical to think of getting engaged in religion in this way. If your fallow ground is broken up, *then* the way to get more feeling, is to go out and see sinners on the road to hell, and talk to them, and guide inquiring souls, and you will get more feelings. You may get into an *excitement* without this breaking up ; you may show a kind of zeal, but it will not last long, and it will not take hold of sinners, unless your hearts are broken up. The reason is that you go about it mechanically, and have not broken up your fallow ground.

4. And now, finally, will you break up your fallow ground? Will you enter upon the course now pointed out, and persevere till you are thoroughly awake? If you fail here, if you do not do this, and get prepared, you can go no further with me in this course of lectures. I have gone with you as far as it is of any use to go, until your fallow ground is broken up. Now, you must make thorough work upon this point, or all I have further to say will do you little good. Nay, it will only harden and make you worse. If, when next Friday night arrives, it finds you with unbroken hearts, you need not expect to be benefited by what I shall say. If you do not set about this work immediately, I shall take it for granted that you do not mean to be revived, that you have forsaken your minister, and mean to let him go up battle alone. If you do not do this, I charge you with having forsaken Christ, with refusing to repent and do your first work. But if you will be prepared to enter upon the work, I propose, God willing, next Friday evening, to lead you into the work of saving sinners.

### QUESTIONS TO CONSIDER

1. What was "fallow ground," in Finney's mind, and how did he tell his listeners to break it up?
2. Why was Finney so interested in helping would-be revival leaders, or revival followers, to do so?

# 11.5 "THE TREE OF INTEMPERANCE" (1855)

Similar to the previous sources in this chapter, the following image, "The Tree of Intemperance," tried to convince Americans of the necessity of moral reform during the nineteenth century. The print was the second of two—the first print was titled "The Tree of Temperance"—published in 1855 by A. D. Fillmore to illustrate the dangers of drinking. The temperance movement, which had close ties to women's anti-domestic violence movement and the Second Great Awakening, gained in power throughout the nineteenth century and eventually culminated the Eighteenth Amendment of 1920. Pay careful attention to the names on the tree's branches and the figures beneath the trees.

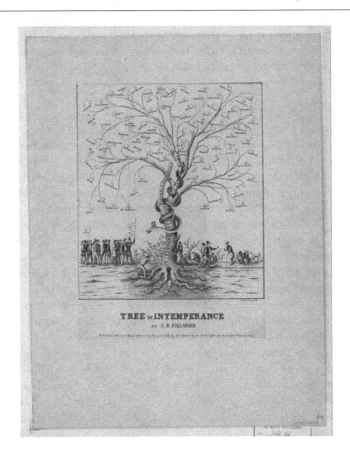

TREE OF INTEMPERANCE
BY A. D. FILLMORE

## QUESTIONS TO CONSIDER

1. What were the evils that resulted from intemperance, according to the image?

2. How were drinkers portrayed?

*Source:* "Tree of Intemperance," http://www.loc.gov/pictures/item/2003689279 (Accessed June 6, 2018).

# 11.6 REBECCA HARDING DAVIS, EXCERPT FROM *LIFE IN THE IRON MILLS* (1861)

Robert Owen's mills (see Reading 11.1) tried to merge industrialization with social uplift, but Rebecca Harding Davis' 1861 novella *Life in the Iron Mills* emphasized the grim experience of industrialization experienced by most nineteenth century factory workers. Davis, a realist author, intended the story to exhibit the moral decay fostered by the American industrial system, which increasingly depended on immigrant labor during the time. *Life in the Iron Mills* was immediately viewed as a new type of literature, one concerned with the daily experience of laborers. In the story, an omniscient narrator introduces the reader to the laborer Hugh Wolfe and Deborah, his cousin. Deborah sets off to take Hugh supper at his factory, and the reader experiences the hellish journey with her. Later, Deborah steals from a wealthy visitor to the mill, and she and Hugh both are caught and imprisoned. At the story's end, Hugh commits suicide in jail.

My story is very simple,—Only what I remember of the life of one of these men,—a furnace-tender in one of Kirby & John's rolling-mills,—Hugh Wolfe. You know the mills? They took the great order for the lower Virginia railroads there last winter; run usually with about a thousand men. I cannot tell why I choose the half-forgotten story of this Wolfe more than that of myriads of these furnace-hands. Perhaps because there is a secret, underlying sympathy between that story and this day with its impure fog and thwarted sunshine,—or perhaps simply for the reason that this house is the one where the Wolfes lived. There were the father and son,—both hands, as I said, in one of Kirby & John's mills for making railroad-iron,—and Deborah, their cousin, a picker in some of the cotton-mills. The house was rented then to half a dozen families. The Wolfes had two of the cellar-rooms. The old man, like many of the puddlers and feeders of the mills, was Welsh,—had spent half of his life in the Cornish tin-mines. You may pick the Welsh emigrants, Cornish miners, out of the throng passing the windows, any day. They are a trifle more filthy; their muscles are not so brawny; they stoop more. When they are drunk, they neither yell, nor shout, nor stagger, but skulk along like beaten hounds. A pure, unmixed blood, I fancy: shows itself in the slight angular bodies and sharply-cut facial lines. It is nearly thirty years since the Wolfes lived here. Their lives were like those of their class: incessant labor, sleeping in kennel-like rooms, eating rank pork and molasses, drinking—God and the distillers only know what; with an occasional night in jail, to atone for some drunken excess. Is that all of their lives?—of the portion given to them and these their duplicates swarming the streets to-day?—nothing beneath?—all? So many a political reformer will tell you,—and many a private reformer, too, who has gone among them with a heart tender with Christ's charity, and come out outraged, hardened.

One rainy night, about eleven o'clock, a crowd of half-clothed women stopped outside of the cellar-door. They were going home from the cotton-mill.

"Good-night, Deb," said one, a mulatto, steadying herself against the gas-post. She needed the post to steady her. So did more than one of them.

"Dah's a ball to Miss Potts' to-night. Ye'd best come."

"Inteet, Deb, if hur'll come, hur'll hef fun," said a shrill Welsh voice in the crowd.

*Source:* Rebecca Harding Davis, *Life in the Iron Mills* (Urbana Champaign: Project Gutenberg, 2008).

Two or three dirty hands were thrust out to catch the gown of the woman, who was groping for the latch of the door.

"No."

"No? Where's Kit Small, then?"

"Begorra! on the spools. Alleys behint, though we helped her, we dud. An wid ye! Let Deb alone! It's on-dacent frettin' a quite body. Be the powers, an we'll have a night of it! there'll be lashin's o' drink,—the Vargent be blessed and praised for't!"

They went on, the mulatto inclining for a moment to show fight, and drag the woman Wolfe off with them; but, being pacified, she staggered away.

Deborah groped her way into the cellar, and, after considerable stumbling, kindled a match, and lighted a tallow dip, that sent a yellow glimmer over the room. It was low, damp,—the earthen floor covered with a green, slimy moss,—a fetid air smothering the breath. Old Wolfe lay asleep on a heap of straw, wrapped in a torn horse-blanket. He was a pale, meek little man, with a white face and red rabbit-eyes. The woman Debo-rah was like him; only her face was even more ghastly, her lips bluer, her eyes more watery. She wore a faded cotton gown and a slouching bonnet. When she walked, one could see that she was deformed, almost a hunch-back. She trod softly, so as not to waken him, and went through into the room beyond. There she found by the half-extinguished fire an iron saucepan filled with cold boiled potatoes, which she put upon a broken chair with a pint-cup of ale. Placing the old candlestick beside this dainty repast, she untied her bonnet, which hung limp and wet over her face, and prepared to eat her supper. It was the first food that had touched her lips since morning. There was enough of it, however: there is not always. She was hungry,—one could see that easily enough,—and not drunk, as most of her companions would have been found at this hour. She did not drink, this woman,—her face told that, too,—nothing stron-ger than ale. Perhaps the weak, flaccid wretch had some stimulant in her pale life to keep her up,—some love or hope, it might be, or urgent need. When that stimulant was gone, she would take to whiskey. Man cannot live by work alone. While she was skinning the potatoes, and munching them, a noise behind her made her stop.

"Janey!" she called, lifting the candle and peering into the darkness. "Janey, are you there?"

A heap of ragged coats was heaved up, and the face of a young girl emerged, staring sleepily at the woman.

"Deborah," she said, at last, "I'm here the night."

"Yes, child. Hur's welcome," she said, quietly eating on.

The girl's face was haggard and sickly; her eyes were heavy with sleep and hunger: real Milesian eyes they were, dark, delicate blue, glooming out from black shadows with a pitiful fright.

"I was alone," she said, timidly.

"Where's the father?" asked Deborah, holding out a potato, which the girl greedily seized.

"He's beyant,—wid Haley,—in the stone house." (Did you ever hear the word tail from an Irish mouth?) "I came here. Hugh told me never to stay me-lone."

"Hugh?"

"Yes."

A vexed frown crossed her face. The girl saw it, and added quickly,—

"I have not seen Hugh the day, Deb. The old man says his watch lasts till the mornin'."

The woman sprang up, and hastily began to ar-range some bread and flitch in a tin pail, and to pour her own measure of ale into a bottle. Tying on her bonnet, she blew out the candle.

"Lay ye down, Janey dear," she said, gently, cover-ing her with the old rags. "Hur can eat the potatoes, if hur's hungry.

"Where are ye goin', Deb? The rain's sharp."

"To the mill, with Hugh's supper."

"Let him bide till th' morn. Sit ye down."

"No, no,"—sharply pushing her off. "The boy'll starve."

She hurried from the cellar, while the child wearily coiled herself up for sleep. The rain was falling heavily, as the woman, pail in hand, emerged from the mouth of the alley, and turned down the narrow street, that stretched out, long and black, miles before her. Here and there a flicker of gas lighted an uncertain space of muddy footwalk and gutter; the long rows of houses, except an occasional lager-bier shop, were closed; now and then she met a band of millhands skulking to or from their work.

Not many even of the inhabitants of a manufac-turing town know the vast machinery of system by which the bodies of workmen are governed, that goes on unceasingly from year to year. The hands of each mill are divided into watches that relieve each other as regularly as the sentinels of an army. By night and day the work goes on, the unsleeping engines groan and shriek, the fiery pools of metal boil and surge. Only for a day in the week, in half-courtesy to public censure, the fires are partially veiled; but as soon as the clock strikes midnight, the great furnaces break forth with renewed fury, the clamor begins with fresh, breathless vigor, the engines sob and shriek like "gods in pain."

As Deborah hurried down through the heavy rain, the noise of these thousand engines sounded through the sleep and shadow of the city like far-off thunder. The mill to which she was going lay on the river, a mile below the city-limits. It was far, and she was weak, aching from standing twelve hours at the spools. Yet it was her almost nightly walk to take this man his supper, though at every square she sat down to rest, and she knew she should receive small word of thanks.

Perhaps, if she had possessed an artist's eye, the picturesque oddity of the scene might have made her step stagger less, and the path seem shorter; but to her the mills were only "summat deilish to look at by night."

The road leading to the mills had been quarried from the solid rock, which rose abrupt and bare on one side of the cinder-covered road, while the river, sluggish and black, crept past on the other. The mills for rolling iron are simply immense tent-like roofs, covering acres of ground, open on every side. Beneath these roofs Deborah looked in on a city of fires, that burned hot and fiercely in the night. Fire in every horrible form: pits of flame waving in the wind; liquid metal-flames writhing in tortuous streams through the sand; wide caldrons filled with boiling fire, over which bent ghastly wretches stirring the strange brewing; and through all, crowds of half-clad men, looking like revengeful ghosts in the red light, hurried, throwing masses of glittering fire. It was like a street in Hell. Even Deborah muttered, as she crept through, "looks like t' Devil's place!" It did,—in more ways than one.

She found the man she was looking for, at last, heaping coal on a furnace. He had not time to eat his supper; so she went behind the furnace, and waited. Only a few men were with him, and they noticed her only by a "Hyur comes t'hunchback, Wolfe."

Deborah was stupid with sleep; her back pained her sharply; and her teeth chattered with cold, with the rain that soaked her clothes and dripped from her at every step. She stood, however, patiently holding the pail, and waiting.

"Hout, woman! ye look like a drowned cat. Come near to the fire,"—said one of the men, approaching to scrape away the ashes.

She shook her head. Wolfe had forgotten her. He turned, hearing the man, and came closer.

"I did no' think; gi' me my supper, woman."

She watched him eat with a painful eagerness. With a woman's quick instinct, she saw that he was not hungry,—was eating to please her. Her pale, watery eyes began to gather a strange light.

"Is't good, Hugh? T' ale was a bit sour, I feared."

"No, good enough." He hesitated a moment. "Ye're tired, poor lass! Bide here till I go. Lay down there on that heap of ash, and go to sleep."

He threw her an old coat for a pillow, and turned to his work. The heap was the refuse of the burnt iron, and was not a hard bed; the half-smothered warmth, too, penetrated her limbs, dulling their pain and cold shiver.

Miserable enough she looked, lying there on the ashes like a limp, dirty rag,—yet not an unfitting figure to crown the scene of hopeless discomfort and veiled crime: more fitting, if one looked deeper into the heart of things, at her thwarted woman's form, her colorless life, her waking stupor that smothered pain and hunger,—even more fit to be a type of her class. Deeper yet if one could look, was there nothing worth reading in this wet, faded thing, halfcovered with ashes? no story of a soul filled with groping passionate love, heroic unselfishness, fierce jealousy? of years of weary trying to please the one human being whom she loved, to gain one look of real heart-kindness from him? If anything like this were hidden beneath the pale, bleared eyes, and dull, washed-out-looking face, no one had ever taken the trouble to read its faint signs: not the half-clothed furnace-tender, Wolfe, certainly. Yet he was kind to her: it was his nature to be kind, even to the very rats that swarmed in the cellar: kind to her in just the same way. She knew that. And it might be that very knowledge had given to her face its apathy and vacancy more than her low, torpid life. One sees that dead, vacant look steal sometimes over the rarest, finest of women's faces,—in the very midst, it may be, of their warmest summer's day; and then one can guess at the secret of intolerable solitude that lies hid beneath the delicate laces and brilliant smile. There was no warmth, no brilliancy, no summer for this woman; so the stupor and vacancy had time to gnaw into her face perpetually. She was young, too, though no one guessed it; so the gnawing was the fiercer.

She lay quiet in the dark corner, listening, through the monotonous din and uncertain glare of the works, to the dull plash of the rain in the far distance, shrinking back whenever the man Wolfe happened to look towards her. She knew, in spite of all his kindness, that there was that in her face and form which made him loathe the sight of her. She felt by instinct, although she could not comprehend it, the finer nature of the man, which made him among his fellow-workmen something unique, set apart. She knew, that, down under all the vileness and coarseness of his life, there was a groping passion for whatever was beautiful and pure, that his soul sickened with disgust at her deformity, even when his words were kindest. Through this dull consciousness, which never left her, came, like a sting, the recollection of the dark blue eyes and lithe figure of the little Irish girl she had left in the cellar. The recollection struck through even her stupid intellect with a vivid glow of beauty and of grace. Little Janey, timid, helpless, clinging to Hugh as her only friend: that was the sharp thought, the bitter thought, that drove into the glazed eyes a fierce light of pain. You laugh at it? Are pain and jealousy less savage realities down here in this place I am taking you to than in your own house or your own heart,—your heart, which they clutch at sometimes? The note is the same, I fancy, be the octave high or low.

If you could go into this mill where Deborah lay, and drag out from the hearts of these men the terrible tragedy of their lives, taking it as a symptom of the disease of their class, no ghost Horror would terrify you more. A reality of soul-starvation, of living death, that meets you every day under the besotted faces on the street,—I can paint nothing of this, only give you the outside outlines of a night, a crisis in the life of one man: whatever muddy depth of soul-history lies beneath you can read according to the eyes God has given you . . .

## QUESTIONS TO CONSIDER

1. How would you describe Deborah's surroundings and the mill?
2. In what ways did Davis use word choice and imagery to inspire the reader to feel sympathy for Hugh and Deborah?

CHAPTER 12

# MANIFEST DESTINY, 1836–1848

## 12.1 EXCERPT FROM *AUTOBIOGRAPHY OF BLACK HAWK* (1833)

Black Hawk (1767–1838) was a Native American Sauk leader who lived in the North American Midwest. He gained much of his political power through his war exploits, notably fighting on the British side during the War of 1812. In a contested 1804 treaty, the Sauk Tribe had given up its land in Illinois and moved west of the Mississippi River. By 1830, Black Hawk decided to try to regain some of the tribe's land and began leading excursions into Illinois. In 1832, he brought a group of 1,500 people into Illinois, which led to a series of military engagements with the Illinois and Michigan militias that became known as the Black Hawk War. (Notably, Abraham Lincoln's only military experience came during this war.) Black Hawk's small band eventually tried to flee north but were captured in August 1832. In 1833, Black Hawk narrated his biography to Antoine Le Claire, who ghost wrote the *Autobiography of Black Hawk,* from which the following excerpt is taken. In it, Black Hawk narrates the end of the war and gives a new perspective on nineteenth-century American expansionism.

Our people were treated very badly by the whites on many occasions. At one time a white man beat one of our women cruelly, for pulling a few suckers of corn out of his field to suck when she was hungry. At another time one of our young men was beat with clubs by two white men, for opening a fence which crossed our road to take his horse through. His shoulder blade was broken and his body badly braised, from the effects of which he soon after died.

Bad and cruel as our people were treated by the whites, not one of them was hurt or molested by our band. I hope this will prove that we are a peaceable people—having permitted ten men to take possession of our corn fields, prevent us from planting corn, burn our lodges, ill-treat our women, and beat to death our men without offering resistance to their barbarous cruelties. This is a lesson worthy for the white man to learn: to use forebearance when injured.

*Source: Autobiography of Ma-ka-tai-me-she-kia-kiak, or Black Hawk* (Oquawka, IL: J. B. Patterson, 1882). Retrieved from the Project Gutenberg website, http://www.gutenberg.org/files/7097/7097-h/7097-h.htm (Accessed June 6, 2018).

We acquainted our agent daily with our situation, and through him the great chief at St. Louis, and hoped that something would be done for us. The whites were complaining at the same time that we were intruding upon their rights. They made it appear that they were the injured party, and we the intruders. They called loudly to the great war chief to protect their property.

How smooth must be the language of the whites, when they can make right look like wrong, and wrong like right. . . . .

We learned during the winter, that part of the land where our village stood had been sold to individuals, and that the trader at Rock Island, Colonel Davenport, had bought the greater part that had been sold. The reason was now plain to me why he urged us to remove. His object, we thought, was to get our lands. We held several councils that winter to determine what we should do. We resolved in one of them, to return to our village as usual in the spring. We concluded that if we were removed by force, that the trader, agent and others must be the cause, and that if they were found guilty of having driven us from our village they should be killed. The trader stood foremost on this list. He had purchased the land on which my lodge stood, and that of our graveyard also. We therefore proposed to kill him and the agent, the interpreter, the great chief at St. Louis, the war chiefs at Forts Armstrong, Rock Island and Keokuk, these being the principal persons to blame for endeavoring to remove us. Our women received bad accounts from the women who had been raising corn at the new village, of the difficulty of breaking the new prairie with hoes, and the small quantity of corn raised. We were nearly in the same condition with regard to the latter, it being the first time I ever knew our people to be in want of provisions.

I prevailed upon some of Keokuk's band to return this spring to the Rock river village, but Keokuk himself would not come. I hoped that he would get permission to go to Washington to settle our affairs with our Great Father. I visited the agent at Rock Island. He was displeased because we had returned to our village, and told me that we must remove to the west of the Mississippi. I told him plainly that we would not. I visited the interpreter at his house, who advised me to do as the agent had directed me. I then went to see the trader and upbraided him for buying our lands. He said that if he had not purchased them some person else would, and that if our Great Father would make an exchange with us, he would willingly give up the land he had purchased to the government. This I thought was fair, and began to think that he had not acted so badly as I had suspected. We again repaired our lodges and built others, as most of our village had been burnt and destroyed. Our women selected small patches to plant corn, where the whites had not taken them in their fences, and worked hard to raise something for our children to subsist upon.

I was told that according to the treaty, we had no right to remain on the lands sold, and that the government would force us to leave them. There was but a small portion however that had been sold, the balance remaining in the hands of the government. We claimed the right, if we had no other, to "live and hunt upon it as long as it remained the property of the government," by a stipulation in the treaty that required us to evacuate it after it had been sold. This was the land that we wished to inhabit and thought we had a right to occupy. . . .

The enemy's encampment was in a skirt of woods near a run, about half a day's travel from Dixon's ferry. We attacked them in the prairie, with a few bushes between us, about sundown, and I expected that my whole party would be killed. I never was so much surprised in all the fighting I have seen, knowing, too, that the Americans generally shoot well, as I was to see this army of several hundreds retreating, without showing fight, and passing immediately through their encampment, I did think they intended to halt there, as the situation would have forbidden attack by my party if their number had not exceeded half of mine, as we would have been compelled to take the open prairie whilst they could have picked trees to shield themselves from our fire.

I was never so much surprised in my life as I was in this attack. An army of three or four hundred men, after having learned that we were sueing for peace, to attempt to kill the flag bearers that had gone unarmed to ask for a meeting of the war chiefs of the two contending parties to hold a council, that I might return to the west side of the Mississippi, to come forward with a full determination to demolish the few braves I had with me, to retreat when they had ten to one, was unaccountable to me. It proved a different spirit from any I had ever before seen among the pale faces. I expected to see them fight as the Americans did with the British during the last war, but they had no such braves among them. At our feast with the Pottowattomies I was convinced that we had been imposed upon by those who had brought in reports of large re-enforcements to my band and resolved not to strike a blow; and in order to get permission from White Beaver to return and re-cross the Mississippi, I sent a flag of peace to the American war chief, who was reported to be close by with his army, expecting that he would convene a council and listen to what we had to say. But this chief, instead of pursuing that honorable and chivalric course, such as I have always practiced, shot down our flag-bearer and thus forced us into war with less than five hundred warriors to contend against three or four thousand soldiers.

The supplies that Neapope and the prophet told us about, and the reinforcements we were to have, were never more heard of, and it is but justice to our British Father to say were never promised, his chief being sent word in lieu of the lies that were brought to me, "for us to remain at peace as we could accomplish nothing but our own ruin by going to war."

What was now to be done? It was worse than folly to turn back and meet an enemy where the odds were so much against us and thereby sacrifice ourselves, our wives and children to the fury of an enemy who had murdered some of our brave and unarmed warriors when they were on a mission to sue for peace.

Having returned to our encampment, and found that all our young men had come in, I sent out spies to watch the movements of the army, and commenced moving up Kishwacokee with the balance of my people. I did not know where to go to find a place of safety for my women and children, but expected to find a good harbor about the head of Rock river. I concluded to go there, and thought my best route would be to go round the head of Kishwacokee, so that the Americans would have some difficulty if they attempted to follow us. . . .

During our encampment at the Four Lakes we were hard pressed to obtain enough to eat to support nature. Situated in a swampy, marshy country, (which had been selected in consequence of the great

difficulty required to gain access thereto,) there was but little game of any sort to be found, and fish were equally scarce. The great distance to any settlement, and the impossibility of bringing supplies therefrom, if any could have been obtained, deterred our young men from making further attempts. We were forced to dig roots and bark trees, to obtain something to satisfy hunger and keep us alive. Several of our old people became so reduced, as to actually die with hunger! Learning that the army had commenced moving, and fearing that they might come upon and surround our encampment, I concluded to remove our women and children across the Mississippi, that they might return to the Sac nation again. Accordingly, on the next day we commenced moving, with five Winnebagoes acting as our guides, intending to descend the Wisconsin.

Neapope, with a party of twenty, remained in our rear, to watch for the enemy, whilst we were proceeding to the Wisconsin, with our women and children. We arrived, and had commenced crossing over to an island, when we discovered a large body of the enemy coming towards us. We were now compelled to fight, or sacrifice our wives and children to the fury of the whites. I met them with fifty warriors, (having left the balance to assist our women and children in crossing) about a mile from the river[.] When an attack immediately commenced, I was mounted on a fine horse, and was pleased to see my warriors so brave. I addressed them in a load voice, telling them to stand their ground and never yield it to the enemy. At this time I was on the rise of a hill, where I wished to form my warriors, that we might have some advantage over the whites. But the enemy succeeded in gaining this point, which compelled us to fall into a deep ravine, from which we continued firing at them and they at us, until it began to grow dark. My horse having been wounded twice during this engagement, and fearing from his loss of blood that he would soon give out, and finding that the enemy would not come near enough to receive our fire, in the dusk of the evening, and knowing that our women and children had had sufficient time to reach the island in the Wisconsin, I ordered my warriors to return, by different routes, and meet me at the Wisconsin, and was astonished to find that the enemy were not disposed to pursue us.

In this skirmish with fifty braves, I defended and accomplished my passage over the Wisconsin, with a loss of only six men, though opposed by a host of mounted militia. I would not have fought there, but to gain time for our women and children to cross to an island. A warrior will duly appreciate the embarrassments I labored under—and whatever may be the sentiments of the white people in relation to this battle, my nation, though fallen, will award to me the reputation of a great brave in conducting it.

The loss of the enemy could not be ascertained by our party; but I am of the opinion that it was much greater, in proportion, than mine. We returned to the Wisconsin and crossed over to our people.

Here some of my people left me, and descended the Wisconsin, hoping to escape to the west side of the Mississippi, that they might return home. I had no objection to their leaving me, as my people were all in a desperate condition, being worn out with traveling and starving with hunger. Our only hope to save ourselves was to get across the Mississippi. But few of this party escaped. Unfortunately for them, a party of soldiers from Prairie du Chien were stationed on the Wisconsin, a short distance from its mouth, who fired upon our distressed people. Some were killed, others drowned, several taken prisoners, and the balance escaped to the woods and perished with hunger. Among this party were a great many women and children.

I was astonished to find that Neapope and his party of spies had not yet come in, they having been left in my rear to bring the news, if the enemy were discovered. It appeared, however, that the whites had come in a different direction and intercepted our trail but a short distance from the place where we first saw them, leaving our spies considerably in the rear. Neapope and one other retired to the Winnebago village, and there remained during the war. The balance of his party, being brave men, and considering our interests as their own, returned, and joined our ranks.

Myself and band having no means to descend the Wisconsin, I started over a rugged country, to go to the Mississippi, intending to cross it and return to my nation. Many of our people were compelled to go on foot, for want of horses, which, in consequence of their having had nothing to eat for a long time, caused our march to be very slow. At length we arrived at the Mississippi, having lost some of our old men and little children, who perished on the way with hunger.

We had been here but a little while before we saw a steamboat (the "Warrior,") coming. I told my braves not to shoot, as I intended going on board, so that we might save our women and children. I knew the captain (Throckmorton) and was determined to give myself up to him. I then sent for my white flag. While the messenger was gone, I took a small piece of white cotton and put it on a pole, and called to the captain of the boat, and told him to send his little canoe ashore and let me come aboard. The people on board asked whether we were Sacs or Winnebagoes. I told a Winnebago to tell them that we were Sacs, and wanted to give ourselves up! A Winnebago on the boat called out to us "to run and hide, that the whites were going to shoot!" About this time one of my braves had jumped into the river, bearing a white flag to the boat, when another sprang in after him and brought him to the shore. The firing then commenced from the boat, which was returned by my braves and continued for some time. Very few of my people were hurt after the first fire, having succeeded in getting behind old logs and trees, which shielded them from the enemy's fire.

The Winnebago on the steamboat must either have misunderstood what was told, or did not tell it to the captain correctly; because I am confident he would not have allowed the soldiers to fire upon us if he had known my wishes. I have always considered him a good man, and too great a brave to fire upon an enemy when sueing for quarters.

After the boat left us, I told my people to cross if they could, and wished; that I intended going into the Chippewa country. Some commenced crossing, and such as had determined to follow them, remained; only three lodges going with me. Next morning, at daybreak, a young man overtook me, and said that all my party had determined to cross the Mississippi—that a number had already got over safely and that he had heard the white army last night within a few miles of them. I now began to fear that the whites would come up with my people and kill them before they could get across. I had determined to go and join the Chippewas; but reflecting that by this I could only save myself, I concluded to return, and die with my people, if the Great Spirit would not give us another victory. During our stay in the thicket, a party of whites came close by us, but passed on without discovering us.

Early in the morning a party of whites being in advance of the army, came upon our people, who were attempting to cross the Mississippi. They tried to give themselves up; the whites paid no attention to their entreaties, but commenced slaughtering them. In a little while the whole army arrived. Our braves, but few in [n]umber, finding that the enemy paid no regard to age or sex, and seeing that they were murdering helpless women and little children, determined to fight until they were killed. As many women as could, commenced swimming the Mississippi, with their children on their backs. A number of them were drowned, and some shot before they could reach the opposite shore.

One of my braves, who gave me this information, piled up some saddles before him, (when the fight commenced), to shield himself from the enemy's fire, and killed three white men. But seeing that the whites were coming too close to him, he crawled to the bank of the [river] without being perceived, and hid himself under the bank until the enemy retired. He then came to me and told me what had been done. After hearing this sorrowful news, I started with my little party to the Winnebago village at Prairie La Cross. On my arrival there I entered the lodge of one of the chiefs, and told him that I wished him to go with me to his father, that I intended giving myself up to the American war chief and die, if the Great Spirit saw proper. He said he would go with me. I then took my medicine bag and addressed the chief. I told him that it was "the soul of the Sac nation—that it never had been dishonored in any battle, take it, it is my life—dearer than life—and give it to the American chief!" He said he would keep it, and take care of it, and if I was suffered to live, he would send it to me.

During my stay at the village, the squaws made me a white dress of deer skin. I then started with several Winnebagoes, and went to their agent, at Prairie du Chien, and gave myself up.

On my arrival there, I found to my sorrow, that a large body of Sioux had pursued and killed a number of our women and children, who had got safely across the Mississippi. The whites ought not to have permitted such conduct, and none but cowards would ever have been guilty of such cruelty, a habit which had always been practiced on our nation by the Sioux.

The massacre, which terminated the war, lasted about two hours. Our loss in killed was about sixty, besides a number that was drowned. The loss of the enemy could not be ascertained by my braves, exactly; but they think that they killed about sixteen during the action.

**QUESTIONS TO CONSIDER**

1. How does Black Hawk view Americans?
2. Does the autobiography make you feel sympathy for Black Hawk?

# 12.2 TEXAS DECLARATION OF INDEPENDENCE (1836)

In 1819, the Adams-Onis Treaty formally divided Texas from the Louisiana Purchase territory of the United States. Two years later, Mexico gained its independence from Spain, and Texas became part of Mexico. Quickly, the Mexican government and Anglo settlers clashed over the acceptability of slavery in Texas and future American immigration into the region. In October 1835, the conflict broke out in open war. Mexican President Antonio López de Santa Anna led his troops into Texas to put down the insurrection and won an early battle at the Alamo, where he executed the remaining American survivors. Santa Anna's treatment of those survivors likely convinced many Texans to join the conflict, however, and Texas eventually gained its independence in April 1836. The Texas Declaration of Independence was ratified in March 1836 to defend the rebellion and make the case for the viability of the Republic of Texas.

When a government has ceased to protect the lives, liberty and property of the people, from whom its legitimate powers are derived, and for the advancement of whose happiness it was instituted, and so far from being a guarantee for the enjoyment of those inestimable and inalienable rights, becomes an instrument in the hands of evil rulers for their oppression.

When the Federal Republican Constitution of their country, which they have sworn to support, no longer has a substantial existence, and the whole nature of their government has been forcibly changed, without their consent, from a restricted federative republic, composed of sovereign states, to a consolidated central military despotism, in which every interest is disregarded but that of the army and the priesthood, both the eternal enemies of civil liberty, the everready minions of power, and the usual instruments of tyrants.

When, long after the spirit of the constitution has departed, moderation is at length so far lost by those in power, that even the semblance of freedom is removed, and the forms themselves of the constitution discontinued, and so far from their petitions and remonstrances being regarded, the agents who bear them are thrown into dungeons, and mercenary armies sent forth to force a new government upon them at the point of the bayonet.

When, in consequence of such acts of malfeasance and abdication on the part of the government, anarchy prevails, and civil society is dissolved into its original elements. In such a crisis, the first law of nature, the right of self-preservation, the inherent and inalienable rights of the people to appeal to first principles, and take their political affairs into their own hands in extreme cases, enjoins it as a right towards themselves, and a sacred obligation to their posterity, to abolish such government, and create another in its stead, calculated to rescue them from impending dangers, and to secure their future welfare and happiness.

Nations, as well as individuals, are amenable for their acts to the public opinion of mankind. A statement of a part of our grievances is therefore submitted to an impartial world, in justification of the hazardous but unavoidable step now taken, of severing our political connection with the Mexican people, and assuming an independent attitude among the nations of the earth.

*Source:* "The Texas Declaration of Independence: March 2, 1836," http://avalon.law.yale.edu/19th_century/texdec.asp (Accessed May 10, 2018).

The Mexican government, by its colonization laws, invited and induced the Anglo-American population of Texas to colonize its wilderness under the pledged faith of a written constitution, that they should continue to enjoy that constitutional liberty and republican government to which they had been habituated in the land of their birth, the United States of America.

In this expectation they have been cruelly disappointed, inasmuch as the Mexican nation has acquiesced in the late changes made in the government by General Antonio Lopez de Santa Anna, who having overturned the constitution of his country, now offers us the cruel alternative, either to abandon our homes, acquired by so many privations, or submit to the most intolerable of all tyranny, the combined despotism of the sword and the priesthood.

It has sacrificed our welfare to the state of Coahuila, by which our interests have been continually depressed through a jealous and partial course of legislation, carried on at a far distant seat of government, by a hostile majority, in an unknown tongue, and this too, notwithstanding we have petitioned in the humblest terms for the establishment of a separate state government, and have, in accordance with the provisions of the national constitution, presented to the general Congress a republican constitution, which was, without just cause, contemptuously rejected.

It incarcered in a dungeon, for a long time, one of our citizens, for no other cause but a zealous endeavor to procure the acceptance of our constitution, and the establishment of a state government.

It has failed and refused to secure, on a firm basis, the right of trial by jury, that palladium of civil liberty, and only safe guarantee for the life, liberty, and property of the citizen.

It has failed to establish any public system of education, although possessed of almost boundless resources, (the public domain,) and although it is an axiom in political science, that unless a people are educated and enlightened, it is idle to expect the continuance of civil liberty, or the capacity for self government.

It has suffered the military commandants, stationed among us, to exercise arbitrary acts of oppression and tyrany, thus trampling upon the most sacred rights of the citizens, and rendering the military superior to the civil power.

It has dissolved, by force of arms, the state Congress of Coahuila and Texas, and obliged our representatives to fly for their lives from the seat of government, thus depriving us of the fundamental political right of representation.

It has demanded the surrender of a number of our citizens, and ordered military detachments to seize and carry them into the Interior for trial, in contempt of the civil authorities, and in defiance of the laws and the constitution.

It has made piratical attacks upon our commerce, by commissioning foreign desperadoes, and authorizing them to seize our vessels, and convey the property of our citizens to far distant ports for confiscation.

It denies us the right of worshipping the Almighty according to the dictates of our own conscience, by the support of a national religion, calculated to promote the temporal interest of its human functionaries, rather than the glory of the true and living God.

It has demanded us to deliver up our arms, which are essential to our defence, the rightful property of freemen, and formidable only to tyrannical governments.

It has invaded our country both by sea and by land, with intent to lay waste our territory, and drive us from our homes; and has now a large mercenary army advancing, to carry on against us a war of extermination.

It has, through its emissaries, incited the merciless savage, with the tomahawk and scalping knife, to massacre the inhabitants of our defenseless frontiers.

It hath been, during the whole time of our connection with it, the contemptible sport and victim of successive military revolutions, and hath continually exhibited every characteristic of a weak, corrupt, and tyranical government.

These, and other grievances, were patiently borne by the people of Texas, untill they reached that point at which forbearance ceases to be a virtue. We then took up arms in defence of the national constitution. We appealed to our Mexican brethren for assistance. Our appeal has been made in vain. Though months have elapsed, no sympathetic response has yet been heard from the Interior. We are, therefore, forced to the melancholy conclusion, that the Mexican people have acquiesced in the destruction of their liberty, and the substitution therfor of a military government; that they are unfit to be free, and incapable of self government.

The necessity of self-preservation, therefore, now decrees our eternal political separation.

We, therefore, the delegates with plenary powers of the people of Texas, in solemn convention assembled, appealing to a candid world for the necessities of our condition, do hereby resolve and declare, that our political connection with the Mexican nation has forever ended, and that the people of Texas do now constitute a free, Sovereign, and independent republic, and are fully invested with all the rights and attributes which properly belong to independent nations; and, conscious of the rectitude of our intentions, we fearlessly and confidently commit the issue to the decision of the Supreme arbiter of the destinies of nations.

**QUESTIONS TO CONSIDER**

1.  What kinds of grievances stand out? How similar is it to the American Declaration of Independence?
2.  How did the writers portray Texas and its Anglo settlers?

# 12.3 MARTIN VAN BUREN, INAUGURAL ADDRESS (1837)

Martin Van Buren (1782–1862) was the eighth President of the United States. Serving only one term in office, Van Buren's tenure was damaged by the Panic of 1837, which set off a five-year economic depression. Van Buren also carried out Andrew Jackson's plans for Native American removal. In his inaugural address, Van Buren promoted American progress and future American expansionism. He also, surprisingly, decided to take a determined position on slavery in the United States. Van Buren's attempted moderation on the slavery matter illustrates the degree to which it would become a major national issue as more states joined the Union. Manifest Destiny became inextricable from the issue of slavery.

Fellow-Citizens:

The practice of all my predecessors imposes on me an obligation I cheerfully fulfill—to accompany the first and solemn act of my public trust with an avowal of the principles that will guide me in performing it and an expression of my feelings on assuming a charge so responsible and vast. In imitating their example I tread in the footsteps of illustrious men, whose superiors it is our happiness to believe are not found on the executive calendar of any country. Among them we recognize the earliest and firmest pillars of the Republic—those by whom our national independence was first declared, him who above all others contributed to establish it on the field of battle, and those whose expanded intellect and patriotism constructed, improved, and perfected the inestimable institutions under which we live. If such men in the position I now occupy felt themselves overwhelmed by a sense of gratitude for this the highest of all marks of their country's confidence, and by a consciousness of

*Source:* "Martin Van Buren Inaugural Address," http://www.presidency.ucsb.edu/ws/index.php?pid=25812 (Accessed May 10, 2018).

their inability adequately to discharge the duties of an office so difficult and exalted, how much more must these considerations affect one who can rely on no such claims for favor or forbearance! Unlike all who have preceded me, the Revolution that gave us existence as one people was achieved at the period of my birth; and whilst I contemplate with grateful reverence that memorable event, I feel that I belong to a later age and that I may not expect my countrymen to weigh my actions with the same kind and partial hand.

So sensibly, fellow-citizens, do these circumstances press themselves upon me that I should not dare to enter upon my path of duty did I not look for the generous aid of those who will be associated with me in the various and coordinate branches of the Government; did I not repose with unwavering reliance on the patriotism, the intelligence, and the kindness of a people who never yet deserted a public servant honestly laboring their cause; and, above all, did I not permit myself humbly to hope for the sustaining support of an ever-watchful and beneficent Providence.

To the confidence and consolation derived from these sources it would be ungrateful not to add those which spring from our present fortunate condition. Though not altogether exempt from embarrassments that disturb our tranquillity at home and threaten it abroad, yet in all the attributes of a great, happy, and flourishing people we stand without a parallel in the world. Abroad we enjoy the respect and, with scarcely an exception, the friendship of every nation; at home, while our Government quietly but efficiently performs the sole legitimate end of political institutions—in doing the greatest good to the greatest number—we present an aggregate of human prosperity surely not elsewhere to be found.

How imperious, then, is the obligation imposed upon every citizen, in his own sphere of action, whether limited or extended, to exert himself in perpetuating a condition of things so singularly happy! All the lessons of history and experience must be lost upon us if we are content to trust alone to the peculiar advantages we happen to possess. Position and climate and the bounteous resources that nature has scattered with so liberal a hand—even the diffused intelligence and elevated character of our people—will avail us nothing if we fail sacredly to uphold those political institutions that were wisely and deliberately formed

with reference to every circumstance that could preserve or might endanger the blessings we enjoy. The thoughtful framers of our Constitution legislated for our country as they found it. Looking upon it with the eyes of statesmen and patriots, they saw all the sources of rapid and wonderful prosperity; but they saw also that various habits, opinions, and institutions peculiar to the various portions of so vast a region were deeply fixed. Distinct sovereignties were in actual existence, whose cordial union was essential to the welfare and happiness of all. Between many of them there was, at least to some extent, a real diversity of interests, liable to be exaggerated through sinister designs; they differed in size, in population, in wealth, and in actual and prospective resources and power; they varied in the character of their industry and staple productions, and [in some] existed domestic institutions which, unwisely disturbed, might endanger the harmony of the whole. Most carefully were all these circumstances weighed, and the foundations of the new Government laid upon principles of reciprocal concession and equitable compromise. The jealousies which the smaller States might entertain of the power of the rest were allayed by a rule of representation confessedly unequal at the time, and designed forever to remain so. A natural fear that the broad scope of general legislation might bear upon and unwisely control particular interests was counteracted by limits strictly drawn around the action of the Federal authority, and to the people and the States was left unimpaired their sovereign power over the innumerable subjects embraced in the internal government of a just republic, excepting such only as necessarily appertain to the concerns of the whole confederacy or its intercourse as a united community with the other nations of the world.

This provident forecast has been verified by time. Half a century, teeming with extraordinary events, and elsewhere producing astonishing results, has passed along, but on our institutions it has left no injurious mark. From a small community we have risen to a people powerful in numbers and in strength; but with our increase has gone hand in hand the progress of just principles. The privileges, civil and religious, of the humblest individual are still sacredly protected at home, and while the valor and fortitude of our people have removed far from us the slightest apprehension of foreign power, they have not yet induced us in a single instance to forget what is right. Our commerce has been extended to the remotest nations; the value and even nature of our productions have been greatly changed; a wide difference has arisen in the relative wealth and resources of every portion of our country; yet the spirit of mutual regard and of faithful adherence to existing compacts has continued to prevail in our councils and never long been absent from our conduct. We have learned by experience a fruitful lesson--that an implicit and undeviating adherence to the principles on which we set out can carry us prosperously onward through all the conflicts of circumstances and vicissitudes inseparable from the lapse of years. . . .

Certain danger was foretold from the extension of our territory, the multiplication of States, and the increase of population. Our system was supposed to be adapted only to boundaries comparatively narrow. These have been widened beyond conjecture; the members of our Confederacy are already doubled, and the numbers of our people are incredibly augmented. The alleged causes of danger have long surpassed anticipation, but none of the consequences have followed. The power and influence of the Republic have arisen to a height obvious to all mankind; respect for its authority was not more apparent at its ancient than it is at its present limits; new and inexhaustible sources of general prosperity have been opened; the effects of distance have been averted by the inventive genius of our people, developed and fostered by the spirit of our institutions; and the enlarged variety and amount of interests, productions, and pursuits have strengthened the chain of mutual dependence and formed a circle of mutual benefits too apparent ever to be overlooked.

In justly balancing the powers of the Federal and State authorities difficulties nearly insurmountable arose at the outset and subsequent collisions were deemed inevitable. Amid these it was scarcely believed possible that a scheme of government so complex in construction could remain uninjured. From time to time embarrassments have certainly occurred; but how just is the confidence of future safety imparted by the knowledge that each in succession has been happily removed! Overlooking partial and temporary evils as inseparable from the practical operation of all human institutions, and looking only to the general result, every patriot has reason to be satisfied. While

the Federal Government has successfully performed its appropriate functions in relation to foreign affairs and concerns evidently national, that of every State has remarkably improved in protecting and developing local interests and individual welfare; and if the vibrations of authority have occasionally tended too much toward one or the other, it is unquestionably certain that the ultimate operation of the entire system has been to strengthen all the existing institutions and to elevate our whole country in prosperity and renown.

The last, perhaps the greatest, of the prominent sources of discord and disaster supposed to lurk in our political condition was the institution of domestic slavery. Our forefathers were deeply impressed with the delicacy of this subject, and they treated it with a forbearance so evidently wise that in spite of every sinister foreboding it never until the present period disturbed the tranquillity of our common country. Such a result is sufficient evidence of the justice and the patriotism of their course; it is evidence not to be mistaken that an adherence to it can prevent all embarrassment from this as well as from every other anticipated cause of difficulty or danger. Have not recent events made it obvious to the slightest reflection that the least deviation from this spirit of forbearance is injurious to every interest, that of humanity included? Amidst the violence of excited passions this generous and fraternal feeling has been sometimes disregarded; and standing as I now do before my countrymen, in this high place of honor and of trust, I can not refrain from anxiously invoking my fellow-citizens never to be deaf to its dictates. Perceiving before my election the deep interest this subject was beginning to excite, I believed it a solemn duty fully to make known my sentiments in regard to it, and now, when every motive for misrepresentation has passed away, I trust that they will be candidly weighed and understood. At least they will be my standard of conduct in the path before me. I then declared that if the desire of those of my countrymen who were favorable to my election was gratified "I must go into the Presidential chair the inflexible and uncompromising opponent of every attempt on the part of Congress to abolish slavery in the District of Columbia against the wishes of the slaveholding States, and also with a determination equally decided to resist the slightest interference with it in the States where it exists." I submitted also to my fellow-citizens, with fullness and frankness, the reasons which led me to this determination. The result authorizes me to believe that they have been approved and are confided in by a majority of the people of the United States, including those whom they most immediately affect. It now only remains to add that no bill conflicting with these views can ever receive my constitutional sanction. These opinions have been adopted in the firm belief that they are in accordance with the spirit that actuated the venerated fathers of the Republic, and that succeeding experience has proved them to be humane, patriotic, expedient, honorable, and just. If the agitation of this subject was intended to reach the stability of our institutions, enough has occurred to show that it has signally failed, and that in this as in every other instance the apprehensions of the timid and the hopes of the wicked for the destruction of our Government are again destined to be disappointed. Here and there, indeed, scenes of dangerous excitement have occurred, terrifying instances of local violence have been witnessed, and a reckless disregard of the consequences of their conduct has exposed individuals to popular indignation; but neither masses of the people nor sections of the country have been swerved from their devotion to the bond of union and the principles it has made sacred. It will be ever thus. Such attempts at dangerous agitation may periodically return, but with each the object will be better understood. That predominating affection for our political system which prevails throughout our territorial limits, that calm and enlightened judgment which ultimately governs our people as one vast body, will always be at hand to resist and control every effort, foreign or domestic, which aims or would lead to overthrow our institutions.

What can be more gratifying than such a retrospect as this? We look back on obstacles avoided and dangers overcome, on expectations more than realized and prosperity perfectly secured. To the hopes of the hostile, the fears of the timid, and the doubts of the anxious actual experience has given the conclusive reply. We have seen time gradually dispel every unfavorable foreboding and our Constitution surmount every adverse circumstance dreaded at the outset as beyond control. Present excitement will at all times magnify present dangers, but true philosophy must teach us that none more threatening than the past can remain to be overcome; and we ought (for we have just reason) to entertain an abiding confidence in the stability of our institutions and an entire conviction that if administered in the true form, character, and spirit in which they were established they are abundantly adequate to preserve to us and our children the rich blessings already derived from them, to make our beloved land for a thousand generations that chosen spot where happiness springs from a perfect equality of political rights.

For myself, therefore, I desire to declare that the principle that will govern me in the high duty to which my country calls me is a strict adherence to the letter and spirit of the Constitution as it was designed by those who framed it. Looking back to it as a sacred instrument carefully and not easily framed; remembering that it was throughout a work of concession and compromise; viewing it as limited to national objects; regarding it as leaving to the people and the States all power not explicitly parted with, I shall endeavor to preserve, protect, and defend it by anxiously referring to its provision for direction in every action. To matters of domestic concernment which it has intrusted to the Federal Government and to such as relate to our intercourse with foreign nations I shall zealously devote myself; beyond those limits I shall never pass. . . .

## QUESTIONS TO CONSIDER

1. What did Van Buren think about expansion?
2. Does Van Buren's slavery strategy seem viable for the time?

# 12.4 JAMES K. POLK, SPEECH ON WAR WITH MEXICO (1846)

After Texas gained its independence in 1836 (see Reading 12.2), it became an independent Republic. The force of American slaveholders who had propelled its revolution, however, closely tied the country to the United States. In 1837, President Andrew Jackson formally recognized Texas as an independent country. In 1845, Congress passed a bill to admit Texas into the United States. Texas voters later approved the bill, and Texas joined the United States as a slaveholding state. Just one year later, the United States and Mexico clashed over the state's borders. President James K. Polk sent a military force into the contested region along the Rio Grande River to provoke a military response from Mexico. His strategy worked, and the two nations went to war. In the following speech, Polk defended his actions to Congress and asked it for a declaration of war against Mexico. Two days later, after an extremely close vote, Congress approve the declaration.

The existing state of the relations between the United States and Mexico renders it proper that I should bring the subject to the consideration of Congress. In my message at the commencement of your present session the state of these relations, the causes which led to the suspension of diplomatic intercourse between the two countries in March, 1845, and the long-continued and unredressed wrongs and injuries committed by the Mexican Government on citizens of the United States in their persons and property were briefly set forth.

As the facts and opinions which were then laid before you were carefully considered, I can not better express my present convictions of the condition of affairs up to that time than by referring you to that communication.

The strong desire to establish peace with Mexico on liberal and honorable terms, and the readiness of this Government to regulate and adjust our boundary and other causes of difference with that power on such fair and equitable principles as would lead to permanent relations of the most friendly nature, induced me in September last to seek the reopening of diplomatic relations between the two countries. Every measure adopted on our part had for its object the furtherance of these desired results. In communicating to Congress a succinct statement of the injuries which we had suffered from Mexico, and which have been accumulating during a period of more than twenty years, every expression that could tend to inflame the people of Mexico or defeat or delay a pacific result was carefully avoided. An envoy of the United States repaired to Mexico with full powers to adjust every existing difference. But though present on the Mexican soil by agreement between the two Governments, invested with full powers, and bearing evidence of the most friendly dispositions, his mission has been unavailing. The Mexican Government not only refused to receive him or listen to his propositions, but after a long-continued series of menaces have at last invaded our territory and shed the blood of our fellow-citizens on our own soil.

It now becomes my duty to state more in detail the origin, progress, and failure of that mission. In

*Source:* "James K. Polk: Special Message to Congress on Mexican Relations," http://www.presidency.ucsb.edu/ws/?pid=67907 (Accessed May 10, 2018).

pursuance of the instructions given in September last, an inquiry was made on the 13th of October, 1845, in the most friendly terms, through our consul in Mexico, of the minister for foreign affairs, whether the Mexican Government "would receive an envoy from the United States intrusted with full powers to adjust all the questions in dispute between the two Governments," with the assurance that "should the answer be in the affirmative such an envoy would be immediately dispatched to Mexico." The Mexican minister on the 15th of October gave an affirmative answer to this inquiry, requesting at the same time that our naval force at Vera Cruz might be withdrawn, lest its continued presence might assume, the appearance of menace and coercion pending the negotiations. This force was immediately withdrawn. On the 10th of November, 1845, Mr. John Slidell, of Louisiana, was commissioned by me as envoy extraordinary and minister plenipotentiary of the United States to Mexico, and was intrusted with full powers to adjust both the questions of the Texas boundary and of indemnification to our citizens. The redress of the wrongs of our citizens naturally and inseparably blended itself with the question of boundary. The settlement of the one question in any correct view of the subject involves that of the other. I could not for a moment entertain the idea that the claims of our much-injured and long-suffering citizens, many of which had existed for more than twenty years, should be postponed or separated from the settlement of the boundary question. . . .

In my message at the commencement of the present session I informed you that upon the earnest appeal both of the Congress and convention of Texas I had ordered an efficient military force to take a position "between the Nueces and the Del Norte." This had become necessary to meet a threatened invasion of Texas by the Mexican forces, for which extensive military preparations had been made. The invasion was threatened solely because Texas had determined, in accordance with a solemn resolution of the Congress of the United States, to annex herself to our Union, and under these circumstances it was plainly our duty to extend our protection over her citizens and soil.

This force was concentrated at Corpus Christi, and remained there until after I had received such information from Mexico as rendered it probable, if not certain, that the Mexican Government would refuse to receive our envoy.

Meantime Texas, by the final action of our Congress, had become an integral part of our Union. The Congress of Texas, by its act of December 19, 1836, had declared the Rio del Norte to be the boundary of that Republic. Its jurisdiction had been extended and exercised beyond the Nueces. The country between that river and the Del Norte had been represented in the Congress and in the convention of Texas, had thus taken part in the act of annexation itself, and is now included within one of our Congressional districts. Our own Congress had, moreover, with great unanimity, by the act approved December 31, 1845, recognized the country beyond the Nueces as a part of our territory by including it within our own revenue system, and a revenue officer to reside within that district has been appointed by and with the advice and consent of the Senate. It became, therefore, of urgent necessity to provide for the defense of that portion of our country. Accordingly, on the 13th of January last instructions were issued to the general in command of these troops to occupy the left bank of the Del Norte. This river, which is the southwestern boundary of the State of Texas, is an exposed frontier. From this quarter invasion was threatened; upon it and in its immediate vicinity, in the judgment of high military experience, are the proper stations for the protecting forces of the Government. In addition to this important consideration, several others occurred to induce this movement. Among these are the facilities afforded by the ports at Brazos Santiago and the mouth of the Del Norte for the reception of supplies by sea, the stronger and more healthful military positions, the convenience for obtaining a ready and a more abundant supply of provisions, water, fuel, and forage, and the advantages which are afforded by the Del Norte in forwarding supplies to such posts as may be established in the interior and upon the Indian frontier.

The movement of the troops to the Del Norte was made by the commanding general under positive instructions to abstain from all aggressive acts toward Mexico or Mexican citizens and to regard the relations between that Republic and the United States as peaceful unless she should declare war or commit acts of hostility indicative of a state of war. He was specially directed to protect private property and respect personal rights.

The Army moved from Corpus Christi on the 11th of March, and on the 28th of that month arrived on the left bank of the Del Norte opposite to Matamoras, where it encamped on a commanding position, which has since been strengthened by the erection of field-works. A depot has also been established at Point Isabel, near the Brazos Santiago, 30 miles in rear of the encampment. The selection of his position was necessarily confided to the judgment of the general in command.

The Mexican forces at Matamoras assumed a belligerent attitude, and on the 12th of April General Ampudia, then in command, notified General Taylor to break up his camp within twenty-four hours and to retire beyond the Nueces River, and in the event of his failure to comply with these demands announced that arms, and arms alone, must decide the question. But no open act of hostility was committed until the 24th of April. On that day General Arista, who had succeeded to the command of the Mexican forces, communicated to General Taylor that "he considered hostilities commenced and should prosecute them." A party of dragoons of 63 men and officers were on the same day dispatched from the American camp up the Rio del Norte, on its left bank, to ascertain whether the Mexican troops had crossed or were preparing to cross the river, "became engaged with a large body of these troops, and after a short affair, in which some 16 were killed and wounded, appear to have been surrounded and compelled to surrender."

The grievous wrongs perpetrated by Mexico upon our citizens throughout a long period of years remain unredressed, and solemn treaties pledging her public faith for this redress have been disregarded. A government either unable or unwilling to enforce the execution of such treaties fails to perform one of its plainest duties.

Our commerce with Mexico has been almost annihilated. It was formerly highly beneficial to both nations, but our merchants have been deterred from prosecuting it by the system of outrage and extortion which the Mexican authorities have pursued against

them, whilst their appeals through their own Government for indemnity have been made in vain. Our forbearance has gone to such an extreme as to be mistaken in its character. Had we acted with vigor in repelling the insults and redressing the injuries inflicted by Mexico at the commencement, we should doubtless have escaped all the difficulties in which we are now involved.

Instead of this, however, we have been exerting our best efforts to propitiate her good will. Upon the pretext that Texas, a nation as independent as herself, thought proper to unite its destinies with our own she has affected to believe that we have severed her rightful territory, and in official proclamations and manifestoes has repeatedly threatened to make war upon us for the purpose of reconquering Texas. In the meantime we have tried every effort at reconciliation. The cup of forbearance had been exhausted even before the recent information from the frontier of the Del Norte. But now, after reiterated menaces, Mexico has passed the boundary of the United States, has invaded our territory and shed American blood upon the American soil. She has proclaimed that hostilities have commenced, and that the two nations are now at war.

As war exists, and, notwithstanding all our efforts to avoid it, exists by the act of Mexico herself, we are called upon by every consideration of duty and patriotism to vindicate with decision the honor, the rights, and the interests of our country.

Anticipating the possibility of a crisis like that which has arrived, instructions were given in August last, "as a precautionary measure" against invasion or threatened invasion, authorizing General Taylor, if the emergency required, to accept volunteers, not from Texas only, but from the States of Louisiana, Alabama, Mississippi, Tennessee, and Kentucky, and corresponding letters were addressed to the respective governors of those States. These instructions were repeated, and in January last, soon after the incorporation of "Texas into our Union of States," General Taylor was further "authorized by the President to make a requisition upon the executive of that State for such of its militia force as may be needed to repel invasion or to secure the country against apprehended invasion." On the 2d day of March he was again reminded, "in the event of the approach of any considerable Mexican force, promptly and efficiently to use the authority with which he was clothed to call to him such auxiliary force as he might need." War actually existing and our territory having been invaded, General Taylor, pursuant to authority vested in him by my direction, has called on the governor of Texas for four regiments of State troops, two to be mounted and two to serve on foot, and on the governor of Louisiana for four regiments of infantry to be sent to him as soon as practicable.

In further vindication of our rights and defense of our territory, I invoke the prompt action of Congress to recognize the existence of the war, and to place at the disposition of the Executive the means of prosecuting the war with vigor, and thus hastening the restoration of peace. To this end I recommend that authority should be given to call into the public service a large body of volunteers to serve for not less than six or twelve months unless sooner discharged. A volunteer force is beyond question more efficient than any other description of citizen soldiers, and it is not to be doubted that a number far beyond that required would readily rush to the field upon the call of their country. I further recommend that a liberal provision be made for sustaining our entire military force and furnishing it with supplies and munitions of war.

The most energetic and prompt measures and the immediate appearance in arms of a large and overpowering force are recommended to Congress as the most certain and efficient means of bringing the existing collision with Mexico to a speedy and successful termination.

In making these recommendations I deem it proper to declare that it is my anxious desire not only to terminate hostilities speedily, but to bring all matters in dispute between this Government and Mexico to an early and amicable adjustment; and in this view I shall be prepared to renew negotiations whenever Mexico shall be ready to receive propositions or to make propositions of her own.

I transmit herewith a copy of the correspondence between our envoy to Mexico and the Mexican minister for foreign affairs, and so much of the correspondence between that envoy and the Secretary of State and between the Secretary of War and the general in command on the Del Norte as is necessary to a full understanding of the subject.

*JAMES K. POLK.*

## QUESTIONS TO CONSIDER

1. How did Polk defend his actions?
2. Do you find Polk's argument persuasive?

# 12.5 FREDERICK DOUGLASS ON WAR IN MEXICO (1848)

By January 1848, the Mexican-American War was close to its end. One month later, the two sides would sign the Treaty of Guadalupe Hidalgo, which gave the United States rights to an enormous tract of land in the southwest—the current states of California, Nevada, and Utah, along with much of New Mexico, Arizona, and Colorado and portions of Texas, Oklahoma, Kansas, and Wyoming— in exchange for about $18 million in financial considerations. The war had proven to be an immense military success. The freed slave and abolitionist Frederick Douglass, however, saw things differently. In his newspaper *The North Star,* he published a major critique of the war on the basis that it would contribute to the spread of slavery. In many ways, Douglass was quite prescient. The contested territory gained by the Treaty of Guadalupe Hidalgo led to a great deal of friction between slaveholding and non-slaveholding states, and the Civil War would erupt just thirteen years later.

From aught that appears in the present position and movements of the executive and cabinet—the proceedings of either branch of the national Congress—the several State Legislatures, North and South—the spirit of the public press—the conduct of leading men, and the general views and feelings of the people of United States at large, slight hope can rationally be predicated of very speedy termination of the present disgraceful, cruel, and iniquitous war with our sister republic. Mexico seems a doomed victim to Anglo Saxon cupidity and love of dominion. The determination of our slaveholding President to his success in wringing from the people men and money to carry it on, is made evident, rather than doubtful, by the puny opposition arrayed against him. No politician of any considerable distinction or eminence, seems willing to hazard his popularity with his party, or stem the fierce current of executive influence, by an open and unqualified disapprobation of the war. None seem willing to take their stand for peace at all risks; and all seem willing that the war should be carried on, in some form or other. If any oppose the President's demands, it is not because they hate the war, but for want of information as to the aims and objects of the war. The boldest

declaration on this point is that of Hon. John P. Hale, which is to the effect that he will not vote a single dollar to the President for carrying on the war, until he shall be fully informed of the purposes and object of the war. Mr. Hale knows, as well as the President can inform him, for what the war is waged; and yet he accompanies his declaration with that prudent proviso. This shows how deep seated and strongly bulwarked is the evil against which we contend. The boldest dare not fully grapple with it.

Meanwhile, "the plot thickens:" the evil spreads. Large demands are made on the national treasury, (to wit: the poor man's pockets.) Eloquent and patriots speeches are made in the Senate, House of Representatives and State Assemblies: Whig as well as Democratic governors stand stoutly up for the war: experienced and hoary-headed strength and ingenuity in devising ways and means for advancing the infernal work: recruiting sergeants and corporals perambulate the land in search of victims for the sword and food for powder. Wherever there is a sink of iniquity, or a den of pollutions, these buzzards may be found in search of their filthy prey. They dive into the run shop, and gambling house, and other sinks too infamous to name, with

*Source:* Frederick Douglass, "The War with Mexico," *The North Star,* January 21, 1848.

swine-like avidity, in pursuit of degraded men to vindicate the insulted honor of our Christian country. Military chieftains and heros multiply, and towering high above the level of common men, are glorified, if not deified, by the people. The whole nation seems to "wonder after these [bloody] beasts." Grasping ambition, tyranic usurpation, atrocious aggression, cruel and haughty pride; spread, and pervade the land. No part of the country can claim entire exemption from its evils. They may be seen as well in the State of New York, as in South Carolina: on the Penobscot, as on the Sabine. The people appear to be completely in the hands of office seekers, demagogues, and political gamblers. Within the bewildering meshes of their political nets, they are worried, confused, and confounded, so that a general outer is heard—"Vigorous prosecution of war!"—"Mexico must be humbled!"—" Conquer a peace!"—" Indemnity!"—"War forced upon us!"—"National honor!"—"The whole of Mexico!"— "Our destiny!"—"This continent!"—"Anglo Saxon blood!"—"More territory!"—"Free institutions!"— "Our country!" till it seems indeed "that justice has fled to brutish beasts, and men have lost their reason." The taste of human blood and the smell of powder seem to have extinguished the senses, seared the people to a degree that may well induce the gloomy apprehension that our nation has fully entered on her downward career, and yielded herself up to the revolting idea of battle and blood. "Fire and sword," are now the choice of our young republic. The loss of thousands of her own men, and the slaughter of tens of thousands of the sons and daughters of Mexico, have rather given edge than dullness to our appetite for fiery conflict and plunder. The civilization of the age, the voice of the world, the sacredness of human life, the tremendous expense, the dangers, hardships, and the deep disgrace which must forever attach to our inhuman course, seem to oppose no availing check to mad spirit of proud ambition, blood, and carnage, let loose in the land.

We have no preference for parties, regarding this slaveholding crusade. The one is as bad as the other. The friends of peace have nothing to hope from either. The Democrats claim the credit of commencing, and the Whigs monopolize the glory of voting supplies and carrying on the war; branding the war as dishonorably commenced, yet boldly persisting in pressing it. If we have any preference of two such parties, that preference inclines to the one whose practice, though wicked, most accord with its professions. We know where to find the so called Democrats. They are the accustomed panderers to slaveholders: nothing is either too mean, too dirty, or infamous for them, when commanded by the merciless man stealers of our country. No one expects any thing honorable or decent from that party, touching human rights. They annexed Texas under the plea of extending the area of freedom. They elected James K. Polk, the slaveholder, as the friend of freedom: and they have backed him up in his Presidential falsehoods. They have used their utmost endeavors to crush the right of speech, abridge the right of petition, and to perpetuate the enslavement of colored people of this country. But we do not intend to go into any examination of parties just now. That we shall have frequent opportunities of doing hereafter. We wish merely to give our readers a general portrait of the present aspect of our country in regard the Mexican war, its designs, and its results, as they have thus far transpired.

Of the settled determination to prosecute the war, there can be to debut: Polk has avowed it; his organs have published it; his supporters have rallied round him; all their actions bend in that direction; and every effort is made to establish their purpose firmly in the hearts of the people, and to harden their hearts for the conflict. All danger must be defied; all suffering despised; all honor eschewed; all mercy dried up; and all the better promotions of the human soul blunted, silenced and repudiated, while all the furies of hell are invoked to guide our hired assassins,—our man-killing machines,—now in and out of Mexico, to the infernal consummation. Qualities of head and heart, principles and maxims, counsels and warnings, which once commanded respect, and secured a national sense of decency must be utterly drowned: age nor sex must exercise any humanizing effect upon our gallant soldiers, or restrain their satanic designs. The groans of slaughtered men, the screams of violated women, and the cries of orphan children, must bring no throb of pity from our national heart, but must rather serve as music to inspire our gallant troops to deeds of atrocious cruelty, lust, and blood. The work is thus laid out, commenced, and is to be continued. Where it will end is known only to the Great Ruler of the Universe: but where the responsibility rests, and upon whom retribution will fall, is sure and certain.

In watching the effects of the war spirit, prominent among them, will be seen not only the subversion of the great principles of Christian morality, but the most horrid blasphemy.

While traveling from Rochester to Victor, a few days ago, we listened to a conversation between two persons of apparent gentility and intelligence, on the subject of the United States' war against Mexico. A wide difference of opinion appeared between them; the one contending for the war, and the other against it. The main argument in favor of the war was the meanness and wickedness of the Mexican people; and, to cap the climax, he gave it as his solemn conviction, that the hand of the Lord was in the work! that the cup of Mexican iniquity was full: and that God was now making use of the Anglo Saxon race as a rod to chastise them! The effect of this religious outthrust was to stun his opponent into silence: he seemed speechless: the ground was too high and holy for him; he did not dare reply to it; and thus the conversation ended. When men charge their sins upon God, argument is idle; rebuke alone is needful; and the poor man, lacking the moral courage to do this, sat silent.

Here, then, we have religion coupled with our murderous designs. We are, in the hands of the great God, a rod to chastise this rebellious people! What say our evangelical elegy to this blasphemy? That clergy seem as silent as the grave; and their silence is the greatest sanction of the crime. They have seen the blood of the innocent poured out like water, and are dumb; they have seen the truth trampled in the dust—right sought by pursuing the wrong—peace sought by prosecuting the war—honor sought buy dishonorable means,—and have not raise a whisper against it: they float down with the multitude in the filthy current of crime, and are hand in hand the guilty. Had the pulpit been faithful we might have been saved from this withering curse. We sometimes fear, that now our case as a nation is hopeless. May God grant otherwise! Our nation seems resolved to rush on in her wicked career, though the road be ditched with human blood, and paved with human skulls. Well, be it so. But, humble as we are, and unavailing as our voice may be, we wish to warn our fellow countrymen, that they may follow the course which they have marked out for themselves; no barrier may be sufficient to obstruct them; they may accomplish all they desire; Mexico may fall before them; she may be conquered and subdued; her government may be annihilated—her name among the great sisterhood of nations blotted out; her separate existence annihilated her rights and power usurped; her people put under the iron arm of a military despotism, and reduced to a condition little better than that endured by the Saxons when vanquished by their Norman invaders; but, so sure as there is a God of justice, we shall no go unpunished; the penalty is certain; we cannot escape; a terrible retribution waits us. We beseech our countrymen to leave off this horrid conflict, abandon their murderous plans, and forsake the way of blood. Peradventure our country may yet be saved. Let the press, the pulpit, the church, the people at large, unite at once; and let petitions flood the halls of Congress by the million, asking for the instant recall of our force from Mexico. This may not save us, but it is our only hope.

## QUESTIONS TO CONSIDER

1. How does Douglass defend his position?
2. Do you find his position convincing?

# 12.6 WILLIAM WALKER, EXCERPT FROM *THE WAR IN NICARAGUA* (1860)

William Walker provides an illuminating coda to the discussion of American expansionism and its relation to slavery. Walker was a filibuster, one of a series of Americans who tried to create slave-holding colonies under their control in the Americas. In 1853, Walker conquered a portion of Baja California, in Mexico, with forty-five men. Just one year later, the Mexican government ejected him from the area. Put on trial in America, a sympathetic jury acquitted Walker of violating the Neutrality Act of 1794, which banned Americans from waging wars against countries "at peace" with the United States. In 1855, Walker turned his sights south toward Nicaragua, then embroiled in a civil war. Walker temporarily allied himself with one faction in the war, then later took control of the country himself after leading his forces to victory. Under Walker's rule, the country reestablished slavery and concentrated power in the hands of a small, white elite in an attempt to ally the country with states in the American South. In 1857, under heavy pressure from Costa Rican, Honduran, Salvadoran, Guatemalan, and American troops, Walker surrendered to a U.S. admiral and returned to America. In 1860, he published *The War in Nicaragua*, a self-aggrandizing account of his exploits and, from which the following document is excerpted. After publishing the book, Walker returned to Central America, where he was captured and executed by Honduran authorities in September 1860.

THE policy of the Walker government was, of course, the same as that of Rivas, so far as the introduction of the white race into Nicaragua was concerned. Bur the administration of Rivas was, from its nature, transitional. It sought to increase the American element without inquiring what place the new people were to occupy in the old society. Rivas and his cabinet felt that Nicaraguan society required reorganization, but they knew not how it was to be accomplished, nor would they have adopted the means necessary for the end event if the proper measures had been pointed out to them. Hence, when the reorganization, not merely of the State, but of the family and of labor, became necessary, another executive than Rivas was not a matter of choice. Not merely the secondary form of the crystal was to be modified, but the primary from was to be radically changed, and for this a new force was to be brought into play. It may be that the reorganization in Nicaragua was attempted too soon ; but those who have read the foregoing pages may judge whether or not the Americans were driven forward by the force of events. Sooner or later the struggle between the old and the new forms of society must inevitable have occurred.

The difference of language between the members of the old society and that portion of the white race, necessarily dominant in the new, while it was a cause keeping the elements apart, afforded also a means of regulating the relations between the several races meeting on the same soil. In order that the laws of the Republic might be thoroughly published, it was decreed that they should be published in English as well as in Spanish. The reason of this was apparent to every one ; but the object of another clause in the same

*Source:* William Walker, *The War in Nicaragua* (Mobile, AL: S. H. Goetzel & Co, 1860), 251–274. Retrieved from the Internet Archive website, https://ia800503.us.archive.org/35/items/warinnicaragua00walk/warinnicaragua00walk.pdf (Accessed June 6, 2018).

decree, "That all documents connected with public affairs shall be of equal value whether written in English or Spanish," was not noticed except by the careful observer. By this clause the proceedings of all the courts, and the record of all the deeds in the State, might be made in English. It was not necessary to decree that all such records should be in English—the mere permission was sufficient to accomplish the object. Lawyers will readily see what an advantage such a clause gave to those speaking both English and Spanish, over those acquainted only with the latter language.

The decree concerning the use of the two languages tended to make the ownership of the lands of the state fall in the hands of those speaking English. But in addition to this, a decree was published declaring the property of all enemies of State forfeited to the Republic, and a Board of commissioners was named "to take possession of, direct, determine upon, and sell all such confiscated or forfeited properties." The Board was given the ordinary power of courts for examining witnesses, and for enforcing obedience to its orders. All property declared confiscated was to be sold soon after the rendition of the judgment, and military scrip was to be received in payment at the sale of such property, thus giving those who had been in the military service of the state an opportunity to secure their pay out of the estates of the persons engaged in the war against them.

The land titles in Nicaragua were in very unsettled condition, and the same system prevailed there as in other Spanish American States. The limits of grants were indeterminate, and there was of course, no registry law. Accordingly, in order to fix the number of outstanding grants from the Republic, a decree was published requiring all claims to land to be recorded within six months, and it was further decreed that after a certain date no conveyance or mortgage should be valid against third parties, unless duly recorded in the district where the land lay. This was a substitution of the English and American system for the rules of the Roman and Continental law. The recording of titles is undoubtedly for the public advantage, and those possessed of good titles to land in Nicaragua would in virtue of this decree have held their possessions by a tenure more certain than ever. But the system was fatal to the bad or uncertain titles. It also gave an advantage to those familiar with the habit of registry.

The general tendency of these several decrees was the same ; they were intended to place a large proportion of the land of the country in the hands of the white race. The military force of the State might, for a time, secure the Americans in the government of the Republic, but in order that their possession of government might be permanent, it was requisite for them to hold the land. . . .

In Nicaragua the negro seems to be in this natural climate. The blacks who have gone thither from Jamaica are healthy, strong and capable of severe labor. They were much employed by the Accessory Transit Company on the San Juan river and at Virgin Bay ; and even on the bungos of the lake and river, they bore the toil and exposure to the sun as well as the natives of the country. In fact, the negro blood seems to assert its superiority over the indigenous Indian of Nicaragua. Some of the negro and mulatto officers in the Legitimist army were remarkable among their fellows for courage and energy, though with these qualities were generally joined cruelty and ferocity.

The advantage of negro slavery in Nicaragua would, therefore, be two-fold ; while it would furnish certain labor for the use of agriculture, it would tend to separate the races and destroy the half-castes who cause the disorder, which has prevailed in the country since the independence. But there are many who, while admitting the advantage of slavery to Nicaragua, think it was impolitic to have attempted its re-establishment at the time the decree of the 22d of September was published. This brings us to consider the decree in its relation with the question of slavery in the United States.

At the time the decree was published it was clear that the Americans in Nicaragua would be called on to defend themselves against the forces of four allied States. Their cause was right and just, but it then appeared to touch themselves only. Up to that time there was no American interest in country, save that of the army and of the Transit Company ; hence it was expedient by some positive act to bind to the cause for which the naturalized Nicaraguans were contending some strong and powerful interest in the United States. The decree, re-establishing slavery while it declared the manner in which the Americans proposed to regenerate Nicaraguan society made them the champions of the Southern States of the Union in the conflict truly styled "irrepressible" between free and slave labor. The policy of the act consisted in pointing out to the Southern States the only means, short of revolution, whereby they can preserve their present social organization.

In 1856, the South began to perceive that all territory hereafter acquired by the federal government, would necessarily enure to the use and benefit of free labor. The immigrant from the free labor States moves easily and readily into the new territories ; and the surplus of population being greater at the North than at the South, the majority in any new territory would certainly be from the anti-slavery region. Besides this, the South has no surplus labor to send westward or southward. On the contrary the Gulf States are crying out for more negroes ; and the uneasiness of Southern society results from the superabundance of its intellect and capital in proportion to its rude labor. It is impossible, in the present condition of affairs, for the South to get the labor [it lacks] ; and the only means of restoring the balance to its industry is to send its unemployed intellect to a field where no political obstacles prevent it from getting the labor it requires.

There are, however, some people in the Southern States who condemn every effort to extend slavery, because they say, it irritates the anti-slavery sentiment, and thus feeds and strengthens hostility to Southern society. With them, the great cure for abolitionism, is rest and inaction on the part of slaveholders. But such are the shallowest of thinkers. It is impossible to keep down the discussion of the slavery question in the United States. The question is one which touches the whole labor of the country, and involves the vital relations of capital with labor. And this is the question which in all ages, and in all countries, has divided states and societies. Hence it is idle to speak of the question being settled ; from the nature of things the contest between free and slave labor is "never ending, still beginning." . . .

. . . [S]lavery is not abnormal to American society. It must be the rule, not the exception. But to keep it so requires effort and labor. The enemies of many and powerful. They are resolute in their determination not merely to limit but to extirpate slavery. The man who leads the free-labor myriads of the United States—he, whose firm will and far-reaching mind do not quail either at the doctrines or the acts to which his political

philosophy logically conducts him, has already declared that he hopes to see the time when the foot of not a slave shall press the continent. Yet the sluggards of slavery say, "a little more rest, a little more folding of the arms to slumber." Strafford sleeps though the axe of the headsman is whetted for his execution.

The contest between free and slave labor in the United States not only touches the interests and destiny of those immediately engaged in the struggle but it affects the fate of the whole continent. The question involved is whether the civilization of the western world shall be European or American. If free labor prevails in its effort to banish slave labor from the continent, the history of American society becomes a faith reflex of European systems and prejudices, without contributing any new ideas, any new sentiments, or any new institutions, to the mental and moral wealth of the world. The necessary consequence of the triumph of free labor will be the destruction, by a slow and cruel process, of the colored races which now inhabit the central and southern portions of the continent. The labor of the inferior race cannot compete with that of the white race unless you give it a white master to direct its energies ; and without such protection as slavery affords, the colored races must inevitably succumb in the struggle with white labor. Hence a Nicaraguan can not be an indifferent spectator of the contest between the two form of labor in the United States ; and deeper yet must be his interest in the matter if born and educated in a slave State of the Union, he revolves in his mind the results which will ensue to the home of his childhood, and the firesides of the friends of his youth, in case victory smiles upon the soldiers of free labor. Do not, therefore, men of the South, deem it the voice of a stranger, or of one without a stake in your country's welfare, which urges you to strike a blow in defense of your honor, no less than of your hearths and your families, ere the blast of the enemy's bugle calls upon you to surrender your arms to an overwhelming force.

## QUESTIONS TO CONSIDER

1. How does Walker defend his efforts?
2. Does this change how you think about Manifest Destiny and American expansionism?

# CHAPTER 13

# THE POLITICS OF SLAVERY, 1848–1860

## 13.1 FREDERICK DOUGLASS, "WHAT TO THE SLAVE IS THE FOURTH OF JULY?" (1852)

Escaped slave and noted abolitionist Frederick Douglass was one of the most powerful orators of his time. (For his views on the Mexican-American War, see Chapter 12, Reading 12.5). On July 5, 1852, Douglass gave a speech to the Ladies' Anti-Slavery Society in Rochester, New York. In the speech, from which the following document is excerpted, Douglass attacked the institution of slavery through the frame of July Fourth. Douglass, a renowned intellectual, drew a clear divide between white society and African American society in the lengthy speech. During the years ahead, Douglass would continue to be active in the abolitionist movement and the women's suffrage movement. In 1872, he became the first African American nominated for Vice President, on the Equal Rights Party ticket. He died in Washington, D.C., in 1895 while attending a meeting of the National Council of Women. "What to the Slave is the Fourth of July?" has come to be known as an essential text for studying the rhetoric of the abolitionist movement.

This, for the purpose of this celebration, is the 4th of July. It if the birthday of your National Independence, and of your political freedom. This, to you, is what the Passover was to the emancipated people of God. It carries your minds back to the day, and to the act of your great deliverance; and to the signs, and to the wonders, associated with that act, and that day. This celebration also marks the beginning of another year of your national life; and reminds you that the Republic of America is now 76 years old. I am glad, fellow-citizens, that your nation is so young. Seventy-six years, though a good old age for a man is but a mere speck in the life of a nation. Three score years and ten is the allotted time for individual men; but nations number their years by thousands. According to this fact; you are even now only in the beginning of you[r] national career, still lingering in the period of childhood. I repeat, I am glad this is so. There is hope in the thought, and hope is much needed, under the dark clouds which lower above the horizon. The eye

*Source:* Frederick Douglass, *Oration Delivered in Corinthian Hall, Rochester, By Frederick Douglass* (Rochester: Lee, Mann & Co., 1852), 4–6, 14–19, 20–21. Retrieved from the Hathi Trust website, https://babel.hathitrust.org/cgi/pt?id=inu.3000000508774 1;view=1up;seq=7 (Accessed June 6, 2018).

of the reformer is met with angry flashes, portending disastrous times, but his heart may well beat lighter at the thought that America is young and that she is still in the impressible stage of her existence. May he not hope that high lessons of wisdom, of justice and of truth, will yet give direction to her destiny? Were the nation older, the patriot's heart might be sadder, and shrouded in gloom, and the hope of its prophets go out in sorrow. There is consolation in the thought, that America is young.—Great steams are not easily turned from channels, worn deep in the course of ages. They may also rise in wrath and fury, and bear away, on their angry waves, the accumulated wealth of years of toil and hardship. They, however, gradually flow back to the same old channel, and flow on as serenely as ever. But, while the river may not be turned aside, it may dry up, and leave nothing behind but the withered branch, and the unsightly rock, to howl in the abyss-sweeping wind, the sad tale of departed glory. As with rivers so with nations.

Fellow-citizens, I shall not presume to dwell at length on the associations that cluster about this day. The simple story of it is, that, 76 years ago, the people of this country were British subjects. The style and title of your "sovereign people" (in which you now glory) was not then born. You were under the British Crown. Your fathers esteemed the English Government as the home government; and England as the fatherland. This home government, you know, although a considerable distance from your home, did, in the exercise of its parental prerogatives, impose upon its colonial children, such restraints, burdens and limitations, as, in its mature judgment, it deemed wise, right and proper. . . .

Fellow-citizens, pardon me, allow me to ask, why am I called upon to speak here to-day? What have I, or those I represent, to do with your national independence? Are the great principles of political freedom and of natural justice, embodied in that Declaration of Independence, extended to us? And am I, therefore, called upon to bring our humble offering to the national alter, and to confess the benefits and express devout gratitude for the blessings resulting from your independence to us?

Would to God, both for your sakes and ours, that an affirmative answer could be truthfully returned to these questions! Then would my task be light, and

my task be light, and my burden easy and delightful. For who is there so cold, that a nation's sympathy could not warm him? Who so obdurate and dead to the claims of gratitude, that would not thankfully acknowledge such priceless benefits? Who so stolid and selfish, that would not give his voice to swell the hallelujahs of a nation's jubilee, when the chains of servitude had been torn from his limbs? I am not that man. In a case like that, the dumb might eloquently speak and the " lame man leap as an hart."

But, such is not the state of the case, I say it with a sad sense of the disparity between us. I am not included within the pale of this glorious anniversary Your high independence only reveals the immensurable distance between us. The blessings in which you, this day, rejoice, are not enjoyed in common. The rich inheritance of justice, liberty, prosperity, and independence bequeathed by your father is shared by you, not by me. The sunlight that brought life and healing to you, has brought stripes and death to me. This Fourth July is *yours*, not *mine*. *You* may rejoice, *I* must mourn. To drag a man in fetters into the grand illuminated temple of liberty, and call upon him to join you in joyous anthems, and call were inhuman mockery and sacrilegious irony. Do you mean, citizens, to mock me, by asking me to speak to-day If so, there is a parallel to your conduct. And let me warn you that it is dangerous to copy the example of a nation whose crimes, towering up to heaven, were thrown down by the breath of the Almighty, burying that nation in irrecoverable ruin. I can to-day take up the plaintive lament of a peeled and woe-smitten people!

"By the rivers of Babylon, there we sat down. Yea! we wept when remembered Zion. We hanged our harps upon the willows in the midst thereof. For there, they that carried us away captive, required of us a song; and they who wasted us required of us mirth, saying Sing us one of the songs of Zion, How can we sign the Lord's song in a strange land? If I forget thee, O Jerusalem, let my right hand forget her cunning. If I do not remember thee, let my tongue cleave to the roof of my month."

Fellow-citizens; above your national, tumultuous joy, I hear the mournful wail of millions! Whose chains, heavy and grievous yesterday, are, to-day, rendered more intolerable by the jubilee shouts that reach them. If I forget, if I do not faithfully remember those bleeding children of sorrow this day, "may my right hand forget her cunning, and may my tongue cleave to the roof of my mouth!" To forget them, to pass lightly over their wrongs, and to chime in with the popular theme, would be treason most scandalous and shocking, and would make me a reproach before God and the world. My subject, then, fellow-citizens, is AMERICA SLAVERY. I shall see, this day, and its popular characteristics, from the slave's pint of view. Standing, there, identified with the American bondman, making his wrongs mine, I do not hesitate to declare, with all my soul, that the character and conduct of this nation never looked blacker to me than of this 4th of July! Whether we turn to the declaration of the past, or to the professions of the present, the conduct of the nation seems equally hideous and revolting. America is false to the past, false to the present, and solemnly binds herself to be false to the future. Standing with God and the cursed and bleeding slave on this occasion, I will, in the name of humanity which is outranged, in the name of liberty which is fettered, in the name of the constitution and the Bible, which are disregarded and trampled upon, dare to call in question and to denounce, with all the emphasis I can command, everything that serves to perpetuate slavery––the great sin and shame of America! "I will not equivocate; I will not excuse;" I will use the severest language I can command; and yet not one word shall escape me that any man, whose judgment is not blinded by prejudice, or who is not at heart a slaveholder, shall not confess to be right and just.

But I fancy I hear some one of my audience say, it is just in this circumstance that you and your brother abolitionists fail to make a favorable impression on the public mind. Would you argue more, and denounce less, would you persuade more, and rebuke less, your cause would be much more likely to succeed. But, I submit, where all is plain there is nothing to be argued. What point in the anti-slavery slavery creed would you have me argue? On what branch of the subject do the people of this country need light? Must I undertake to prove that the slave is a man? That point is conceded already. Nobody doubts it. The slaveholders themselves acknowledge it in the enactment of laws for their government. They acknowledge it in the enactment of laws for their government. They acknowledge

it when they punish disobedience on the part of the slave. There are seventy-two crimes in the State of Virginia, which, if committed by a black man, (no matter how ignorant he be,) subject him to the punishment of death; while only two of the same crimes will subject a white man to the like punishment.—What is this but acknowledgement that the slave is a moral, intellectual and responsible and being. The manhood of the slave is conceded. It is admitted in the fact that Southern statute books are covered with enactments forbidding, under severe fines and penalties, the teaching of the slave to read or to write.—When you can point to any such laws, in reference to beasts of the field, then I may consent to argue the manhood of the slave. When the dogs in your streets, when the fowls of the air, when the cattle on your hills, when the fish of the sea, and the reptiles that crawl, shall be unable to distinguish the slave from a brute, then will I argue with you that the slave is a man!

For the present, it is enough to affirm the equal manhood of the negro race. Is it not astonishing that, while we are ploughing, planting and reaping, using all kinds of mechanical tools, erecting houses, constructing bridges, building ships, working in metals of brass, iron, copper, silver and gold; that, while we are reading, writing and cyphering, acting as clerks, merchants and secretaries, having among us lawyers, doctors, ministers, poets, authors, editors, orators and teachers; that, while we are engaged in all manner of enterprises common to other men, digging gold in California, capturing the whale in the Pacific, feeding sheep and cattle on the hill-side, living, moving, acting, thinking, planning, living in families as husbands, wives and children, and, above all, confessing and worshipping the Christian's God, and looking hopefully for life and immortality beyond the grave, we are called upon to prove that we are men!

Would you have me argue that man is entitled to liberty? That he is the rightful owner of his own body? You have already declared it. Must I argue the wrongfulness of slavery? Is that a question for Republicans? Is it to be settled by the rules of logic and argumentation, as a matter beset with great difficulty, involving a doubtful application of the principle of justice, hard to be understood? How should I look to-day in the presence of Americans, dividing, and subdividing a discourse, to show that men have a natural right to freedom? speaking of it relatively, and positively, negatively, and affirmatively. |To do so, would be to make myself ridiculous, and to offer an insult to your understanding.— There is not a man beneath the canopy of heaven, that does not know slavery is wrong *for him.* . . .

What, to the American slave, is your 4th of July? I answer; a day that reveals to him, more than all other days in the year, the gross injustice and cruelty to which he is the constant victim. To him, your celebration is a sham; your boasted liberty, an unholy license; your national greatness, swelling vanity; your sounds of rejoicing are empty and heartless; your denunciations of tyrants, brass fronted impudence; your shouts of liberty and equality, hollow mockery; your prayers and hymns, your sermons and thanksgivings, with all your religious parade, and solemnity, are, to him, mere bombast, fraud, deception, impiety, and hypocrisy—a thin veil to cover up crimes which would disgrace a nation of savages. There is not a nation on the earth guilty of practices more shocking and bloody, than are the people of these United States, at this very hour.

Go where you may, search where you will, roam through all the monarchies and despotisms of the old world, travel through South America, search out every abuse, and when you have found the last, lay your facts by the side of the every day practices of this nation, and you will say with me that, for revolting barbarity and shameless hypocrisy, America reigns without a rival.

**QUESTIONS TO CONSIDER**

1. Why is the Fourth of July a valuable frame for Douglass' analysis?
2. Douglass often uses "you" in the text. Why does he do this, and how effective is it?

# 13.2 GEORGE FITZHUGH, EXCERPT FROM *SOCIOLOGY FOR THE SOUTH* (1854)

George Fitzhugh (1806–1881) was a southern sociologist who emerged as one of the most prominent defenders of slavery in the antebellum period. A lawyer and painter, Fitzhugh became controversial in the 1850s for his pro-slavery works. In his writings, Fitzhugh claimed that northern factory workers lived desperate lives of poverty, whereas southern slaves were well treated. Fitzhugh's 1854 *Sociology for the South* enlarged his accusations against on northern society to include attacks on free labor and the ideology of capitalism more broadly. Fitzhugh also supported white slavery as well, and he called for a world economy supported by slave labor. After publishing *Sociology for the South,* Fitzhugh traveled throughout the United States to defend his arguments; his aggressive, public personality lent him a degree of fame in his own time.

Now it has been the practice in all countries and in all ages, in some degree, to accommodate the amount and character of government control to the wants, intelligence, and moral capacities of the nations or individuals to be governed. A highly moral and intellectual people, like the free citizens of ancient Athens, are best governed by a democracy. For a less moral and intellectual one, a limited and constitutional

*Source:* George Fitzhugh, *Sociology for the South: On the Failure of Free Society* (Richmond: A. Morris, 1854), 82–89, 164–168.

monarchy will answer. For a people either very ignorant or very wicked, nothing short of military despotism will suffice. So among individuals, the most moral and well-informed members of society require no other government than law. They are capable of reading and understanding the law, and have sufficient self-control and virtuous disposition to obey it. Children cannot be governed by mere law; first, because they do not understand it, and secondly, because they are so much under the influence of impulse, passion and appetite, that they want sufficient self-control to be deterred or governed by the distant and doubtful penalties of the law. They must be constantly controlled by parents or guardians, whose will and orders shall stand in the place of law for them. Very wicked men must be put into penitentiaries; lunatics into asylums, and the most wild of them into straight jackets, just as the most wicked of the sane are manacled with irons; and idiots must have committees to govern and take care of them. Now, it is clear the Athenian democracy would not suit a negro nation, nor will the government of mere law suffice for the individual negro. He is but a grown up child, and must be governed as a child, not as a lunatic or criminal. The master occupies towards him the place of parent or guardian. We shall not dwell on this view, for no one will differ with us who thinks as we do of the negro's capacity, and we might argue till dooms-day, in vain, with those who have a high opinion of the negro's moral and intellectual capacity.

Secondly. The negro is improvident; will not lay up in summer for the wants of winter; will not accumulate in youth for the exigencies of age. He would become an insufferable burden to society. Society has the right to prevent this, and can only do so by subjecting him to domestic slavery.

In the last place, and living in their midst, they would be far outstripped or outwitted in the chase of free competition. Gradual but certain extermination would be their fate. We presume the maddest abolitionist does not think the negro's providence of habits and money-making capacity at all to compare to those of the whites. This defect of character would alone justify enslaving him, if he is to remain here. In Africa or the West Indies, he would become idolatrous, savage and cannibal, or be devoured by savages and cannibals. At the North he would freeze or starve.

We would remind those who deprecate and sympathize with negro slavery, that his slavery here relives him from a far more cruel slavery in Africa, or from idolatry and cannibalism, and every brutal vice and crime that can disgrace humanity; and that it Christianizes, protects, supports and civilizes him; that it governs him far better than free laborers at the North are governed. There, wife-murder has become a mere holiday pastime; and where so many wives are murdered, almost all must be brutally treated. Nay, more: men who dill their wives or treat them brutally, must be ready for all kinds of crime, and the calendar of crime at the North proves the inference to be correct. Negroes never kill their wives. If it be objected that legally they have no wives, then we reply, that in an experience of more than forty years, we never yet heard of a negro man killing a negro woman. Our negroes are not only better off as to physical comfort than free laborers, but their moral condition is better. . . .

Negro slavery would be changed immediately to some form of peonage, serfdom or villienage, if the negroes were sufficiently intelligent and provident to manage a farm. No one would have the labor and trouble of management, if his negroes would pay in hires and rents one-half what free tenants pay in rent in Europe. Every negro in the South would be soon liberated, if he would take liberty on the terms that white tenants hold it. The fact that he cannot enjoy liberty on such terms, seems conclusive that he is only fit to be a slave.

But for the assaults of the abolitionists, much would have been done ere this to regulate and improve Southern slavery. Our negro mechanics do not work so hard, have many more privileges and holidays, and are better fed and clothed than field hands, and are yet more valuable to their masters. The slaves of the improve Southern slavery. Our negro mechanics do not work so hard, have many more privileges and holidays, and are better fed and clothed than field hands, and are yet more valuable to their masters. The slaves of the South are cheated of their rights by the purchase of Northern manufactures which they could produce. Besides, if we would employ our slaves in the coarser processes of the mechanic arts and manufactures, such as brick making, getting and hewing timber for ships and houses, iron mining and smelting, coal mining, grading railroads and plank roads, in the manufacture of cotton, tobacco, &c., we would find a vent in new employment for their increase, more humane and more profitable than the vent afforded by new states and territories. The nice and finishing processes of manufacture and mechanics should be reserved for the whites, who only are fitted for them, and thus, by diversifying pursuits and cutting off dependence on the North, we might benefit and advance the interests of our whole population. Exclusive agriculture has depressed and impoverished the South. We will not here dilate on this topic, because we intend to make it the subject of a separate essay. Free trade doctrines, not slavery, have made the South agricultural and dependent, given her a sparse and ignorant population, ruined her cities, and expelled her people.

Would the abolitionists approve of a system of society that set white children free, and remitted them at the age of fourteen, males and females, to all the rights, both as to person and property, which belong to adults? Would it be criminal or praiseworthy to do so? Criminal, of course. Now, are the average of negroes equal in information, in native intelligence, in prudence or providence, to well-informed white children of fourteen? We who have lived with them for forty years, think not. The competition of the world would be too much for the children. They would be cheated out of their property and debased in their morals. Yet they would meet every where with sympathizing friends of their own color, ready to aid, advise and assist them. The negro would be exposed to the same competition and greater temptations, with no greater ability to contend with them, with these additional difficulties. He would be welcome nowhere; meet with thousands of enemies and no friends. If he went North, the white laborers would kick him and cuff him, and drive him out of employment. If he went to Africa, the savages would cook him and eat him. If he went to the West Indies, they would not let him in, or if they did, they would soon make of him a savage and idolater.

We have a further question to ask. If it be right and incumbent to subject children to the authority of parents and guardians, and idiots and lunatics to committees, would it not be equally right and incumbent to give the free negroes masters, until at least they arrive at years of discretion, which very few ever did or will attain? What is the difference between the authority of a parent and of a master? Neither pay wages, and each is entitled to the services of those subject to him. The father may not sell his child forever, but may hire him out till he is twenty-one. The free negro's master may also be restrained from selling. Let him stand in loco parentis, and call him papa instead of master. Look closely into slavery, and you will see nothing so hideous in it; or if you do, you will find plenty of it at home in its most hideous form. . . .

. . . What is the mental condition of the free laborer? Is he exempt from the cares that beset wealth and power, and plant thorns in the path of royalty?

Poor men have families as well as the rich, and they love those families more than rich men, because they have little else to love. The smiles of their wives and the prattle of their children, when they return from labor at night, compensate, in some degree, for the want of those luxuries which greet the rich, but which render them less keenly alive to the pleasures of domestic affection. Their love is divided between their possessions and their families; the poor man's love is intensely concentrated on his wife and children. Wife and children do not always smile and prattle. Want makes them sad and serious. Cold and hunger and nakedness give them haggard looks, and then the poor man's heart bleeds at night as he tosses on his restless pillow. They are often delicate and sometimes sick. The parent must go out to toil to provide for them, nevertheless. He cannot watch over their sick beds like the rich. Apprehension does not sweeten and lighten his labors. Nor does loss of rest in watching and nursing a sick wife or child better fit him to earn his wages the next day. The poor have not the cares of wealth, but the greater cares of being without it. They have no houses, know not when they may be turned out of rented ones, or when, or on what terms they may rent another. This must be looked to and provided for. The head of the family gets sick sometimes, too. Wages cease. Does it soothe fever and assuage pain to look at a destitute family, or to reflect on the greater destitution that awaits them, if he, the parent, should die? Is he in health and getting good wages—the competition of fellow-laborers may any day reduce his wages or turn him out of employment. The poor free man has all the cares of the rich, and a thousand more besides. When the labors of the day are ended, domestic anxieties and cares begin. The usual, the ordinary, the normal condition of the whole laboring class, is that of physical suffering, cankering, corroding care, and mental apprehension and pain. The poor houses and poor rates prove this. The ragged beggar children in the streets, and their suffering parents pining in cellars and garrets, attest it. Destitute France, poor Scotland, and starving Ireland proclaim it. The concurrent testimony of all history and of all statistics, for three centuries, leave no room for cavil or for doubt. Why, in this age of progress, are the great majority of mankind, in free countries, doomed to live in penitential pains and purgatorial agony? They, the artificers of every luxury, of every comfort, and every necessary of life, see the idle enjoying the fruits of their toil. Is there a just God in Heaven, and does he see, approve and ordain all this? Has it ever been thus? If so, God delights in human agony, and created man to punish him. All other animals enjoy life, and did God make man after his own image, that life should be a pain and a torture to him? Bad as the laboring man's condition is now, those who live in free society tell us it was far worse formerly. He used to be a slave, and they say slavery is a far worse condition to the laborer than liberty. Well, for the argument, we grant it. His condition was worse throughout all past time in slavery, than now with liberty. Is it consistent with the harmony of nature, or the wisdom and mercy of God, that such a being should be placed in this would, and placed, too, at the head of it? It is rank Diabolism to admit such a conclusion. None but Lucifer would have made such a world.

God made no such world! He instituted slavery from the first, as he instituted marriage and parental authority. Profane, presumptuous, ignorant man, in attempting to improve, has marred and defaced the work of his Creator. Wife and children, although not free, are relieved from care and anxiety, supported and protected, and their situation is as happy and desirable as that of the husband and parent. In this we see the doings of a wise and just God. The slave, too, when the night comes, may lie down in peace. He has a master to watch over and take care of him. If he be sick, that master will provide for him. If his family be sick, his master and mistress sympathise with his affliction, and procure medical aid for the sick. And when he comes to die, he feels that his family will be provided for. He does all the labor of life; his master bears all its corroding cares and anxieties. Here, again, we see harmonious relations, consistent with the wisdom and mercy of God. We see an equal and even-handed justice meted out to all alike, and we see life itself no longer a terrestrial purgatory; but a season of joy and sorrow to the rich and the poor.

Man is naturally associative, because isolated and alone he is helpless. The object of all associations, form States to Temperance societies, is mutual insurance. Man does not feel the advantage of State insurance, until he is driven to the poor house. House insurance companies and life insurance companies often fail; and when successful, only insure against a class of misfortunes. The insurance of Trade Unions, Odd Fellows, and Temperance societies, is wholly inadequate. Slavery insurance never fails, and covers all losses and all misfortunes. Domestic slavery is nature's mutual insurance society; art in vain attempts to imitate it, or to supply its place.

## QUESTIONS TO CONSIDER

1.  How did Fitzhugh defend slavery?
2.  How did Fitzhugh attack northern capitalism?

# 13.3 HINTON ROWAN HELPER, EXCERPT FROM
## *THE IMPENDING CRISIS OF THE SOUTH* (1857)

Hinton Rowan Helper (1829–1909), a southerner like Fitzhugh, drew the opposite conclusions from slavery. Born in North Carolina, Helper migrated to California during the Gold Rush but quickly returned east after failing to find success. In 1857, Helper published *The Impending Crisis of the South,* an attack on the slave system from a southerner's viewpoint. The book was immediately successful and helped to spur the widening divisions between northern and southern viewpoints. After the Civil War, Helper emerged as a fervent white supremacist and argued that all former slaves should be expelled from the United States. He even supported a plan to build a railroad between North and South America so that the United States might more easily lure white migrants and eject blacks. He committed suicide in Washington, D.C., in 1909.

### THE FREE AND THE SLAVE STATES

It is a fact well known to every intelligent Southerner that we are compelled to go to the North for almost every article of utility and adornment, from matches, shoepegs and paintings up to cotton-mills, steamships and statuary; that we have no foreign trade, no princely merchants, nor respectable artists; that, in comparison with the free states, we contribute nothing to the literature, polite arts and inventions of the age; that, for want of profitable employment at home, large numbers of our native population find themselves necessitated to emigrate to the West, whilst the free states retain not only the larger proportion of those born within their own limits, but induce, annually, hundreds of thousands of foreigners to settle and remain amongst them; that almost everything produced at the North meets with ready sale, while, at the same time, there is no demand, even among our own citizens, for the productions of Southern industry; that, owing to the absence of a proper system of business amongst us, the North becomes, in one way or another, the proprietor and dispenser of all our floating wealth, and that we are dependent on Northern capitalists for the means necessary to build our railroads, canals and other public improvements; that if we want to visit a foreign country, even though it may lie directly South of us, we find no convenient way of getting there except by taking passage through a Northern port; and that nearly all the profits arising from the exchange of commodities, from insurance and shipping offices, and from the thousand and one industrial pursuits of the country, accrue to the North, and are there invested in the erection of those magnificent cities and stupendous works of art which dazzle the eyes of the South, and attest the superiority of free institutions!

The North is the Mecca of our merchants, and to it they must and do make two pilgrimages per annum—one in the spring and one in the fall. All our commercial, mechanical, manufactural, and literary supplies come from there. We want Bibles, brooms, buckets and books, and we go to the North; we want pens, ink, paper, wafers and envelopes, and we go to the North; we want shoes, hats, handkerchiefs, umbrellas and pocket knives, and we go to the North; we want furniture, crockery, glassware and pianos, and we go to

*Source:* Hinton Rowan Helper, *The Impending Crisis of the South: How to Meet It* (New York: A. B. Burdick, 1859). Retrieved from the Project Gutenberg website, http://www.gutenberg.org/files/36055/36055-h/36055-h.htm (Accessed June 6, 2018).

the North; we want toys, primers, school books, fashionable apparel, machinery, medicines, tombstones, and a thousand other things, and we go to the North for them all. Instead of keeping our money in circulation at home, by patronizing our own mechanics, manufacturers, and laborers, we send it all away to the North, and there it remains; it never falls into our hands again.

In one way or another we are more or less subservient to the North every day of our lives. In infancy we are swaddled in Northern muslin; in childhood we are humored with Northern gewgaws; in youth we are instructed out of Northern books; at the age of maturity we sow our "wild oats" on Northern soil; in middle-life we exhaust our wealth, energies and talents in the dishonorable vocation of entailing our dependence on our children and on our children's children, and, to the neglect of our own interests and the interests of those around us, in giving aid and succor to every department of Northern power; in the decline of life we remedy our eye-sight with Northern spectacles, and support our infirmities with Northern canes; in old age we are drugged with Northern physic; and, finally, when we die, our inanimate bodies, shrouded in Northern cambric, are stretched upon the bier, borne to the grave in a Northern carriage, entombed with a Northern spade, and memorized with a Northern slab!

But it can hardly be necessary to say more in illustration of this unmanly and unnational dependence, which is so glaring that it cannot fail to be apparent to even the most careless and superficial observer. All the world sees, or ought to see, that in a commercial, mechanical, manufactural, financial, and literary point of view, we are as helpless as babes; that, in comparison with the Free States, our agricultural resources have been greatly exaggerated, misunderstood and mismanaged; and that, instead of cultivating among ourselves a wise policy of mutual assistance and co-operation with respect to individuals, and of self-reliance with respect to the South at large, instead of giving countenance and encouragement to the industrial enterprises projected in our midst, and instead of building up, aggrandizing and beautifying our own States, cities and towns, we have been spending our substance at the North, and are daily augmenting and strengthening

the very power which now has us so completely under its thumb.

It thus appears, in view of the preceding statistical facts and arguments, that the South, at one time the superior of the North in almost all the ennobling pursuits and conditions of life, has fallen far behind her competitor, and now ranks more as the dependency of a mother country than as the equal confederate of free and independent States. Following the order of our task, the next duty that devolves upon us is to trace out the causes which have conspired to bring about this important change, and to place on record the reasons, as we understand them[.]

## WHY THE NORTH HAS SURPASSED THE SOUTH

And now that we have come to the very heart and soul of our subject, we feel no disposition to mince matters, but mean to speak plainly, and to the point, without any equivocation, mental reservation, or secret evasion whatever. The son of a venerated parent, who, while he lived, was a considerate and merciful slaveholder, a native of the South, born and bred in North Carolina, of a family whose home has been in the valley of the Yadkin for nearly a century and a half, a Southerner by instinct and by all the influences of thought, habits, and kindred, and with the desire and fixed purpose to reside permanently within the limits of the South, and with the expectation of dying there also—we feel that we have the right to express our opinion, however humble or unimportant it may be, on any and every question that affects the public good; and, so help us God, "sink or swim, live or die, survive or perish," we are determined to exercise that right with manly firmness, and without fear, favor or affection.

And now to the point. In our opinion, an opinion which has been formed from data obtained by assiduous researches, and comparisons, from laborious investigation, logical reasoning, and earnest reflection, the causes which have impeded the progress and prosperity of the South, which have dwindled our commerce, and other similar pursuits, into the most contemptible insignificance; sunk a large majority of our people in galling poverty and ignorance, rendered a small minority conceited and tyrannical, and driven the rest away from their homes; entailed upon us a humiliating dependence on the Free States; disgraced us in the recesses of our own souls, and brought us under reproach in the eyes of all civilized and enlightened nations—may all be traced to one common source, and there find solution in the most hateful and horrible word, that was ever incorporated into the vocabulary of human economy—*Slavery*!

Reared amidst the institution of slavery, believing it to be wrong both in principle and in practice, and having seen and felt its evil influences upon individuals, communities and states, we deem it a duty, no less than a privilege, to enter our protest against it, and to use our most strenuous efforts to overturn and abolish it! Then we are an abolitionist? Yes! not merely a freesoiler, but an abolitionist, in the fullest sense of the term. We are not only in favor of keeping slavery out of the territories, but, carrying our opposition to the institution a step further, we here unhesitatingly declare ourself in favor of its immediate and unconditional abolition, in every state in this confederacy, where it now exists! Patriotism makes us a freesoiler; state pride makes us an emancipationist; a profound sense of duty to the South makes us an abolitionist; a reasonable degree of fellow feeling for the negro, makes us a colonizationist. With the free state men in Kansas and Nebraska, we sympathize with all our heart. We love the whole country, the great family of states and territories, one and inseparable, and would have the word Liberty engraved as an appropriate and truthful motto, on the escutcheon of every member of the confederacy. We love freedom, we hate slavery, and rather than give up the one or submit to the other, we will forfeit the pound of flesh nearest our heart. Is this sufficiently explicit and categorical? If not, we hold ourself in readiness at all times, to return a prompt reply to any proper question that may be propounded.

Our repugnance to the institution of slavery, springs from no one-sided idea, or sickly sentimentality. We have not been hasty in making up our mind on the subject; we have jumped at no conclusions; we have acted with perfect calmness and deliberation; we have carefully considered, and examined the reasons for and against the institution, and have also taken into account the probable consequences of our decision.

The more we investigate the matter, the deeper becomes the conviction that we are right; and with this to impel and sustain us, we pursue our labor with love, with hope, and with constantly renewing vigor.

That we shall encounter opposition we consider as certain; perhaps we may even be subjected to insult and violence. From the conceited and cruel oligarchy of the South, we could look for nothing less. But we shall shrink from no responsibility, and do nothing unbecoming a man; we know how to repel indignity, and if assaulted, shall not fail to make the blow recoil upon the aggressor's head. The road we have to travel may be a rough one, but no impediment shall cause us to falter in our course. The line of our duty is clearly defined, and it is our intention to follow it faithfully, or die in the attempt.

But, thanks to heaven, we have no ominous forebodings of the result of the contest now pending between Liberty and Slavery in this confederacy. Though neither a prophet nor the son of a prophet, our vision is sufficiently penetrative to divine the future so far as to be able to see that the "peculiar institution" has but a short, and, as heretofore, inglorious existence before it. Time, the righter of every wrong, is ripening events for the desired consummation of our labors and the fulfillment of our cherished hopes. Each revolving year brings nearer the inevitable crisis. The sooner it comes the better; may heaven, through our humble efforts, hasten its advent.

The first and most sacred duty of every Southerner, who has the honor and the interest of his country at heart, is to declare himself an unqualified and uncompromising abolitionist. No conditional or half-way declaration will avail; no mere threatening demonstration will succeed. With those who desire to be instrumental in bringing about the triumph of liberty over slavery, there should be neither evasion, vacillation, nor equivocation. We should listen to no modifying terms or compromises that may be proposed by the proprietors of the unprofitable and ungodly institution. Nothing short of the complete abolition of slavery can save the South from falling into the vortex of utter ruin. Too long have we yielded a submissive obedience to the tyrannical domination of an inflated oligarchy; too long have we tolerated their arrogance and self-conceit; too long have we submitted to their unjust and savage exactions. Let us now wrest from them the sceptre of power, establish liberty and equal rights throughout the land, and henceforth and forever guard our legislative halls from the pollutions and usurpations of pro-slavery demagogues.

**QUESTIONS TO CONSIDER**

1. How did Helper support his argument against slavery?
2. Why do you think the book was so immediately successful?

# 13.4 CHARLES SUMNER, "THE CRIME AGAINST KANSAS" (1856)

Charles Sumner (1811–1874) opposed slavery from the northern perspective. A Republican Senator from Massachusetts, Sumner became known as one of the most powerful anti-slavery speakers in Congress. In 1856, Kansas became embroiled in a war, termed "Bleeding Kansas," between pro-slavery and anti-slavery factions. Because the 1854 Kansas-Nebraska Act ruled that the territory's settlers would decide Kansas' fate as a slave or a free state, the war had very real consequences. Though Kansas joined the Union as a free state in 1861, violence would last until the end of the Civil War. In 1856, Sumner took to the Senate podium to argue that Kansas should be able to immediately join the Union as a free state. In his speech "The Crime Against Kansas," Sumner condemned the Kansas-Nebraska Act and slavery more generally. He especially singled out Andrew Butler, a South Carolina Senator who had previously castigated the Republican Party for its anti-slavery stance, and Stephen Douglas, the Illinois Senator who championed popular sovereignty. Two days after Sumner's inflammatory speech, Preston Brooks, a U.S. Representative from South Carolina, beat Sumner unconscious with his cane in the Senate chamber. Brooks continued to beat Sumner until his cane broke. Sumner spent months in the hospital and did not return to the Senate until 1859. Sumner's caning probably led to a shift in the Republican Party toward a more full embrace of anti-slavery views.

The wickedness which I now begin to expose is immeasurably aggravated by the motive which prompted it. Not in any common lust for power did this uncommon tragedy have its origin. It is the rape of a virgin Territory, compelling it to the hateful embrace of Slavery; and it may be clearly traced to a depraved longing for a new slave State, the hideous offspring of such a crime, in the hope of adding to the power of slavery in the National Government. Yes, Sir, when the whole world, alike Christian and Turk, is rising up to condemn this wrong, making it a hissing to the nations, here in our Republic, *force*—aye, Sir, FORCE,—is openly employed in compelling Kansas to this pollution, and all for the sake of political power. There is the simple fact, which you will vainly attempt to deny, but which in itself presents an essential wickedness that makes other public crimes seem like public virtues.

*Source:* Charles Sumner, "The Crime Against Kansas, May 19th–20th, 1856." From *Charles Sumner: His Complete Works* (Boston: Lee and Shepard, 1900), vol. 5, pp. 140–146.

This enormity, vast beyond comparison, swells to dimensions of crime which the imagination toils in vain to grasp, when it is understood that for this purpose are hazarded the horrors of intestine feud, not only in this distant Territory, but everywhere throughout the country. The muster has begun. The strife is no longer local but national. Even now, while I speak, portents lower in the horizon, threatening to darken the land, which already palpitates with the mutterings of civil war. The fury of the propagandists, and the calm determination of their opponents, are diffused from the distant Territory over wide-spread communities, and the whole country, in all its extent, marshalling hostile divisions, and foreshadowing a conflict which, unless happily averted by the triumph of Freedom, will become war,—fratricidal, parricidal war,—with an accumulated wickedness beyond that of any war in human annals, justly provoking the avenging Pen of History, and constituting a strife such as was pictured by the Roman historian, more than *foreign*, more than *social*, more than *civil*, being something compounded of all these, and in itself more than war. . . .

Before entering upon the argument, I must say something of a general character, particularly in response to what has fallen from Senators who have raised themselves to eminence on this floor in championship of human wrong; I mean the Senator from South Carolina, [Mr. BUTLER], and the Senator from Illinois, [Mr. DOUGLAS], who, though unlike as Don Quixote and Sancho Panza, yet, like this couple, sally forth together in the same adventure. I regret much to miss the elder Senator from his seat; but the cause, against which he has run a tilt with such ebullition of animosity, demands that the opportunity of exposing him should not be lost; and it is for the cause that I speak. The Senator from South Carolina has read many books of chivalry, and believes himself a chivalrous knight, with sentiments of honor and courage. Of course he has chosen a mistress to whom he has made his vows, and who, though ugly to others, is always lovely to him; though polluted in the sight of the world, is chaste in his sight— I mean the harlot, Slavery. For her his tongue is always profuse in words. Let her be impeached in character, or any proposition be made to shut her out from the extension of her wantonness, and no extravagance of manner or hardihood of assertion is too great for this

Senator . . . The asserted rights of Slavery, which shock equality of all kinds, are cloaked by a fantastic claim of equality. If the Slave States cannot enjoy what, in mockery of the great fathers of the Republic, he misnames Equality under the Constitution,—in other words, the full power in the National territories to compel fellowmen to unpaid toil, to separate husband and wife, and to sell little children at the auction-block,—then, Sir, the chivalric Senator will conduct the State of South Carolina out of the Union! Heroic knight! Exalted Senator! A second Moses come for a second exodus!

Not content with this poor menace, which we have been twice told was "measured," the Senator, in the unrestrained chivalry of his nature, has undertaken to apply opprobrious words to those who differ from him on this floor. He calls them "sectional and fanatical"; and resistance to the usurpation of Kansas he denounces as "an uncalculated fanaticism." . . . He is the uncompromising, unblushing representative on this floor of a flagrant *sectionalism*, now domineering over the Republic,—and yet, with a ludicrous ignorance of his own position, unable to see himself as others see him, or with an effrontery which even his white head ought not to protect from rebuke, he applies to those here who resist his *sectionalism* the very epithet which designates himself. The men who strive to bring back the Government to its original policy, when Freedom and not Slavery was national, while Slavery and not Freedom was sectional, he arraigns as *sectional*. This will not do. It involves too great a perversion of terms. I tell that Senator that it is to himself, and to the "organization" of which he is the "committed advocate," that his epithet belongs. I now fasten it upon them. For myself, I care little for names; but since the question is raised here, I affirm that the Republican party of the Union is in no just sense *sectional*, but, more than any other party, *national*,—and that it now goes forth to dislodge from the high places that tyrannical sectionalism of which the Senator from South Carolina is one of the maddest zealots.

## QUESTIONS TO CONSIDER

1. Why does Sumner focus on Southern "chivalry"?
2. Do you find Sumner's anti–popular sovereignty stance convincing?

# 13.5 JOHN BROWN, SPEECH TO THE COURT AT HIS TRIAL (1859)

John Brown (1800–1859) was a radical abolitionist, of the mind that only violent action could end the scourge of slavery. In 1846, Brown moved to Springfield, Massachusetts, a hotbed of the anti-slavery movement. After Congress passed the 1850 Fugitive Slave Act, Brown founded the League of Gileadites, a militant abolitionist group. During the "Bleeding Kansas" crisis, he moved to the territory to fight the pro-slavery forces. In 1856, after pro-slavery militias sacked Lawrence, Kansas, Brown and a small group of his allies killed five pro-slavery settlers near Pottawatomie Creek—they killed three of the settlers with broadswords—in an incident that came to be known as the Pottawatomie Massacre. Three years later, after spending time raising money and gathering weapons, Brown led an ill-fated attack on the Federal arsenal at Harper's Ferry, Virginia. His goal was to seize the weapons stored there and to arm slaves with them. Though Brown and his allies easily captured the arsenal building, Federal forces quickly closed in on them, killed some of the men (including Brown's sons Watson and Oliver), and captured the rest. On November 2, 1859, a jury convicted Brown of murder, treason, and conspiracy and sentenced him to death; he gave the following speech before he received the sentence. In the years that followed, Brown would become a martyr for anti-slavery sentiment.

I have, may it please the Court, a few words to say.

In the first place, I deny every thing but what I have already admitted, of a design on my part to *free Slaves*. I intended, certainly, to have made a clean thing of that matter, as I did last winter, when I went into Missouri, and there took Slaves, without the snapping of a gun on either side, moving them through the country, and finally leaving them in Canada. I desired to have done the same thing again, on a much larger scale. *That was all I intended.* I never did intend murder, or treason, or the destruction of property, or to excite or incite slaves to rebellion, or to make insurrection.

I have another objection, and that is, that it is *unjust* that I should suffer such a penalty. Had I interfered in the manner, and which I admit has been fairly proved,—for I admire the truthfulness and candor of the greater portion of the witnesses who have testified in this case,—had I so interfered in behalf of the rich, the Powerful, the Intelligent, the so-called Great, or in behalf of any of their friends, either father, mother, brother, sister, wife, or children, or any of *that* class, and suffered and sacrificed what I have in this interference, *it would have been all right.* Every man in this Court would have deemed it an act worthy a reward, rather than a punishment.

This Court acknowledges too, as I suppose, the validity of the Law of God. I saw a book kissed, which I suppose to be the Bible, or at least the New Testament, which teaches me that, "All things whatsoever I would that men should do to me, I should do even so to them." It teaches me further, to "Remember them that are in bonds, as bound with them. "I endeavored to act up to that instruction. I say I am yet too young to understand that God is any *respecter of persons.* I believe

*Source:* "Address of John Brown to the Virginia Court," https://cdn.loc.gov/service/rbc/rbpe/rbpe06/rbpe065/06500500/06500500.pdf (Accessed June 6, 2018).

that to have interfered as I have done, as I have always freely admitted I have done, in behalf of his *despised poor*, I have done no wrong, but RIGHT.

Now, if it is deemed necessary that I should forfeit my life, for the furtherance of the ends of justice, and MINGLE MY BLOOD FURTHER WITH THE BLOOD OF MY CHILDREN, and with the blood of millions in the Slave country, whose rights are disregarded by wicked, cruel, and unjust enactments,—I say, LET IT BE DONE.

Let me say one word further: I feel entirely satisfied with the treatment I have received on my trial. Considering all the circumstances, it has been more generous than I expected; but I feel no consciousness of guilt. I have stated from the first what was my *intention*, and what was not. I never had any design against the liberty of any person, nor any disposition to commit treason, or excite Slaves to rebel, or make any general insurrection. I never encouraged any man to do so, but always discouraged any idea of that kind.

Let me say something, also, in regard to the statements made by some of those who were connected with me. I hear that it has been stated by some of them, that I have induced them to join me; but the contrary is true. I do not say this to injure them, but as regarding their weakness. Not one but joined me of his own accord, and the greater part at their own expense. A number of them I never saw and never had a word of conversation with, till the day they came to me, and that was for the purpose I have stated. Now I have done.

**QUESTIONS TO CONSIDER**

1. How did Brown "object" to his conviction?
2. Does the speech read as the speech of a man who wanted to be a martyr?

# 13.6 EXCERPTS FROM CONFEDERATE STATES' SECESSION STATEMENTS (1861)

On December 20, 1860, South Carolina became the first state to secede. Over the next 15 months, ten others joined South Carolina. Collectively, the seceding states formed the Confederate States of America. In the following document, you will read excerpts from the documents of secession issued by Georgia, Mississippi, South Carolina, and Virginia. Play close attention to the language used by the four seceding states.

## GEORGIA

The people of Georgia having dissolved their political connection with the Government of the United States of America, present to their confederates and the world the causes which have led to the separation.

For the last ten years we have had numerous and serious causes of complaint against our non-slave-holding confederate States with reference to the subject of African slavery. They have endeavored to weaken our security, to disturb our domestic peace and tranquility,

*Source:* "The Declaration of Causes of Seceding States," https://www.battlefields.org/learn/primary-sources/declaration-causes-seceding-states#Georgia (Accessed May 19, 2018).

and persistently refused to comply with their express constitutional obligations to us in reference to that property, and by the use of their power in the Federal Government have striven to deprive us of an equal enjoyment of the common Territories of the Republic. This hostile policy of our confederates has been pursued with every circumstance of aggravation which could arouse the passions and excite the hatred of our people, and has placed the two sections of the Union for many years past in the condition of virtual civil war. Our people, still attached to the Union from habit and national traditions, and averse to change, hoped that time, reason, and argument would bring, if not redress, at least exemption from further insults, injuries, and dangers. Recent events have fully dissipated all such hopes and demonstrated the necessity of separation.

Our Northern confederates, after a full and calm hearing of all the facts, after a fair warning of our purpose not to submit to the rule of the authors of all these wrongs and injuries, have by a large majority committed the Government of the United States into their hands. The people of Georgia, after an equally full and fair and deliberate hearing of the case, have declared with equal firmness that they shall not rule over them. . . .

## MISSISSIPPI

*A Declaration of the Immediate Causes which Induce and Justify the Secession of the State of Mississippi from the Federal Union.*

In the momentous step which our State has taken of dissolving its connection with the government of which we so long formed a part, it is but just that we should declare the prominent reasons which have induced our course.

Our position is thoroughly identified with the institution of slavery—the greatest material interest of the world. Its labor supplies the product which constitutes by far the largest and most important portions of commerce of the earth. These products are peculiar to the climate verging on the tropical regions, and by an imperious law of nature, none but the black race can bear exposure to the tropical sun. These products have become necessities of the world, and a blow at

slavery is a blow at commerce and civilization. That blow has been long aimed at the institution, and was at the point of reaching its consummation. There was no choice left us but submission to the mandates of abolition, or a dissolution of the Union, whose principles had been subverted to work out our ruin. That we do not overstate the dangers to our institution, a reference to a few facts will sufficiently prove.

The hostility to this institution commenced before the adoption of the Constitution, and was manifested in the well-known Ordinance of 1787, in regard to the Northwestern Territory.

The feeling increased, until, in 1819–20, it deprived the South of more than half the vast territory acquired from France.

The same hostility dismembered Texas and seized upon all the territory acquired from Mexico.

It has grown until it denies the right of property in slaves, and refuses protection to that right on the high seas, in the Territories, and wherever the government of the United States had jurisdiction.

It refuses the admission of new slave States into the Union, and seeks to extinguish it by confining it within its present limits, denying the power of expansion.

It tramples the original equality of the South under foot.

It has nullified the Fugitive Slave Law in almost every free State in the Union, and has utterly broken the compact which our fathers pledged their faith to maintain.

It advocates negro equality, socially and politically, and promotes insurrection and incendiarism in our midst.

It has enlisted its press, its pulpit and its schools against us, until the whole popular mind of the North is excited and inflamed with prejudice.

It has made combinations and formed associations to carry out its schemes of emancipation in the States and wherever else slavery exists.

It seeks not to elevate or to support the slave, but to destroy his present condition without providing a better.

It has invaded a State, and invested with the honors of martyrdom the wretch whose purpose was to apply flames to our dwellings, and the weapons of destruction to our lives.

It has broken every compact into which it has entered for our security.

It has given indubitable evidence of its design to ruin our agriculture, to prostrate our industrial pursuits and to destroy our social system.

It knows no relenting or hesitation in its purposes; it stops not in its march of aggression, and leaves us no room to hope for cessation or for pause.

It has recently obtained control of the Government, by the prosecution of its unhallowed schemes, and destroyed the last expectation of living together in friendship and brotherhood.

Utter subjugation awaits us in the Union, if we should consent longer to remain in it. It is not a matter of choice, but of necessity. We must either submit to degradation, and to the loss of property worth four billions of money, or we must secede from the Union framed by our fathers, to secure this as well as every other species of property. For far less cause than this, our fathers separated from the Crown of England.

Our decision is made. We follow their footsteps. We embrace the alternative of separation; and for the reasons here stated, we resolve to maintain our rights with the full consciousness of the justice of our course, and the undoubting belief of our ability to maintain it.

## SOUTH CAROLINA

*Declaration of the Immediate Causes Which Induce and Justify the Secession of South Carolina from the Federal Union*

The people of the State of South Carolina, in Convention assembled, on the 26th day of April, A.D., 1852, declared that the frequent violations of the Constitution of the United States, by the Federal Government, and its encroachments upon the reserved rights of the States, fully justified this State in then withdrawing from the Federal Union; but in deference to the opinions and wishes of the other slaveholding States, she forbore at that time to exercise this right. Since that time, these encroachments have continued to increase, and further forbearance ceases to be a virtue.

And now the State of South Carolina having resumed her separate and equal place among nations, deems it due to herself, to the remaining United States of America, and to the nations of the world, that she

should declare the immediate causes which have led to this act. . . .

The ends for which the Constitution was framed are declared by itself to be "to form a more perfect union, establish justice, insure domestic tranquility, provide for the common defence, promote the general welfare, and secure the blessings of liberty to ourselves and our posterity."

These ends it endeavored to accomplish by a Federal Government, in which each State was recognized as an equal, and had separate control over its own institutions. The right of property in slaves was recognized by giving to free persons distinct political rights, by giving them the right to represent, and burthening them with direct taxes for three-fifths of their slaves; by authorizing the importation of slaves for twenty years; and by stipulating for the rendition of fugitives from labor.

We affirm that these ends for which this Government was instituted have been defeated, and the Government itself has been made destructive of them by the action of the non-slaveholding States. Those States have assume[d] the right of deciding upon the propriety of our domestic institutions; and have denied the rights of property established in fifteen of the States and recognized by the Constitution; they have denounced as sinful the institution of slavery; they have permitted open establishment among them of societies, whose avowed object is to disturb the peace and to eloign the property of the citizens of other States. They have encouraged and assisted thousands of our slaves to leave their homes; and those who remain, have been incited by emissaries, books and pictures to servile insurrection.

For twenty-five years this agitation has been steadily increasing, until it has now secured to its aid the power of the common Government. Observing the *forms* [emphasis in the original] of the Constitution, a sectional party has found within that Article establishing the Executive Department, the means of subverting the Constitution itself. A geographical line has been drawn across the Union, and all the States north of that line have united in the election of a man to the high office of President of the United States, whose opinions and purposes are hostile to slavery. He is to be entrusted with the administration of the common Government, because he has declared that that "Government cannot endure permanently half slave, half free," and that the public mind must rest in the belief that slavery is in the course of ultimate extinction.

This sectional combination for the submersion of the Constitution, has been aided in some of the States by elevating to citizenship, persons who, by the supreme law of the land, are incapable of becoming citizens; and their votes have been used to inaugurate a new policy, hostile to the South, and destructive of its beliefs and safety.

On the 4th day of March next, this party will take possession of the Government. It has announced that the South shall be excluded from the common territory, that the judicial tribunals shall be made sectional, and that a war must be waged against slavery until it shall cease throughout the United States.

The guaranties of the Constitution will then no longer exist; the equal rights of the States will be lost. The slaveholding States will no longer have the power of self-government, or self-protection, and the Federal Government will have become their enemy.

Sectional interest and animosity will deepen the irritation, and all hope of remedy is rendered vain, by the fact that public opinion at the North has invested a great political error with the sanction of more erroneous religious belief.

We, therefore, the People of South Carolina, by our delegates in Convention assembled, appealing to the Supreme Judge of the world for the rectitude of our intentions, have solemnly declared that the Union heretofore existing between this State and the other States of North America, is dissolved, and that the State of South Carolina has resumed her position among the nations of the world, as a separate and independent State; with full power to levy war, conclude peace, contract alliances, establish commerce, and to do all other acts and things which independent States may of right do.

## VIRGINIA

AN ORDINANCE TO REPEAL THE RATIFICATION OF THE CONSTITUTION OF THE UNITED STATES OF AMERICA BY THE STATE OF VIRGINIA, AND TO RESUME ALL THE RIGHTS AND POWERS GRANTED UNDER SAID CONSTITUTION.

The people of Virginia, in their ratification of the Constitution of the United States of America, adopted by them in Convention on the twenty-fifth day of June, in the year of our Lord one thousand seven hundred and eighty-eight, having declared that the powers granted under the said Constitution were derived from the people of the United States, and might be resumed whensoever the same should be perverted to their injury and oppression; and the Federal Government, having perverted said powers, *not only to the injury of the people of Virginia, but to the oppression of the Southern Slaveholding States*.

Now, therefore, we, the people of Virginia, do declare and ordain that the ordinance adopted by the people of this State in Convention, on the twenty-fifth day of June, eighty-eight, whereby the Constitution of the United States of America was ratified, and all acts of the General Assembly of this State, ratifying or adopting amendments to said Constitution, are hereby repealed and abrogated; that the Union between the State of Virginia and the other States under the Constitution aforesaid, is hereby dissolved, and that the State of Virginia is in the full possession and exercise of all the rights of sovereignty which belong and appertain to a free and independent State. And they do further declare that the said Constitution of the United States of America is no longer binding on any of the citizens of this State.

### QUESTIONS TO CONSIDER

1. What common themes emerge from the statements?
2. How did the seceding states justify their actions? Do you find their rhetoric convincing?

# CHAPTER 14

# A WAR FOR UNION AND EMANCIPATION, 1861–1865

## 14.1 "JOHN BROWN'S BODY," LYRICS (1861)

After John Brown's execution (see Chapter 13, Reading 13.5), he became a martyr for the abolitionist cause. The following song—"John Brown's Body"—became a Union Army marching tune during the Civil War. Many different sets of lyrics emerged. The following version was written by poet Julia Ward Howe, who felt inspired to write new lyrics after hearing Union Soldiers singing the song.

John Brown's body lies a mouldering in the grave,
John Brown's body lies a mouldering in the grave,
John Brown's body lies a mouldering in the grave,
   His soul's marching on!

Chorus.
Glory Hally, Hallelujah! Glory Hally, Hallelujah!
   Glory
      Hally, Hallelujah!
His soul's marching on!

He's gone to be a soldier in the army of our Lord,
He's gone to be a soldier in the army of our Lord,
He's gone to be a soldier in the army of our Lord,
   His soul's marching on!

Chorus: Glory Hally, Hallelujah! Glory Hally,
   Hallelujah!
      Glory Hally, Hallelujah!
His soul's marching on!

John Brown's knapsack is strapped upon his
   back,
John Brown's knapsack is strapped upon his back,
John Brown's knapsack is strapped upon his back,
   His soul's marching on!

Chorus: Glory Hally, Hallelujah! Glory
   Hallelujah!
      Glory Hally, Hallelujah!
His soul's marching on!

His pet lamps will meet him on the way, —
His pet lamps will meet him on the way, —
His pet lamps will meet him on the way, —
   They go marching on!

Chorus: Glory Hally, Hallelujah! Glory Hally
   Hallelujah!
      Glory Hally, Hallelujah!
They go marching on!

*Source:* "John Brown Song," http://www.loc.gov/teachers/lyrical/songs/docs/john_brown.pdf (Accessed June 6, 2018).

They will hang Jeff Davis to a tree!
They will hang Jeff Davis to a tree!
They will hang Jeff Davis to a tree!
    As they march along!

Chorus: Glory Hally, Hallelujah! Glory Hally,
    Hallelujah!
      Glory Hally, Hallelujah!
    As they march along!

Now, three rousing cheers for the Union!
Now, three rousing cheers for the Union!
Now, three rousing cheers for the Union!
    As we are marching on!

Chorus: Glory Hally, Hallelujah! Glory Hally,
    Hallelujah!
      Glory Hally, Hallelujah!
    Hip, hip, hip, hip, Hurrah!

**QUESTIONS TO CONSIDER**

1. How do the lyrics contribute to the idea of John Brown as a martyr?
2. Why do you think the song has remained popular to this day?

# 14.2 ABRAHAM LINCOLN, "GETTYSBURG ADDRESS" (1863)

On November 19, 1863, President Abraham Lincoln arrived in Gettysburg, Pennsylvania, to commemorate the Union soldiers killed in the Battle of Gettysburg four months previously and to consecrate the new National Cemetery at Gettysburg for those dead soldiers. The man who addressed the crowd before Lincoln, American politician Edward Everett, droned on for two hours. Lincoln spoke for two minutes. Marvelously summarizing the Civil War struggle and encapsulating the Union Army's broader aims, Lincoln's "Gettysburg Address" has come to be recognized as one of the greatest American speeches.

Four score and seven years ago our fathers brought forth, upon this continent, a new nation, conceived in Liberty, and dedicated to the proposition that all men are created equal.

Now we are engaged in a great civil war, testing whether that nation, or any nation, so conceived, and so dedicated, can long endure. We are met here on a great battle-field of that war. We have come to dedicate a portion of it as a final resting place for those who here gave their lives that that nation might live. It is altogether fitting and proper that we should do this.

But in a larger sense we can not dedicate — we can not consecrate — we can not hallow this ground. The brave men, living and dead, who struggled here, have consecrated it far above our poor power to add or detract. The world will little note, nor long remember, what we say here, but can never forget what they did here. It is for us, the living, rather to be dedicated here to the unfinished work which they have, thus far, so nobly carried on. It is rather for us to be here dedicated to the great task remaining before us — that from these honored dead we take increased devotion to the that

*Source:* "Abraham Lincoln, Draft of Gettysburg Address, Hay Copy (November 1863)," https://cdn.loc.gov/service/mss/mal/435/4356600/4356600.pdf (Accessed June 6, 2018).

cause for which they here gave the last full measure of devotion — that we here highly resolve that these dead shall not have died in vain; that this nation shall have a new birth of freedom; and that this government of the people, by the people, shall not perish from the earth.

**QUESTIONS TO CONSIDER**

1. How did Lincoln define the Union's central aims in fighting the Civil War?
2. What did Lincoln mean by a "new birth of freedom"?

# 14.3 WALT WHITMAN, "THE GREAT ARMY OF THE SICK" (1863)

Poet and journalist Walt Whitman (1819–1892), probably best known for his 1855 collection *Leaves of Grass,* worked as a nurse in Union Army hospitals during the Civil War. In 1863, he published "The Great Army of the Sick," a narrative of the horrors he found in those hospitals. While Whitman withheld some of the worst of the horrors from his readers, the account still gives insight into the human toll the Civil War took on soldiers of both sides. In many ways, the Civil War was the first modern war, and its human causalities bore the brunt of such modernity.

**WASHINGTON, MONDAY, FEB. 23, 1863.**

The military hospitals, convalescent camps, &c. in Washington and its neighborhood sometimes contain over fifty thousand sick and wounded men. Every form of wound, (the mere sight of some of them having been known to make a tolerably hardy visitor faint away,) every kind of malady, like a long procession, with typhoid fever and diarrhoea at the head as leaders, are here in steady motion. The soldier's hospital! how many sleepless nights how many woman's tears, how many long and aching hours and days of suspense, from every one of the Middle, Eastern and Western States, have concentrated here! Our own New-York, in the form of hundreds and thousands of her young men, may consider herself here—Pennsylvania, Ohio, Indiana and all the West and Northwest the same—and all the New-England States the same.

Upon a few of these hospitals I have been almost daily calling as a missionary, on my own account, for the sustenance and consolation of some of the most needy cases of sick and dying men, for the last two months. One has much to learn in order to do good in these places. Great tact is required. These are not like other hospitals. By far the greatest proportion (I should say five-sixths) of the patients are American young men, intelligent, of independent spirit, tender feelings, used to a hardy and healthy life; largely the farmers are represented by their sons—largely the mechanics and workingmen of the cities. Then they are *soldiers.* All these points must be borne in mind.

People through our Northern cities have little or no idea of the great and prominent feature which these military hospitals and convalescent camps make in and around Washington. There are not merely two or three or a dozen, but some fifty of them, of different

*Source:* Walt Whitman, "The Great Army of the Sick," from the *New York Times,* February 26, 1863, reprinted in Louis P. Masur, ed., *The Real War Will Never Get in the Books,* pp. 258–262, and elsewhere.

degrees of capacity. Some have a thousand and more patients. The newspapers here find it necessary to print every day a directory of the hospitals; a long list, something like what a directory of the churches would be in New-York, Philadelphia or Boston.

## BARRACKS ADOPTED BY GOVERNMENT

The Government, (which really tries, I think, to do the best and quickest it can for these sad necessities,) is gradually settling down to adopt the plan of placing the hospitals in clusters of one-story wooden barracks, with their accompanying tents and sheds for cooking and all needed purposes. Taking all things into consideration, no doubt these are best adapted to the purpose; better than using churches and large public buildings like the Patent Office. These sheds now adopted are long, one-story edifices, sometimes ranged along in a row, with their heads to the street, and numbered either alphabetically, Wards A, or B, C, D and so on; or Wards 1, 2, 3, &c. The middle one will be marked by a flagstaff, and is the office of the establishment, with rooms for the Ward Surgeons, &c. One of these sheds or wards, will contain sixty cots— sometimes, on an emergency, they move them close together, and crowd in more. Some of the barracks are larger, with, of course more inmates. Frequently, there are tents, more comfortable here than one might think, whatever they may be down in the army.

Each ward has a Ward-master, and generally a nurse for every ten or twelve men. A Ward Surgeon has, generally, two wards—although this varies. Some of the wards have a woman nurse—the Armory-square wards have some very good ones. The one in Ward E is one of the best.

## THE PATENT OFFICE

A few weeks ago the vast area of the second story of that noblest of Washington buildings, the Patent Office, was crowded close with rows of sick, badly wounded and dying soldiers. They were placed in three very large apartments. I went there several times. It was a strange, solemn and, with all its features of suffering and death, a sort of fascinating sight. I went sometimes at night, to soothe and relieve particular cases; some, I found, needed a little cheering up and friendly consolation at that time, for they went to sleep better afterward. Two

of the immense apartments are filled with high and ponderous glass cases, crowded with models in miniature of every kind of utensil, machine or invention, it ever entered into the mind of man to conceive; and with curiosities and foreign presents. Between these cases were lateral openings, perhaps eight feet wide, and quite deep, and in these were placed many of the sick; besides a great long double row of them up and down through the middle of the hall. Many of them were very bad cases, wounds and amputations. Then there was a gallery running above the hall, in which there were beds also. It was, indeed, a curious scene at night, when lit up. The glass cases, the beds, the sick, the gallery above and the marble pavement under foot—the suffering, and the fortitude to bear it in various degrees—occasionally, from some, the groan that could not be repressed—sometimes a poor fellow dying, with emaciated face and glassy eye, the nurse by his side, the doctor also there, but no friend, no relative—such were the sights but lately in the Patent Office. The wounded have since been removed from there, and it is now vacant again.

Of course, there are among these thousands of prostrated soldiers in hospital here, all sorts of individual cases. On recurring to my note-book, I am puzzled which cases to select to illustrate the average of these young men and their experiences. I may here say, too, in general terms, that I could not wish for more candor and manliness, among all their sufferings, than I find among them.

## CASE OF J. A. H., OF COMPANY C, TWENTY-NINTH MASSACHUSETTS

Take this case in Ward 6, Campbell Hospital—a young man from Plymouth Country, Massachusetts; a farmer's son, aged about 20 or 21, a soldierly American young fellow, but with sensitive and tender feelings. Most of December and January last, he lay very low, and for quite a while I never expected he would recover. He had become prostrated with an obstinate diarrhoea; his stomach would hardly keep the least thing down, he was vomiting half the time. But that was hardly the worst of it. Let me tell his story—it is but one of thousands.

He had been some time sick with his regiment in the field, in front, but did his duty as long as he could—was in the battle of Fredericksburgh—soon after was put in the regimental hospital. He kept getting worse—could not eat anything they had there—the doctor told him nothing could be done for him there—the poor fellow had fever also—received (perhaps it could not be helped) little or no attention—lay on the ground getting worse. Toward the latter part of December, very much enfeebled, he was sent up from the front, from Falmouth Station, in an open platform car; (such as hogs are transported upon north,) and dumped with a crowd of others on the boat at Aquia Creek, falling down like a rag where they deposited him, too weak and sick to sit up or help himself at all. No one spoke to him, or assisted him—he had nothing to eat or drink—was used (amid the great crowds of sick) either with perfect indifference, or, as in two or three instances, with heartless brutality.

On the boat, when night came and the air grew chilly, he tried a long time to undo the blankets he had in his knapsack, but was too feeble. He asked one of the employees, who was moving around deck, for a moment's assistance, to get the blankets. The man asked him back if he could not get them himself? He answered no, he had been trying for more than half an hour, and found himself too weak. The man rejoined, he might then go without them, and walked off. So H. lay, chilled and damp, on deck all night, without anything under or over him, while two good blankets were within reach. It caused him a great injury—nearly cost him his life.

Arrived at Washington, he was brought ashore and again left on the wharf, or above it, amid the great crowds, as before, without any nourishment—not a drink for his parched mouth—no kind hand offered to cover his face from the forenoon sun. Conveyed at last some two miles by ambulance to the hospital, and assigned a bed, (bed 47, ward 6, Campbell Hospital, January and February, 1863,) he fell down exhausted upon the bed; but the Ward-master (he has since been changed) came to him with a growling order to get up—the rules, he said, permitted no man to lie down in that way with his old clothes on—he must sit up—must first go to the bath-room, be washed, and have his clothes completely changed. (A very good rule, properly applied.) He was taken to the bath-room and scrubbed well with cold water. The attendants, callous

for a while, were soon alarmed, for suddenly the half-frozen and lifeless body fell limpsy in their hands, and they hurried it back to the cot, plainly insensible, perhaps dying.

Poor boy! the long train of exhaustion, deprivation, rudeness, no food, no friendly word or deed, but all kinds of upstart airs, and impudent, unfeeling speeches and deeds, from all kinds of small officials, (and some big ones,) cutting like razors into that sensitive heart, had at last done the job. He now lay, at times out of his head, but quite silent, asking nothing of anyone, for some days, with death getting a closer and surer grip upon him—he cared not, or rather he welcomed death. His heart was broken. He felt the struggle to keep up any longer to be useless. God, the world, humanity—all had abandoned him. It would feel so good to shut his eyes forever on the cruel things around him and toward him.

As luck would have it, at this time, I found him. I was passing down Ward No. 6 one day, about dusk (4th of January, I think,) and noticed his glassy eyes with a look of despair and hopelessness, sunk low in his thin pallid-brown young face. One learns to divine quickly in the hospital, and as I stopped by him and spoke some commonplace remark, (to which he made no reply,) I saw as I looked that it was a case for ministering to the affections first, and other nourishment and medicines afterward. I sat down by him without any fuss—talked a little—soon saw that it did him good—led him to talk a little himself—got him somewhat interested—wrote a letter for him to his folks in Massachusetts, (to L. H. CAMPBELL, Plymouth County,)— soothed him down as I saw he was getting a little too much agitated, and tears in his eyes—gave him some small gifts, and told him I should come again soon. (He has told me since that this little visit, at that hour, just saved him—a day more, and it would have been perhaps too late.)

Of course I did not forget him, for he was a young fellow to interest any one. He remained very sick—vomiting much every day, frequent diarrhoea, and also something like bronchitis, the doctor said. For a while I visited him almost every day—cheered him up—took him some little gifts, and gave him small sums of money, (he relished a drink of new milk, when it was brought through the ward for sale.) For a couple of weeks his condition was uncertain— sometimes I thought there was no chance for him at all. But of late he is doing better—is up and dressed, and goes around more and more (Feb. 21) every day. He will not die, but will recover.

The other evening, passing through the ward, he called me—he wanted to say a few words, particular. I sat down by his side on the cot, in the dimness of the long ward, with the wounded soldiers there in their beds, ranging up and down. H. told me I had saved his life. He was in the deepest earnest about it. It was one of those things that repay a soldiers' hospital missionary a thousand-fold—one of the hours he never forgets.

## THE FIELD IS LARGE, THE REAPERS FEW

A benevolent person with the right qualities and tact, cannot perhaps make a better investment of himself, at present, anywhere upon the varied surface of the whole of this big world, than in these same military hospitals, among such thousands of most interesting young men. The army is very young—and so much more American than I supposed. Reader, how can I describe to you the mute appealing look that rolls and moves from many a manly eye, from many a sick cot, following you as you walk slowly down one of these wards? To see these, and to be incapable of responding to them, except in a few cases, (so very few compared to the whole of the suffering men,) is enough to make one's heart crack. I go through in some cases cheering up the men; distributing now and then little sums of money—and regularly, letter-paper and envelopes, oranges, tobacco, jellies, &c., &c.

## OFFICIAL AIRS AND HARSHNESS

Many things invite comment, and some of them sharp criticism, in these hospitals. The Government, as I said, is anxious and liberal in its practice toward its sick; but the work has to be left, in its personal application to the men, to hundreds of officials of one grade or another about the hospitals, who are sometimes entirely lacking in the right qualities. There are tyrants and shysters in all positions, and especially those dressed in subordinate authority. Some of the ward doctors are careless, rude, capricious, needlessly strict. One I found who prohibited the men from all enlivening amusements; I found him sending men to the guard-house for the most trifling offence. In general, perhaps, the officials—especially the new ones, with their straps or badges—put on too many airs. Of all places in the world, the hospitals of American young men and soldiers, wounded in the volunteer service of their country, ought to be exempt from mere conventional military airs and etiquette of shoulder-straps. But they are not exempt.

## QUESTIONS TO CONSIDER

1. What can you glean about life for Civil War soldiers from the reading?
2. Do you think any of Whitman's descriptions would have been especially surprising to his readers?

# 14.4 LOUISA MAY ALCOTT, EXCERPT FROM *HOSPITAL SKETCHES* (1863)

Like Whitman, Louisa May Alcott, famed author of *Little Women,* spent time during the Civil War working as a volunteer nurse for the Union Army in a hospital near Washington D.C. Published in 1863, Hospital Sketches was based on letters she sent home during that time. The work was an immediate success and raised Alcott's literary stature. The following excerpt comes from Chapter III, "A Day," which recounts the events that occurred after a group of wounded men are brought to the hospital. The excerpt raises interesting questions about gender, memory, and experience during the Civil War.

"THEY'VE come! they've come! hurry up, ladies—you're wanted."

"Who have come? the rebels?"

This sudden summons in the gray dawn was somewhat startling to a three days' nurse like myself, and, as the thundering knock came at our door, I sprang up in my bed, prepared

> "To gird my woman's form,
> And on the ramparts die,"

if necessary; but my room-mate took it more coolly, and, as she began a rapid toilet, answered my bewildered question,—

"Bless you, no child; it's the wounded from Fredericksburg; forty ambulances are at the door, and we shall have our hands full in fifteen minutes."

"What shall we have to do?"

"Wash, dress, feed, warm and nurse them for the next three months, I dare say. Eighty beds are ready, and we were getting impatient for the men to come. Now you will begin to see hospital life in earnest, for you won't probably find time to sit down all day, and may think yourself fortunate if you get to bed by midnight. Come to me in the ball-room when you are ready; the worst cases are always carried there, and I shall need your help."

So saying, the energetic little woman twirled her hair into a button at the back of her head, in a "cleared for action" sort of style, and vanished, wrestling her way into a feminine kind of pea-jacket as she went.

I am free to confess that I had a realizing sense of the fact that my hospital bed was not a bed of roses just then, or the prospect before me one of unmingled rapture. My three days' experiences had begun with a death, and, owing to the defalcation of another nurse, a somewhat abrupt plunge into the superintendence of a ward containing forty beds, where I spent my shining hours washing faces, serving rations, giving medicine, and sitting in a very hard chair, with pneumonia on one side, diptheria on the other, five typhoids on the opposite, and a dozen dilapidated patriots, hopping, lying, and lounging about, all staring more or less at the new "nuss," who suffered untold agonies, but concealed them under as matronly an aspect as a spinster could assume, and blundered through her trying labors with a Spartan firmness, which I hope they appreciated, but am afraid they didn't. Having a taste for "ghastliness," I had rather longed for the wounded to arrive, for rheumatism was n't heroic, neither was liver

*Source:* Louisa May Alcott, *Hospital Sketches,* http://digital.library.upenn.edu/women/alcott/sketches/sketches.html#31 (Accessed June 6, 2018).

complaint, or measles; even fever had lost its charms since "bathing burning brows" had been used up in romances, real and ideal; but when I peeped into the dusky street lined with what I at first had innocently called market carts, now unloading their sad freight at our door, I recalled sundry reminiscences I had heard from nurses of longer standing, my ardor experienced a sudden chill, and I indulged in a most unpatriotic wish that I was safe at home again, with a quiet day before me, and no necessity for being hustled up, as if I were a hen and had only to hop off my roost, give my plumage a peck, and be ready for action. A second bang at the door sent this recreant desire to the right about, as a little woolly head popped in, and Joey, (a six years' old contraband,) announced—

"Miss Blank is jes' wild fer ye, and says fly round right away. They's comin' in, I tell yer, heaps on 'em— one was took out dead, and I see him,—hi! warn't he a goner!"

With which cheerful intelligence the imp scuttled away, singing like a blackbird, and I followed, feeling that Richard was *not* himself again, and wouldn't be for a long time to come.

The first thing I met was a regiment of the vilest odors that ever assaulted the human nose, and took it by storm. Cologne, with its seven and seventy evil savors, was a posy-bed to it; and the worst of this affliction was, every one had assured me that it was a chronic weakness of all hospitals, and I must bear it. I did, armed with lavender water, with which I so besprinkled myself and premises, that, like my friend Sairy, I was soon known among my patients as "the nurse with the bottle." Having been run over by three excited surgeons, bumped against by migratory coal-hods, water-pails, and small boys, nearly scalded by an avalanche of newly-filled tea-pots, and hopelessly entangled in a knot of colored sisters coming to wash, I progressed by slow stages up stairs and down, till the main hall was reached, and I paused to take breath and a survey. There they were! "our brave boys," as the papers justly call them, for cowards could hardly have been so riddled with shot and shell, so torn and shattered, nor have borne suffering for which we have no name, with an uncomplaining fortitude, which made one glad to cherish each as a brother. In they came, some on stretchers, some in men's arms, some feebly

staggering along propped on rude crutches, and one lay stark and still with covered face, as a comrade gave his name to be recorded before they carried him away to the dead house. All was hurry and confusion; the hall was full of these wrecks of humanity, for the most exhausted could not reach a bed till duly ticketed and registered; the walls were lined with rows of such as could sit, the floor covered with the more disabled, the steps and doorways filled with helpers and lookers on; the sound of many feet and voices made that usually quiet hour as noisy as noon; and, in the midst of it all, the matron's motherly face brought more comfort to many a poor soul, than the cordial draughts she administered, or the cheery words that welcomed all, making of the hospital a home.

The sight of several stretchers, each with its legless, armless, or desperately wounded occupant, entering my ward, admonished me that I was there to work, not to wonder or weep; so I corked up my feelings, and returned to the path of duty, which was rather "a hard road to travel" just then. The house had been a hotel before hospitals were needed, and many of the doors still bore their old names; some not so inappropriate as might be imagined, for my ward was in truth a *ball-room*, if gun-shot wounds could christen it. Forty beds were prepared, many already tenanted by tired men who fell down anywhere, and drowsed till the smell of food roused them. Round the great stove was gathered the dreariest group I ever saw—ragged, gaunt and pale, mud to the knees, with bloody bandages untouched since put on days before; many bundled up in blankets, coats being lost or useless; and all wearing that disheartened look which proclaimed defeat, more plainly than any telegram of the Burnside blunder. I pitied them so much, I dared not speak to them, though, remembering all they had been through since the route at Fredericksburg, I yearned to serve the dreariest of them all. Presently, Miss Blank tore me from my refuge behind piles of one-sleeved shirts, odd socks, bandages and lint; put basin, sponge, towels, and a block of brown soap into my hands, with these appalling directions:

"Come, my dear, begin to wash as fast as you can. Tell them to take off socks, coats and shirts, scrub them well, put on clean shirts, and the attendants will finish them off, and lay them in bed."

If she had requested me to shave them all, or dance a hornpipe on the stove funnel, I should have been less staggered; but to scrub some dozen lords of creation at a moment's notice, was really—really—. However, there was no time for nonsense, and, having resolved when I came to do everything I was bid, I drowned my scruples in my wash-bowl, clutched my soap manfully, and, assuming a business-like air, made a dab at the first dirty specimen I saw, bent on performing my task *vi et armis* if necessary. I chanced to light on a withered old Irishman, wounded in the head, which caused that portion of his frame to be tastefully laid out like a garden, the bandages being the walks, his hair the shrubbery. He was so overpowered by the honor of having a lady wash him, as he expressed it, that he did nothing but roll up his eyes, and bless me, in an irresistible style which was too much for my sense of the ludicrous; so we laughed together, and when I knelt down to take off his shoes, he "flopped" also, and wouldn't hear of my touching "them dirty craters. May your bed above be aisy darlin', for the day's work ye ar doon!—Whoosh! there ye are, and bedad, it's hard tellin' which is the dirtiest, the fut or the shoe." It was; and if he hadn't been to the fore, I should have gone on pulling, under the impression that the "fut" was a boot, for trousers, socks, shoes and legs were a mass of mud. This comical tableau produced a general grin, at which propitious beginning I took heart and scrubbed away like any tidy parent on a Saturday night. Some of them took the performance like sleepy children, leaning their tired heads against me as I worked, others looked grimly scandalized, and several of the roughest colored like bashful girls. One wore a soiled little bag about his neck, and, as I moved it, to bathe his wounded breast, I said,

"Your talisman didn't save you, did it?"

"Well, I reckon it did, marm, for that shot would a gone a couple a inches deeper but for my old mammy's camphor bag," answered the cheerful philosopher.

Another, with a gun-shot wound through the cheek, asked for a looking-glass, and when I brought one, regarded his swollen face with a dolorous expression, as he muttered—

"I vow to gosh, that's too bad! I warn't a bad looking chap before, and now I'm done for; won't there be a thunderin' scar? and what on earth will Josephine Skinner say?"

He looked up at me with his one eye so appealingly, that I controlled my risibles, and assured him that if Josephine was a girl of sense, she would admire the honorable scar, as a lasting proof that he had faced the enemy, for all women thought a wound the best decoration a brave soldier could wear. I hope Miss Skinner verified the good opinion I so rashly expressed of her, but I shall never know. . . .

All having eaten, drank, and rested, the surgeons began their rounds; and I took my first lesson in the art of dressing wounds. It wasn't a festive scene, by any means; for Dr P., whose Aid I constituted myself, fell to work with a vigor which soon convinced me that I was a weaker vessel, though nothing would have induced me to confess it then. He had served in the Crimea, and seemed to regard a dilapidated body very much as I should have regarded a damaged garment; and, turning up his cuffs, whipped out a very unpleasant looking housewife, cutting, sawing, patching and piecing, with the enthusiasm of an accomplished surgical seamstress; explaining the process, in scientific terms, to the patient, meantime; which, of course, was immensely cheering and comfortable. There was an uncanny sort of fascination in watching him, as he peered and probed into the mechanism of those wonderful bodies, whose mysteries he understood so well. The more intricate the wound, the better he liked it. A poor private, with both legs off, and shot through the lungs, possessed more attractions for him than a dozen generals, slightly scratched in some "masterly retreat;" and had any one appeared in small pieces, requesting to be put together again, he would have considered it a special dispensation.

The amputations were reserved till the morrow, and the merciful magic of ether was not thought necessary that day, so the poor souls had to bear their pains as best they might. It is all very well to talk of the patience of woman; and far be it from me to pluck that feather from her cap, for, heaven knows, she isn't allowed to wear many; but the patient endurance of these men, under trials of the flesh, was truly wonderful. Their fortitude seemed contagious, and scarcely a cry escaped them, though I often longed to groan for them, when pride kept their white lips shut, while great drops stood upon their foreheads, and the bed shook with the irrepressible tremor of their tortured bodies. One or two Irishmen anathematized the doctors with the frankness of their nation, and ordered the Virgin to stand by them, as if she had been the wedded Biddy to whom they could administer the poker, if she didn't; but, as a general thing, the work went on in silence, broken only by some quiet request for roller, instruments, or plaster, a sigh from the patient, or a sympathizing murmur from the nurse.

It was long past noon before these repairs were even partially made; and, having got the bodies of my boys into something like order, the next task was to minister to their minds, by writing letters to the anxious souls at home; answering questions, reading papers, taking possession of money and valuables; for the eighth commandment was reduced to a very fragmentary condition, both by the blacks and whites, who ornamented our hospital with their presence. Pocket books, purses, miniatures, and watches, were sealed up, labelled, and handed over to the matron, till such times as the owners thereof were ready to depart homeward or campward again. The letters dictated to me, and revised by me, that afternoon, would have made an excellent chapter for some future history of the war; for, like that which Thackeray's "Ensign Spooney" wrote his mother just before Waterloo, they were "full of affection, pluck, and bad spelling;" nearly all giving lively accounts of the battle, and ending with a somewhat sudden plunge from patriotism to provender, desiring "Marm," "Mary Ann," or "Aunt Peters," to send along some pies, pickles, sweet stuff, and apples, "to yourn in haste," Joe, Sam, or Ned, as the case might be.

My little Sergeant insisted on trying to scribble something with his left hand, and patiently accomplished some half dozen lines of hieroglyphics, which he gave me to fold and direct, with a boyish blush, that rendered a glimpse of "My Dearest Jane," unnecessary, to assure me that the heroic lad had been more successful in the service of Commander-in-Chief Cupid than that of Gen. Mars; and a charming little romance blossomed instanter in Nurse Periwinkle's romantic fancy, though no further confidences were made that day, for Sergeant fell asleep, and, judging from his tranquil face, visited his absent sweetheart in the pleasant land of dreams.

At five o'clock a great bell rang, and the attendants flew, not to arms, but to their trays, to bring up supper, when a second uproar announced that it was ready. The new comers woke at the sound; and I presently discovered that it took a very bad wound to incapacitate the defenders of the faith for the consumption of their rations; the amount that some of them sequestered was amazing; but when I suggested the probability of a famine hereafter, to the matron, that motherly lady cried out: "Bless their hearts, why shouldn't they eat? It's their only amusement; so fill every one, and, if there's not enough ready to-night, I'll lend my share to the Lord by giving it to the boys." And, whipping up her coffee-pot and plate of toast, she gladdened the eyes and stomachs of two or three dissatisfied heroes, by serving them with a liberal hand; and I haven't the slightest doubt that, having cast her bread upon the waters, it came back buttered, as another large-hearted old lady was wont to say.

Then came the doctor's evening visit; the administration of medicines; washing feverish faces; smoothing tumbled beds; wetting wounds; singing lullabies; and preparations for the night. By twelve, the last labor of love was done; the last "good night" spoken; and, if any needed a reward for that day's work, they surely received it, in the silent eloquence of those long lines of faces, showing pale and peaceful in the shaded rooms, as we quitted them, followed by grateful glances that lighted us to bed, where rest, the sweetest, made our pillows soft, while Night and Nature took our places, filling that great house of pain with the healing miracles of Sleep, and his diviner brother, Death.

### QUESTIONS TO CONSIDER

1. How does Alcott view the Civil War? What difficulties does she note in being a nurse?
2. Is *Hospital Sketches* effective at getting us to grasp the experience of the Civil War?

# 14.5 FOUR CIVIL WAR PHOTOGRAPHS (1861–1865)

The Civil War was the first major war to be comprehensively photographed. Photographers such as Matthew Brady photographed battlefields, hospitals, and wounded men. Therefore, they created an extensive catalogue of the damage the Civil War wrought on soldiers, civilian populations, and the American landscape. The following four images illustrate the broad scope of this photography. The first shows the Civil War battlefield at Antietam, where over 22,000 people died in the single bloodiest day of the war. The second shows a set of surgical photographs: two skulls featuring bullet wounds and two men with amputated legs. The third shows the infamous Confederate prison at Andersonville, Georgia, where over 31,000 Union soldiers endured horrifying conditions. The last shows the damage wrought by a Union campaign towards the end of the war and the fires set by retreating Confederate troops.

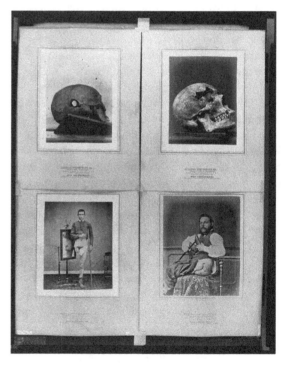

*Source:* "Civil War Glass Negatives and Related Prints," http://www.loc.gov/pictures/collection/cwp/ (Accessed June 6, 2018).

**QUESTIONS TO CONSIDER**

1. How might photography have changed the way civilians thought about the Civil War?

2. What stands out to you about the photographs?

# 14.6 SARAH MORGAN DAWSON, EXCERPT FROM *A CONFEDERATE GIRL'S DIARY* (1913)

Sarah Morgan Dawson (1842–1909) was born in New Orleans and later moved to Baton Rouge, Louisiana. During the Civil War, Dawson began writing a diary to recount her experiences. She lived through difficult times during the Civil War. Three of her brothers died, as did her father. In 1862, the Union Army captured and sacked her family's Baton Rouge home, and Sarah, her mother, and her sisters abandoned it, later moving to Union-occupied New Orleans. After the Civil War, Dawson became a relatively prominent newspaper writer and a women's suffrage activist. Her diary was published posthumously in 1913. In the excerpt you will read, Dawson recounts preparations for the arrival of the Union Army early in the Civil War, her reaction to occupation, and her thoughts after Robert E. Lee surrendered on April 9, 1865. Dawson's diary provides another perspective on the war and a unique view of Union occupation.

**APRIL 26TH, 1862**

There is no word in the English language that can express the state in which we are, and have been, these last three days. Day before yesterday, news came early in the morning of three of the enemy's boats passing the Forts, and then the excitement began. It increased

*Source:* Sarah Morgan Dawson, *A Confederate Girl's Diary* (Boston: Houghton Mifflin Company, 1913), 16–30, 435–440. Retrieved from the Internet Archive website, https://ia600305.us.archive.org/11/items/confederategirlsdaws/confederategirlsdaws.pdf (Accessed June 6, 2018).

rapidly on hearing of the sinking of eight of our gun-boats in the engagement, the capture of the Forts, and last night, of the burning of the wharves and cotton in the city while the Yankees where taking possession. To-day, the excitement has reached the point of delirium. I believe I am one of the most self-possessed in my small circle; and yet I feel such a craving for news of Miriam, and mother, and Jimmy, who are in the city, that I suppose I am as wild as the rest. It is nonsense to tell me I am cool, with all these patriotic and enthusi-astic sentiments. Nothing can positively ascertained, save that our gunboats are sunk, and theirs are coming up to the city. Everything else has been contradicted until we really do not know whether the city has been taken or not. We only know we had best be prepared for anything. So day before yesterday, Lilly and I sewed up our jewelry, which may be of use if we have to fly. I vow I will not move one step, unless carried away. Come what will, here I remain.

We went this morning to see the cotton burning—a sight never before witnessed, and probably never again to be seen. Wagons, drays,—everything that can driven or rolled,—were loaded with the bales and taken a few squares back to burn on the commons. Negroes were running around, cutting them piling them up, and setting then afire. All were as busy as though their salvation depended on disappointing the Yankees. Later, Charlie sent for us to come to the river and see him fire a flatboat loaded with the pre-cious material for which the Yankees are risking their bodies and souls. Up and down the levee, as far as we could see, negroes were rolling it down to the brink of the river where they would set them afire and push the bales in to float burning down the tide. Each sent up its wreath of smoke and looked like a tiny steamer puffing away. Only I doubt that from the source to the mouth of the river there are as many boats afloat on the Mississippi. The flatboat was piled with as many bales as it could hold without sinking. Most of them were cut open, while negroes staved in the heads of barrels of alcohol, whiskey, etc., and dashed bucketsful over the cotton. Others built up little chimneys of pine every few feet, lined with pine, knots and loose cotton, to burn more quickly. There, piled the length of the whole levee, or burning in the river, lay the work of thousands of negroes for more than a year past. It had come from every side. Men stood by who owned the cotton that was burning or waiting to burn. They either helped, or looked on cheerfully. Charlie owned but sixteen bales—a matter of some fifteen hundred dol-lars; but he was the head man of the whole affair, and burned his own, as well as the property of others. A single barrel of whiskey that was thrown on the cotton, cost the man who gave it one hundred and twenty-five dollars, (It shows what a nation in earnest is capable of doing.) Only two men got on the flatboat with Char-lie when it was ready. It was towed to the middle of the river, set afire in every place, and then they jumped into a little skiff fastened in front, and rowed to land. The cotton floated down the Mississippi one sheet of living flame, even in the sunlight. It would have been grand at night. But then we will have fun watching it this evening anyway; for they cannot get through to-day, though no time is to be lost. Hundreds of bales remained untouched. An incredible amount of prop-erty has been destroyed to-day; but no one be-grudges it. Every grog-shop has been emptied, and gutters and pavements are floating with liquors of all kinds. So that if the Yankees are fond of strong drink, they will fare ill. . . .

## MAY 5TH

Vile old Yankee boats, four in number, passed up this morning without stopping. After all our excitement, this "silent contempt" annihilated me! What in the world do they mean? The river was covered with burn-ing cotton; perhaps they want to see where it came from.

## MAY 9TH

Our lawful (?) owners have at last arrived. About sunset, day before yesterday, the Iroquois anchored here, and a graceful young Federal stepped ashore, carrying a Yankee flag over his shoulder, and asked the way to the Mayor's office. I like the style! If we girls of Baton Rouge had been at the landing, instead of the men, that Yankee would never have insulted us by flying his flag in our faces! *We* would have opposed his landing except under a flag of truce; but the men let him alone, and he even found a poor Dutchman will-ing to show him the road!

He did not accomplish much; said a formal demand would be made next day, and asked if it was safe for the men to come ashore and buy a few necessaries, when he was assured the air of Baton Rouge was very unhealthy for Yankee soldiers at night. He promised very magnanimously not to shell us out if we did not molest him; but I notice none of them dare set their feet on *terra firma*, except the officer who has now called three times on the Mayor, and who is said to tremble visibly as he walks the streets.

Last evening came the demand: the town must be surrendered immediately; the Federal flag Must be raised; they would grant us the same terms they granted New Orleans. Jolly terms those were! The answer was worthy of a southerner. It was, "The town was defenseless; if we had cannon, there were not men enough to resist; but if forty vessels lay at the landing,—it was intimated we were in their power, and more ships coming up,—we would not surrender; if they wanted, they might come and Take us; if they wished the Federal flag hoisted over the Arsenal, they might put it up for themselves, the town had no control over Government property." Glorious! What a pity they did not shell the town! But they are taking us at our word, and this morning they are landing at the Garrison.

"All devices, signs, and flags of the Confederacy shall be suppressed." So says Picayune Butler. *Good.* I devote all my red, white, and blue silk to the manufacture of Confederate flags. As soon as one is confiscated, I make another, until my ribbon is exhausted, when I will sport a duster emblazoned in high colors, "Hurra! For the Bonny blue flag!" Henceforth, I wear one pinned to my bosom — not a duster, but a little flag; the man who says take it off will have to pull it off for himself; the man who dares attempt it — well! a pistol in my pocket fills up the gap. I am capables, too.

This is a dreadful war, to make even the hearts of women so bitter! I hardly know myself these last few weeks. I, who have such a horror of bloodshed, consider even killing in self-defense murder, who cannot with them the slightest evil, whose only prayer is to have them sent back in peace to their own country,—*I* talk of killing them! For what else do I wear a pistol and carving-knife? I am afraid I *will* try them on the first one who says an insolent world to me. Yes, and repent for it ever after in sack-cloth and ashes. *O!* if I was only a man! Then I could don the breeches, and slay them with a will! If some few Southern women

were in the ranks, they could set the men an example they would not blush to follow. Pshaw! There are *no* women here! We are *all* men!

## MAY 10TH

. . . And this is WAR! Heaven save me from like scenes and experiences again. I was wild with excitement last night when Miriam described how the soldiers, marching to the depot, waved their hats to the crowds of women and children, shouting, "God bless you, ladies! We will fight for you!" and they, waving their handkerchiefs, sobbed with one voice, "God bless you, Soldiers! Fight for us!"

We, too, have been having our fun. Early in the evening four more gunboats sailed up here. We saw them from the corner, three squares off, crowded with men even up in the riggings. The American flag was flying from every peak. It was received in profound silence, by the hundreds gathered on the banks. I could hardly refrain from a groan. Much as I once loved that flag, I hate it now! I came back and made myself a Confederate flag about five inches long, slipped the staff in my belt, pinned the flag to my shoulder, and walked downtown, to the consternation of women and children, who expected something awful to follow. An old negro cried, "My young missus got her flag flying', anyhow!" Nettie made one and hid it in the folds of her dress. But we were the only two who ventured. We went to the State House terrace, and took a good look at the Brooklyn which was crowded with people who took a good look at us, likewise. The picket stationed at the Garrison took alarm at half a dozen men on horse-back and ran, saying that the citizens were attacking. The kind officers aboard the ship sent us word that if they were molested, the town would be shelled. Let them! Butchers! Does it take thirty thousand men and millions of dollars to murder defenseless women and children? O the great nation! Bravo!

## MAY 11TH

I—I am disgusted with myself. No unusual thing, but I am *peculiarly* disgusted this time. Last evening, I went to Mrs. Brunot's, without an idea of going beyond, with my flag flying again. They were all going to the State House, so I went with them; to my great distress, some fifteen or twenty Federal officers were standing on the first terrace, stared at like wild beasts by the curious crowd. I had not expected to meet them, and felt a painful conviction that I was unnecessarily attracting attention, by an unladylike display of defiance, from the crowd gathered there. But what was I to do? I felt humiliated, conspicuous, everything that is painful and disagreeable; but—strike my colors in the face of the enemy? Never! Nettie and Sophie had them, too, but that was no consolation for the shame I suffered by such a display so totally distasteful to me. How I wished myself away, and chafed at my folly, and hated myself for being there, and everyone for seeing me. I hope it will be a lesson to me always to remember a lady can gain nothing by such display.

I was not ashamed of the flag of my country,—I proved that by never attempting to remove it in spite of my mortification,—but I was ashamed of my position; for these are evidently gentlemen, not the Billy Wilson's crew we were threatened with. Fine, noble-looking men they were, showing refinement and gentlemanly bearing in every motion. One cannot help but admire such foes! They set us an example worthy of our imitation, and one we would be benefited by following. They come as visitors without either pretensions to superiority, or the insolence of conquerors; they walk quietly their way, offering no annoyance to the citizens, though they themselves are stared at most unmercifully, and pursued by crowds of ragged little boys, while even men gape at them with open mouths. They prove themselves gentlemen, while many of our citizens have proved themselves boors, and I admire them for their conduct. With a conviction that I had allowed myself to be influenced by bigoted, narrow-minded people, in believing them to be unworthy of respect or regard, I came home wonderfully changed in all my newly acquired sentiments, resolved never more to wound their feelings, who were so careful of ours, by such unnecessary display. And I hung my flag on the parlor mantel, there to wave, if it will, in the shades of private life; but to make a show, make me conspicuous and ill at ease, as I was yesterday,—never again! . . .

### APRIL 19TH, 1865

"All things are taken from us, and become portions and parcels of the dreadful pasts." . . .

Thursday the 13th came the dreadful tidings of the surrender of Lee and his army on the 9th. Everybody cried, but I would not, satisfied that God will still save us, even though all should apparently be lost. Followed at intervals of two or three hours by the announcement of the capture of Richmond, Selma, Mobile, and Johnston's army, even the stanchest Southerners were hopeless. Every one proclaimed Peace, and the only matter under consideration was whether Jeff Davis, all politicians, every man above the rank of Captain in the army and above that of Lieutenant in the navy, should be hanged immediately, or *some* graciously pardoned. Henry Ward Beecher humanely pleaded mercy for us, supported by a small minority. Davis and all leading men *must* be executed; the blood of the others would serve to irrigate the country. Under this lively prospect, Peace, blessed Peace! was the cry. I whispered, "Never! Let a great earthquake swallow us up first! Let us leave our land and emigrate to any desert spot of the earth rather than return to the Union, even as it Was!"

Six days this has lasted. Blessed with the silently obstinate disposition, I would not dispute, but felt my heart swell, repeating, "God is our refuge and our strength, a very present help in time of trouble," and could not for an instant believe this could end in an overthrow.

This morning, when I went down to breakfast at seven, Brother read the announcement of the assassination of Lincoln and Secretary Seward.

"Vengeance is mine; I will repay, saith the "Lord." This is murder! God have mercy on those who did it! Charlotte Corday killed Marat in his bath, and is held up in history as one of Liberty's martyrs, and one of the heroines of her country. To me, it is all murder. Let historians extol blood-shedding; it is woman's place to abhor it. And because I know that they would have apotheosized any man who had crucified Jeff Davis, I abhor this, and call it foul murder, unworthy of our cause—and God grant it was only the temporary insanity of a desperate man that committed this crime! Let not his blood be visited on our nation, Lord!

Across the way, a large building, undoubtedly inhabited by officers, is being draped in black. Immense streamers of black and white hang from the balcony. Downtown, I understand, all shops are closed, and all wrapped in mourning. And I hardly dare pray God to bless us, with the crape hanging over the way. It would have been banners, if our President had been killed, thought!

## SATURDAY, 22D APRIL

To see a whole city draped in mourning is certainly an imposing spectacle, and becomes almost grand when it is considered as an expression of universal affliction. So it is, in one sense. For the more violently "Secesh" the inmates, the more thankful they are for Lincoln's death, the more profusely the houses are decked with the emblems of woe. They all look to me like "not sorry for him, but dreadfully grieved to be forced to this demonstration." So all things have indeed assumed a funereal aspect. Men who have hated Lincoln with all their souls, under terror of confiscation and imprisonment which they *understand* is the alternative, tie black crape from every practicable knob and point to save their homes. Last evening the B——s were all in tears, preparing their mourning. What sensibility! What patriotism! a stranger would have exclaimed. But Bella's first remark was: "Is it not horrible? This vile, *vile* old crape! Think of hanging it out when—" Tears of rage finished the sentence. One would have thought pity for the murdered man had very little to do with it. . . .

## TUESDAY, MAY 2D, 1865

While praying for the return of those who have fought so nobly for us, how I have dreaded their first days at home! Since the boys died, I have constantly thought of what pain it would bring to see their comrades return without them—to see families reunited, and know that ours never could be again, save in heaven. Last Saturday, the 29th of April, seven hundred and fifty paroled Louisianians from Lee's army were brought here—the sole survivors of ten regiments who left four years ago so full of hope and determination. On the 29th of April, 1861, George left New Orleans with his regiment. On the fourth anniversary of that day, they came back; but George and Gibbes have long been lying in their graves. . . .

## JUNE 15TH

Our Confederacy has gone with one crash—the report of the pistol fired at Lincoln.

## QUESTIONS TO CONSIDER

1. What stands out in Dawson's recollection?
2. Does the reading change how you think about the Civil War?

# CHAPTER 15

# RECONSTRUCTING A NATION, 1865–1877

## 15.1 JOURDON ANDERSON, LETTER TO HIS FORMER SLAVEOWNER (1864)

Jourdon Anderson (1825–1907) was born in Tennessee, where he was enslaved on various plantations until 1864, when Union soldiers freed him. Subsequently, Anderson moved to Dayton, Ohio, where he worked in various positions and eventually settled as a church maintenance man in 1894. In July 1865, Anderson's former owner, P. H. Anderson, wrote Jourdon to ask him to return to Tennessee and work on the plantation. Jourdon's response became immediately celebrated for Jourdon's careful demands and sarcastic tone. P. H. Anderson later sold his plantation at a major loss in order to escape debt, and he died at age 44 just two years later.

*To my old Master,* COLONEL P. H. ANDERSON, *Big Spring, Tennessee.*

SIR: I got your letter, and was glad to find that you had not forgotten Jourdon, and that you wanted me to come back and live with you again, promising to do better for me than anybody else can. I have often felt uneasy about you. I thought the Yankees would have hung you long before this, for harboring Rebs they found at your house. I suppose they never heard about your going to Colonel Martin's to kill the Union soldier that was left by his company in their stable. Although you shot at me twice before I left you, I did not want to hear of your being hurt, and am glad you are still living. It would do me good to go back to the dear old home again, and see Miss Mary and Miss Martha and Allen, Esther, Green, and Lee. Give my love to them all, and tell them I hope we will meet in the better world, if not in this. I would have gone back to see you all when I was working in the Nashville Hospital, but one of the neighbors told me that Henry intended to shoot me if he ever got a chance.

I want to know particularly what the good chance is you propose to give me. I am doing tolerably well here. I get twenty-five dollars a month, with

*Source:* L. Maria Child, ed., *The Freedmen's Book* (Boston: Ticknor and Fields, 1865), 265–267. Retrieved from the Internet Archive website, https://babel.hathitrust.org/cgi/pt?id=hvd.32044013553797;view=1up;seq=7 (Accessed June 6, 20188).

victuals and clothing; have a comfortable home for Mandy,—the folks call her Mrs. Anderson,—and the children—Milly, Jane, and Grundy—go to school and are learning well. The teacher says Grundy has a head for a preacher. They go to Sunday School, and Mandy and me attend church regularly. We are kindly treated. Sometimes we overhear others saying, "Them colored people were slaves" down in Tennessee. The children feel hurt when they hear such remarks; but I tell them it was no disgrace in Tennessee to belong to Colonel Anderson. Many darkeys would have been proud, as I used to be, to call you master. Now if you will write and say what wages you will give me, I will be better able to decide whether it would be to my advantage to move back again.

As to my freedom, which you say I can have, there is nothing to be gained on that score, as I got my free papers in 1864 from the Provost-Marshal-General of the Department of Nashville. Mandy says she would be afraid to go back without some proof that you were disposed to treat us justly and kindly; and we have concluded to test your sincerity by asking you to send us our wages for the time we served you. This will make us forget and forgive old scores, and rely on your justice and friendship in the future. I served you faithfully for thirty-two years, and Mandy twenty years. At twenty-five dollars a month for me, and two dollars a week for Mandy, our earnings would amount to eleven thousand six hundred and eighty dollars. Add to this the interest for the time our wages have been kept back, and deduct what you paid for our clothing, and three doctor's visits to me, and pulling a tooth for Mandy, and the balance will show what we are in justice entitled to. Please send the money by Adams's Express, in care of V. Winters, Esq., Dayton, Ohio. If you fail to pay us for faithful labors in the past, we can have little faith in your promises in the future. We trust the good Maker has opened your eyes to the wrongs which you and your fathers have done to me and my fathers, in making us toil for you for generations without recompense. Here I draw my wages every Saturday night; but in Tennessee there was never any pay-day for the negroes any more than for the horses and cows. Surely there will be a day of reckoning for those who defraud the laborer of his hire.

In answering this letter, please state if there would be any safety for my Milly and Jane, who are now grown up, and both good-looking girls. You know how it was with poor Matilda and Catherine. I would rather stay here and starve—and die, if it come to that—than have my girls brought to shame by the violence and wickedness of their young masters. You will also please state if there has been any schools opened for the colored children in your neighborhood. The great desire of my life now is to give my children an education, and have them form virtuous habits.

Say howdy to George Carter, and thank him for taking the pistol from you when you were shooting at me.

*From your old servant,*
*JOURDON ANDERSON.*

**QUESTIONS TO CONSIDER**

1. Are Anderson's demands serious?
2. Why do you think Anderson's letter became so celebrated?

# 15.2 ABRAHAM LINCOLN'S LAST PUBLIC ADDRESS (1865)

On April 11, 1865, two days after Robert E. Lee surrendered, President Abraham Lincoln spoke from a White House balcony to a crowd of hundreds who had assembled on the lawn below. Far from delivering the joyful speech those in the crowd had expected, Lincoln chose a somber tone in his prepared remarks, and he discussed his strategy toward reincorporating southern states into the Union. Just three days later, John Wilkes Booth shot Lincoln in the back of the head as the President was watching the play "My American Cousin" at Ford's theatre. Lincoln succumbed to his wounds the following morning. This speech, then, provides the clearest hints of Lincoln's potential Reconstruction strategy, one likely more moderate than Radical Republicans would have preferred it to be.

We meet this evening, not in sorrow, but in gladness of heart. The evacuation of Petersburg and Richmond, and the surrender of the principal insurgent army, give hope of a righteous and speedy peace whose joyous expression can not be restrained. In the midst of this, however, He, from Whom all blessings flow, must not be forgotten. A call for a national thanksgiving is being prepared, and will be duly promulgated. Nor must those whose harder part gives us the cause of rejoicing, be overlooked. Their honors must not be parcelled out with others. I myself, was near the front, and had the high pleasure of transmitting much of the good news to you; but no part of the honor, for plan or execution, is mine. To Gen. Grant, his skilful officers, and brave men, all belongs. The gallant Navy stood ready, but was not in reach to take active part.

By these recent successes the re-inauguration of the national authority—reconstruction—which has had a large share of thought from the first, is pressed much more closely upon our attention. It is fraught with great difficulty. Unlike the case of a war between independent nations, there is no authorized organ for us to treat with. No one man has authority to give up the rebellion for any other man. We simply must begin with, and mould from, disorganized and discordant elements. Nor is it a small additional embarrassment that we, the loyal people, differ among ourselves as to the mode, manner, and means of reconstruction.

As a general rule, I abstain from reading the reports of attacks upon myself, wishing not to be provoked by that to which I can not properly offer an answer. In spite of this precaution, however, it comes to my knowledge that I am much censured for some supposed agency in setting up, and seeking to sustain, the new State Government of Louisiana. In this I have done just so much as, and no more than, the public knows. In the Annual Message of Dec. 1863 and accompanying Proclamation, I presented *a* plan of re-construction (as the phrase goes) which, I promised, if adopted by any State, should be acceptable to, and sustained by, the Executive government of the nation. I distinctly stated that this was not the only plan which might possibly be acceptable; and I also distinctly protested that the Executive claimed no right to say when, or whether members should be admitted to seats in Congress from such States. This plan was, in advance, submitted to the then Cabinet, and distinctly approved by every member of it. One of them

*Source: Collected Works of Abraham Lincoln, Volume VIII* (Ann Arbor: University of Michigan Digital Library Production Services, 2001), **https://quod.lib.umich.edu/l/lincoln/lincoln8/1:850?rgn=div1;singlegenre=All;sort=occur;subview=detail;type=simple;view=fulltext;q1=April+11%2C+1865** (Accessed June 6, 2018).

suggested that I should then, and in that connection, apply the Emancipation Proclamation to the theretofore excepted parts of Virginia and Louisiana; that I should drop the suggestion about apprenticeship for freed-people, and that I should omit the protest against my own power, in regard to the admission of members to Congress; but even he approved every part and parcel of the plan which has since been employed or touched by the action of Louisiana. The new constitution of Louisiana, declaring emancipation for the whole State, practically applies the Proclamation to the part previously excepted. It does not adopt apprenticeship for freed-people; and it is silent, as it could not well be otherwise, about the admission of members to Congress. So that, as it applies to Louisiana, every member of the Cabinet fully approved the plan. The Message went to Congress, and I received many commendations of the plan, written and verbal; and not a single objection to it, from any professed emancipationist, came to my knowledge, until after the news reached Washington that the people of Louisiana had begun to move in accordance with it. From about July 1862, I had corresponded with different persons, supposed to be interested, seeking a reconstruction of a State government for Louisiana. When the Message of 1863, with the plan before mentioned, reached New-Orleans, Gen. Banks wrote me that he was confident the people, with his military co-operation, would reconstruct, substantially on that plan. I wrote him, and some of them to try it; they tried it, and the result is known. Such only has been my agency in getting up the Louisiana government. As to sustaining it, my promise is out, as before stated. But, as bad promises are better broken than kept, I shall treat this as a bad promise, and break it, whenever I shall be convinced that keeping it is adverse to the public interest. But I have not yet been so convinced.

I have been shown a letter on this subject, supposed to be an able one, in which the writer expresses regret that my mind has not seemed to be definitely fixed on the question whether the seceded States, so called, are in the Union or out of it. It would perhaps, add astonishment to his regret, were he to learn that since I have found professed Union men endeavoring to make that question, I have *purposely* forborne any public expression upon it. As appears to me that question has not

been, nor yet is, a practically material one, and that any discussion of it, while it thus remains practically immaterial, could have no effect other than the mischievous one of dividing our friends. As yet, whatever it may hereafter become, that question is bad, as the basis of a controversy, and good for nothing at all—a merely pernicious abstraction.

We all agree that the seceded States, so called, are out of their proper practical relation with the Union; and that the sole object of the government, civil and military, in regard to those States is to again get them into that proper practical relation. I believe it is not only possible, but in fact, easier, to do this, without deciding, or even considering, whether these states have even been out of the Union, than with it. Finding themselves safely at home, it would be utterly immaterial whether they had ever been abroad. Let us all join in doing the acts necessary to restoring the proper practical relations between these states and the Union; and each forever after, innocently indulge his own opinion whether, in doing the acts, he brought the States from without, into the Union, or only gave them proper assistance, they never having been out of it.

The amount of constituency, so to to [*sic*] speak, on which the new Louisiana government rests, would be more satisfactory to all, if it contained fifty, thirty, or even twenty thousand, instead of only about twelve thousand, as it does. It is also unsatisfactory to some that the elective franchise is not given to the colored man. I would myself prefer that it were now conferred on the very intelligent, and on those who serve our cause as soldiers. Still the question is not whether the Louisiana government, as it stands, is quite all that is desirable. The question is "Will it be wiser to take it as it is, and help to improve it; or to reject, and disperse it?" "Can Louisiana be brought into proper practical relation with the Union *sooner* by *sustaining*, or by *discarding* her new State Government?"

Some twelve thousand voters in the heretofore slave-state of Louisiana have sworn allegiance to the Union, assumed to be the rightful political power of the State, held elections, organized a State government, adopted a free-state constitution, giving the benefit of public schools equally to black and white, and empowering the Legislature to confer the elective franchise upon the colored man. Their Legislature has already voted to ratify the constitutional amendment recently passed by Congress, abolishing slavery throughout the nation. These twelve thousand persons are thus fully committed to the Union, and to perpetual freedom in the state—committed to the very things, and nearly all the things the nation wants—and they ask the nations recognition, and it's assistance to make good their committal. Now, if we reject, and spurn them, we do our utmost to disorganize and disperse them. We in effect say to the white men "You are worthless, or worse—we will neither help you, nor be helped by you." To the blacks we say "This cup of liberty which these, your old masters, hold to your lips, we will dash from you, and leave you to the chances of gathering the spilled and scattered contents in some vague and undefined when, where, and how." If this course, discouraging and paralyzing both white and black, has any tendency to bring Louisiana into proper practical relations with the Union, I have, so far, been unable to perceive it. If, on the contrary, we recognize, and sustain the new government of Louisiana the converse of all this is made true. We encourage the hearts, and nerve the arms of the twelve thousand to adhere to their work, and argue for it, and proselyte for it, and fight for it, and feed it, and grow it, and ripen it to a complete success. The colored man too, in seeing all united for him, is inspired with vigilance, and energy, and daring, to the same end. Grant that he desires the elective franchise, will he not attain it sooner by saving the already advanced steps toward it, than by running backward over them? Concede that the new government of Louisiana is only to what it should be as the egg is to the fowl, we shall sooner have the fowl by hatching the egg than by smashing it? Again, if we reject Louisiana, we also reject one vote in favor of the proposed amendment to the national constitution. To meet this proposition, it has been argued that no more than three fourths of those States which have not attempted secession are necessary to validly ratify the amendment. I do not commit myself against this, further than to say that such a ratification would be questionable, and sure to be persistently questioned; while a ratification by three fourths of all the States would be unquestioned and unquestionable.

I repeat the question. "Can Louisiana be brought into proper practical relation with the Union *sooner* by *sustaining* or by *discarding* her new State Government?

What has been said of Louisiana will apply generally to other States. And yet so great peculiarities pertain to each state; and such important and sudden changes occur in the same state; and, withal, so new and unprecedented is the whole case, that no exclusive, and inflexible plan can safely be prescribed as to details and colatterals. Such exclusive, and inflexible plan, would surely become a new entanglement. Important principles may, and must, be inflexible.

In the present "*situation*" as the phrase goes, it may be my duty to make some new announcement to the people of the South. I am considering, and shall not fail to act, when satisfied that action will be proper.

**QUESTIONS TO CONSIDER**

1. What was Lincoln's view of African American rights in the years to come?
2. Which strategy do you think Lincoln would have taken toward Reconstruction? What do you think of this strategy?

# 15.3 FREEDMEN'S BUREAU BILL TEXT (1865)

In 1865, Congress established the Freedmen's Bureau, formally titled the Bureau of Refugees, Freedmen, and Abandoned Lands. As you will read, the bill aimed to reunite African American families displaced by the war, provide humanitarian aid to African Americans, educate former slaves, assure fair labor conditions for those who returned to work for wages on plantations, and encourage positive relations between former slaves and whites. For the next seven years, the Bureau became an important, controversial part of Reconstruction. Former Confederate states fought the Bureau by issuing Black Codes, which aimed to keep African Americans in semi-bondage. The Ku Klux Klan terrorized Bureau supporters and employees alike. In 1872, Congress did not renew the program, but it remained an important symbol of attempted Federal Reconstruction action.

### CHAP. XC.—*AN ACT TO ESTABLISH A BUREAU FOR THE RELIEF OF FREEDMEN AND REFUGEES.*

*Be it enacted by the Senate and House of Representatives of the United States of America in Congress assembled,* That there is hereby established in the War Department, to continue during the present war of rebellion, and for one year thereafter, a bureau of refugees, freedmen, and abandoned lands, to which shall be committed, as hereinafter provided, the supervision and management of all abandoned lands, and the control of all subjects relating to refugees and freedmen from rebel states, or from any district of country within the territory embraced in the operations of the army, under such rules and regulations as may be prescribed by the head of the bureau and approved by the President. The Said bureau shall be under the management and control of a commissioner to be appointed by the President, by and with the advice and consent of the Senate, whose compensation shall be three thousand dollars per annum, and such number of clerks as may be assigned to him by the Secretary of War, not exceeding one chief clerk, two of the fourth class, two of the third class, and five of the first class. And the commissioner and all persons appointed under this act, shall, before entering upon their duties, take the oath of office prescribed in an act entitled "An act to prescribe an oath of office, and for other purposes," approved July second, eighteen hundred and sixty-two, and the commissioner and the chief clerk shall, before entering upon their duties, give bonds to the treasurer of the United States, the former in the sum of fifty thousand dollars, and the latter in the sum of ten thousand dollars, conditioned for the faithful discharge of their duties respectively, with securities to be approved as sufficient by the Attorney-General, which bonds shall be filed in the office of the first comptroller of the treasury, to be by him put in suit for the benefit of any injured party upon any breach of the conditions thereof.

SEC. 2. *And be it further enacted,* That the Secretary of War may direct such issues of provisions, clothing, and fuel, as he may deem needful for the immediate and temporary shelter and supply of destitute and suffering refugees and freedmen and their wives and children, under such rules and regulations as he may direct.

*Source: An Act to Establish a Bureau for the Relief of Freedmen and Refugees,* 38th Congress, Session II, *Congressional Globe* (March 3, 1865), 507–509.

SEC. 3. *And be it further enacted*, That the President may, by and with the advice and consent of the Senate, appoint an assistant commissioner for each of the states declared to be in insurrection, not exceeding ten in number, who shall, under the direction of the commissioner, aid in the execution of the provisions of this act; and he shall give a bond to the Treasurer of the United States, in the sum of twenty thousand dollars, in the form and manner prescribed in the first section of this act. And any military officer may be detailed and assigned to duty under this act without increase of pay or allowances. The commissioner shall, before the commencement of each regular session of congress, make full report of his proceedings with exhibits of the state of his accounts to the President, who shall communicate the same to congress, and shall also make special reports whenever required to do so by the President or either house of congress; and the assistant commissioners shall make quarterly reports of their proceedings to the commissioner, and also such other special reports as from time to time may be required.

SEC. 4. *And be it further enacted*, That the commissioner, under the direction of the President, shall have authority to set apart, for the use of loyal refugees and freedmen, such tracts of land. Within the insurrectionary states as shall have been abandoned, or to which the United States shall have acquired title by confiscation or sale, or otherwise, and to every male citizen, whether refugee or freedman, as aforesaid, there shall be assigned not more than forty acres of such land, and the person to whom it was so assigned shall be protected in the use and enjoyment of the land for the term of three years at an annual rent not exceeding six per centum upon the value of such land, as it was appraised by the state authorities in the year eighteen hundred and sixty, for the purpose of taxation, and in case no such appraisal can be found, then the rental shall be based upon the estimated value of the land in said year, to be ascertained in such manner as the commissioner may by regulation prescribe. At the end of said term, or at any time during said term, the occupants of any parcels so assigned may purchase the land and receive such title thereto as the United States can convey, upon paying therefore the value of the land, as ascertained and fixed for the purpose of determining the annual rent aforesaid.

SEC. 5. *And be it further enacted*, That all acts and parts of acts Repealing inconsistent with the provisions of this act, are hereby repealed.

APPROVED, March 3, 1865.

## QUESTIONS TO CONSIDER

1. What did the Bill do?
2. Do you think the Bill was an overreach of Federal power?

# 15.4 ANDREW JOHNSON DEFENDS PASSIVE RECONSTRUCTION POLICIES (1866)

Andrew Johnson (1808–875) became President after Lincoln's 1865 assassination. Lincoln had added the Democratic Johnson, a U.S. Senator from Tennessee, to his National Union Party ticket to propagate a bipartisan message during the 1864 election. Upon assuming the Presidency, Johnson quickly tried to reincorporate former Confederate states into the Union. He clashed with Radical Republicans, such as Thaddeus Stevens (see Reading 15.5), who desired a slower reincorporation policy that was more punitive toward previous Confederate politicians and ensured greater African American rights. In 1867, Johnson vetoed the First Reconstruction Act, which placed the Confederacy under martial law and required former Confederate states to ratify the Fourteenth Amendment in order to rejoin the Union. Congress then overrode his veto, and the House of Representatives impeached Johnson, though the Senate later acquitted him. Johnson delivered the following speech during an ill-fated speaking tour he completed in 1866 to try to rouse support for his non-punitive Reconstruction plans. Johnson later failed in his bid to receive the 1868 Democratic nomination for President, but he pardoned all major Confederate officials before leaving office.

Fellow Citizens of Cleveland:—It is not for the purpose of making a speech I came here to-night. I am aware of the great curiosity that exists on the part of strangers in reference to seeing individuals who are here amongst us. [Louder.] You must remember there are a good many people here to-night, and it requires a great voice to reach the utmost verge of this vast audience. I have used my voice so constantly for some days past that I do know as I shall be able to make you all hear, but I will do my best to make myself heard.

What I am going to say is: There is a large number here who would like to see General Grant, and hear him speak, and hear what he would have to say; but the fact is General Grant is not here. He is extremely ill. His health will not permit of his appearing before this audience to-night. It would be a greater pleasure to me to see him here and have him speak than to make a speech of my own. So then it will not be expected that he will be here to-night, & you cannot see him on account of his extreme indisposition.

Fellow Citizens: In being before you to-night it is not for the purpose of making a speech, but simply to make your acquaintance, and while I am telling you how to do, and at the same time tell you goodbye. We are here to-night on our tour towards a sister State for the purpose of participating in and witnessing the laying of the chief corner stone over a monument to one of our fellow citizens who is no more. It is not necessary for me to mention the name of Stephen A. Douglas to the citizens of Ohio. It is a name familiar to you all, and being on a tour to participate in the ceremonies, and passing through your State and section of country and witnessing the demonstration and manifestation of regard & respect which has been paid to me, I am free to say to you that so far as I am concerned, and I think I am speaking for all the company, when I say we feel extremely gratified and flattered at the demonstration made by the country through which we have passed, and in being flattered, I want to state at the same time that I don't consider that

*Source:* Andrew Johnson speech included in 40th Congress, 2d Session, *Supplement to the Congressional Globe* (April 3, 1868), 109–110.

entirely personal, but as evidence of what is pervading the public mind, that there is a great issue before the country, and that this demonstration of feeling, is more than anything else, an indication of a deep interest among the great mass of the people in regard to all these great questions that agitate the public mind. In coming before you to-night, I come before you as an American citizen, and not simply as your Chief Magistrate. I claim to be a citizen of the Southern States, and an inhabitant of one of the States of the Union. I know that it has been said, and contended for on the part of some, that I was an alien, for I did not reside in any one of the States of the Union, and therefore I could not be Chief Magistrate, though the States declared I was.

But all that was necessary was simply to introduce a resolution declaring the office vacant or depose the occupant, or under some pretext to prefer articles of impeachment, & the individual who occupies the Chief Magistracy would be deposed and deprived of power.

But, fellow-citizens, a short time since you had a ticket before you for the Presidency and Vice Presidency; I was placed upon that ticket, in conjunction with a distinguished fellow citizen who is now no more. (Voice, "a great misfortune too"). I know there are some who will exclaim, "unfortunate." I admit the ways of Providence are mysterious and unfortunate but uncontrolable by those who would exclaim unfortunate. I was going to say my countrymen, but a short time since, I was selected and placed upon a ticket. There was a platform prepared and adopted by those who placed me upon it, and now, notwithstanding all kinds of misrepresentation: notwithstanding since after the sluice of misrepresentation has been poured out, notwithstanding a subsidized gang of hirelings have traduced me and maligned me ever since I have entered upon the discharge of my official duties, yet I will say had my predecessor have lived, the vials of wrath would have been poured out on him (cries of never, never, never.) I come here to-night in passing along, and being called upon, for the purpose of exchanging opinions and views as time would permit, and to ascertain if we could who was in the wrong.

I appear before you to-night and I want to say this: that I have lived and been among all American people,

and have represented them in some capacity for the last twenty-five years. And where is the man living, or the woman in the community, that I have wronged, or where is the person that can place their finger upon one single hair breadth of deviation from one single pledge I have made, or one single violation of the Constitution of the country. What tongue does he speak? What religion does he profess? Let him come forward and place his finger upon one pledge I have violated. (A voice, "Hang Jeff Davis"): (Mr. President resumes.) Hang Jeff Davis? Hang Jeff Davis? Why don't you? (Applause.) Why don't you? (Applause.) Have you not got the Court? Have you not got the Court? Have not you got the Attorney General? Who is your Chief Justice— and that refused to sit upon the trial? (Applause.) I am not the Prosecuting Attorney. I am not the jury. But I will tell you what I did do: I called upon your Congress, that is trying to break up the Government, (immense applause.) Yes, did your Congress order hanging Jeff Davis? (Prolonged applause, mingled with hisses.)

But, fellow citizens, we had as well let feelings and prejudices pass; let passion subside; let reason resume her empire. In presenting myself to you in the few remarks I intended to make, my intention was to address myself to your judgment and to your good sense, and not to your anger or the malignity of your hearts. This was my object in presenting myself on this occasion, and at the same time to tell you good-bye. I have heard the remark made in this crowd to-night. "Traitor, traitor!" (Prolonged confusion.) My countrymen, will you hear me for my cause? For the Constitution of my country? I want to know when, where and under what circumstances Andrew Johnson, either as Chief Executive, or in any other capacity over violated the Constitution of his country. Let me ask this large and intelligent audience here to-night, if your Secretary of State, who served four years under Mr. Lincoln, who was placed under the butcher's blow and exposed to the assassin's knife, when he turned traitor. If I were disposed to play orator, and deal in declamation, here to-night. I would imitate one of the ancient tragedies we have such account of—I would take William HSeward and open to you the scars he has received. I would exhibit his bloody garment and show the rent caused by the assassin's knife. [Three cheers for Seward.] Yes, I would unfold his bloody garments here to-night and ask who had committed treason. I would ask why Jeff Davis was not hung? Why don't you hang Thad Stevens and Wendell Phillips? I can tell you, my countrymen I have been fighting traitors in the South, [prolonged applause,] and they have been whipped, and say they were wrong, acknowledge their error and accept the terms of the Constitution.

And now as I pass around the circle, having fought traitors at the South, I am prepared to fight traitors at the North. God being willing with your help ["You can't have it." and prolonged confusion,] they would be crushed worse than the traitors of the South, and this glorious Union of ours will be preserved. In coming here to-night, it was not coming as Chief Magistrate of twenty-five States, but I come here as the Chief Magistrate of thirty-six States. I came here to-night with the flag of my country in my hand, with a constellation of thirty-six and not twenty-five stars. I came here to-night with the Constitution of my country intact,

determined to defend the Constitution, let the consequences be what they may. I came here to-night for the Union: the entire circle of these States. [A Voice, "How many States made you President?"] How many States made me President? Was you against secession? Do you want to dissolve the Union? [A voice, No.] Then I am President of the whole United States, and I will tell you one thing. I understand the discordant notes in this audience here to-night. And I will tell you furthermore, that he that is opposed to the restoration of the Government and the union of the States, is as great a traitor as Jeff Davis, and I am against both of them. I fought traitors at the South, now I fight them at the North. (Immense applause.)

### QUESTIONS TO CONSIDER

1. How did Johnson defend himself?
2. Do you find the speech to be persuasive?

# 15.5 THADDEUS STEVENS' SPEECH ON RECONSTRUCTION (1867)

Thaddeus Stevens (1792–1868) held very different views than Johnson (see Reading 15.4). A member of the U.S. House of Representatives from Pennsylvania, Stevens was a "Radical Republican" who demanded a stronger version of Federal Reconstruction in order to punish prominent Confederates and secure African American rights after the war. Stevens, who found Lincoln's delayed acceptance of complete abolitionism to be appalling, especially clashed with President Andrew Johnson, who advocated friendly policies toward the former Confederacy. In January 1867, Stevens delivered the following speech. In it, he demanded greater Federal action to quell southern dissent and violence toward Freedmen. Two months later, Stevens led the effort in the House of Representatives to remove Johnson from office via impeachment. Stevens passed away in 1868, shortly after the Senate acquitted Johnson in its impeachment trial.

*Source:* Beverly Wilson Palmer, ed., *The Selected Papers of Thaddeus Stevens, Volume II* (Pittsburgh: University of Pittsburgh Press, 1998), 211–221.

Mr. Speaker, I am very anxious that this bill should be proceeded with until finally acted upon. I desire that as early as possible, without curtailing debate, this House shall come to some conclusion as to what shall be done with the rebel States. This becomes more and more necessary every day; and the late decision of the Supreme Court of the United States has rendered immediate action by Congress upon the question of the establishment of governments in the rebel States absolutely indispensable.

That decision, although in terms perhaps not as infamous as the Dred Scott decision, is yet far more dangerous in its operation upon the lives and liberties of the loyal men of this country. That decision has taken away every protection in every one of these rebel States from every loyal man, black or white, who resides there. That decision has unsheathed the dagger of the assassin, and places the knife of the rebel at the throat of every man who dares proclaim himself to be now, or to have been heretofore, a loyal Union man. If the doctrine enunciated in that decision be true, never were the people of any country anywhere, or at any time, in such terrible peril as are our loyal brethren at the South, whether they be black or white, whether they go there from the North or are natives of the rebel States.

Now, Mr. Speaker, unless Congress proceeds at once to do something to protect these people from the barbarians who are now daily murdering them; who are murdering the loyal whites daily and daily putting into secret graves not only hundreds but thousands of the colored people of that country; unless Congress proceeds at once to adopt some means for their protection, I ask you and every man who loves liberty whether we will not be liable to the just censure of the world for our negligence or our cowardice or our want of ability to do so?

Now, sir, it is for these reasons that I insist on the passage of some such measure as this. This is a bill designed to enable loyal men, so far as I could discriminate them in these States, to form governments which shall be in loyal hands, that they may protect themselves from such outrages as I have mentioned. . . .

. . . May I ask, without offense, will Congress have the courage to do its duty? Or will it be deterred by the clamor of ignorance, bigotry, and despotism from perfecting a revolution begun without their consent, but which ought not to be ended without their full participation and concurrence? Possibly the people would not have inaugurated this revolution to correct the palpable incongruities and despotic provisions of the Constitution; but having it forced upon them, will they be so unwise as to suffer it to subside without erecting this nation into a perfect Republic?

Since the surrender of the armies of the confederate States of America a little has been done toward establishing this Government upon the true principles of liberty and justice; and but a little if we stop here. We have broken the material shackles of four million slaves. We have unchained them from the stake so as to allow them locomotion, provided they do not walk in paths which are trod by white men. We have allowed them the unwonted privilege of attending church, if they can do so without offending the sight of their former masters. We have even given them that highest and most agreeable evidence of liberty as defined by the "great plebeian," the "right to work." But in what have we enlarged their liberty of thought? In what have we taught them the science and granted them the privilege of self-government? We have imposed upon them the privilege of fighting our battles, of dying in defense of freedom, and of bearing their equal portion of taxes; but where have we given them the privilege of ever participating in the formation of the laws for the government of their native land? By what civil weapon have we enabled them to defend themselves against oppression and injustice? Call you this liberty? Call you this a free Republic where four millions are subjects but not citizens? Then Persia, with her kings and satraps, was free; then Turkey is free! Their subjects had liberty of motion and of labor, but the laws were made without and against their will; but I must declare that, in my judgment, they were as really free governments as ours is to-day. I know they had fewer rulers and more subjects, but those rulers were no more despotic that ours, and their subjects had just as large privileges in governing the country as ours have. Think not I would slander my native land; I would reform it. Twenty years ago I denounced it as a despotism. Then, twenty million white men enchained four million black men. I pronounce it no nearer to a true Republic now when twenty-five million of a privileged class exclude five million from all participation in the rights of government.

The freedom of a Government does not depend upon the quality of its laws, but upon the power that has the right to enact them. During the dictatorship of Pericles his laws were just, but Greece was not free. During the last century Russia has been blessed with most remarkable emperors, who have generally decreed wise and just laws, but Russia is not free.

No Government can be free that does not allow all its citizens to participate in the formation and execution of her laws. There are degrees of tyranny. But every other government is despotism. It has always been observed that the larger the number of the rulers the more cruel the treatment of the subject races. It were better for the black man if he were governed by one king than by twenty million. . . .

But it will be said, as it has been said, "This is negro equality!" What is negro equality, about which so much is said by knaves, and some of which is believed by men who are not fools? It means, as understood by honest Republicans, just this much, and no more: every man, no matter what his race or color; every earthly being who has an immortal soul, has an equal right to justice, honesty, and fair play with every other man; and the law should secure him these rights. The same law which condemns or acquits an African should condemn or acquit a white man. The same law which gives a verdict in a white man's favor should give a verdict in a black man's favor on the same state of facts. Such is the law of God and such ought to be the law of man. The doctrine does not mean that a negro shall sit on the same seat or eat at the same table with a white man. That is a matter of taste which every man must decide for himself. The law has nothing to do with it. If there be any who are afraid of the rivalry of the black man in office or in business, I have only to advise them to try and beat their competitor in knowledge and business capacity, and there is no danger that his white neighbors will prefer his African rival to himself. I know there is between those who are influenced by this cry of "negro equality" and the opinion that there is still danger that the negro will be the smartest,

for I never saw even a contraband slave that had not more sense than such men.

There are those who admit the justice and ultimate utility of granting impartial suffrage to all men, but they think it is impolitic. An ancient philosopher, whose antagonist admitted that what he required was just but deemed it impolitic, asked him: "Do you believe in Hades?" I would say to those above referred to, who admit the justice of human equality before the law but doubt its policy: "Do you believe in hell?"

How do you answer the principle inscribed in our political scripture, "That to secure these rights governments are instituted among men, deriving their just powers from the consent of the governed?" Without such consent government is a tyranny, and you exercising it are tyrants. Of course, this does not admit malefactors to power, or there would soon be no penal laws and society would become an anarchy. But this step forward is an assault upon ignorance and prejudice, and timid men shrink from it. Are such men fit to sit in the places of statesmen?

There are periods in the history of nations when statesmen can make themselves names for posterity; but such occasions are never improved by cowards. In the acquisition of true fame courage is just as necessary in the civilian as in the military hero. In the Reformation there were men engaged as able and perhaps more learned than Martin Luther. Melancthon and others were ripe scholars and sincere reformers, but none of them had his courage. He alone was willing to go where duty called though "devils were as thick as the tiles on the houses." And Luther is the great luminary of the Reformation, around whom the others revolve as satellites and shine by his light. We may not aspire to fame. But great events fix the eye of history on small objects and magnify their meanness. Let us at least escape that condition.

### QUESTIONS TO CONSIDER

1. How did Stevens make his case for greater Federal action?
2. Do you find the speech to be persuasive?

# 15.6 ULYSSES S. GRANT, "USE OF THE ARMY IN CERTAIN OF THE SOUTHERN STATES" (1876)

Ulysses S. Grant (1822–1885) was the Commanding General of the Union Army at the end of the Civil War and the eighteenth President of the United States. In the 1868 election, Grant defeated Democrat Horatio Seymour by a wide margin and, once in office, worked with his fellow Republicans to secure the rights gained by Union victory in the Civil War. In 1970, he campaigned for the ratification of the Fifteenth Amendment, which prohibited denying suffrage based on "race, color, or previous condition of servitude." Grant continued to struggle, however, with southern violence toward both freed slaves and the state Republican governments that protected them. In 1876, Grant delivered the following speech. In it, he defended sending the military into Virginia, South Carolina, Louisiana, and Florida to protect African American voting right, quell violence, and protect Republican governments in those states. Grant's presidency was undone by a series of corruption strategies that involved senior officials in his administration. His successor, Rutherford B. Hayes, ended the Federal military occupation of the South.

To the House of Representatives :

On the 9th day of December, 1876, the following resolution of the House of Representatives was received, viz :

*Resolved*, That the President be requested, if not incompatible with the public interest, to transmit to this House copies of any and all orders or directions emanating from him or from either of the Executive Departments of the Government to any military commander or civil officer, with reference to the service of the Army, or any portion thereof, in the States of Virginia, South Carolina, Louisiana, and Florida, since the 1st of August last, together with reports, by telegraph or otherwise, from either or any of said military commanders or civil officers.

It was immediately, or soon thereafter, referred to the Secretary of War and the Attorney-General, the custodians of all retained copies of "orders or directions" given by the executive department of the Government covered by the above inquiry, together with all information upon which such "orders or directions" were given.

The information, it will be observed, is voluminous, and, with the limited clerical force in the Department of Justice, has consumed the time up to the present. Many of the communications accompanying this have been already made public in connection with messages heretofore sent to Congress. This class of information includes the important documents received from the governor of South Carolina, and sent to Congress with my message on the subject of the Hamburgh massacre ; also the documents accompanying my response to the resolution of the House of Representatives in regard to the soldiers stationed at Petersburgh.

There have also come to me and to the Department of Justice, from time to time, other earnest written communications from persons holding public trusts and from others residing in the South, some of which I append hereto as bearing upon the precarious

*Source:* Ulysses S. Grant, "Use of the Army in Certain of the Southern States," 44th Congress, 2d Session, *Congressional Globe* (January 24, 1877), 1–4.

condition of the public peace in those States. These communications I have reason to regard as made by respectable and responsible men. Many of them deprecate the publication of their names as involving danger to them personally,

The reports heretofore made by committees of Congress of the results of their inquiries in Mississippi and in Louisiana, and the newspapers of several States recommending "the Mississippi plan," have also furnished important data for estimating the danger to the public peace and order in those States.

It is enough to say that these different kinds and sources of evidence have left no doubt whatever in my mind that intimidation has been used, and actual violence, to an extent requiring the aid of the United States Government, where it was practicable to furnish such aid, in South Carolina, in Florida, and in Louisiana, as well as in Mississippi, in Alabama, and in Georgia.

The troops of the United States have been but sparingly used, and in no case so as to interfere with the free exercise of the right of suffrage. Very few troops were available for the purpose of preventing or suppressing the violence and intimidation existing in the States above named. In no case except that of South Carolina was the number of soldiers in any State increased in anticipation of the election, saving that twenty-four men and an officer were sent from Fort Foote to Petersburgh, Va., where disturbances were threatened prior to the election.

No troops were stationed at the voting-places. In Florida and in Louisiana, respectively, the small number of soldiers already in the said States were stationed at such points in each State as were most threatened with violence, where they might be available as a *posse* for the officer whose duty it was to preserve the peace and prevent intimidation of voters, Such a disposition of the troops seemed to me reasonable, and justified by law and precedent, while its omission would have been inconsistent with the constitutional duty of the President of the United States "to take care that the laws be faithfully executed." The statute expressly forbids the bringing of troops to the polls, "except where it is necessary to keep the peace," implying that to keep the peace it may be done. But this even, so far as I am advised, has not in any case been done. The Stationing

of a company or part of a company in the vicinity, where they would be available to prevent riot, has been the only use made of troops prior to and at the time of the elections. Where so stationed, they could be called, in an emergency requiring it, by a marshal or deputy marshal as a *posse* to aid in suppressing unlawful violence. The evidence which has come to me has left me no ground to doubt that if there had been more military force available, it would have been my duty to have disposed of it in several States with a view to the prevention of the violence and intimidation which have undoubtedly contributed to the defeat of the election-law in Mississippi, Alabama, and Georgia, as well as in South Carolina, Louisiana, and Florida.

By article 4, section 4, of the Constitution, "The United States shall guarantee to every State in this Union a republican form of government, and on application of the legislature, or of the executive, (when the legislature cannot be convened,) shall protect each of them against domestic violence."

By act of Congress (R. S. U. S., sec, 1034,1035) the President, in case of "insurrection in any State," or of "unlawful obstruction to the enforcement of the laws of the United States by the ordinary course of judicial proceedings," or whenever "domestic violence in any State so obstructs the execution of the laws thereof, and of the United States, as to deprive any portion of the people of such State" of their civil or political rights, is authorized to employ such parts of the land and naval forces as he may deem necessary to enforce the execution of the laws and preserve the peace, and sustain the authority of the State and of the United States. Acting under this title (69) of the Revised Statutes, United States, I accompanied the sending of troops to South Carolina with a proclamation such as is therein prescribed.

The President is also authorized by act of Congress "to employ such part of the land or naval forces of the United States" ✳ ✳ "as shall be necessary to prevent the violation and to enforce the due execution of the provisions" of Title 24 of the Revised Statutes of the United States for the protection of the civil rights of citizens, among which is the provision against conspiracies "to prevent by force, intimidation, or threat, any citizen who is lawfully entitled to vote, from giving his support or advocacy in a legal manner toward or in favor of the election of any lawfully qualified person as an elector for President or Vice President, or as a member of Congress of the United States." (U. S. Rev. Stat., 1989.)

In cases falling under this title I have not considered it necessary to issue a proclamation to precede or accompany the employment of such part of the Army as seemed to be necessary.

In case of insurrection against a State government, or against the Government of the United States, a proclamation is appropriate ; but in keeping the peace of the United States at an election at which members of Congress are elected, no such call from the State or proclamation by the President is prescribed by statute or required by precedent.

In the case of South Carolina, insurrection and domestic violence against the State government were clearly shown, and the application of the governor founded thereon was duly presented, and I could not deny his constitutional request without abandoning my duty as the Executive of the National Government.

The companies stationed in the other States have been employed to secure the better execution of the laws of the United States and to preserve the peace of the United States.

After the election had been had, and where violence was apprehended by which the returns from the counties and precincts might be destroyed, troops were ordered to the State of Florida, and those already in Louisiana were ordered to the points in greatest danger of violence.

I have not employed troops on slight occasions, nor in any case where it has not been necessary to the enforcement of the laws of the United States. In this I have been guided by the Constitution and the laws which have been enacted and the precedents which have been formed under it.

It has been necessary to employ troops occasionally to overcome resistance to the internal-revenue laws, from the time of the resistance to the collection of the whisky-tax in Pennsylvania, under Washington, to the present time.

In 1854, when it was apprehended that resistance would be made in Boston to the seizure and return to his master of a fugitive slave, the troops there stationed were employed to enforce the master's right under the Constitution, and troops stationed at New York were ordered to be in readiness to go to Boston if it should prove to be necessary.

In 1859, when John Brown with a small number of men made his attack upon Harper's Ferry, the President ordered United States troops to assist in the apprehension and suppression of him and his party, without a formal call of the legislature or governor of Virginia, and without proclamation of the President.

Without citing further instances, in which the Executive has exercised his power as commander of the Army and Navy to prevent or suppress resistance to the laws of the United States, or where he has exercised like authority in obedience to a call from a State to suppress insurrection, I desire to assure both Congress and the country that it has been my purpose to administer the executive powers of the Government fairly, and in no instance to disregard or transcend the limits of the Constitution.

## QUESTIONS TO CONSIDER

1. How did Grant make the case for Federal military involvement in the South?
2. Do you find the speech to be persuasive?